Hitchcock and the Methods of Suspense

WILLIAM HARE

Foreword by Robert Kendall

McFarland & Company, Inc., Publishers
Jefferson, North Carolina, and London

LIBRARY OF CONGRESS CATALOGUING-IN-PUBLICATION DATA

Hare, William, 1942–
    Hitchcock and the methods of suspense / William Hare ; foreword by
Robert Kendall.
        p.   cm.
    Includes bibliographical references and index.

    ISBN-13: 978-0-7864-2560-0
    ISBN-10: 0-7864-2560-1
    (softcover : 50# alkaline paper) ∞

    1. Hitchcock, Alfred, 1899–1980— Criticism and interpretation.
    2. Suspense in motion pictures, television, etc.   I. Title
    PN1998.3.H58H37   2007
    791.4302'33092 — dc22   2006036817

British Library cataloguing data are available

On the cover: Jospeh Cotten, Teresa Wright, Macdonald Carey
in *Shadow of a Doubt* (1943)

Manufactured in the United States of America

McFarland & Company, Inc., Publishers
  Box 611, Jefferson, North Carolina 28640
    www.mcfarlandpub.com

#75088016

To Ken Annakin, Hazel Court, Robert
Kendall and Ken Mogg, whose lives intersected in
various ways with Alfred Hitchcock, and who were
kind enough to share their memories and experiences.

Table of Contents

Foreword
by Robert Kendall

Having enjoyed the unique films of Alfred Hitchcock, it was a wonderful moment as a member of the press to have the opportunity to meet and speak with the master of movie suspense on two separate occasions.

So it is with great pleasure that I read film historian William Hare's book on Alfred Hitchcock, with his comprehensive analysis of the director's greatest films.

As the head of a drama department at a San Fernando Valley, California, high school, I was fascinated by my student's reactions to various Hitchcock films.

Alfred Hitchcock's films and television shows were favorites of my students because he knew how to entertain his audiences. In his memorable press conference before the release of his final film, *Family Plot*, Hitchcock entertained with his wonderful wit, answering some rather tactless press questions with keen insight and humor, and captivating his audience while keeping the entire media contingent listening and laughing.

Directors, actors and writers, as well as teachers of drama and cinema at high schools and colleges, such as the University of Southern California, where I received cinema and television training, could benefit from the insights provided by this book as required reading. It would prove enormously helpful with its behind the scenes insights into the film and television industries.

In the golden era of motion pictures the finest creative minds often worked for years to prepare one motion picture for production. That is precisely why great film masterpieces need to be viewed repeatedly. There is so much meaning packed into these films that they cannot be fully appreciated through a single viewing.

Movie audiences watching Hitchcock films can learn something new and gain appreciable insight with each additional viewing. Reading Hare's book explains what to look for in these famous films.

Introduction

This book's genesis resulted in part from a trip to the Salvador Dalí Museum in Saint Petersburg, Florida. After the tour guide introduced himself to the group he made a statement that, after reflection, prompted me to apply it to Alfred Hitchcock and his work.

While aware even before my visit to that museum that the famous Spanish painter and Hitchcock had joined forces on one occasion, for *Spellbound*, when Dalí supplied the art for the famous dream sequence of Gregory Peck, this was not what triggered the linkage between the two creative geniuses. It was a statement the guide made when he began launching into his informative presentation that caused me to eventually think about Hitchcock and apply it to a creative effort of my own.

"Dalí's engineering background, coupled with his creative skills, enabled him to provide original works with differing looks depending on the perspective," the guide explained. "Because Dalí's works were so original and varied in detail we take one work at a time and explain it, after which we then move on to another one."

The guide's words reverberated in my ears long after my visit to the Dalí Museum. I soon realized that these words also applied to Alfred Hitchcock. The film craftsman known as the Master presented varying perspectives and combined the thematically unique with the familiar, providing filmgoers with a sense of the new and provocative in a setting familiar enough to provide spontaneous identification.

Hitchcock was like another brilliant contemporary filmmaker who shared his British roots, David Lean, in that from their early youths they were fascinated by the camera and what it could accomplish within the framework of a story. Neither one could conceive of becoming anything other than what they ultimately became, film craftsmen, and how much richer we all are as a result.

For Hitchcock a film's origin resided in its rich imagery. This confounded prominent mystery author Raymond Chandler during their sole collaboration, *Strangers on a Train*. Chandler was used to writing a script through presenting characters in well-plotted stories. When Hitchcock commenced from a different method — by beginning with various shots of Washington, D.C., showcasing fascinating historical sites — a nonplussed Chandler asked, "Why do you need me?" Hitchcock had a different way of operating, aware that what set the film industry apart from other creative endeavors was the camera, and he constantly explored more daring ways to use it within the framework of an entertaining story.

An important aspect of Hitchcock film exploration involved probing the psychological depths of the human mind. A full chapter is devoted to the period following World War II when psychoanalysis began to fascinate the elite of the Hollywood film community. When Hitchcock's then creative partner David O. Selznick became a patient of psychiatrist Dr. May Romm and quickly developed a fascination with the subject, he found an interested Alfred Hitchcock prepared to undertake a film involving psychoanalysis. Selznick's close friend and frequent collaborator Ben Hecht, one of Hollywood's most successful and prolific screenwriters, and someone who had, like Selznick, undergone psychotherapy, was eager to jump on the bandwagon. The synergistic result was *Spellbound*, one of Hitchcock's most successful films and one that continues to entertain new admirers of the Master's work.

Once Hitchcock had successfully explored the human mind in *Spellbound* he would revisit the same territory, with brilliant results, via *Notorious*, *Vertigo* and *Psycho*. Probing the mind enhanced viewer interest in analyzing the intriguing array of characters Hitchcock presented in his films. In the manner of successful people in all fields, when Hitchcock discovered a winning formula it would be retooled for continuing success.

David O. Selznick was a formative influence on the great director in his early Hollywood period after the legendary producer of *Gone with the Wind* enticed him out of London. While the relationship between two of the film industry's strong-willed figures was rocky, Hitchcock was benefited by a meticulous precision at analyzing scripts. Hitchcock's finished products were often appreciably enhanced by recommendations within the outpourings of Selznick's long memos.

Alfred Hitchcock recognized that audiences loved nothing more than being spoofed in the framework of an evolving suspense story. Consequently, he found limitless ways of accomplishing this objective through a brilliant 53-film career, culminating with the 1976 release of *Family Plot*, which ended, appropriately enough, with phony psychic Barbara Harris winking at the audience after carrying out her final spoof.

The beauty of Alfred Hitchcock's successful approach to filmmaking was an ability to please theater patrons at two levels. For those who wanted strictly to be entertained he supplied a constellation of what were called Hitchcock

Roman candles, special effects and visual tricks and twists designed to entertain. For those who wanted to explore beyond that level he supplied well-crafted stories rich in characterization and meaning, keeping critics and historians occupied interpreting the dimensions of opulently visual film presentations.

Chapter 1 begins with a thorough discussion of *The 39 Steps* and its linkage to developing events in England. It was adapted from a John Buchan novel, a renowned spy thriller author in Britain that Hitchcock had read as a young boy. This great film, along with *The Lady Vanishes*, *Foreign Correspondent* and *Saboteur*, represented Hitchcock's keen awareness of the developing world conflict in the various stages preparatory to full-fledged battle. The bridge is then made into Chapter 2 with Hitchcock's arrival in Hollywood after signing a contract with David O. Selznick. While Hitchcock expressed dissatisfaction with their first joint effort, *Rebecca*, which was adapted from a gothic novel penned by Daphne du Maurier, believing that it bore more of Selznick's imprint than his own, the 1940 release features the inimitable combination of the Master's grasp of suspense along with intensely evocative cinematography. The result of the often stormy collaboration was an Academy Award for Best Picture, which constituted a double for Selznick since he had won for *Gone with the Wind* one year earlier.

Shadow of a Doubt has been classified as Hitchcock's first homage to his new home of America. He called it his favorite film experience due to the small-town hospitality the people and authorities of Santa Rosa, California, displayed toward Hitchcock and the film's performers and crew. The 1943 release presented an intimate study of a psychotic killer of rich widows in Joseph Cotten. This is a character type Hitchcock would display repeatedly in other films, providing memorable challenges for performers such as Robert Walker, Anthony Perkins and Barry Foster. *Shadow of a Doubt* is the subject of Chapter 3.

By the conclusion of World War II the Hollywood film community had become enraptured with psychiatry and, more specifically, psychoanalysis, which became a popular topic at cocktail and dinner parties among the upper echelon of the industry. Chapter 4 details how the keen interest of Selznick and his best friend, prominent film writer Ben Hecht, resulted in two Hitchcock successes. Chapter 5 delineates how Hitchcock joined forces with Selznick and Hecht to achieve an international blockbuster triumph with the 1945 release *Spellbound*, in which psychiatrist Ingrid Bergman sought to cure Gregory Peck of amnesia and prove that he was innocent of the charge of murder. Selznick, concentrating on his production of *Duel in the Sun*, relinquished all involvement in *Notorious*, in which Hitchcock joined forces again with screenwriter Hecht to produce one of the director's enduring masterpieces in 1946.

In this suspenseful psychological drama federal agent Cary Grant seeks to save Ingrid Bergman's life after she has, on Grant's recommendation, infiltrated a Nazi spy ring in Rio de Janeiro and married master scientist Claude Rains. The race is on to stop Rains and his colleagues before he can create a bomb that will alter the post-war balance of power. In this film Rains plays the role of a "mamma's boy," a character trait to which Hitchcock would return in fleshing out certain villains. These two psychological classics are covered in Chapter 5.

Returning to the psychological and psychopathic roots of *Shadow of a Doubt*, Hitchcock crafted releases in 1948 and 1949 that showed warped but fascinating killers at work. *Rope* was loosely based on the Leopold-Loeb thrill killing of a vulnerable young student, and starred John Dall and Farley Granger as brilliant and ruthless killers with superiority complexes. Their former philosophy professor, played by James Stewart, ultimately solves the crime.

Granger, as the more passive of the killer duo, was used by Hitchcock to play the role of an innocent victim in the adaptation of the Patricia Highsmith novel *Strangers on a Train*. His character played superbly opposite Robert Walker in his most unforgettable role. Tragically, Walker would be dead by the time plaudits came his way after the film's release. Walker emerged as one of Hitchcock's most memorable psycho killers. Chapter 6 is comprised of an examination of *Rope* and *Strangers on a Train*.

Strangers on a Train marked the only time that Hitchcock would work with suspense writing legend Raymond Chandler; their clashes while working on the screenplay often made the battles between the director and Selznick during the filming of *Rebecca* appear tame. *Strangers on a Train* was one of Hitchcock's films that did not achieve initial box office success but eventually attained classic status. Hitchcock would pull out of his temporary box office slump, however, with a 1954 release featuring two of the most dynamic Hollywood stars ever to be showcased before a camera.

James Stewart, who to various people at different times constituted America's favorite son or next door neighbor, was paired with Grace Kelly, the beautiful and elegant blonde who ultimately left Hollywood to become a princess, in *Rear Window*. The film swiftly became one of Hitchcock's most successful box office achievements, as well as being one of his most skillful cinema presentations. Hitchcock's interest in depicting the fascinating psychological depths of human beings during periods of acute tension, commencing with the end of World War II with *Spellbound*, was pursued with a new twist in *Rear Window*. This time, rather than focusing on serial killers like those portrayed by Joseph Cotten and Robert Walker, an attempt to assist a troubled soul in the manner of psychiatrist Ingrid Bergman assisting Gregory Peck in *Spellbound*, or assistance being rendered to Bergman by Cary Grant in *Notorious*, in *Rear Window* Hitchcock tackled voyeurism in the venue of a suspense vehicle with a uniquely presented element of romance.

Hitchcock, with the able assistance of scenarist John Michael Hayes, adapted a novella by famous New York mystery author Cornell Woolrich while applying a shrewd new touch. In the novella the narrator and main character (portrayed by Stewart in the film) is laid up with a broken leg and spends his days and nights looking out the window to pass the time. Ultimately he observes strange conduct that he believes encompasses murder. Hitchcock and Hayes cleverly wove a romantic element between Stewart and Grace Kelly into the story, with a voyeuristic twist.

Kelly's character, depicted as a popular Manhattan cover girl, was created along the lines of screenwriter Hayes's own beautiful blonde cover girl wife Mel. While Kelly pursues Stewart for marriage, he is nervously reluctant, believing that an action magazine photographer like himself is too distantly removed from her world of martini lunches and champagne dinners perfection of cover girl Kelly. At one point, during his uncomfortable period of escape, he becomes entranced with the seductive movements of the shapely ballet dancer living across the courtyard who he appropriately nicknames "Miss Torso," arousing disgusted concern from Kelly. Eventually, they are able to solve the murder of the wife of Lars Thorwald (Raymond Burr) committed by her ruthless husband, but not before Stewart almost loses his life in the process.

The other film that comprises Chapter 7 along with *Rear Window* is a remake of Hitchcock's 1934 film made during his London phase, *The Man Who Knew Too Much*. A chief difference distinguishing the two versions stems from the technical advances made in the industry during a period just short of a generation, as Hitchcock uses deliciously glossy color to develop a stirring mystery theme set in exotic Morocco and fascinating London, the city where the director was born, raised and launched his career. The 1956 release's chances for box office success were enhanced by pairing James Stewart with Doris Day, one of the reigning female box office giants of the fifties.

The psychological element shrewdly explored by Hitchcock and scenarist John Michael Hayes centers on the McKenna family of Indianapolis, comprised of Stewart, Day and son Christopher Olsen. At the film's outset the McKennas appear indomitably successful, but one tragic event — the young son's kidnapping within a broad international spy context in which a prominent European political leader is targeted for death — grimly reminds the McKennas of how vulnerable they are in an imperfect world rife with crime and uncertainty. Stewart is a successful doctor, and the family is celebrating in Morocco following the conclusion of an international medical convention in Paris. The family appears on top of the world until the young son is apprehended. They then must overcome their shock and adopt a position of astute teamwork to save the lives of Olsen and the political leader targeted for assassination.

Discussion of *The Man Who Knew Too Much* is enhanced by the insights of Ken Mogg, one of the leading experts on Alfred Hitchcock and his films. Australian Mogg runs the successful and popular The MacGuffin Web Page, "Where Hitchcock scholars meet." The Stewart-Day film evokes significant meaning for Mogg, who was exposed to Hitchcock's genius one evening at a Boy Scout hall where *The Man Who Knew Too Much* was showing. Mogg colorfully describes that memorable evening and the impact it had on him, resulting in a lifelong interest in Hitchcock and his films. Mogg's insights on the pulse-pounding scene at Royal Albert Hall when Day saves the life of the intended assassination target, as well as the important story elements surrounding it, are fascinating.

Chapter 8 is highlighted by an analysis of the film that numerous Hitchcock scholars, historians and fans have classified as the finest work of the director's distinguished career. The 1957 release *Vertigo* reunited Hitchcock with James Stewart, teaming him with one of Hitchcock's memorable blonde leading ladies, Kim Novak, who had recently soared to success in *Picnic*. *Vertigo* is a daring exploration of voyeurism, a theme that had earlier been such an important element in *Rear Window*, and in addition its rich photogenic setting of San Francisco provides some of the most dazzling color in all of Hitchcock's films. It is bolstered by one of filmdom's most brilliant musical scores, supplied by Bernard Herrmann.

Vertigo, adapted by scenarists Alec Coppel and Samuel Taylor from a novel by French author Pierre Boileau, delivered two thematic tours de force. Retired San Francisco police detective Stewart is a man known for his Scottish practicality, but he ultimately hurls all caution to the winds in falling head over heels in love with a woman who never existed. Tom Helmore, a former college classmate of Stewart's, inveigles him to follow the woman he declares to be his wife through the streets of San Francisco, explaining that the spirit of a deceased ancestor she never met or knows anything about haunts her. Helmore tells Stewart he fears that his wife will commit suicide, as had the ancestor, and that she is even the same age as the tragic suicide victim.

Kim Novak plays a challenging dual role split into the film's two segments, the first as the woman who does not exist, when she portrays herself as the aristocratic wife of Helmore. Stewart then meets the real person, who was working as a department store sales clerk, and seeks to remake her into the pretended figure who had been a pawn, along with the retired detective, of Helmore. Their assistance, with Stewart's being totally unwilling, enables the suave and cunning Helmore to commit the perfect crime as he kills his real wife.

The second thematic tour de force of *Vertigo* is the criminal persona of Helmore. Never in any other memorable film would viewers see a ruthless killer who is seen on camera as an unfailingly decent and courteous man without his other side ever being revealed by his actions, save a brief flashback when Novak confirms Stewart's ultimate suspicions. By film's end the ingenious Helmore has destroyed three lives, adding those of Stewart and Novak to the wife he murdered, and has left America to live luxuriously with riches inherited from the woman he murdered. The Helmore character is one of several instances in *Vertigo* where viewers are invited to fill in blanks to provide answers to probing questions for which the story supplies no answers.

North by Northwest is the other film carefully examined in Chapter 8. Cary Grant, whose charismatic international stardom helped propel *Notorious* to astounding success, helps Hitchcock craft another winner. Grant's co-star is Eva Marie Saint, and their roles and the story structure are reminiscent of Hitchcock's 1935 international blockbuster *The 39 Steps*. Eva Marie Saint emerges as another dazzling Hitchcock "cool blonde" in the mold of Madeleine Carroll, Grace Kelly and the Kim Novak figure of the first half of *Vertigo*, while spy James Mason, who is Saint's lover in the early stages of the film, is a shrewd and controlling villain reminiscent of Tom Helmore and the dominance he holds over Kim Novak in *Vertigo*.

Chapter 9 features *Psycho*, the low-budget blockbuster that surprised Hitchcock more than any other. Paramount gave Hitchcock a smaller budget with which to work after he experienced some box office reversals. The wily director emerged with the film that became the most popular of his career and is an authentic cult classic. The famous shower scene in which psychopathic killer Anthony Perkins stabs Janet Leigh to death has emerged as not only the director's most famous scene, but also arguably the best known cinematic sequence anyone has ever done. The film has a lot to say about American social mores and emerges as another example of Hitchcock reworking the same psychotic killer scenario, this time built around demented mamma's boy Anthony Perkins, that bore tangible results in *Shadow of a Doubt* and *Strangers on a Train*.

The book's final chapter deals with Hitchcock's mature phase and reveals an inventive artist who was never content to sit back on his laurels, and was ever cognizant of changing times and circumstances, adjusting his technique and story development accordingly. Chapter 10 begins with the 1963 release *The Birds*, an allegory, yet at the same time a chronicle of the human condition during a tense period of history in which the world stood on the brink of war during the October 1962 Cuban Missile Crisis. This was also the period in which the ecology movement was born, and *The Birds*, using destructive cohesive attacks by winged creatures, makes viewers aware of the potential destruction of the planet. Veteran British director Ken Annakin describes visiting the set of *The Birds* at the invitation of Tippi Hedren, the blonde female lead. Hitchcock told Annakin that anything was possible on film.

The second film covered in Chapter 10 is *Frenzy*, a 1972 release that provided Hitchcock with one last opportunity to make a film in London. *Frenzy* is also the final time that Hitchcock would revisit his familiar theme of building a film around the exploits of a psychotic killer. British stage acting veteran Barry Foster falls into the familiar heading of a Hitchcock villain who is also a mamma's boy, characteristic of Claude Rains, Robert Walker and Anthony Perkins. It is also noteworthy that Foster is a greengrocer in the then popular marketing venue of Covent Garden, in that this was the profession of Hitchcock's father in London.

Frenzy saw Hitchcock take violence and voyeurism to depths well beyond what he had previously plumbed. Hitchcock was an artist of his time, as violence was explored in the period by Sergio Leone in the low-budget Italian "spaghetti westerns" that catapulted Clint Eastwood to international stardom, and the successful Dino De Laurentis *Death Wish* series saw Charles Bronson's career skyrocket to new levels of popularity.

During this same period Hitchcock's celebrity status was substantially enhanced through his on-screen appearances introducing and adding postscripts to dramas on the popular network television program *Alfred Hitchcock Presents*. Readers are taken into that scene through the illuminating insights of British actress Hazel Court, who recounts her appearance on the show playing the wife of Laurence Harvey, as well as meeting future husband Don Taylor for the first time when he directed her on another segment.

The final segment of the chapter is devoted to Hitchcock's last film and the press party and major satellite news conference that preceded the filming and release of *Family Plot* in 1976. Universal pulled out all stops to publicize what would be the Master's final film. Robert Kendall, who had begun an acting career at Universal shortly after World War II, returned to the studio to cover both the unique graveyard party given on Universal's lot and the news conference in which Hitchcock's superb wit was on ample display in answering the questions of media representatives throughout America. Kendall recreates the colorful drama of the occasions and recounts his own conversations with Hitchcock.

Another personal firsthand account presented in the chapter concerning *Family Plot* involves the trip Ken Mogg took to America from Australia. Mogg visited the locations of *Vertigo* and *The Birds*. While in Southern California he viewed Hitchcock in action directing a scene from *Family Plot*. The Kendall and Mogg accounts reveal important elements of the distinctive Hitchcock style.

Ken Annakin provides valuable insight into a vital area of Hitchcock's technique. Alfred Hitchcock was an ardent believer in the storyboard method, in which he worked with a talented artist who then sketched out scenes prior to filming. Annakin became versed in the technique while directing such major Disney hits as *The Swiss Family Robinson*, which was the only 1960 film to gross higher than Hitchcock's *Psycho*, and *The Third Man on the Mountain*. Walt Disney was a firm believer in storyboard technique and insisted that directors of his films employ it. Annakin provides an analysis of the benefits derived from storyboarding.

While this book does not include all of Hitchcock's films, the work's central ambition is to provide an understanding of the Hitchcock filmmaking process. The emphasis is on films that represented Hitchcock's basic style and received solid acclaim over a period of time. As so representative of other forms of art, some of Hitchcock's most brilliant creative efforts were not among his most well-received works initially. Through the passage of time, however, such celebrated works as *Vertigo*, *Strangers on a Train* and *Rope* have garnered the classical status deserved for their creative ingenuity.

1

A Breakthrough Spy Adventure:
The 39 Steps (1935)

What is drama but life with the dull bits cut out?
— Alfred Hitchcock

The exceedingly visual Alfred Hitchcock was such a natural for filmmaking that many are unaware that he did not explode onto the scene to be instantly discovered for his genius, enduring happily thereafter on a vaunted cinema pedestal. Depending upon how his career is measured, and what previous efforts are counted, it was in the vicinity of Hitchcock's twentieth film that his major breakthrough occurred, vaulting him into the top ranks of world cinema. That does not mean that he did not thereafter experience his share of ups and downs, consistent with any prolific creative force, no matter how talented. After one 1935 triumph, however, Hitchcock would emerge as and remain a major film talent for the remainder of his professional life.

Hitchcock's major international breakthrough film came after he completed a picture that is highly acclaimed today, the 1934 release *The Man Who Knew Too Much*. The film represented an early triumph for the brilliant character performer Peter Lorre and also starred Leslie Banks and Edna Best. While it received great attention and has also been cited as an international breakthrough vehicle for Hitchcock, it was nonetheless distributed as a second feature, billed with an A release that is long forgotten.

In being relegated to second feature status with the highly regarded *The Man Who Knew Too Much*, Hitchcock suffered a fate customary of creators who are ahead of their time and place. Michael Balcon, head of Gaumont-British, operating out of its studio at Shepherd's Bush in Southwest London, had provided Hitchcock with a home. In the course of his activity Hitchcock ran afoul of C.M. Woolf, financier of Balcon's distribution arm. Toward the end of March 1925, producer Balcon held a screening for the press and theater exhibitors of *The Pleasure Garden*, the first film directed solely by Hitchcock, then in his mid–

twenties. The film, featuring American silent star Virginia Valli, was lauded by an anonymous reviewer in the March 25 edition of *Bioscope* as "A powerful and interesting story."

C.M. Woolf found *The Pleasure Garden* troubling. The distribution financier thought the film would confuse and upset audiences, with such strange shots as overhead views of a spiral staircase, odd angles and shadows, high contrasts in lighting, and low angle shots of chorines' legs as they descended to stage level.

The studious Hitchcock had learned a great deal about creating atmosphere with light and shadow and with striking camera angles during his formative years, when he was fortunate to be able to work and observe in Berlin, the European capital of filmmaking. Hitchcock learned about sophisticated camera technique by observing master German directors such as F.W. Murnau and Fritz Lang.

While Woolf was quick to acknowledge that the Hitchcock characteristics he criticized might be staples in the work of artistic German film directors, English audiences were not accustomed to them. Hitchcock biographer Donald Spoto noted, "British moviegoers ... were accustomed to the rather more simple views presented by American melodrama and by the static, brightly lit drawing-room comedies and romances served up by British studios."

Woolf felt strongly enough about Hitchcock's technique to persuade Michael Balcon that circulating *The Pleasure Garden* would endanger bookings for several of his other movies that were already successful releases. As a result of this steady opposition the negative and prints of Hitchcock's first complete film were banished to the studio storeroom. Critic Cedric Belfrage took umbrage with the production decision, indicating in *Picturegoer* that the move surprised him. "Hitchcock has such a complete grasp of film technique that he is able to take far more control of his production than the average director of four times his experience," Belfrage wrote. "The fact is that he has crammed twenty years of experience into five years of practice, while his youth is a tremendous asset towards freshness of treatment." Despite such a ringing endorsement, Woolf remained adamant, banishing a film embodying innovative technique, just what British audiences needed, to the sidelines.

The unfortunate experience surrounding *The Pleasure Garden* underscores a major battle that continues to be fought today in the upper strata of moviemaking. It is further underscored by the fact that the then-daringly fresh aspects of Hitchcock's technique would be the traits that won places in the hearts and minds of critics such as Belfrage, along with sophisticated elements of the moviegoing public. Hitchcock's effective use of lighting and manipulation of camera as a flexible, moving, often surprising vehicle of cinematic expression were the dual traits he exercised to climb to cinematic greatness. Hitchcock had run headlong into a battle pitting an innovative creative artist against an unimaginative production business type looking exclusively at "the bottom line," fearing that new concepts would rock the boat and contribute to diminished box office returns.

Woolf would continue to serve as an obstacle to Hitchcock in his rise up the ladder under Balcon at Gaumont-British. Still skeptical of Hitchcock's style, it was C.M. Woolf who subjected *The Man Who Knew Too Much* to second feature status. Hitchcock then propelled himself out of the Woolf box with his breakthrough triumph in *The 39 Steps.*

The MacGuffin Film

With Hitchcock such a frequently discussed figure in film circles, a word taken from an old Scottish story has become increasingly associated with him. The word "MacGuffin" is so closely associated with Hitchcock's mastery of the adventure thriller that it has been chosen as a name for a website devoted to serious researchers and students of his films. Hitchcock historian Steven DeRosa states, "Although popularized by Hitchcock, the term [MacGuffin] is credited to Angus MacPhail, chief story editor at Gaumont-British [and sometime writing collaborator], and was derived from an anecdote...."

The anecdote involves two men traveling by train from London to Scotland. One man notices a long, oddly wrapped parcel in the overhead storage compartment. His curiosity leads to a brief dialogue exchange that has etched its way into cinema annals.

"What have you there?" one man asks.

"Oh, that's a MacGuffin," his companion replies.

"What's a MacGuffin?"

"It's a device for trapping lions in the Scottish Highlands."

"But there aren't any lions in the Scottish Highlands."

"Well, then, I guess that's no MacGuffin."

Hitchcock used the story as a symbol. His wry humor adapted the word MacGuffin to mean a device used to propel an adventure story along. As Donald Spoto explains, "The point is that a MacGuffin is neither relevant, important, nor, finally, any of one's business. It simply gets the story going. In the case of *The 39 Steps,* the MacGuffin is a secret formula — the specifications for a line of fighter planes."

Using the same parlance as befits a romantic Don Juan, the chase is the thing. The title *The 39 Steps* comes from the name of an international spy organization committed to obtaining vital specifications about a line of British fighter planes and transporting it to an unnamed enemy nation bent on world conquest. One hunted man, played by Robert Donat, has pieced together bit by bit the insidious plot. A victim of circumstance, he battles seemingly overwhelming forces seeking his destruction by exercising humankind's most basic instinct, that of survival.

The Author and Tradition

As a young man Hitchcock's tastes, unsurprisingly, often involved reading spy adventures. A top author of the genre was John Buchan, who was a worthy recipient of an appellation often applied with tiring redundance, that of renaissance man. At a time when he was also expressing an interest in Edgar Allan Poe's stories and poetry, young Hitchcock read *The Thirty-Nine Steps*. Its focus on an international spy apparatus was typical of the time of publication, 1914, the World War I period.

Buchan's stories were popular among young readers during the time of Hitchcock's youth. Writing spy adventures was only one of many career hats the versatile Buchan wore during his life. The Scotland-born Buchan initially practiced law. During World War I he became Britain's Director of Information. Along with authoring many spy adventure stories, Buchan forged a political career as a Member of Parliament for the Scottish Universities. Eventually, after becoming a baron and assuming the title of Lord Tweedsmuir, Buchan was appointed Governor-General of Canada. Ross MacDonald, then a student at Western Ontario University and ultimately the creator of the highly successful Lew Archer detective series, credited a lecture he heard Buchan deliver as his career inspiration.

John Buchan was described by friend and admirer A.L. Rowse as a man "who could never resist a challenge." In later life, while Governor-General of Canada and a sick man, Buchan, after returning from an exhausting tour in the Arctic, decided to surmount the formidable challenge posed by Bear Mountain above the Mackenzie River. "The rock was rotten and slanting the wrong way," Buchan told Rowse, "but I took it cautiously and had no difficulties, except at the very top where there is an overhang. I managed to drag up an Indian so that he could give me a back, and wriggled my way up. The rest of my staff, including an inspector of police, got stuck on the lower rocks and had to be rescued by ropes!"

Buchan's influence on Hitchcock was established on a firm bedrock of British adventure story tradition. The adventure Buchan pursued in the spy world was embraced by Arthur Conan Doyle in the detective sphere with the Sherlock Holmes series. Hitchcock saw this influence as indigenously British.

"John Buchan had a big influence on me," Hitchcock said, "but more than that, I think that the attack on the whole of the subject matter is strictly English. Where sometimes one gets into difficulties with the American people is that they want everything spelled out; and they worry about content. I don't worry about content at all. The film can be about anything you like, so long as I'm making that audience react in a certain way to whatever I put on the screen. If you begin to worry about the details of what the papers are about that the spies are trying to steal, that's a lot of nonsense: I can't be bothered about what the papers are, what the spies are after. I often fall foul of critics who criticize content instead of technique."

In that Hitchcock's career fell into two distinct areas, the earlier British phase and the American period commencing with his arrival in the United States in 1939, he noted in an interview with Huw Wheldon the distinctions separating the two bodies of work. "Well, as the French say, the early English period is quite different from the American period," Hitchcock observed. "There was much more spontaneity, I suppose, and more instinct at work in the English period, but more calculation in the American period. That is the main difference."

Babe in the Woods Adventure Hero

While the book Buchan wrote was altered significantly from the movie directed by Hitchcock, as will be addressed shortly, one basic element remained the same: the major figure and his central posture. Richard Hannay, played by handsome and debonair British Midlander Robert Donat, was what one could term a Babe in the Woods Adventure Hero. In that sphere the Hannay character differs markedly from Alec Leamas, the major figure played by Richard Burton in another memorable British spy drama released thirty years later, *The Spy Who Came in from the Cold*. In the latter film, directed by American Martin Ritt, Burton's Alec Leamas is a burnt out British spy operative who has gone to seed from the driving force of alcohol occasioned by the troubling anarchistic pit into which he has fallen. This resulted from engaging in such numerous switches and ideological legerdemain that he is left an embittered man who believes in nothing. It was a mood translated to the screen from the gripping novel by John Le Carre, who, as Donald Cornwell, was a British intelligence operative. Cornwell–Le Carre understood the unique type of frustration endured by forces who are manipulators and victims at the same time. When Leamas is selected for a unique assignment, taking him to East Germany, he is used by his superiors, but understands the dimensions of the plan taking shape.

Donat's Richard Hannay is a discernibly different spy adventurer. While the foreboding Burton is a seasoned professional who understands the rules of the game he plays, Donat is a total novice who falls into the fray by a twist of fate. Burton is used by his British handlers, but as a professional who ultimately understands what is happening. He is an antihero, a frustrated man caught up in a bitter vortex of multiple dealings. The film was praised by critics for superbly capturing Cold War angst. Hannay as a Babe in the Woods Adventure Hero possesses a spontaneity an embittered veteran of the spy wars such as Leamis lost years earlier, being replaced by a sullen, thoroughly cynical anarchy.

Given Hannay's lack of facts, he must piece things together on the spur of the moment. While a novice in the field of spy adventure, what makes him a fascinating figure in *The 39 Steps* is his creative intelligence. He relies on his instincts, directed by a spontaneous intelligence, to accomplish two important objectives: 1) stay alive in a rising tide of ruthless efforts to kill him because of what he came to know through happenstance, and 2) his correlative effort to stay alive through learning all he can about the forces seeking to do him in and resolving the mystery by turning the tables on his pursuers.

Open Spaces Claustrophobia

Hannay is pursued amid the Scottish moors, providing the always visual Hitchcock with a sweeping backdrop to frame his swift plot action. Given such a sprawling setting, Hitchcock is able to employ the concept of Open Spaces Claustrophobia. The concept embodies a grand irony — while open spaces are thought of as protecting through expansion, in this case the greater the amount of space, the more suffocated the film's central figure becomes.

Open Spaces Claustrophobia was a natural ploy for film noir and its savage existential irony inherent in pitting an individual against the forces of nature. The ploy succeeded brilliantly in two noir films, one American, the other British. The 1949 RKO release *They Live by Night* saw director Nicholas Ray zero in through the intimacy of an all-seeing camera on tragic young Depression loser Bowie, played by Farley Granger, who starred in two Hitchcock films, *Rope* and *Strangers on a Train*. After the death of his two older and brutally ruthless former prison inmates, Granger is a man on the run. They had forced him into a life of crime as a bank robber after freeing him during a prison break. The term he was serving was for a crime he did not commit.

Wanted by the law, and with his ruthless mentors both dead, Bowie is forced, along with his wife, played by the sensitive Cathy O'Donnell, into a life on the run as vigilant law enforcement authorities pursue him. Ray's intimate portrait of an increasingly frustrated Bowie, alone against the forces of authority, is set against a scenic tableau of the trapped ex-bank robber moving anxiously from place to place. Helicopter shots show the barren dusty expanses, with Bowie moving restlessly, knowing time is his ultimate enemy.

Across the Bridge, a 1957 British film, captured the agonized plight of international financier Carl Schaffner trapped in a small Mexico border town. Rod Steiger brilliantly evoked the desperation of the haunted Schaffner, who cannot cross the border into Texas and America since a Scotland Yard operative is waiting, prepared to take him back to England to stand trial on fraud charges. He is forced to sleep outdoors, his only friend a dog named Dolores. The unscrupulous local police chief, seeking to control Schaffner's life and grab his fortune, denies him the basic elements of food and shelter.

Schaffner sleeps in open spaces but is trapped in the same kind of hellish claustrophobia endured by Farley Granger as the hunted Bowie eight years earlier in *They Live by Night*. Director Ken Annakin uses the camera's eye to show Steiger as a man lying helplessly in dusty wasteland while his world collapses on all sides. Like John Le Carre, who wrote *The Spy Who Came in from the Cold*, Graham Greene, whose short story was adapted to the screen in *Across the Bridge*, had also been a British intelligence operative. That experience assisted these authors in becoming effective chroniclers of a chaotic world with darkened hues, where events are so frequently the opposite of what they appear to be.

The background of an author often provides a significant clue to a story's objective, as well as its technique. Such was the case with Le Carre and Greene — and with John Buchan. Buchan looms as a product of his times whose experience shaped his development of *The Thirty-Nine Steps*. Douglas Fairbanks, Jr. reveals in his poignant 1988 autobiography, *Salad Days*, volume one, just how intimately familiar Buchan was with his subject matter in *The Thirty-Nine Steps* and his many other adventure stories. "When we had first worked together a few years back on a couple of scripts for Criterion [Productions, the film actor's company]," Fairbanks said, "I knew him only as the famous author of *The Thirty-Nine Steps* and all those wonderful Greenmantle action stories. I knew he was venerated by the literati of Great Britain and had served in a high ceremonial post under the crown of Scotland. I knew him as a small, wiry man with a soft accent and an intriguing quiet personality. I did not *know* until recently that he had been the head of Britain's secret intelligence service — the MI-5 — for some time."

More Timely Than Ever

While Hitchcock initially read *The Thirty-Nine Steps* as a schoolboy when it was first published in 1914, the book had an even more timely ring when he brought the film to the screen twenty-one years later. The international spy activities resonated in the atmosphere of World War I when Buchan wrote the story, but its message was enhanced within the framework of Britain just prior to its involvement in the Battle of Britain in the context of World War II. With the sound of war drums moving closer as the activities of dictators Adolf Hitler in Germany and Benito Mussolini in Italy assumed an increasing boldness and aggressiveness, in Britain there was a movement, headed by a handsome and charismatic figure, that was generating concern within and outside power portals.

Sir Oswald Mosley was born in 1896 to a highly prominent Staffordshire County family. He graduated from Sandhurst, Britain's version of West Point, which Winston Churchill had attended earlier. Excelling both intellectually and as an athlete, the dynamic Mosley was a young man in a hurry. He was elected to the House of Commons in 1918 and took his seat as the body's youngest member.

Mosley's dissatisfaction with the current political system was accented by impatient calls to action, culminating in frequent party switching. After starting as a Conservative he would move to Labour, then become briefly an Independent before launching his own organization, the New Party. When Britain became immersed in the throes of the worldwide Depression Mosley presented a bold plan for economic action. A man ahead of his time, he incorporated many ideas that would later be popularly associated with distinguished economist John Maynard Keynes. Criticizing the parliamentary structure as too archaic to deal with Britain's current economic needs, Mosley's plan for action called for the creation of an economic board with broad powers.

When Britain, which was not hit as hard by the Depression as America and the European heartland, made a spirited recovery from the worst of its difficulties, Mosley's movement swung away from economics into an area of great concern. A trip to Italy convinced Mosley that Benito Mussolini was investing his country with a governing efficiency and unity of spirit that he admired. He created the British Union of Fascists. Mosley attracted to his ranks sturdy men of action like himself who wore uniforms and marched in jack-booted militaristic lockstep, and came to be known as the Blackshirts. Fights often broke out at party rallies. One of the highest-pitched battles occurred during an Albert Hall rally. The famous Kensington concert hall was used by Hitchcock as the dramatic centerpiece for assassination attempts of world statesmen in both his 1934 and 1956 versions of *The Man Who Knew Too Much*. Blackshirts used truncheons in battles in which leader Mosley also became physically involved.

The Anti-Semitic Factor

Buchan's book registered a ringing prescience in one area that was a far more paramount force twenty-one years later than when it was initially published. Richard Hannay, the book's innocent hero, becomes drawn into the spy world after returning to his Portland Place flat and being confronted by Scudder, a mysterious neighbor from America whose intense comments about sinister international forces that threaten his life extend into the area of anti–Semitism.

On page 4, Buchan penned the following chilling words from an emotional monologue launched by Scudder:

> "Do you wonder?" he cried. "For three hundred years they have been persecuted, and this is the return match for the pogroms. The Jew is everywhere, but you have to go far down the backstairs to find him. Take any big Teutonic business concern. If you have dealings with it the first man you meet is Prince von and zu Something, an elegant young man who talks Eton-and-Harrow English. But he cuts no ice. If your business is big, you get behind him and find a prognathous Westphalian with a retreating brow and the manners of a hog. He is the German business man that gives your English papers the shakes. But if you're on the biggest kind of job and are bound

Opposite: Early Suspense Blockbuster — Robert Donat and Madeleine Carroll were the appealing stars of Hitchcock's adaptation of John Buchan's suspense novel *The Thirty-Nine Steps*. The film's enormous success enhanced Hitchcock's international reputation.

Handcuffed TO THE GIRL WHO DOUBLE-CROSSED HIM

The "Monte Cristo" hero...
The MAN who put
the MAN in roMANce.

ROBERT   MADELEINE
DONAT CARROLL
in
THE 39 STEPS

Directed by ALFRED HITCHCOCK
Director of The Man Who Knew Too Much

A GB PRODUCTION

A HUNDRED STEPS AHEAD OF ANY PICTURE THIS YEAR

to get to the real boss, ten to one you are brought up against a little, white-faced Jew in a bath-chair with an eye like a rattlesnake. Yes, sir, he is the man who is ruling the world just now, and he has a knife in the Empire of the Tsar, because his aunt was outraged and his father flogged in some one-horse location on the Volga."

The chief reason why Richard Hannay is initially disinclined to take Scudder seriously is due to such commentary, which he regards as sheer bombast. The strong anti–Semitic tone of Scudder carries a particularly chilling ring in the wake of ongoing events in mid-thirties Germany, with the heavily bigoted overtones of the ruling Third Reich.

At the time that Buchan penned *The Thirty-Nine Steps*, in Russia a fraudulent anti–Semitic hate tract known as *Protocols of the Elders of Zion* had gained great popularity. It became known as "the anti–Semites' bible" and was exploited for propagandistic purposes by the Third Reich. A knowledgeable man of state such as Buchan could be expected to know about it, and his reference to the conspiratorial accusations of the paranoiac Scudder probably held the twin objective of a warning to enlightened people as to what might lie ahead as well as an opportunity to ridicule such beliefs in print. While Mosley's group had initially devoted itself to largely economic issues, in time its message began to assume a loathsome anti–Semitic as well as anti-foreign bent, along with a foreboding militarism.

Mosley's Blackshirts were not ultimately reduced to obscurity until Britain became locked in conflict with Hitler's Third Reich. After the Conservative and Labour parties formed a political union declaring non-opposition to each other until the end of the war, the British Union of Fascists ran slates of so-called peace candidates in national elections.

The Blackshirt element was making its presence felt in Britain at the time that Hitchcock made *The 39 Steps*. Seeing uniformed para-militarists on English streets shifted more attention to what was happening there and related it to unfolding activities in Germany and Italy. Such events made moviegoers all the more empathic with Richard Hannay's adventures as he battles an unidentified unscrupulous international force intent on world conquest.

Probably for visual reasons, Alfred Hitchcock changed the word "Thirty-Nine" in the book's title to the number. There is a greater visual urgency bestowed on the strength of the shorter, more succinct impact of *The 39 Steps*. Succinctness is a hallmark throughout as Hannay moves with a surging urgency. The swift pacing, along with Hitchcock's busy camera, enhances the paramount element of the film's plot — that this is a man with very little time to uncover the truth and save his life in the process.

From Book to Film

While the main story line of Richard Hannay's frantic chase to avoid death from sinister spy forces or capture by police were retained, significant changes were made to Buchan's story by the time the film reached the screen. Some of the changes related to perceptible differences between a reading and cinematic experience, while others appear to have conformed to definite story plotting ideas characteristic of a highly stylistic director.

In Buchan's book the reader is exposed to quite a bit about Richard Hannay, whose manner and spirited activities appear reflective of the fascinating, multi-faceted author who penned the story. Hannay the literary hero has led a fascinating life. He uses colorful experiences to entertain by anecdote, working himself into the good graces of people he encounters. This bent is exercised with diplomatic aplomb while Hannay, having escaped from his Portland Place flat following the murder of former neighbor Scudder, is living by his wits as police authorities and spy operatives close in on him.

It is anything but surprising that a proud Scot such as John Buchan would set much of the story's intrigue in a series of chase sequences in which the peripatetic Hannay moves through the heather of the moors. Adventurous mountain climber Buchan is at home in this world, the difference being that his literary hero is forced to thread his way through an obstacle course at which the specter of death lurks at each point.

Hannay is resourceful by necessity, as evidenced in some graphic writing by an author with an affinity for mountain climbing: "I dropped out of sight behind the skyline. That way was shut to me, and I must try the bigger hills to the south beyond the highway. The car I had noticed was getting nearer, but it was still a long way off with some very steep gradients before it. I ran hard, crouching low except in the hollows, and as I ran I kept scanning the brow of the hill before me. Was it imagination, or did I see figures, one, two, perhaps more — moving in a glen beyond the stream?"

"If you are hemmed in on all sides in a patch of land there is only one chance of escape. You must stay in the patch, and let your enemies search it and not find you. That was good sense, but how on earth was I to escape notice in that table-cloth of a place? I would have buried myself to the neck in mud or lain below water or climbed the tallest tree. But there was not a stick of wood, the bog-holes were little puddles, the stream was a slender trickle. There was nothing but short heather, and bare hill bent, and the white highway."

Hannay's hectic ordeal prompts him to long for the simpler things in life. He ruefully admits, under the duress of a hunted man and feeling acute hunger pains, how wrong he was to take for granted the fine food his manservant would prepare for him. If only he could savor the scent and luxuriate in the taste of some bacon and eggs at that trouble-filled moment, he ruminates. Hannay's first-person account rendered amid great duress reveals his life of travel as a mining engineer. He regales those he meets with accounts from his days in outposts such as South Africa, India or Rhodesia. Along with missing the simple pleasures of regular food, Hannay expresses guilt over the melancholy boredom he was experiencing in London before being propelled by fate into his frantic battle for survival. Hannay recounts the ennui of a London club man, existing in the cloistered settings of plush drawing rooms, martinis and cigars among the city's social elite. Digging his way through the moors, looking bedraggled and unkempt, he marvels at the irony as he recollects what it was like in his sedately aristocratic milieu before his spirited adventures began.

Filling in the Blanks

The first-person account of Richard Hannay developed in Buchan's spy thriller is detailed in a way that Hitchcock's hero is not. The wily Hitchcock is a director who invites audience members to fill in blanks, and they are numerous with protagonist Richard Hannay. The audience is told nothing about Hannay other than that he is a visitor to London from Montreal. Hitchcock, through a combination of story and visual technique, enables viewers to conclude that Hannay is a prosperous and apparently well educated man. His Portland Mansions residence at Portland Place invites an inference of affluence, despite an understandable spartan-like ambience of a bachelor flat. Portland Place is located off Oxford and Regent streets at the beginning of London's West End, where the main quarters of the British Broadcasting Corporation is situated. When the audience first sets its collective eye on Hannay, he is well dressed. His upper-class accent and articulateness reveal him as well-bred.

Hannay falls into what would later become a familiar pattern for Hitchcock in mysteries of the innocent novice being thrust into a vortex of international spy intrigue that he must piece together based on developing experiences. Twenty-four years later Hitchcock's *North by Northwest* teaming of Cary Grant and Eva Marie Saint would prompt references to it as the director's "American *39 Steps*." In 1937, just two years after *The 39 Steps* was released, Hitchcock in *Young and Innocent* presented Derrick de Marney as a victim of circumstance in danger of being overwhelmed by forces beyond his control in the same manner as Robert Donat in the earlier film. In 1934's *The Man Who Knew Too Much*, which preceded by one year *The 39 Steps*, Leslie Banks and Edna Best, as husband and wife, are thrust into the brutal world of espionage when their daughter, Nova Pilbeam, is kidnapped by a gang of international incorrigibles led by a ruthless Peter Lorre. Pilbeam would reemerge two years later in *Young and Innocent* as a supportive tower of strength to Derrick de Marney. A generation after the original version of *The Man Who Knew Too Much* was released, Hitchcock remade it with Jimmy Stewart and Doris Day as the victimized parents. Hitchcock's 1942 war espionage film, *Saboteur*, follows an identical theme as an innocent Glendale, California, aircraft worker, played by Robert Cummings, is pursued by a nest of Nazi spies, led by a smarmy and megalomaniacal Otto Kruger, as Priscilla Lane supplies support.

Introducing Donat

Hitchcock introduces Robert Donat as Richard Hannay in a manner that blends intrigue with tantalizing mystery. The audience sees the back of a man in a black overcoat as he moves toward his seat, then sits down in a packed London music hall. Through a sequence showing the main character in his initial action, audience members are invited to step into his shoes. As Donat is experiencing his first action in the film, so is his audience.

One of the film's key characters is introduced in the person of Mr. Memory, played by Wylie Watson. The character is based on an actual British performer, Datas. Hitchcock in his youth saw him perform his amazing memory feats. When Mr. Memory begins answering questions the first element of conflict, a Hitchcock staple he uses to both entertain and tease his audiences, emerges in the ranks of audience members. A sharp contrast is evident between the suit-attired portion of the audience and the wisecracking hecklers wearing caps and sporting Cockney accents. Some audience members are interested in testing his phenomenal memory, but are in conflict with the poorer element, whose members tease with irreverent wisecracks, being admonished by the master of ceremonies.

Donat, in the role of Richard Hannay, is cleverly introduced to the audience as a visitor to London when he asks a question of Mr. Memory, "How far is Winnipeg from Montreal?" After Mr. Memory delivers a smiling welcome to the Canadian visitor, he supplies the correct answer.

The crowd finally assumes the roar of an angry collective animal ready to spring on its prey. Hitchcock's busy camera pans to brawling audience members swinging arms and tumbling to the ground. The brawling ends when two gunshots are fired. The audience moves hastily toward the exits, with Hannay among their ranks. The pandemonium erupting in a theater conjures up memories of Hitchcock's memorable Albert Hall scenes depicting assassination attempts in the two versions of *The Man Who Knew Too Much.*

Scuttling Scudder

As Hannay moves quickly toward the nearest exit in the midst of the maelstrom he falls into the arms of another swiftly departing patron, a slender, aristocratically beautiful brunette woman in her middle thirties, played with the proper measure of enigmatic intrigue by Lucie Mannheim. A measure of urgency is evident in her request to accompany Hannay home. He obliges with the reply, "It's your funeral." We will learn later that a carefree kidding remark contains a note of chilling irony. They board a bus and emerge at Portland Place.

The script reaches a point of sharp diversion with the supplanting of the fearful paranoiac American Scudder in favor of Lucie Mannheim's character. Her thick European accent is reminiscent of the exoticism prevalent in the mid-thirties with Greta Garbo. Mannheim, who spent most of her cinema career alternating between West Germany and England, exhibits the proper measure of spy intrigue from the outset of her brief but highly memorable performance, which provides a pivotal mainspring to all that will follow. The name she assumes carries the ring of a Hitchcock tease—Annabella Smith. The first name conveys a note of foreign intrigue while that of Smith resounds with an American typicality.

When Smith arrives at Hannay's flat a conflict develops. Surely one of the advantages Hitchcock recognized in the spy adventure, along with the obvious conflict of unscrupulous hunters and innocent hunted, is the sub-compartmentalized tension within the main anxiety of conflict. This stems from the disbelief of certain individuals to accept what appears to them to be a far-fetched premise of foreign spy intrigue.

When the telephone rings Annabella implores Hannay not to answer it. She asks that the mirror in the living room be turned toward the wall. They move into the kitchen, where there are no windows. Smith explains that she had fired the shots in the music hall to create a disruption so that she could escape her pursuers, two men seeking to kill her. One brief look out the window convinces Hannay—he sees the two men standing beneath a street light, a contrast of light against a backdrop of darkness. He exclaims, "You win." With quick effectiveness it is demonstrated that the mysterious, exotic woman is speaking the truth.

Introducing His MacGuffin

Hitchcock sees that his MacGuffin or plot key is quickly introduced. The name of the ruthless spy organization of which exotic foreign agent Annabella Smith has run afoul carries connotations of international intrigue:

SMITH: Have you heard of the 39 Steps?
HANNAY: No, what's that—a pub?
SMITH: Never mind. But what you are laughing at just now is true. These men will stop at nothing. I am the only person who can stop them. If they are not stopped, it is only a matter of days, perhaps hours, before the secret is out of the country.
HANNAY: Well, why don't you phone the police or something?
SMITH: 'Cause they wouldn't believe me any more than you did. And if they did, how long do you think it would take to get them going? These men act quickly. You don't know how clever their chief is.

Annabella Smith is unable to provide the name of the master spy. She is, however, able to supply a vital clue. "He has a dozen names, and he can look like a hundred people," the apprehensive Annabella exclaims, "but one thing he cannot disguise—this: part of his little finger is missing—so if ever you should meet a man with no top joint there, be careful, my friend."

The exotic brunette with the fascinating accent tells Hannay that the goal of the organization is the theft of crucial documents from the War Ministry. The documents will then be spirited out of England and deposited in the hands of an unnamed enemy. In allowing the audience to guess, Hitchcock is engaging in one of his frequent ploys, that of allowing his audience to fill in blanks. Early in the film Hitchcock, with some carefully constructed dialogue, has provided the thematic blueprint for his movie. All of the following action to the film's conclusion is constructed around the elucidated principles:

1) The existence of a merciless spy organization called the 39 Steps which will stop at nothing to achieve its ends.
2) It is in England to collect top secret information from the War Ministry and place it in the hands of the nation's enemies.
3) Dangerous uncertainty and the hovering threat of death have invaded the life of Richard Hannay, resulting from his association with the mysterious Annabella Smith.

By then his beautiful guest has made her point. His attention is fixed on the gravity of the situation as her problem has now become his own. After preparing a meal of haddock for himself and his guest, Hannay behaves as the perfect gentleman, agreeing to sleep on the living room couch and donating the use of the only bed in his bachelor digs to the brunette.

Murder and the First Identity Switch

As the camera displays a highly revealing open window where white curtains flutter in early morning darkness, Annabella staggers into the living room. The same knife that Hannay had used to cut bread as he was preparing the evening meal is stuck in her back. "Clear out, Hannay!" she implores. "They'll get you next." The telephone rings, sounding a fresh alarm. He peers with apprehensive anticipation through the window, observing the same two men as before.

Annabella's image is superimposed on screen, conveying a ghostly image. Her words of warning return. We hear her once again exclaim, "What you are laughing at just now is true. These men will stop at nothing."

Hannay is able to remove from Annabella's clutching grasp a map of Scotland. A place named Alt-na-Shellach is circled, supplying his only working clue. The basic story elements are in place. The discernibly Hitchcock phase of the film, the feverish cat-and-mouse chases amid human conflicts, commences. Once more the ghost-like image of Annabella is superimposed over the map, symbolically spelling out where the basic story conflict lies. Hannay recounts her haunting words of warning: "There's a man in Scotland whom I must visit next if anything is to be done. It's only a matter of days, perhaps hours, before the secret is out of the country. The police will not believe me any more than you did. I tell you, these men act quickly, quickly, quickly."

While Donat as Hannay is caught flat-footed by emerging events, and is a pure novice being pushed by fate into the eye of an international spy whirlwind, he remains a man of crafty intelligence. This native intelligence, coupled with his survivor's instinct, carries the story forward. Hannay becomes a man of shifting identities, supplying a plausible story for each situation. His first identity shift, which saves his life, occurs only after he is the victim of a boomerang of fate. When Annabella Smith had truthfully explained her plight to him, Richard Hannay was openly skeptical. He sees that his best means of escape is through obtaining assistance from the white-uniformed milkman making his early rounds. When the rattled victim of circumstance explains the blunt truth to the milkman, played by Frederick Piper, he laughs, responding that he could never believe such an obviously contrived story. Donat's statement of fact is greeted by the milkman in the same fashion as the no-frills account rendered by the now deceased Mannheim.

The quick resourcefulness that provides Richard Hannay with repeated escapes from harm's way surfaces as he contrives a story the milkman readily believes. He explains that a jealous husband threatens his well-being and that he had been involved in a liaison with his wife, who lives on the first floor. "Why didn't you tell me before, old fellow?" the milkman replies, reprimanding Hannay in a friendly manner for having previously told such an implausible story.

The milkman offers Hannay use of his uniform, container and bottles as he makes his getaway, fooling his would-be killers. He makes his way to Euston Station, where he boards the Flying Scotsman train and heads for the destination where he hopes he will unlock the mystery surrounding the 39 Steps. The spies pursue fleetingly, running down the tracks and losing the race to the departing train.

The quick cut transition between the whistle of the Flying Scotsman and the discovery of the female spy's body is one of the niftiest of Hitchcock's career. When Hannay's cleaning lady discovers Smith's body she opens her mouth wide in a state of panic. Before the audience can hear her impending scream, however, it is preempted by the ensuing train whistle and the image of the Flying Scotsman rolling down the tracks.

Contrasting Humor and a Cool Blonde

Alfred Hitchcock's British phase, as he noted, revealed a penchant for steady action recorded with a busy camera featuring numerous settings and activities, in contrast to his later American phase and a greater emphasis on the psychological. Contrasts are needed in films such as *The 39 Steps*, featuring a man seeking to avoid death. Hitchcock uses humor to lighten the situation. Often it is etched with irony or satire of various dimensions.

With the healthy dose of death and spies early in the film, Hitchcock sees Hannay's train ride to Scotland as an opportunity to lighten the material, giving his audience a break. Donat shares the compartment with two middle-aged salesmen. They become immersed in conversation about the women's corsets one of the men is selling. The middle-aged men's eyes twinkle as a salesman removes corsets from his case. They resemble pubescent adolescents at a peep show as their minds engage in libidinous fantasy. When the train stops the compartment's only other passenger apart from Hannay departs stiffly. He is a minister who has sat in silence while the libidinous salesmen discussed women's corsets.

One of the men buys a newspaper from a vendor walking along the track, a transaction conducted through an open train window. When the journey resumes, a discussion ensues over the newspaper's headline story of the "Portland Place Murder," which includes a picture of Richard Hannay. He quickly steps out of the compartment, fearing detection.

Hannay observes a group of plainclothes officers moving along the aisle, carefully observing passengers in compartments. Seeking to elude them, Hannay dons a new identity, that of a young lover sharing a passionate embrace with his girlfriend. His problem stems from a discernible lack of cooperation from the young woman he chooses to aid him in his effort to elude authorities.

With time at a premium, Hannay darts into a compartment occupied by Pamela (Madeleine Carroll). He throws his arms around her and delivers a passionate kiss, which prompts one of the officers who looks inside to joke about the intensity of the lovers. Hannay apologizes, honestly explaining his plight. He meets with the same response he received after he told the blunt truth to the milkman in his flat before making his escape.

Moments later the authorities question Hannay and Pamela as they seek the Portland Place murder suspect. "This is the man you want, I think," a revulsion-filled and disbelieving Pamela exclaims. There is no doubt in her mind, since Hannay had, during his lengthy proclamation of innocence, told her his name. Her steadfastness is convincing evidence that she believes Richard Hannay is guilty of murder.

Hannay is able to make a swift escape by darting down the hall, opening a door, and catapulting to the ground. He now literally finds himself on Scottish soil as the chase continues.

Madeleine Carroll's appearance holds great symbolic significance in the history of Hitchcock's films. It marks the first in a tradition, the introduction of the "cool blonde" in his films. She remains the only British blonde of this distinction, the others surfacing in the director's later Hollywood period. Grace Kelly lent her elegant beauty to three Hitchcock films, all released in the span of one year — *Dial M for Murder* and *Rear Window* in 1954, and *To Catch a Thief* in

1955. Eva Marie Saint starred opposite Cary Grant in the American equivalent of *The 39 Steps* and the action-laden *North by Northwest* (1959), and Tippi Hedren starred in *The Birds* (1963) and *Marnie* (1964). Kim Novak's role in *Vertigo* (1958) requires an asterisk since her coolness in trapping Jimmy Stewart through seduction in the film's first half is part of a successful act, as will be later explained, while the real character emerging in the second half, a frightened, tormented young woman, is the antithesis of cool.

When Hannay escapes from the train he rapidly assumes his third identity since his embarkation by the hand of fate into the spy world. He approaches a crofter (Scottish tenant farmer) and introduces himself as an automobile mechanic seeking work. The crofter, portrayed by John Laurie, explains that the area already has a mechanic. Hannay learns that there is one new person in the area, a professor living fourteen miles away. The question that emerges is whether this could be the head of the 39 Steps. Despite Hannay's eagerness to continue his journey, darkness is descending and the journey will have to wait until the next day. He makes a deal with the crofter to have dinner and sleep there that night.

Of Love and Marriage

In addition to the swiftly paced spy story, Hitchcock along the way makes points about love and marriage. Hannay blunders when he meets the stern crofter's wife, believing her to be the man's daughter due to a substantial age difference. The petite and sensitive young wife is played by Peggy Ashcroft, a British legend of the stage who early in her remarkable career was already playing opposite Paul Robeson in London's West End as Desdemona in *Othello*. While most of the career of the grand lady who would ultimately become Dame Peggy Ashcroft would take place on the London stage, at 77 she secured an Oscar for Best Supporting Actress in the role of Mrs. Moore, the British visitor to India, in David Lean's last film, *A Passage to India* (1984).

John Laurie, a noted Shakespearean actor on the British stage, as the crofter represents a stern stiffness reflective of religious dogmatism. Scotland is the land of John Knox, and many of his adherents practice a rigorous brand of Presbyterian conservatism. The character could also be associated with Hitchcock's Catholic youth and his Jesuit education. The marriage is one of convenience, with Ashcroft obviously feeling trapped. In her few moments alone with Hannay, toward whom she feels a bond of kinship as well as physical attraction, she speaks glowingly of a happier period in her native Glasgow, recounting fine shops and cinemas, when she was happy in the pulse of city life. When her dour husband emerges, Hannay, to protect Margaret (Ashcroft), who has voiced views her husband would find heretical, explains his preference for city life. "God made the country," John (Laurie) sternly replies.

Popular Team — Two stars from the English Midlands, Robert Donat and Madeleine Carroll, provided the proper chemistry to help make Hitchcock's 1935 British release, *The 39 Steps*, a luminous success. Four years later Donat would secure Best Actor Academy Award honors for *Goodbye, Mr. Chips* over Clark Gable in *Gone with the Wind*.

Authorities arrive early in the morning to apprehend Hannay, who is warned by Margaret. After John accuses the pair of making love behind his back, Hannay explains that he is wanted for a murder he did not commit. He gives the crofter money to send the police away. Instead John later bargains with authorities, and Margaret, seeing his treachery, urges Hannay to leave quickly. Her last tender look in his direction indicates the love she feels for a man who will treat her with respect. She gives Hannay her husband's overcoat as a final gesture, hopefully making it easier for him to avoid detection.

Meeting the Man

Richard Hannay next emerges at the home of the man known to the community as Professor Jordan, a stately structure scenically situated in the moors. Professor Jordan sends his wife out of the room, talking in privacy to the fugitive. Godfrey Tearle, playing Professor Jordan, hears Hannay out. Despite Hannay's referring to himself as Hammond, marking identity change number four for the resourceful survivor, Professor Jordan immediately knows who he is. He inveigles Hannay to relate all he knows about the beautiful spy who was killed in his flat. As Hannay begins to tell him about the unique physical characteristic of the leader of the 39 Steps, Jordan holds out his hand with the missing finger joint. It graphically reveals him to be the treacherous spy master Annabella Smith described.

The Professor ultimately pulls a gun on Hannay. After giving him a chance to kill himself, which is spurned, he fires. Hannay hits the ground. Is his life over?

We do not have long to wait as, following a quick cut, Hannay is seen explaining what has happened to Sheriff Watson (Frank Cellier), sheriff of the nearest town. The crofter had placed his hymn book in an inside pocket of his overcoat. The bullet penetrated the thick book, saving Hannay, who was moved to another room. When the opportunity surfaced he stole out of the house, lifted spy master Jordan's car, and drove to the police station.

As befitting a spy adventure, once the hero appears to have made progress, the hand of a stern fate intervenes. Hannay has no sooner finished his story than authorities arrive to take him away. Sheriff Watson scoffs that he never believed Hannay's story and that Professor Jordan is his best friend in town.

Hannay crashes out the window before he can be arrested. He undergoes another identity switch, his fifth, as he blends into a crowd of Salvation Army marchers who walk in unison down the town's main street while the band plays a religious hymn. Soon he is into identity six as he darts into a building where a political rally is in progress. He is mistaken for the parliamentary candidate who is expected to speak and is led to the podium. He begins speaking and launches excitedly into impromptu oration that quickly wins over the crowd.

While as gripping entertainment it can stand on its own with no ulterior motivation, a question looms, given the climate of the times. This was a period when Hitler was launching lengthy Sunday orations in concert with torchlight parades at Nuremberg, and Mussolini was delivering stem-winding speeches in Rome's Victor Emanuel Square. Also, the brilliant British orator Sir Oswald Mosley was captivating throngs at Albert Hall and elsewhere. It could accordingly be asked: Could Donat's success in promptly winning over the crowd with his passionate speech be a message from Hitchcock about mass psychology? Is he warning the public against being easily fooled by impassioned rhetoric? Could this scene be a warning for humankind about the tragedies that can befall the world if crowds are taken in by the glib oratory of charismatic speakers?

Despite his convincing efforts, Donat is not destined to avoid detection for long. As he continues his speech Madeleine Carroll enters, along with two men. She had observed Donat's exit through the window of the police station and has led the men to him.

The scene's clever technique is reminiscent of a comparable one in another great British film, Carol Reed's *The Third Man* (1949). Both scenes are interesting due to the fact that the on-screen audiences are unaware of what is really happening. With Donat he is improvising to gain at least temporary safety. In *The Third Man* the American character played by Joseph Cotten is pursued by ruthless Viennese racketeers. As he delivers a lecture to an audience on the topic of literature, writer Cotten is engaged in conversation with one of the spies about his next project. The conversation is in reality not about an upcoming fiction work, but is related to Cotten's unwanted investigation of the alleged murder of his friend, played by Orson Welles. The body in question is not actually that of Welles' character, and Cotten, despite his investigative clumsiness, threatens a thriving criminal enterprise run by Welles.

Conflict with a Cool Blonde

When Hannay is taken into custody by the two men, who have been directed there by Pamela, he implores her once more to believe him. As on the previous occasion, she refuses. The skillful insertion of the cool blonde into the film provides an added dramatic dimension beyond the meeting between Hannay and Scudder in Buchan's novel. As the men lead Hannay away, he is handcuffed to Pamela in a ploy described by one of the men as precautionary.

As they travel along a dirt road in an evening fog, with their next stop presumably Inverarry, Pamela remarks that they are heading in the wrong direction. Hannay correctly concludes that they are not in the hands of the local police, but have been apprehended by two spies. He surmises that they are heading toward the so-called Professor's residence.

At that juncture the vehicle comes to a stop as a large contingent of bleating sheep cross their path. As the spies exit, attempting to get the sheep under control and forge a path to continue, Hannay quickly leaps out of the car, compelling Pamela to accompany him despite her protests.

Not only has Hitchcock brought a statuesque blonde of outstanding beauty into the cast, he has linked her by handcuffs to the story's hero, someone she initially distrusts. While she protests loudly, her opposition will eventually begin to dissipate, especially when he later teases her about his family's proud history in brutal crime, including his illustrious Uncle Penruddy, the "Cornish Blue-beard," whose exploits have resulted in a statue showcasing at Madam Tussauds. When they locate an inn, the couple steps inside and Hannay engages in yet another identity switch as he announces that he and Pamela are newlyweds.

While dramatic conflict is present in their association through much of the picture, the longer the relationship between Donat and Carroll develops, the more it becomes apparent that their carping and insult hurling demonstrates high-spirited mutual attraction. The husband and wife innkeepers become immediate romantics, admiring the younger couple for the passion they appear to share.

Hitchcock scuttled Scudder, replacing him with the beautiful and exotic brunette spy played by Lucie Mannheim. He then brings in another beautiful woman, this time a contrasting blonde, in the form of the elegant Carroll. Hitchcock's voyeuristic camera's eye gives audiences a look at Carroll's sleekly toned legs in a close-up after a stocking tear. He provides many close-ups of her face, displaying an elegant beauty accented by finely-chiseled cheekbones.

"It is strange," Hitchcock told Norah Baring in a 1935 *Film Pictorial* interview, "how very well Madeleine fitted into the part. I had heard a lot about her as a tall, cold, blonde beauty." Hitchcock had seldom seen her on the screen, evaluating her via photographs, which he felt revealed a beauty that was "very cold." At their first meeting she impressed him as "perfectly natural" and possessing "a great sense of humor."

A star beginning in silent days, Madeleine Carroll fell into the catch–22 of many beautiful screen stars. While beauty attracts attention and is showcased, too often it becomes the sole focus and scant if any attention is paid to the other attributes of an actress. Hitchcock believed that this was a dilemma confronting Carroll.

"In her case her obvious good looks had nearly been her downfall," Hitchcock explained to Baring. "It is very hard with merely the material of good looks to create a character, especially when they are completely devitalized by absence of action.... After meeting her I made up my mind to present her to the public as her *natural* self.... In *The 39 Steps* the public is seeing a Madeleine Carroll who has no time to be calm and serene. She is far too busy racing over moors, rushing up and down embankments, and scrambling over rocks."

A Midlands Starring Duo

The dapper Donat and cameo-like, elegant Carroll make a striking couple. The relationship that develops from early distrust on her part to ultimate romance as the camera reveals them holding hands at film's end is one of the strongest points of the film. Donat and Carroll were both born and raised in the British Midlands. Donat's roots were in Manchester while Carroll grew up in

West Bromwich in Staffordshire. The success of *The 39 Steps* mightily enhanced both of their careers.

With his broad-shouldered muscularity and finely-trimmed mustache, Robert Donat could pass as a British Clark Gable. The American star figured in his career, but not due to on-screen linkage. At the 1939 Oscar presentations it was Donat who secured Best Actor honors for his role as master of a boys' school in *Goodbye, Mr. Chips*, winning over Gable, who was nominated for his role as Rhett Butler in *Gone with the Wind*. Donat also rendered a stellar performance in the highly-acclaimed *The Winslow Boy* (1950), in which he is cast as a barrister who defends an innocent Naval cadet accused of stealing. Donat's tragic career handicap, which cut his life short and diminished his acting opportunities, was a serious asthmatic condition.

As for Carroll, Hitchcock was sufficiently pleased with her performance opposite Donat to cast her as the female lead for his next film, *Secret Agent*, in which she starred opposite John Gielgud, Peter Lorre and Robert Young. This film was also released in 1935, and saw Hitchcock returning to the same spy adventure terrain which was paying handsome dividends for the director during the thirties. Carroll's two roles for Hitchcock prompted keen interest from Hollywood, culminating in a contract at Twentieth Century–Fox. Twentieth boss Darryl F. Zanuck put her immediately to work starring opposite Tyrone Power in the 1936 drama *Lloyds of London*. The following year she appeared opposite Dick Powell and Alice Faye in *Every Night at Eight*, and Ronald Colman and Douglas Fairbanks, Jr., in *The Prisoner of Zenda*.

The tide shifts dramatically in the Carroll-Donat relationship after she is able to work her way out of the handcuffs, severing her bond to the wanted man. She slips out of the room they share, but stops on the stairwell as she listens to a telephone conversation of one of the spies, who is searching for Donat. He talks to a fellow spy on the telephone and reveals the name of the 39 Steps. She learns by listening that the man known as the Professor has already left home and "will be picking up our friend at the London Palladium on the way out."

Hitchcock's Ode to Marriage and Romance

In addition to providing rapidly paced drama, Hitchcock in *The 39 Steps* has much to say, always succinctly, about marriage and romance. The Buchan novel was very much a man's story focusing on Richard Hannay's escapes. There is nothing resembling a glamorous woman presented in his spy adventure. Hitchcock, by adding a romantic element, has generated additional audience interest. The relationships displayed include:

1) The original meeting between the exotically beautiful brunette spy and

the story's hero. While Richard Hannay finds Annabella Smith fascinating and is very much aware of her beauty, no relationship is possible as she is brutally murdered hours after they meet under tense and trying circumstances. The meeting, however, is a basic link holding the story together since their interlude has exposed him to danger.

2) After the murder of Smith, Hannay is compelled to use his resourcefulness to gain cooperation from the milkman by telling him he is seeking to escape from a jealous husband following a romantic encounter with his wife, which causes the other man, himself admittedly very much married, to laugh and commiserate. He then provides cooperation.

3) The salesmen on the train, who supply comedic relief lustfully discussing women's corsets while a clergyman sits silently in the compartment, looking stone-faced.

4) The meeting with the tortured and sensitive Peggy Ashcroft, trapped in a marriage presumably formed by convenience to a cold, fanatically religious older man. When the crofter inquires about his missing hymn book and learns from his wife that she gave his overcoat, and the hymn book inside, to Hannay, he brutally slaps her. Ashcroft's longing look toward Donat at his early morning departure reveals her wish for an opportunity for a relationship with him.

5) The family relationship involving Godfrey Tearle as the Professor and his wife and daughter. Tearle delivers a passionless parting kiss of formality to his wife, played by Helen Haye, on announcing he is leaving for London on business. His relationship with his daughter is also stiffly formal. Family life appears rigidly formal. The Professor's is a marriage and family life of proper convenience with no apparent warmth.

6) The husband and wife innkeepers. Hitchcock appreciates that as innkeepers they live vicariously as perpetual observers. They are gregarious people who appreciate romance. This trait saves Hannay and Pamela. When the spies order drinks they begin asking questions. The wily wife uses her intuition to conclude that they are up to no good and concerned about apprehending Donat. She springs into action, giving the men back the crown they used to pay for the liquor, explaining that they must leave and that the establishment is not about to serve patrons beyond the legal closing time.

7) The integral relationship that begins with high-spirited feuding and ends with the prospect of romance between Robert Donat and Madeleine Carroll's characters. By building conflict into such a developing relationship, with the added dimension of handcuffs providing an enforced unity, a clever dimension has been added to the drama. While many events occur, it is but a brief time between Donat's lament of "There are twenty million women in this island and I've got to be chained to you" to their hand holding at the film's conclusion.

A Neatly Wrapped,
Symmetrical Conclusion

One final fiery exchange occurs between the couple when Carroll does not tell Donat about the spies and her belief in his innocence until morning. She recognized his need for sleep after his many harrowing experiences, but is sharply reprimanded due to the time lost. From that point forward they are a united front as they begin their journey to London.

The story ends with a neatly wrapped, symmetrical conclusion in that the finale occurs at a theater. Significantly, the event occurs at the Palladium, situated just off Regent and Oxford streets, no more than a five minute walk from Portland Place and Donat's Portland Mansions flat, where the swirl of events intensified with Annabella Smith's murder. The movie began with Hannay attending the music hall, where gunshots were heard and the escaping main character fell literally into the arms of the exotic spy destined for death and linking him to danger.

Humor is supplied with the name of the show at the Palladium. It is called *Crazy Month*. Pamela remarks to Hannay that it "suits you."

A clever thematic thread of *The 39 Steps* is how Hannay begins periodically humming a tune, doing so for the first time when he is handcuffed to Pamela and in the custody of the spies seeking to take them to the Professor. He hums it later when he is with Pamela at the inn. "I can't get that tune out of my head," he exclaims in bafflement.

The tune is a unifying element, as recognized by Hannay when he hears it at the Palladium and observes Wylie Watson as Mr. Memory. A close-up of the hand with the missing finger joint reveals the presence of the unscrupulous Professor Jordan. The story elements blend in a dramatic conclusion. The police seek to arrest Hannay. He darts away and shouts the most important question of the film, "What are the 39 Steps?"

When Mr. Memory replies, he is shot by Professor Jordan, who then leaps from his box onto the stage and is quickly apprehended by the police. The stricken Mr. Memory is carried backstage, where he supplies the formula in its entirety. He refers to it as the toughest challenge of his career. Hitchcock keeps the action proceeding as Mr. Memory makes his final declaration before dying amid the high-stepping kicks of a female dance chorus performing to lively orchestra music.

The Vital Hitchcock Touches

A tangible sign of true craftsmanship involves taking a story provided for readers and transmitting it into an entertaining film vehicle. Charles Bennett, who adapted Buchan's story to the screen with Hitchcock, stated, "I thought the fundamental idea [of the book], the guy on the run from the police *and* from the heavies at the same time, was a very good idea to base a film on. Our film, though, had practically nothing to do with his novel. His novel had no women in it, or anything like that, for example. And so, we had to come up with an entirely different story, in a way. Try reading the book and you'll see what I mean."

Hitchcock took Buchan's plot of the man on the run in the Scottish moors, sought by international spies and the police, while cherry picking points along the way. One significant alteration from Buchan's novel was the meaning of the 39 Steps. It is the name of the spy organization in the film, while in the book Buchan uses it as a clue from Scudder. Richard Hannay finally figures out its significance, the number of steps to the waiting boat that will transport spies from England. Hannay ultimately posits the port from which the getaway is planned, a deductive logic exercise reminiscent of Arthur Conan Doyle's Sherlock Holmes.

The clever trademark of Professor Jordan, the finger with the missing joint, appeared in the novel in a different manner. Buchan has Hannay describe a conflict one of his characters was engaged in which left a hand bereft of finger joints.

Since the action proceeds at such a breakneck pace, it is difficult to discern all the dramatic and sociological points made in the film without studying it. To say so much within an economy of words and images, maintaining a brisk pace throughout, embodies exemplary film craftsmanship, which was clearly on display in *The 39 Steps*.

Hitchcock followed with fidelity his spy adventure formula for all but one of his remaining films in his British phase. He teamed with writer Charles Bennett, who had worked with him on *The Man Who Knew Too Much* (1934), on *Secret Agent* (1935), *Sabotage* (1936), and *Young and Innocent* (1938). *The Lady Vanishes* (1938) utilized the writing team of Sidney Gilliat and Frank Launder. The famous British writing team went on to pen what has been termed the sequel to *The Lady Vanishes* with *Night Train to Munich* (1940), directed by Carol Reed.

If working in two Hitchcock spy adventures paved the way for Madeleine Carroll to go to Hollywood, films in that successful vernacular facilitated the famous director's ultimate move to the cinema capital. Hitchcock signed a contract with David O. Selznick, who blazed to fame as a young producer with *Gone with the Wind*. The first film in their frequently rocky collaboration would emerge as a classic, one that found Hitchcock departing from the spy adventure realm by facing a fresh double challenge, but never sacrificing a scintilla of suspense in the finished product.

2

America, Selznick and a Gothic Challenge: *Rebecca* (1940)

It was so long that I've just now finished it. I think it'd make a very good film. I'd call it The Longest Story Ever Told. — Alfred Hitchcock in 1969 describing a memo sent to him by producer David O. Selznick on June 12, 1939.

David O. Selznick was a producer who disdained sleep for creative activity when the mood arose, which was frequently. Charles Bennett, the most prolific scenarist of Hitchcock films during his London period, recounted a discussion involving his collaborator, who was still in London while the writer was busily at work on the other side of the Atlantic. "I was loaned to write a picture for Selznick called *The Young in Heart*," Bennett remarked, "and one night, during one of those all-night story conferences which David loved, and we all loathed, he said, 'It's been suggested I should bring over one of these two directors from Gaumont-British, Alfred Hitchcock or Robert Stevenson. Which should I bring?' I said, 'Bring both.'"

Hitchcock first came to the United States in June 1938 to sign a contract with Selznick. There had been earlier American approaches from Universal and Sam Goldwyn, but during that period Hitchcock was under contract to either Gaumont-British or ABC in England. The move became more propitious when Hitchcock's Gaumont-British producer and benefactor, Michael Balcon, left the studio.

"In those days I was called England's 'ace' director," Hitchcock recalled, "and it was through David O. Selznick's brother, the agent Myron Selznick, with whom I'd been acquainted over many years, that I received an offer from David Selznick to come out to Hollywood...."

Selznick was accordingly pleased with his acquisition of Hitchcock in that shortly after he affixed his signature to a contract with the American producer, Hitchcock secured a prestigious New York Film Critics' Award for Best Director for one of his most celebrated spy adventures, *The Lady Vanishes*, which also secured British "Film of the Year" honors. The briskly paced 1938 drama starred Michael Redgrave and Margaret Lockwood, with brilliant support from Dame May Whitty, Paul Lukas, Cecil Parker and Linden Travers. The film is also significant to British film enthusiasts in that it marked the first appearance of the hilarious team of Charter and Caldicott, played by Basil Radford and Naunton Wayne. While a perilous world edges closer to war, Radford and Wayne remain obsessive nationalistic cricket fanatics, supplying a spirited dose of Hitchcock's noted comic relief.

Just before leaving England, after he had returned following signing his contract with Selznick, Hitchcock received a message from the producer. The first film he was supposed to direct had been canceled in place of another project. Hitchcock was initially slated to direct *Titanic*. "In *Titanic* there was only one scene that engaged me," Hitchcock recollected in a 1972 interview, "and if I had made that film I would have made it for that scene: a group of men playing cards at a table. On the table there is a glass of whisky. Close-up of the glass. We see the liquid start to tip. We hear someone laugh!"

The project that Selznick had chosen for Hitchcock's American debut was *Rebecca*, a gothic novel by a famous British author who would place her indelible stamp on that genre in the manner that Agatha Christie dominated the mystery field. Daphne du Maurier was a familiar name to Alfred Hitchcock, apart from the fact that he had already adapted one of her stories to the screen — *Jamaica Inn*, a 1939 release starring Charles Laughton and Leslie Banks, along with a youthful Irish-bred redhead cast in her first important role, Maureen O'Hara. As a young film director in London, Hitchcock struck up a cordial acquaintance with Gerald du Maurier, the future writer's father, who was a prominent stage actor and playwright. A legendary practical joker as well as a man eager to make an impression, Hitchcock commanded the famous actor's attention one evening in 1928. As Donald Spoto wrote, du Maurier "returned to his dressing room after a successful opening night to find not flowers or a congratulatory telegram, but a horse waiting in the cramped quarters. It must have cost Hitchcock a considerable sum, du Maurier guessed — but it must have been worth every shilling to be remembered as the donor of so bizarre and unforgettable memento."

In addition to her professional link to Hitchcock, Daphne du Maurier bore a personal connection to Britain's other leading film director during Hitchcock's British period, Carol Reed, and her association with him established a pattern for du Maurier's subsequent life. At the time her father was starring on the London stage, Carol Reed, seven years Hitchcock's junior, was launching an artistic career as an actor and stage manager, preparation for his subsequent film career that culminated in being knighted, an honor bestowed upon Hitchcock as well as du Maurier, who would ultimately become Dame Daphne. Reed fell in love with the attractive, quiet, and sensitive du Maurier and hoped to marry her. While throbbing London was Reed's world, the introverted du Maurier ultimately abandoned the city of her birth for the quieter splendors of Cornwall, the idyllic Southwest England seaside community which is a popular vacation spot for Britain's city folk. While Reed would ultimately marry two beautiful film actresses, Diana Wynyard and Penelope Dudley-Ward, du Maurier settled down in Cornwall and married a former army officer. Cornwall serves as the backdrop for *Rebecca*.

A Major Departure

The 39 Steps was an example of vintage Hitchcock filmmaking in his Gaumont-British phase. As Charles Bennett remarked, in Hitchcock's successful breakthrough film they had taken great liberties with John Buchan's novel. Upon entering his new professional relationship in Hollywood, however, Hitchcock found that the producer-oriented philosophy of Selznick applied. While *The 39 Steps* had also been a successful novel, Hitchcock drew a distinction between a story on paper and his idea of emphasizing visual imagery and rapid scene pacing to keep theatergoers entertained.

"Selznick had just made *Gone with the Wind* and he had a very strong theory that a best-seller should be adhered to, because readers had their favorite scenes and if you left any of them out they would be disappointed," Hitchcock explained. "He accordingly followed the book of *Rebecca* closely, sometimes I felt *too* closely. I felt that one would like to have got more movement into it, rather than have many static scenes. It was a novel, whichever way you look at it, and the plot had certain holes."

One of the main holes of the novel according to Hitchcock stemmed from Rebecca, the deceased wife of Maxim de Winter, the major male figure, being washed up in a boat in the middle of the story. "So, on the same night that he killed his wife," Hitchcock said, "by some good fortune another woman was washed up on the shore several miles away. Nobody ever realizes this, it's obscured by the general overall interest in the surface story."

While Selznick paid Hitchcock deference by allowing him more latitude than he had any other director, the producer continued to adhere to his central premise that, in filming a successful literary work, audiences should see on screen basically the same story that had become successful in print. On June 12, 1938, as Selznick continued to work on *Gone with the Wind*, Hitchcock arrived at the studio and received a package from the producer. A treatment far more lengthy than normal, which had evolved from an outline written by Hitchcock and his two most famous female story collaborators, his wife Alma and protégée Joan Harrison, had been sent to Selznick. A normal treatment consists of about fifty scene descriptions in fewer pages. Hitchcock provided a far more comprehensively detailed treatment containing several hundred scenes, each with precise specifications for the dialogue, action, and camera placement. This was how he had prepared his English films and he looked forward to receiving prompt approval from Selznick and the announcement of a July shooting date.

Hitchcock opened the package and read a memo so lengthy that he commented tongue-in-cheek, three decades later in 1969, "it was so long that I've just now finished reading it. I think it'd make a very good film. I'd call it *The Longest Story Ever Told*."

While Hitchcock could employ his famous wry wit when speaking of the Selznick memo thirty years later, it was anything but grist for the humor mill at the time. Selznick disapproved of Hitchcock's treatment of the best-selling novel from beginning to end. Selznick took strong exception in particular to the director's beginning scene, in which the smoke from Maxim de Winter's cigar makes his fellow passengers nauseous on a Riviera boating excursion. (Donald Spoto has cited the scene as an apparent reflection of the director's fearful memories of motion sickness.) "I think the scenes of seasickness are cheap," Selznick wrote, "and old-fashioned in the bargain." He then restated his principal objective from the posture of a powerful producer with a fixed objective. "We bought *Rebecca*, and we intend to make *Rebecca*," Selznick insisted, "not a distorted and vulgarized version of a provenly [sic] successful work."

This would be but one shot fired over the bow in a continuing clash between two strong-willed individuals used to exercising firm control. While Hitchcock would retrospectively dismiss *Rebecca* with the belief that it was not a personalized vehicle bearing his unique imprint, a view certainly stemming from his ongoing creative conflicts with Selznick, the film displayed his characteristic style.

Fundamental irony arises from this production known for creative conflict between two strong-willed Hollywood figures when a line of dialogue uttered by Joan Fontaine addresses the question of how a creative force leaves his or her imprint on a work of art. In a 1972 interview for the French publication *Ecran*, long after the dust had settled, and seven years after Selznick's death, Hitchcock was asked an astute question about whether his auteur theory of filmmaking was voiced by Fontaine ("My father always painted the same flower because he thought that when an artist had found his subject he had only one desire — to paint nothing else"). Hitchcock's response could serve as a guidepost to his style and philosophy of filmmaking:

"Yes, that is very evident with painters. We can see it clearly when we visit a museum. Looking at paintings by different masters, we notice that each of them has his own style. We recognize at one glance a Rousseau, a Van Gogh, a Klee. So I ask myself why one should not always recognize the mark of a director or a filmmaker (I do not like the word 'director' because I find this term incorrect and prefer the label 'filmmaker'). I believe that one of the main reasons for this difficulty in identifying the quality of the film they are making generally depends on the quality and importance of the subject matter. As for me, the content of a story, the plot, does not interest me at all. It's the manner of recounting that fascinates me. What attracts me is to discover what will provoke a strong emotion in the viewer and how to make the viewer feel it."

Hitchcock elucidated further, explaining that "in all artistic domains we attempt to create an emotion." He sees the process as evoking a reaction, no matter which reflex is stimulated. Audiences respond by taking a position, whether it is one of hate or love. This response "signifies that one is no longer indifferent."

While Hitchcock might have entertained doubts that his unique vision was stamped indelibly on the screen in the wake of his producer's quest for fidelity to the work from which the film was adapted, the master's touch is definitely present. The only way Selznick could have prevented such a result was to have replaced Hitchcock. Removing the Hitchcock imprint would be comparable to upstaging Robert Mitchum or John Wayne. Just as these actors offered their own unique styles, so did Alfred Hitchcock symbolically wield his own stylized paint brush, ending with onscreen portraits digging into the deepest recesses of the characters via the telling scrutiny of his camera shots. If Van Goghs are clearly recognizable by style, so are haunting portraits of a tormented Laurence Olivier or Joan Fontaine. They are revealed in mixtures of shadow and light, with the artistry of George Barnes' camera displaying their innermost thoughts as filmgoers wonder just what torments them or whether these torments can be satisfactorily resolved by the film's end.

Fontaine and the Process of Selection

Hitchcock demonstrated his casting astuteness, an important instinct in the repertoire of any genius director—or filmmaker, as he preferred—in selecting Joan Fontaine. The choice occurred following a long process he did not need. Selznick's flamboyance surfaced during the selection process. The publicity-conscious producer had received significant attention with his earlier quest to find the perfect Scarlett O'Hara for *Gone with the Wind*. While Vivien Leigh was ultimately cast, the list of those who also tested embodied a who's who of the screen's present and future leading ladies, including Katharine Hepburn, Bette Davis, Joan Crawford, Susan Hayward, Lana Turner and Paulette Goddard. Selznick sent a score of actresses before the camera to test for the role of Mrs. de Winter. Hitchcock not only argued with Selznick over possibilities, he was only one of three directors involved in analyzing the actresses, as the producer brought in consultants. George Cukor and John Cromwell, two directors whose judgments were valued by Selznick, were also included.

By August 19 the choice had been narrowed to Anne Baxter, Margaret Sullavan, and two talented sisters who would eventually both receive Best Actress Oscars, Olivia de Havilland and Joan Fontaine. Vivien Leigh, Loretta Young, Susan Hayward, Lana Turner, Virginia Mayo and Geraldine Fitzgerald had also been tested. Olivia de Havilland was reluctant to compete with her sister for the role. She had just completed *Gone with the Wind* under Selznick and recognized that her own opportunities had thus far been more significant than those of her sister. Baxter, at 16, was eliminated due to her youth.

The two persons whose creativity Hitchcock would rely upon most during his life, wife Alma Reville Hitchcock and Joan Harrison, reached a casting conclusion with which neither the director, the producer, nor the two directorial consultants, Cukor and Cromwell, agreed. Alma and Harrison preferred Baxter, even at 16, to Fontaine, whom they found "too coy and simpering to a degree that is intolerable." Hitchcock's female brain trust found Margaret Sullavan "far ahead of either."

Selznick rejected Sullavan, believing that the actress, known for onscreen fire, lacked credibility in a role calling for extreme passivity. By the end of August Selznick and the three directors considered Fontaine to be the best candidate, and asked her to do another test. She politely responded that, while honored to accept the role, she would not comply with the request. Fontaine was slated to marry actor Brian Aherne on August 19, then leave on her honeymoon. With filming time drawing near, Selznick wired Fontaine the day after her wedding, requesting that she return on Labor Day for final wardrobe fittings and the start of principal photography.

Hitchcock and the entire production received a damaging shock when, on September 1, Germany invaded Poland. Two days later England declared war on Germany. Filming began September 8 amid concerns on the part of Hitchcock and the largely British cast that London would be bombed. Hitchcock fear for his family in England, and concerned about the inexperience of his leading lady. With all the problems and distractions, filming progress was uncharacteristically slow for the first few weeks.

An Invisible MacGuffin

While *Rebecca*, Hitchcock's American debut, featured a story by a prominent British author set in idyllic Cornwall, and an appropriately English cast, one aspect of the production was decidedly American. This element, which would benefit Hitchcock then and in the future, was American production technology. With more capital available than in England, where more penny pinching was necessary, the highly visual Hitchcock received a beneficial thrust. Opportunities were endless, and Hitchcock took advantage of American film technology to provide the best and most varied shots, with just the proper mixture of light and darkness to set the appropriate mood. He now had the chance to put more of a Hitchcock auteur touch on a film than he ever had in London, despite the presence of David O. Selznick. With the continuing turf battles he was then waging with Selznick for creative control, it was difficult for him to see it, even years later.

There was another reason why Hitchcock would later be dismissive of *Rebecca*, and consider it as lying outside the realm of his basic oeuvre — the subject matter. Here was a gothic novel being translated to the screen. It was written by a woman, and was characteristic of gothic works and their female viewpoint and audience. Hitchcock had chalked up an impressive record in England doing fast-paced thrillers more generally embracing a male viewpoint. While at first glance *Rebecca* would constitute a significant change, in the overall scheme, as analyzed by William Rothman, "the Hollywood studio made it possible for Hitchcock to orchestrate the elements of cinematic expression to create incredibly rich and resonant emotional effects.... It is in America that Hitchcock solves the problem of exploiting the resources of the Hitchcock thriller while addressing the means of its conditions." In Rothman's view, Hitchcock's first American movie "clearly reveals Hitchcock's excitement at discovering the emotional weight, the sheer power, he can give to sounds and images by utilizing the sophisticated technology newly available to him."

Whether viewers were transfixed on Robert Donat darting through the Scottish moors to save his life and solve the mystery of *The 39 Steps* or Laurence Olivier and Joan Fontaine seeking meaning in their lives amid the sometimes isolated splendor of Manderley in *Rebecca*, the basic Hitchcock staples of action and conflict, generating story tension, were manifest. At one point while viewing the film, a frustrated Selznick, despite numerous interruptions and dissatisfaction with scenes he witnessed, exclaimed that the film exemplified "jigsaw cutting." What he observed in the rushes was that the film was developing a Hitchcock personality. Stories, to Hitchcock, involved visual flashes, which carried the story and its surrounding action from scene to scene. What looked to Selznick like a jigsaw puzzle was a flowing scenic pattern moving from one dramatic confrontation to another. The blandness one often finds in the gothic style of storytelling was replaced by Hitchcock's electricity. He would visit this type of story only on this occasion, but would invest it with his distinctive imprint.

While Michael Hogan and Philip MacDonald also worked on the script, final credits were shared by Joan Harrison and a towering figure whose career embraced several arenas, Robert Sherwood. Sherwood was the only writer to earn Pulitzer Prizes as both a playwright and historian, and he won an Oscar for Best Screenplay as well. He wrote such stage hits as *The Petrified Forest* and *Waterloo Bridge*, both of which were adapted to the screen. Sherwood's historical work, *Roosevelt and Hopkins*, won a Pulitzer as he detailed the relationship between President Franklin Delano Roosevelt and his principal aide Harry Hopkins. Sherwood worked for a time in the White House and wrote some of Roosevelt's most important speeches. Sherwood and Harrison would be nominated for an Oscar for *Rebecca*, and Sherwood would secure one six years later for penning Sam Goldwyn's most celebrated film, *The Best Years of Our Lives*, directed by William Wyler.

The Hitchcock MacGuffin emerging in the *Rebecca* script was unique. This

MacGuffin could be classified as invisible. It is the mystery revolving around someone who is not alive and is never seen (even in flashback), yet is perpetually referred to throughout the movie. The unseen presence of Rebecca, Maxim de Winter's first wife, hovers like an unshakable ghost over the proceedings. It is understood by de Winter and his young wife that they can never experience marital bliss unless the presence and overpowering aura of the first wife is banished.

In a traditional mystery adventure, solving a crime is complicated by obstacles appearing at cleverly timed intervals to enhance dramatic impact. In *Rebecca* the constant presence of Mrs. Danvers, played by prominent British Shakespearean player Judith Anderson, proves a continuing obstacle. While Mr. and Mrs. de Winter seek to put the tragic first marriage behind them, Mrs. Danvers devotes her unceasing energies toward preserving the image and memory of the first Mrs. de Winter, a woman she looks upon as a veritable goddess.

A Rousing Beginning

Hitchcock's first scene contains a solid dramatic hook, arousing audience interest. In that it is superior to the opening in the original treatment harshly criticized by Selznick, it could be conjectured that the producer, despite Hitchcock's disgust over his frequent criticisms and intrusions, might have helped the director in the manner of a coach who angers an athlete by profuse criticism, thereby urging the individual on to greater effort.

The story is shown in flashback. The first scene, narrated by Fontaine, generates immediate intrigue. The camera pans over the sprawling estate of Manderley. Its once well-tended lawns have given way to weeds. The once proud edifice is worn and ravaged by fire. It is falling apart, in an unoccupied state, a relic from another era. The shot is reminiscent of another film classic released one year after *Rebecca*, *Citizen Kane*, with director and star Orson Welles' rendering of newspaper publishing mogul Charles Foster Kane's then badly worn Xanadu.

A quick cut shows Maxim de Winter (Laurence Olivier) standing amid rocks on a precipice overlooking the crashing waves of the Mediterranean. His tragic and forlorn expression prompts a young woman walking nearby, played by Joan Fontaine, to call out a warning to him as a brief and dramatic scene unfolds, one that defines the characters in a cleverly succinct manner:

WOMAN: No! Stop!
MAN: What the devil are you shouting about? Who are you? What are you staring at?
WOMAN: I'm sorry, I didn't mean to stare, but I, I only thought...
MAN: Oh, you did, did you? Well, what are you doing here?
WOMAN: I was only walking.
MAN: Well, get on with your walking and don't hang about here screaming.

The man's manner bears the imprint of an aristocrat, one used to giving orders. The young woman, painfully shy and insecure, appears to be someone used to taking orders. This point is emphasized when they meet again in the next scene, which occurs in the lobby of an elegant Monte Carlo hotel, where they are both staying under different circumstances. The scene provides Hitchcock with an opportunity to engage in social satire while the personas of the film's main characters are further delineated.

Supplying comedic relief while furnishing needed dramatic contrast is Florence Bates, who looms as the curse of the aristocratic class. Bates was a Los Angeles lawyer who, in her early forties, began acting at the then popular Hollywood talent showcase of Pasadena Playhouse. So well was she received for her convincing performance as a spoiled, highly obtrusive, nouveau riche dowager with a penchant for social climbing that she would receive numerous opportunities to play such parts in future films. When she notices celebrated aristocrat Maxim de Winter walking near where she is sitting, Bates, who plays the role of Mrs. Edyth Van Hopper, calls out to him. Before de Winter appears she speaks with cold condescension to her perpetually abused paid companion Fontaine, who displays the essential submissiveness pseudo-aristocratic Van Hopper demands.

Without appearing rude, de Winter spurns suggestions from social climbing Van Hopper for further involvement. Van Hopper ignores her servant, but the aristocrat brings her into the conversation. He deepens his mystique with one telling line, uttered appropriately on his departure, "I'm afraid I cling to the old motto: 'He travels fastest who travels alone.'" When he leaves, Van Hopper, as would be expected, upbraids her assistant for unwarranted intervention in the conversation, a hilarious criticism in that de Winter plainly found the young servant more interesting than her boorish employer.

When the excessively crude Mrs. Van Hopper contracts a cold, her experience is played out with comedic gusto. When she is administered a pill by a female attendant, the wealthy dowager makes a face and gulps down a chocolate. At another point she puts out a cigarette in her cold cream.

While the plot-lightening comedy is employed, the story develops on another level. As her employer lies in her room nursing a cold, a relationship develops between enigmatic loner de Winter and the young woman. She is never given a name, which invites viewers to fill in blanks about her. The obvious conclusion is that this is a young woman who has received a series of bad breaks, culminating in the submissive posture of catering to a wealthy woman's every demand. To disguise what she is doing, Fontaine dons a white tennis outfit and carries a racquet, explaining she is taking lessons from the hotel's tennis pro. The extent of her involvement with the wealthy aristocrat is demonstrated when Mrs. Van Hopper, due to the frequency of the presumed lessons, wonders aloud if she is engaged in romance with her tennis instructor.

A Split Second Decision

No sooner does Mrs. Van Hopper recover from her illness than an early critical point in the drama emerges. She receives a telephone call from her daughter explaining that she is going to be married. Van Hopper tells Fontaine that they must leave for the airport immediately and fly back to her New York home. While the dowager waits in the taxi, Fontaine takes the opportunity to say goodbye to de Winter. She describes the misery she will encounter returning to the U.S. with Van Hopper. He replies with a question: "Which would you prefer? New York or Manderley?" He asks the question off-screen, from the bathroom, prompting her to think he wants her to return to his home with him for another reason, most ostensibly as an employee. The response is understandable in view of her submissive plight. She cannot at that point conceive of his question as a proposal. He finally states bluntly, "I'm asking you to marry me, you little fool."

After de Winter explains the situation to Mrs. Van Hopper, the overbearing employer takes one last opportunity to deliver a stinging rebuke to her assistant. She concludes that the empty house de Winter has been maintaining since his wife's death has left him nearly "off his head." Van Hopper's parting goodbye and good luck are delivered with customary condescension. One can see the frightened young girl's fears increase as she anticipates the new world into which she is plunging, as her life takes an abrupt, unanticipated u-turn via a marriage to a bona fide man of mystery.

A Name and New Duties

Following a brief, no-frills Monte Carlo wedding, the film's leading female character acquires a name. She is thereafter Mrs. Maxim de Winter, with all the new responsibilities the name and position attached to it entail. When they arrive at Manderley her eyes widen as she takes in the estate's vast splendor for the first time. Her reaction there and inside, when she is introduced to the staff of servants, reveals her anxiety at being thrust into a position for which she is totally unprepared. Her frightened youth and absence of confidence, combined with de Winter's brief temper tantrums, characteristic of her first meeting with him, serve as audience teasers through which the patented Hitchcock suspense pattern gradually emerges. Hitchcock uses one towering character as an ideal spin-off to generate suspense.

Judith Anderson could not have fit Alfred Hitchcock's plans any better had she been fashioned from a dream. He had every reason to consider her an answer to a director's prayer since she filled the pivotal role required to buttress his element of suspense. This was not a spy adventure, as he had been accustomed to making in his native England; and producer Selznick in his stinging memo had told Hitchcock that the film scenario required fidelity to the original novel. All the same, suspense was Hitchcock's game and he found a way to incorporate it into the gothic story. George Barnes' camera uses dark shadowy hues to play off the black dress that the eerie housekeeper Mrs. Danvers wears, leaving a macabre impression. This, coupled with her iceberg exterior, presents dramatic tension whenever Mrs. Danvers encounters the lady of the house, who is plainly uncomfortable in her presence.

A clash of contrasting wills erupts as Mrs. de Winter seeks to adjust to her new role as lady of the manor and the frosty housekeeper is determined to break her. It is immediately revealed that the housekeeper's devotion to the late Mrs. de Winter is nothing short of worshipful, but in a manner that appears ghoulish. Anything the terrifying Danvers does reflects ghoulishness. The awesome task confronting the young bride is further manifested by the sheer size of the Cornwall estate, which threatens to overwhelm the new Mrs. de Winter.

The overpowering magnitude of what Mrs. de Winter confronts is exemplified by two events. She picks up the telephone and responds, "Mrs. de Winter? Oh, I'm afraid you've made a mistake. Mrs. de Winter has been dead for over a year. Oh, I mean..." Mrs. Danvers, observing her mistake and corresponding discomfort, explains that it was the gardener asking for instructions. The memory of Rebecca, reinforced with hypnotic eeriness by Mrs. Danvers, causes the young woman to forget that *she* is now Mrs. de Winter.

A problem arises at Manderley when the young wife breaks a treasured ceramic china cupid. Terrified of being discovered, she hides the pieces of the broken statue in the back of Rebecca's desk drawer. When the object turns up missing, Danvers levels an accusation of theft at a servant. As she discusses the matter with Maxim de Winter, with his wife sitting nearby, the young wife confesses the error. The fact that she owns up to her embarrassing circumstance under the cold eye of Danvers further heightens her insecurity.

Drawing Sides

In the manner of a tug-of-war suspense drama, with two sides in conflict, the new Mrs. de Winter has her support network, but even then the circumstances are extenuating. Maxim's sister, Beatrice Lacy (played by Gladys Cooper), exudes a gentle manner, and kindly exhorts the frightened newlywed to adjust to her new station and surroundings. Before their first meeting, however, a situation occurs that causes awkwardness. It involves Beatrice's husband, Major Giles Lacy, played by Nigel Bruce, who gained fame as the often bumbling foil Dr. Watson opposite Basil Rathbone's Sherlock Holmes in the 1940s film series about Arthur Conan Doyle's fabled detective. Hitchcock uses the opportunity to provide a humorous break while making a story point.

As Mrs. de Winter is moving toward Giles and Beatrice, and thought to be out of earshot, she overhears him exclaim that he believed she was an ex-chorus girl. "He picked her up in the south of France, didn't he?" Giles cites as rationale. As soon as he finishes his comment Mrs. de Winter suddenly appears, prompting embarrassment on all sides. A twofold objective is served here, with Bruce, who played a bumbler in so many films, providing a comedic break with his comment denoting the French Riviera as a place for attractive young gold diggers, which by no means describes Fontaine. The dramatic point is embodied in Fontaine's uncomfortable reaction in the wake of skepticism about her marriage to the reclusive Maxim.

Mrs. de Winter's other household ally is the estate's manager, Frank Crawley, played by Reginald Denny. Though he provides moral support and comforting words in the manner of Beatrice, Mrs. de Winter is nonetheless jolted when, after asking him what Rebecca was like, he responds candidly that she was probably the most beautiful woman he had ever seen. Her agonized expression reveals the length of Rebecca's shadow, underscoring the ponderous prospect of her ever living up to expectations at Manderley.

The team of Mrs. de Winter, Beatrice, and Frank are confronted with the dark specter of a potent foe in Danvers, whose persona takes on the might of a formidable military power. Her bearing is ghostly and intimidating. One can see her dissolving into an apparition and joining forces with Rebecca or, on the other hand, Rebecca returning to earth, so powerful is the twin presence conjured up by the dominant figure of Anderson. Her casting appears all the more shrewd because Anderson, while born in Australia, carved out a niche in England as one of its foremost stage performers. As well as gaining fame for her role in *Medea*, she ran the gamut in Shakespearean drama. Not only was she a superb Lady Macbeth, her strong stage presence enabled her to function as a splendid Hamlet as well. This foreboding strength registers on camera in *Rebecca* as she intimidates the self-conscious young wife seeking to take the place of a woman seemingly stronger in death than in life.

Manipulating a Ghost and Filling in Blanks

As Hitchcock historian Ken Mogg observed, "The woman called Rebecca fascinates us — without our ever seeing her — but the logic of the film requires that she be repudiated." The need for Maxim and Mrs. de Winter to put Rebecca behind them if they are to enjoy anything resembling a successful marriage emerges in contrast with the conflicting necessity of Danvers to maintain the virtually deified status of the dead woman at Manderley.

Danvers' strategy, linked to her slavish devotion to the deceased Rebecca, involves a campaign to make Mrs. de Winter feel totally unworthy of taking the departed woman's place. She shows her new mistress a painting, suggesting she wear the identical dress style to a costume party the couple is hosting. Maxim turns ashen when he sees her wearing the dress, demanding that she remove it immediately. Mrs. de Winter learns that Rebecca had worn the identical dress. A badgering Danvers reduces her to tears by cruelly stating that her own presence in the dress could not compare to that of Rebecca's.

More psychological warfare is applied when Danvers shows the young woman the west wing bedroom of Manderley. She effusively reveals that this room offers the best view on the estate, the only one that looks out onto the nearby sea. It is lavishly appointed, just as when Rebecca occupied it, a point Danvers is only too happy to make. The monogrammed silk pillow on the bed bears the letter "R." Danvers ghoulishly delights in cordoning off the room, maintaining it as a monument to the spirit whose presence engulfs Manderley, assisted mightily by her efforts.

Hitchcock manipulates a psychological opportunity to excellent advantage in moving the gothic mystery forward. Danvers, whose own foreboding aura is nothing short of ghostly, prompts the aura of a dead woman, through making Rebecca's image constantly felt, to the point where she is more alive and present in certain psychological ways than the flesh and blood occupants of Manderley. Through this device Hitchcock also exploits another trait he springs on his audience, that of filling in blanks. The imaginations of moviegoers are tweaked repeatedly by all the talk about Rebecca, and the manner in which her life and world impact upon others, particularly Danvers, the second Mrs. de Winter, and Maxim. This is an ultimate fill-in-the-blank situation that the master director will never repeat in any other film. The movie title bears her name, her aura is present everywhere, and she is discussed with great frequency, but we never set eyes on her. While it would have been possible to present Rebecca in flashback, to do so would sacrifice the unique imprint the film establishes. Hitchcock has worked audience curiosity to the maximum, letting viewers create Rebecca from clues they glean from his film.

A Warning to Stay Away

Mrs. de Winter learns that Manderley's west wing is not the only place that has been declared off limits. As she takes a walk with her husband, she observes their dog Jasper dart down to the cove, in the direction of a beach house situated next to the sea. When she suggests adventuring to the area her husband dismisses the idea, explaining that it is a dull, uninteresting stretch of sand, just like any other. Her curiosity has been piqued, however, and she proceeds alone to the cottage. She then encounters a strange, large-eyed man with an ethereal look and a voice to match, later learning that he is "Barmy" Ben, a deranged drifter. He is played by Leonard Carey with an otherworldliness that invests him with every bit as much of a ghostly persona as the departed Rebecca.

Just as Rebecca has left her indelible presence on Manderley, the same applies to the cottage. Mrs. de Winter learns that the cottage was occupied by

Rebecca, a logical nearby retreat from Manderley since her boat was moored next to it. While the new bride is later told by Frank that Ben is harmless enough, his manner is frightening. He stares hauntingly into the distance and exclaims, "She's gone in the sea, ain't she? She'll come back no more."

When Mrs. de Winter catches up with Maxim heading back to the mansion, he erupts, telling her that the cottage contains tragic memories. "Don't you go there again, you hear!" Maxim angrily scolds. The profound sorrow he feels is disclosed with a blunt manifestation of his mind-set. "We should have stayed away," he hurtfully proclaims. "We should never have come back to Manderley. Oh, what a fool I was."

Mrs. de Winter's sympathetic confidante, estate manager Frank Crawley, played by Denny, fills the young woman in on an important detail, which makes her aware of her husband's dread concerning the beach cottage. She is told that Rebecca died in a tragic boating accident. As the story evolves, Mrs. de Winter, in the manner of Maxim, becomes haunted by the spirit of his first wife. Rebecca's ghostly presence assumes a massive weight threatening to drag them down.

Another mysterious link to Rebecca's past surfaces with the appearance of Jack Favell. He arrives when Maxim is in London on business. The casting selection of George Sanders could not have been more ideal. Ten years later Sanders would receive a Best Supporting Actor Academy Award for his role in *All About Eve*, the masterpiece of Joseph Mankiewicz, who directed and wrote the script. In *Eve* Sanders played Anne Baxter's Svengali-like co-conspirator and sadistic lover, Addison DeWitt, a Broadway theater columnist whose pen drips bile, his superiority complex affixed to an anarchistic world view. He assumes the same level of bilious insouciance in *Rebecca*, dramatically entering the house by slipping in through the window as he refers to the new Mrs. de Winter as "the little bride" and "Cinderella." As for himself, he is a "lonely old bachelor."

Mrs. de Winter becomes intrigued by Favell when the omnipresent Mrs. Danvers regards his appearance with awkward diffidence. Before he leaves, Favell refers to himself as "Rebecca's favorite cousin," wearing his characteristic sardonic smile. After he departs Danvers warns Mrs. de Winter not to mention Favell's visit to the lord of the manor.

Retaining Mystery Technique

While Hitchcock sought to retain the fidelity of a gothic novel revealing an essentially female viewpoint, he applied his characteristic mystery technique to a different realm. Viewers can be thankful that he did so, since the suspense level, operating concomitantly with the shadowy close-ups of characters caught under the spell of a spirit seemingly more active and overpowering in death, is gradually accelerated, leading to the film's resolution. If George Bernard Shaw has been depicted as pulling strings like a puppet master, carefully controlling the movements of the characters he constructed for the London stage, the same applies to Londoner Hitchcock as he weaves his own indelible spell over moviegoers.

The story structure for *Rebecca* can be boiled down thematically:

1) Mysterious man haunted by initially unseen forces finds romance with a frightened girl with zero self-esteem.
2) Couple moves to large estate that appears haunted by the overpowering presence of the deceased first wife, threatening their chance to forge a successful marriage.
3) An eerie presence looms in the housekeeper, whose devotion to the dead woman parallels idolatry, clashing with the need of the newlyweds to put the influence of the deceased wife behind them.
4) The effort to remove the dead weight of uncertainty stemming from unanswered questions about the dead woman, whose presence grows under the steady hand of the ghoulish housekeeper.
5) The gradual surfacing of facts pertaining to the dead woman as the audience sees this exploration of truth from the eyes of the tormented second wife.
6) A constant battle of competing forces to learn the truth, which will hopefully set the married couple free.

An Eruption of Forces

One of the most difficult yet potentially rewarding cinematic achievements is the dramatic double — provide one scene of heart-wrenching drama followed immediately by a swift story spin, then another equally compelling dramatic sequence. Hitchcock pulls off this double in commanding fashion, pushing his audience to the edge of their seats, where they will hold on for dear life until the film's conclusion.

The fiendish Mrs. Danvers has been weaving her insidious web of destruction since the new Mrs. de Winter's arrival. She seeks to seize an opportunity to destroy her when the younger woman is in an agitated psychological state. Danvers pushes mightily to convince the frightened young woman that she will never replace Rebecca and would be better off— for her sake as well as that of others — to end her life, capitalizing on her absence of confidence and self-esteem. The destructive effort is undertaken, appropriately, in the west wing, the exclusive province of the departed Rebecca. The window is open and Mrs. de Winter stands facing the sea below.

The scene is masterfully executed for what is absent as much as what is present. There are none of the loud histrionics, the shouts and tears, that would accompany such an effort in lesser hands. The sheer subtlety of the drama overpowers. The diabolical Danvers speaks softly, but with requisite authority. Her tone is matter of fact, coaxing the crushed young woman with a message that all hope is gone. Meanwhile, the crashing waves of the stormy sea beckon below.

Danvers diabolically intones: "Why don't you go? Why don't you leave Manderley? He doesn't need you. He's got his memories. He doesn't love you — he wants to be alone with her. You've nothing to stay for. You've nothing to live for really, have you? Look down there. It's easy, isn't it? Why don't you? Why don't you? Go on. Go on. Don't be afraid!"

A look of fearful desperation overwhelms Mrs. de Winter. Will she, in her trance-like state, plunge out the window and snuff out her life? A rapid-fire transition occurs at that tense moment, snapping her to quick attention. Flares erupt in the air, accompanied by shouts of "Shipwreck! Ship on the rocks!" A storm at sea results in the washing up of a sunken boat. The jolting event brings a tortured Mrs. de Winter out of her trance. She sees her husband leaving the house to investigate.

As she searches for Maxim on the beach, the ghost-like Ben appears. He is aware of the boat washing up on shore. "She won't come back, will she?" Ben asks Mrs. de Winter, a clear reference to Rebecca. "You said so."

Eventually the young woman finds Maxim de Winter alone with his tormented thoughts in the beach house that was once the province of Rebecca. "Rebecca has won," he tells his wife with tragic resolution. "Her shadow has been between us all the time."

A Devastating Plot Twist

The audience has earlier been jolted by the near suicide of the young wife, followed by the swift transition of the boat's discovery. Now, in the quiet of the beach house, with a Rebecca-laden tension overpowering the de Winters, viewers are devastated by a cleverly constructed plot twist. A sorrowful Mrs. de Winter, feeling trapped and vulnerable in what she sees as an inevitably losing battle with a dead woman, hears a jolting revelation from her husband. With the unflagging propaganda of Mrs. Danvers ringing in her ears, the young and vulnerable wife has reason to believe that Maxim is carrying a ponderous torch, an unshakable love for the romanticized Rebecca. He stares at her with fire in his eyes and emphatically declares, "I hated her!"

Maxim painfully relates the facts of his first marriage, culminating with the confrontation resulting in Rebecca's death. It is here that screenwriter Robert Sherwood and Hitchcock were compelled to change events related in the Daphne du Maurier novel. The Breen Office, imposing strict censorship guidelines, insisted that a murderer ultimately pay the price, and in the book an enraged Maxim de Winter kills Rebecca. In their beach house discussion Maxim explains that Rebecca had been unfaithful throughout their marriage. She maintained a flat in London and would stay away for long periods of time. Rebecca became involved with the sardonic Jack Favell, recalling references to his being Rebecca's "favorite cousin."

Maxim decides to bring an end to the dalliance in a beach house confrontation. He tells his wife that he was aware that Rebecca and Favell used the beach house for liaisons, and after learning in advance of their next meeting, he decides to intervene and kill them both. On his arrival, however, Favell is not there, but Rebecca is, leading to a bitter confrontation in which she not only taunts him about her affair, but announces that she is carrying another man's child, leading him to conclude that the father is Favell.

The impactful scene, from which the story will move toward its resolution, is the eye opener for a stunned Mrs. de Winter, who sees that things were anything other than they appeared to be. Illusion generated by the wicked Mrs. Danvers is supplanted by piercing reality. Maxim then reveals the confrontation's critical moment: "She was smiling: 'Well Max. What are you going to do about it? Aren't you going to kill me?' I suppose I must have gone mad for a moment. I must have struck her. She stood staring at me. She looked almost triumphant. Then she started toward me again, smiling. Suddenly she stumbled and fell. When I looked down, ages later it seemed, she was lying on the floor. She'd struck her head on a heavy piece of ship's tackle. I remember wondering why she was still smiling. Then I realized she was dead."

The audience sees the transformation of a fearful young bride into a mature woman prepared to comfort her husband at a critical moment. Later Maxim will tell her that she no longer has the same youthful look of inexperience he had encountered when he met her in Monte Carlo. Events have seasoned her. When she tells her husband that Rebecca's death was an accident, he concurs, but regards the situation as impossible, since he sought to cover up the circumstances of her death. Mrs. de Winter hugs her husband comfortingly and responds, "No, no. She hasn't won. No matter what happens now, she hasn't won."

The Inquest and Resolution

The film intricately uncovers fact after fact, dispelling the idea that Maxim loved Rebecca by revealing that he actually detested her. Once this informational bombshell is dropped, it is followed by another — his fear that he will be accused of killing her. This then sets up the film's resolution, dissecting the mystery surrounding Rebecca, who dominates thoughts and actions at Manderley long after her body has passed from the earth.

One of the film industry's enduring British character actors then enters the scene, veteran C. Aubrey Smith, who, as Colonel Julyan, is Chief Constable for the county. The question of the boat washing up ashore and the surfacing of the body of the real Rebecca necessitates an inquest. It is one of two notable inquests in Hitchcock films. Each is unforgettably dramatic, but for different reasons. The other inquest occurs in *Vertigo*, with Jimmy Stewart held up to embarrassment. In *Rebecca* Colonel Julyan respects de Winter, whose family is one of the most influential, as well as prosperous, in the county. While he appears to outwardly sympathize with the wealthy aristocrat, it is obvious that he takes his responsibilities seriously and will pursue facts to a logical conclusion.

As the film moves to its finale, its two villains, Danvers and Favell, play significant roles. Through their key involvements in the drama the good versus evil, truth versus falsity equations so characteristic of mystery drama in general and Hitchcock in particular can be played out through extended suspense. The wily Hitchcock teases to the very end.

While Maxim implores his wife to stay away from the inquest, she insists on accompanying him. At a key moment, as he testifies, she faints. When the inquest adjourns for its luncheon break following her collapse, husband and wife retire to their limousine to indulge in a lunch prepared by a Manderley servant.

Favell invites himself into the car, begins munching on a chicken drumstick, then coolly proceeds to blackmail the man he has conspired with Rebecca to cuckold. The George Sanders clever brand of consummate nastiness spins into high gear. Favell notes that 1) he is tired of having to rely on an often tedious job of a motor car salesman, 2) he yearns for independent wealth, 3) Maxim de Winter can help him acquire it, 4) he can supply the requisite proof that Rebecca had anything but suicide on her mind when she died, and 5) he just happens to possess a letter, the last written by her prior to her death, that amply illustrates the point.

Rather than being intimidated, de Winter decides it is time to meet with the Constable. The men adjourn to the meeting room of the local pub. De Winter informs Colonel Julyan of what has occurred. He urges Julyan to command the blackmailer to hand over the potential evidence in question, which he does. The letter reads: "Jack, darling. I've just seen the doctor and I'm going down to Manderley right away. I shall be at the cottage all this evening, and shall leave the door open to you. I have something terribly important to tell you. Rebecca."

At one stage in the discussion, with Favell hurling accusatory darts at de Winter, suggesting he is a murderer, the aristocrat punches him. He knocks Favell to the ground, bloodying his lip. Favell coolly rises, telling de Winter his temper will be the "end of him," another dart. Did he kill Rebecca in a blind rage?

When the inquest resumes, Mrs. Danvers is called to the stand. Favell is concerned about her assisting him to provide a motive for Maxim killing Rebecca. The mention of the possibility of de Winter killing Rebecca prompts the housekeeper to blurt out the name of "Dr. Baker" as the person Rebecca visited in London the day of her death.

The action thereupon shifts to London, with a prompt trip in order as Colonel Julyan, along with de Winter and Favell, travel there. They are then shown into Dr. Baker's office. It is located in Shepherds Bush, situated in Southwest London. This is a significant career setting for Hitchcock since it was in Shepherds Bush that Gaumont-British Studios were located. It was there that, under producer Michael Balcon, Hitchcock attained directing stardom. Balcon had earlier launched the young director's career at Gainsborough.

A Secret Unveiled, Destruction Unleashed

The reason for Maxim de Winter's hatred for his former wife, along with his dread of even discussing her, is documented when the mystery of her death is solved in the office of Dr. Baker. Before the issue is resolved, however, the habitually obnoxious Favell refers to the doctor's modest office as "a dump," expressing surprise that his lover Rebecca would ever go there.

Playing the role of Dr. Baker was Leo G. Carroll, a distinguished character actor who would play significant roles in three other of Hitchcock's most enduring films, *Spellbound*, *Strangers on a Train* and *North by Northwest*. Carroll would become one of the major stars of television's early days in his role as Cosmo Topper in the successful *Topper* series. When Colonel Julyan begins the questioning the group is initially jolted upon learning that Dr. Baker had no Rebecca de Winter on his patient registry. When he checks his patient list for the fateful day, the question is answered and a psychological point is made. The name of "Danvers" appears. This reestablishes the close link between the two women, which has been further strengthened in death by the wicked housekeeper's obsession.

The height of Rebecca's unrelenting hatred toward her husband is revealed when Dr. Baker explains her situation. She was far from the vigorous woman others thought her to be, someone preparing to have a child, in the process potentially turning the world of Manderley upside down. It is learned that she was suffering from inoperable cancer. Dr. Baker reveals, "When I told her it was a matter of months, she said, 'Oh no, doctor, not that long.'"

Rebecca's seething hatred, coupled with her cunning strategy, become clear with Dr. Baker's disclosure. By taunting Maxim with false but enraging information her objective is exposed, that of goading him into killing her. That way his life would be destroyed.

When the group adjourns Favell is unflappable. His unprincipled nature allows him to shrug off the incident. There is no doubt that he will move on to more mischief, probably sooner than later. He laughs off the fact that his car is illegally parked. When Colonel Julyan refuses a ride back to Cornwall with de Winter, explaining his desire to remain in London before returning, Favell offers to take him to dinner. The Chief Constable promptly spurns his offer. He had told Favell earlier that he did not approve of blackmail, and it is obvious that his opinion of the unscrupulous car dealer parallels that held by de Winter.

As the group breaks up, Favell steps into a phone booth and places a call to Mrs. Danvers. The crushing news fills Danvers with all-consuming despair. The cutting words, delivered coolly by Favell, embody a declaration that now "Maxim and that dear little bride of his will be able to stay on at Manderley and live happily ever after."

A cold-eyed, fiendishly determined Danvers is then observed walking through the darkened hallways of Manderley with a lighted candle. She proceeds to set Manderley aflame. This is a logical response within her demented psyche. She has lost all control with the resolution of the grand mystery hovering over Manderley. Also, the woman she had deified was revealed to be mortal after all. The steely veneer Danvers hoped would not be penetrated was thoroughly destroyed with one revelation from Dr. Baker.

The fire that ensues puts David O. Selznick in a unique category. It is doubtful that any future film producer will ever experience, just as no one had prior to *Rebecca*, back to back jackpot successes spectacularly buttressed by raging infernos. Selznick's *Gone with the Wind* showcased Atlanta burning in vivid technicolor. His next film, the gothic masterpiece *Rebecca*, provides another consuming fire, this time in black and white. Considering that the latter film is a stark mood piece, the white flames of *Rebecca*, rather than the red flames seen in the earlier Selznick masterpiece, appear thematically correct.

A final master touch was provided by Hitchcock. The west wing, Rebecca's private province in death as well as life, is under siege. As it is being consumed by the incessant inferno the camera closes in on the silk pillow with the "R" monogram. It represents cinema symbolism at its most powerful. While Danvers perishes in the flames, the last vestige of Rebecca's link to Manderley is destroyed. The scene is reminiscent of the symbolism employed by Orson Welles in *Citizen Kane*, released one year later, as the mystery of "Rosebud" is revealed with the destruction by fire of the sled newspaper tycoon Charles Foster Kane owned as a boy, which he considered his last truly individual possession.

Maxim de Winter — who has arrived just in time to watch his family's estate burn to the ground — and his new wife will have the opportunity to live their life together, removed from the suffocating image of the departed Rebecca and away from the memories of Manderley. Its destruction symbolizes that the past has been extinguished by destructive fire.

Life Imitates Art

Joan Fontaine, a young actress in her early twenties, received the opportunity of a lifetime when she starred in a film adapted by a dual Pulitzer winner from a novel by England's premier gothic author of the time. It was produced by the celebrated young man in a hurry who had just delivered *Gone with the Wind* to audiences. The film was directed by his newest contract acquisition, a

British legend in his own time making his American debut, while her male starring counterpart was one of the most exciting talents to cross the Atlantic from London to Hollywood in years, fresh from his role as the haunted Heathcliff in the 1939 William Wyler triumph produced by Samuel Goldwyn, *Wuthering Heights*. All the same, her account of filming *Rebecca* could be summarized in the title of her 1978 autobiography, *No Bed of Roses*.

The way in which Fontaine was initially introduced to the role in the film that would prove her starring breakthrough was nothing short of storybook opportunity. "I had met Paulette Goddard one night at Charlie Chaplin's the year before," Fontaine related, "a night that was to change the course of my career. At dinner, where Paulette presided, though it remained a mystery whether she was Mrs. Chaplin or not, I found myself seated next to a heavyset, bespectacled gentleman who seemed particularly knowledgeable and pleasant. Soon we were chattering about the current best sellers. I mentioned that I had just read *Rebecca* by Daphne de Maurier and thought it would make an excellent movie. My dinner partner gazed at me through his lenses. 'I just bought the novel today. My name is David Selznick.' Who was I and would I like to test for the part of 'I' de Winter? Would I!"

Alfred Hitchcock occupied a special place in Fontaine's estimation for his ability to work with actors. "Before George Cukor, I'd never worked with an 'actor's director' and have worked with few since," the star candidly asserted. "Most of them, like George Stevens, knew the camera well, but once George said, 'Action,' the actor was supposed to know his lines and make the best of them on his own. On the other hand, Hitch had a good ear. He had patience, authority. He had taste. Most of all, he had imagination. We liked each other and I knew he was rooting for me. He had a strange way of going about it, as actors who have worked with him have verified. His technique was 'Divide and conquer.' He wanted total loyalty, but only to him."

While the young actress felt good that director Hitchcock was on her side, trouble loomed in the form of her male lead, the dynamic Olivier. Hitchcock confided to Fontaine during the first week of filming that Olivier was disappointed that his fiancée, Vivien Leigh, had been bypassed for the role. He later related that Olivier had spoken to him again about Fontaine, this time stating bluntly that she was "awful" and that "Vivien was the only one who should play opposite him." Reports from the Goldwyn Studios set of *Wuthering Heights* revealed that Olivier had lobbied director William Wyler to cast Vivien Leigh in place of his leading lady, Merle Oberon.

Fontaine conceded that she could hardly be friends with Olivier after learning about his conspiratorial action, but the friction extended beyond his complaints to Hitchcock. One morning, less than six weeks following Fontaine's marriage to Brian Aherne, Olivier blew a take and erupted with a four-letter word. While conceding that she had seen the word scrawled a few times on walls, Fontaine had never heard it spoken aloud, and registered an expression of shock.

Hitchcock observed it, and sought to caution his male star.

"I say, Larry old boy, do be careful," Hitchcock said. "Joan is just a new bride."

Turning toward his leading lady, Olivier asked, "Who's the chap you married?"

"Brian Aherne," the young bride proudly boasted.

"Couldn't you do better than that?" Olivier snapped as he strode off.

Joan Fontaine conceded that Olivier's nasty retort shattered her. As to Olivier's claim that his fiancée should have played the female lead in *Rebecca*, the demure, sensitive Fontaine proved a better choice for the unique role of a tender-hearted, frequently hurt young woman experiencing the pangs of adjusting to a new life which appears well beyond her. Leigh was fresh from her celebrated triumph which would win her a Best Actress Oscar for *Gone with the Wind*, in which she played a mercurial firebrand. Even by exercising the most disciplined performing technique it is difficult to envision the charismatic Leigh displaying the level of unique, submissive vulnerability and overall sensitivity realized by Fontaine. Also, with the image of Leigh as Scarlett O'Hara fresh in mind, the film audience would find it difficult empathizing with her in such a totally different role, so strong was her performance as the never-say-die, "tomorrow is another day" heroine of Selznick's spectacle.

The British Colony

The sensitive Fontaine received another jolt on the set after Hitchcock graciously threw a surprise birthday party for his leading lady. While surrounded by Hitchcock and the entire film crew, Fontaine noticed that Reginald Denny was the only actor present. Denny informed her that the party had been delayed one hour, in the course of which numerous telephone calls had been placed to Judith Anderson's dressing room, where the other performers had congregated. "The British brigade couldn't be bothered to attend my surprise party," Fontaine exclaimed.

Fontaine's experience with Hollywood's British Colony left her with an empathic ally in Hitchcock. Almost fifty years after starring in *Rebecca*, urbane woman of the world Fontaine told Gregory Speck in a 1987 interview for, appropriately enough, *Interview* magazine, "Hitch liked to ridicule people because he felt a very strong class distinction between himself and others. He was a cockney of no background whatsoever who was surrounded by all these Mayfair actors."

The leading lady's assessment is borne out by accounts from Donald Spoto and others that, during this early period of adjustment for Hitchcock to his new home of America, rather than seeking association with Hollywood's British Colony, he and wife Alma developed a fast friendship with a film couple typifying

Middle America. The Hitchcocks enjoyed entertaining Ohioan Clark Gable, and Carole Lombard, who was from Indianapolis. Hitch particularly enjoyed the periods of the Gables' visits when, after young daughter Pat had been put to bed for the evening, he could make Hollywood's most glamorous couple laugh by telling risqué jokes. It was that close bond of friendship with the Gables that led to the director making his sole foray into the realm of comedy at RKO with the 1942 release *Mr. and Mrs. Smith*, in which Lombard, the industry's most successful madcap comedienne, appeared opposite Robert Montgomery and Gene Raymond.

Fontaine received a Best Actress Academy Award nomination for *Rebecca* but didn't win. She would only have to wait for her next film, another Hitchcock vehicle, to cop a coveted statuette one year later — for *Suspicion*. "*Suspicion* works well as a teasing comedy-thriller," Ken Mogg reveals, "but Hitchcock would have preferred something more extreme. He had wanted Johnnie to be the wife-murderer of the source novel, in which he's also a philanderer and a mass poisoner."

RKO had imposed the altered ending on Hitchcock. The unsatisfactory conclusion of a story in which clues consistently point toward the ruthless gold-digger husband Johnny Aysgarth, played by Cary Grant, planning to murder his wife Lina McLaidlaw, portrayed by Fontaine, was tacked on to preserve a popular leading man from obloquy — the result of studio timidity. According to Fontaine, "He [Grant] did kill me in the original cut, but at the preview, the audience objected, so they had to reshoot it. We were told later that the audience simply refused to accept him as the murderer. In the new version, the film just stops — without the proper ending."

The rapid progress of Fontaine towards stardom validated the judgment of Hitchcock and Selznick in signing her over a host of bigger names for *Rebecca*. While winning the Oscar for *Suspicion*, she also received the New York Film Critics Award. She would secure the same honor from the New York Film Critics the next year, 1942, for *This Above All*. In 1943 she would win her third New York Film Critics award in a row for *The Constant Nymph* while also securing another Oscar nomination. Fontaine capped off her highly productive early forties phase with a 1944 RKO triumph opposite Orson Welles, playing another vulnerable young woman in a British setting, in *Jane Eyre*. Based on the novel by Charlotte Brontë, the film was directed by Robert Stevenson, who had emigrated from London to Hollywood at the same time as Hitchcock.

Hitchcock and Selznick

While Hitchcock would later be admired by producers and studio heads for completing pictures ahead of schedule and under budget, *Rebecca* was finished at a cost of $1,280,000, some $513,000 over the original budget. The early delays were a factor. The conflict between director and producer was also an element, with certain scenes being reshot as a result of Selznick's demands. The numerous discussions between Hitchcock and Selznick prompted further delays. All the same, after all the delays and confrontations between two headstrong creative forces, *Rebecca* had the look and feel of a spectacle, in the Selznick tradition of *Gone with the Wind* and his later 1946 color epic *Duel in the Sun*, while also bearing a Hitchcock imprint.

Hitchcock won a significant creative clash over how to properly employ symbolism during the crucial fire sequence. The showcasing of the white silk pillow with the "R" monogram was, as noted earlier, symbolically evocative in the same way as Orson Welles' clever invocation of the burning sled of his youth, "Rosebud," one year later in *Citizen Kane*. The raging west wing fire marked the ultimate destruction of Rebecca as a presence. This strong presence was extinguished only with the destruction of Manderley.

Selznick had a different idea. He suggested the letter "R" curling upward in smoke into the dark air. In a recent Public Broadcasting System *American Masters* presentation, "Hitchcock and Selznick," director and film historian Peter Bogdanovich provided one of the documentary's highlights with a hilarious imitation of Hitchcock, his trademark cockney accent ridiculing Selznick's idea of smoke curling upward in the letter "R" from the chimney.

Many film historians have noted that Hitchcock felt understandable disappointment when David O. Selznick mounted the stage on Oscar night to receive a statuette as producer of that year's Best Picture, while the director, despite being honored for his first American effort with a nomination, lost out to John Ford for *The Grapes of Wrath*. The Academy would never again offer such recognition to Hitchcock in the succeeding four decades of his career, as *Rebecca* was the only one of the director's films to secure a Best Picture nomination. As for Selznick, he holds a unique distinction in cinema history for being the only back-to-back Best Picture honoree. Having achieved this distinction before his fortieth birthday, Selznick, years later, lamented to Gregory Peck that by achieving what he had so early, it was well-nigh impossible for him to equal, much less surpass, his efforts as a young man.

Hitchcock could also receive credit for helping Joan Fontaine in her first major film effort. Her sensitive portrayals made her the most significant dramatic actress of the 1940–1944 period, as acknowledged not only by the Academy, but by the prestigious New York Film Critics Circle as well. While she would be criticized in some quarters for a performance that was excessively withdrawn, and co-star Laurence Olivier was cited for being overly stiff, had the attentive Hitchcock believed this to be the case, different results would have been achieved. In deference to the performers and Hitchcock, Fontaine and Olivier played their parts within the credible structure of their respective characters. Fontaine for much of the film was a frightened young woman and showed it onscreen. Olivier, laboring under the overpowering ghostly shadow of a woman whose image became even more dominant in death, demonstrated a stiff awkwardness at times which was reflective of his character.

The film's other Oscar recipient was George Barnes for his black and white cinematography, which effectively conveyed Manderley as a hallowed hall of an increasingly receding British past haunted by Rebecca's ghostly specter, replete with accompanying shadowy darkness. Out of those dark shadows came the film's most haunting onscreen entity, the macabre creature in black, Mrs. Danvers. Judith Anderson received a highly deserved Best Supporting Actress nomination for investing the role with a chilling presence accented by a perpetual death consciousness. Audience members could see Danvers symbolically holding hands with Rebecca, who towered over Manderley in death.

In Daphne du Maurier's novel, Danvers was introduced to readers like this: "Someone advanced from the sea of faces, someone tall and gaunt, dressed in deep black..." In guiding the project from book to film, Hitchcock used his skilled director's touch to move a character with overpowering presence on the printed page of a gripping gothic novel to the screen. The camera of George Barnes reveals a cavernous interior of what increasingly takes on the presence of a haunted house, as reflected by dark, shadowy hues and a humorless housekeeper in black. Anderson in silence can evoke more chilling impact than most performers delivering lengthy monologues. The encompassing darkness is then augmented by the increasingly haunted presences of Fontaine and Olivier. It is thoroughly credible when Olivier later in the film states with abject defeat that Rebecca "has won."

Just four years after her triumph in *Rebecca*, Anderson received plaudits for her role in a film in which Clifton Webb attacks Dana Andrews for "falling in love with a ghost" in *Laura*. Anderson plays Mrs. Treadwell, aunt to Gene Tierney, cast as Laura Hunt, who is believed to have been murdered, a mistaken impression that dominates the first half of the film.

As for *Rebecca*, it had the look of a Selznick spectacle, right down to the fire sequence. It had the feel of a Hitchcock product. His camerawork and pacing provided *Rebecca* with the same stamp of an evolving thriller as that found on his two previous celebrated British works, *The 39 Steps* and *The Lady Vanishes*. A spy setting was replaced by the ambience of a gothic Cornwall estate as a tormented aristocrat and his initially frightened young wife gradually unlock the mysteries behind the mysterious Rebecca de Winter.

While Hitchcock's American debut film was reflective of a setting he could have expected had he stayed in England, the director would soon score brilliantly with a taut drama that secured his objective of depicting small town Americana, a contrast of good pitted against evil, highlighted by a visit from a man who, at his worst, could have terrified even Mrs. Danvers.

3

Tranquility in
the Midst of War

Shadow of a Doubt *is one of my favorite pictures.*
— Alfred Hitchcock

With Hitchcock adjusting to a new country and responding to the differences between the British and American film industries, it would be a while before he would have the opportunity to move into a truly American phase. After *Rebecca* was finished, Selznick, noted for his loanout skills and the profits derived by shuffling his talented contractees around various Hollywood studios, put Hitchcock to work with producer Walter Wanger on *Foreign Correspondent.* Apart from resenting the money Selznick made for loaning him out, Hitchcock was happy to be free from working with a producer noted for his numerous demands on directors and his micromanaging involvement in the creative end of his projects.

Foreign Correspondent, which starred Joel McCrea and Laraine Day, was the kind of film that, like *Rebecca,* would be easy to associate with Hitchcock's British phase. While filmed at Goldwyn Studios, the story's setting was Holland. Though the force opposing freedom in the drama is clearly Nazi Germany, no country or political system is identified. *Foreign Correspondent* was fine-tuned along the way to conform to then occurring events amid the advancing war clouds of Europe. The film's conclusion reveals Hitchcock's beloved England under siege. *Foreign Correspondent* was unabashed propaganda-cum-entertainment designed to alert Americans and a world citizenry to the onrushing menace of Nazism.

Joel McCrea plays a somewhat indolent, easygoing nice guy American journalist sent to Europe who becomes ensnared in the deadly world of international espionage. His essential trusting nature makes him unaware that the man assigned to him as a bodyguard is actually attempting to kill him, and is slow to observe that Herbert Marshall, father of the woman with whom he falls in love (played by Laraine Day) is far from what he purports to be. Rather than heading an international peace organization, as Marshall purports to be doing, he is actually a spy working for the enemy.

Foreign Correspondent, while filmed entirely at Samuel Goldwyn Studios, conveys the look of Europe under imminent siege, bolstered by Hitchcock's elaborate set pieces and the contribution of brilliant set designer William Cameron Menzies. The impending threat is psychologically emphasized by cramped enclosures, from the newspaper office to the London and Amsterdam hotels, from the foreboding windmill interior to the traumatic airplane crash into the sea viewed from a cramped cockpit. Activities build to a climax and culminate in survivors clinging desperately to a piece of fuselage in an endless sea. The survival scene presaged Hitchcock's 1944 release, *Lifeboat*, which takes place in a floating craft where a group of wartime survivors seek to endure in the face of life-threatening elements.

In *Foreign Correspondent*, Joel McCrea is cast in the familiar Hitchcock role of an innocent thrown into a sea of international political conflict well beyond his depth of understanding but determined to endure. He seeks to survive in tandem with a beautiful woman, reflective of Robert Donat and Madeleine Carroll in *The 39 Steps*, Robert Cummings and Priscilla Lane in *Saboteur*, James Stewart and Doris Day in the remake of *The Man Who Knew Too Much*, and Cary Grant alongside Eva Marie Saint in *North by Northwest*.

In the case of Alfred Hitchcock, who was born and raised in London and sought to adapt to his new home in America, *Foreign Correspondent* proved to be personally symbolic. This duality was perceived by Donald Spoto, who wrote, "In spite of its mostly European setting, the leading man is American and the whole tone and texture of the picture celebrates American simplicity, American savvy, and American courage. That's what the producer and studio wanted, and that's what Hitchcock delivered with a benign vengeance."

The success of the film in achieving its objective was recognized by someone who profoundly understood propaganda, and who became an unlikely fan of *Foreign Correspondent*. Joseph Goebbels, Hitler's Minister of Propaganda, saluted *Foreign Correspondent* as a masterpiece. It became one of his favorite films and he viewed it frequently in his office.

A Film Shrouded in Doubt

While 1940 found Hitchcock in his new country turning out two films characteristic of products he might easily have crafted during his British period, *Rebecca* and *Foreign Correspondent*, the following year found more of the same with *Suspicion*, shot on the RKO lot but with a British setting and two of Hollywood's most notable English stars, Cary Grant and Joan Fontaine. While Fontaine, who had received a Best Actress Oscar nomination for *Rebecca* under Hitchcock's direction, would win the coveted statuette for *Suspicion*, the film would be perhaps the most controversial of Hitchcock's long career, as well as one riddled with production untidiness highly uncharacteristic of his works.

Hitchcock was noted for meticulously crafting each film, down to camera angles, using a detailed storyboard technique. He considered his plan a foolproof mechanism wherein, once the finished script was completed, the production process proceeded on automatic pilot. "The production is finished and it's time to move on to another project," Hitchcock would say after a script was completed. Some critics would question the process, preferring more spontaneity on the set from the director, while Hitchcock, by then bored with the process, would often fall asleep. Hitchcock's supporters would present as corroborative evidence the fact that his projects were delivered on time and within budgetary designs. With Hitchcock, meticulousness meant thrift, a quality notably lacking in some of the most creative film directors.

A cardinal Hitchcock sin was in evidence on the RKO set as *Suspicion* was being filmed. The normal iron clad rule of having a finished script before filming began was undercut by a sea of uncertainty that, at its worst, saw Hitchcock suffer a breakdown, resulting in the production shutting down. Leading lady Fontaine, complaining that Hitchcock was not providing her with the kind of careful attention he had provided during *Rebecca*, suffered from a bout of indisposition as the huge question mark remained concerning how the film would end. A further compounding irony was that the two women with whom Hitchcock bore the closest professional identity during his long career, his wife Alma Reville Hitchcock and Joan Harrison, who began as his secretary in London and would eventually become producer of his popular television program during the fifties, were the scenarists of *Suspicion*.

Despite the suspenseful drama and excellent acting rapport between Cary Grant and Joan Fontaine, *Suspicion* is the Hitchcock film shrouded in collective audience doubt relating to its unsatisfactory ending. While all signs point toward Grant being a charming schemer and murderer with a design to eliminate his wife for her money, it was decided that the highly popular British actor could not portray a killer.

The conclusion of *Suspicion*, in which Grant's character is vindicated, appears contrived and was an unwieldy compromise catering to popular tastes as well as the omnipresent hobgoblin film enforcer, the Breen Office. Hitchcock sought to provide an ending in which Fontaine's character, desperately in love with that of Grant and depressed by his criminal designs, decides to end her life by taking poison but, prior to doing so, writes a letter to her mother revealing her husband's true nature. The prevailing film code would permit suicide only in instances where a character's sin was being expiated, which was not the case in *Suspicion*.

Controversy and dissatisfaction regarding the end of *Suspicion* continues to this day. Had Hitchcock been permitted to exercise his unfettered discretion the situation would have been more satisfactorily resolved. His eminently plausible ending would have proven more satisfying, had it been incorporated into the film. He put the issue in perspective:

> *Suspicion* suffered from a compromised ending because the star, Cary Grant, obviously cannot be a murderer. The original ending had the wife dying from a poisoned glass of milk given her by her homicidal husband. Of course it was impossible to use that in the film, but I did have an ending whereby the wife now knows that she's married to a murderer who's going to kill her, so she writes a letter to her mother saying, "I don't want to live any more, I'm in love with him, he's going to kill me, but I think society should be protected." She writes the letter, seals it, puts it beside the bed, and when he brings up the fatal glass of milk she says, "Would you post that letter for me?" So she drinks the milk and dies. Then you fade out and fade in again on one shot: Cary Grant walking down the street whistling very cheerfully and popping the letter in the box. But I couldn't use that ending either.

The other Hitchcock 1941 release, also an RKO product, was *Mr. and Mrs. Smith*, the master filmmaker's only venture into comedy. It remained for the director to put his own suspense imprint on a characteristically American project, something Hitchcock watchers would not identify with his British period. At first blush his next American project, *Saboteur*, might appear to qualify as a new beginning. It was not only set in America, the climactic, nail-biting sequence took place at the Statue of Liberty, one of the nation's most familiar icons along with the Capitol Building and the White House in Washington, D.C.

When all was said and done, *Saboteur*, despite its American setting, was perceived by many as Hitchcock resorting to his old British bag of tricks. As in *Foreign Correspondent*, the film deals with Nazis seeking to undermine freedom. Unable to secure the services of Gary Cooper, who turned the role down, as he had earlier rejected the male lead in *Foreign Correspondent*, Hitchcock settled for Robert Cummings as his leading man. A victim of circumstances, Cummings' character becomes entwined in a labyrinthian pattern of espionage originating from his work in a Glendale, California, aircraft plant. He later meets Priscilla Lane, who, in the manner of Madeleine Carroll in *The 39 Steps*, is initially distrustful of the man with whom she becomes interlinked by fate. *Saboteur* was seen as a return to the picaresque form of Hitchcock's brilliant triumph from his British days, *The 39 Steps*, while film critics Rohmer and Chabrol summarized it as "a potpourri of his English works."

While choppy and episodic, the heralded statue of liberty scene at the close of *Saboteur* is one of the most creatively imaginative ever filmed by Hitchcock or any other director. Norman Lloyd played the role of the Nazi saboteur who plunges to his death, despite a valiant effort to save him by Robert Cummings, with the proper measure of enigmatic hostility.

It was in the following year, 1943, that a film was released that served as Hitchcock's ode to his new home. It dealt with madness, and the male lead carried off the portrait convincingly within the confines of small town America, being ultimately thwarted by his own niece, who idolized him. With noir consciousness extending beyond the earlier detective roots of Chandler and Ham-

mett to the Park Avenue world of Waldo Lydecker and beyond, it was anticipated that suspense master Hitchcock, with his instinct for tapping into the psyches of troubled inhabitants of the shadowy underbelly of society, would enter
the scene with his unencumbered creative flourish.

Darkness Lurking in Small Town America

Santa Rosa, a quiet town some 40 miles north of San Francisco, was the
perfect American city from which Hitchcock could launch into a new thematic
American phase. Filming occurred far from the bombs shelling his native England
during a period of great conflict in which, by then, his adopted nation was very
much involved. *Shadow of a Doubt* was the result, a film Hitchcock considered
one of his personal favorites.

If small, laidback Santa Rosa was the perfect locale for Hitchcock's first truly
American venture, the selection of Thornton Wilder as scenarist was equally apt.
Hitchcock was impressed by Wilder's 1940 ode to small town America, *Our
Town*, set in New Hampshire and starring youthful lead players William Holden
and Martha Scott. While *Our Town* represented a capsulized look at American
small town serenity, master of mystery Hitchcock wove a different creative fabric in the brilliant film noir classic, *Shadow of a Doubt*.

The Use of Doubles

Shadow of a Doubt incorporated a technique often employed by Hitchcock
in his mystery films. Hitchcock was born at the end of the nineteenth century,
1899, and utilized a device that was popular with Victorian writers such as Robert
Louis Stevenson (in *The Strange Case of Dr. Jekyll and Mr. Hyde*) and Oscar
Wilde (in *The Picture of Dorian Gray*)—that of the double. In the aforementioned classic works authors Stevenson and Wilde penned psychologically fascinating studies of characters with split personalities. Perceived on a broader scale,
the individuals represented the duality of the world itself, where a kindly and
organized realm of existence functions alongside one of cruelty and chaotic uncertainty.

Hitchcock biographer Donald Spoto believed that the director's own life
was strongly governed by such a pronounced pattern of duality, that he recognized it, and found the theme fascinating from a personal standpoint. After all,
as Spoto pointed out, Hitchcock was a Victorian Catholic who on one level conveyed an image of meticulous correctness, and on another delightedly
overindulged in food and alcohol while enjoying ribald toilet humor. On the
one hand he could demonstrate great love and affection toward those he loved,
notably wife Alma and daughter Patricia, while on the other he could evidence

a cruel and cold indifference, virtually ignoring them as well as others toward whom he bore genuine feeling.

Shadow of a Doubt had its origin in a nine-page treatment by Gordon McDonell, whose wife was then story editor for David O. Selznick during the period when Hitchcock was being frequently loaned out by the crafty producer. Mrs. McDonell met Hitchcock at the Brown Derby in Beverly Hills and informed him of her husband's idea, which the director suggested she type out. She did and it was acquired for Hitchcock. "Then I invited Thornton Wilder to come out and do the script because, as the author of *Our Town*, he was the best available example of a writer of Americana," Hitchcock explained. "We used to talk in the morning and he'd write in the afternoon. He didn't work in continuity either, he jumped around."

Even before Wilder arrived, Santa Rosa had been selected as the locale for the drama. Wilder and Hitchcock studied the town carefully. Hitchcock noted that he "constantly used local citizens in the cast." The definitive example was the casting of a young girl whose father owned a small store Hitchcock visited, which reminded him of that owned by his own father. The result was a brilliant performance by Edna May Wonacott as Ann Newton, the younger sister of Teresa Wright, a bespectacled, book-devouring, no-nonsense youngster who, like Hitchcock, has a penchant for Sir Walter Scott. While Wilder's efforts mainly lay in the realm of character development and mood, it was Hitchcock's faithful and talented wife, Alma Reville, and short story writer Sally Benson, who shaped the story into a finished script.

The doubles element of the film begins with two characters bearing the same name. Selznick contract player Joseph Cotten portrays the worldly Uncle Charlie, who comes to stay with the Newton family in Santa Rosa. His arrival is enthusiastically welcomed by Teresa Wright, named after Uncle Charlie, the younger brother her mother Emma (played by stage actress Patricia Collinge) willingly admits to having spoiled.

Uncle Charlie is, on the surface, a charming and debonair man of the world, but there exists within him a side to be fully explored during his stay in Santa Rose with the Newtons, that of a rageful, anti-social, unregenerate serial murderer of wealthy middle-aged widows. It remains for Wright as Young Charlie, whose blood line and psychical bond to the uncle she initially adores invests her with a capability above all others to understand him as well as to flush out the total entity of the man, to eventually learn his darkest innermost secrets while her mother and the rest of the Newton family remain unaware of his murderous side.

A Psychic Connection

While films dealing with psychic subject matter are far from rare today, the focus placed on the subject of mutual mental telepathy in the early phase of

Shadow of a Doubt was unusual for the early forties. A frustrated Teresa Wright, a sensitive and highly intelligent high school student, is focusing on the drabness of life early in the film. Her mother expresses concern. Wright, a twinkle surfacing in her eyes, decides to send a telegram to Uncle Charlie and ask him to visit. There is already a telegram waiting for the Newtons at the telegraph office, which is from Uncle Charlie, announcing that he will be coming to visit for an extended period of time.

Joseph Cotten and Teresa Wright interact with empathic brilliance as two individuals who, in certain contexts, embody alter egos of one another. Their empathy ends in the fact that Cotten embodies evil and finds the world a foul, rotten place, whereas Wright, while possessing a superior intellect capable of recognizing that all is not well with the world, embodies the idealism of a young woman appealing to and identifying with the positive side of the human experience. What prompts the emotional volcano within Wright is the increasing awareness that the uncle she idolizes is the polar opposite of what she envisioned him to be. She soon learns, much to her sorrow, that the charming, engaging exterior revealed by Uncle Charlie is not only a false front, but a deadly one designed to lure wealthy women into a vulnerable position prior to strangling them.

Cotten's outwardly engaging manner and dexterous charm in the role make him the kind of killer Hitchcock loved to showcase. A killer with charm is much more likely to be successful than an obvious, hideously repulsive type, which prompts women in particular to recoil. *Shadow of a Doubt* was based on the case of the "Merry Widow Murderer," Earle Leonard Nelson, a serial strangler from the twenties. Cotten delivered one of his finest performances as the complex killer, who veers alternately between the bubbly outer facade and the antisocial strangler whose hatred for women is matched only by his contempt for society at large.

Courtly Virginian Cotten enjoyed a banner 1940s period in which the Mercury Theater product starred with his youthful mentor, director and co-star Orson Welles, in *Citizen Kane* in 1941, then starred under Welles's direction in *The Magnificent Ambersons* one year later. After *Shadow of a Doubt* he starred in 1944 productions opposite Ingrid Bergman in *Gaslight* and Claudette Colbert in *Since You Went Away*. He would do three major films with Jennifer Jones, *Love Letters* in 1945, *Duel in the Sun* in 1946, and *Portrait of Jenny* in 1948. He starred opposite Loretta Young in her Oscar-winning role in *The Farmer's Daughter* in 1947 and ended 1949 unsuccessfully pursuing Alida Valli and ultimately turning in old friend Orson Welles to the police in the brilliant noir epic, *The Third Man*.

Cotten expressed concern to Hitchcock that, as an actor who had never previously played a murderer, he was unsure of just what a serial killer was like and what demeanor one should carry in such a role. The actor described the character he portrayed as "a man high on the most wanted list of the FBI and

Arousing suspicion — A dapper Joseph Cotten has just deposited a large sum of money at the bank where his brother-in-law, played by veteran character actor Henry Travers, right, is employed. Instead of indicating joy or gratitude over the substantial deposit, however, niece Teresa Wright and her father express surprise over his bizarre behavior in a scene from *Shadow of a Doubt*, which was shot on location in Santa Rosa near San Francisco.

one with a most complex philosophy, which advocated the annihilation of rich widows whose greedy ambitions had rewarded their husbands with expensive funerals."

Hitchcock suggested an experiment. The two men got into Cotten's car. As he was driving Hitchcock into town the director confided that, despite having taught both his wife and daughter to drive in the privacy of their own driveway, he had never driven a car due to experiencing "a real panic" anytime he saw a policeman. Hitchcock also explained the psychological motivation driving the man known as "the Merry Widow Murderer": "Uncle Charlie feels no guilt at all. To him, the elimination of his widows is a dedication, an important sociological contribution to civilization."

Hitchcock had Cotten transport him to Rodeo Drive in Beverly Hills, after which the director put his actor through a psychological exercise. "Take a look at the men you pass and let me know when you spot a murderer," Hitchcock said after Cotten had parked and the two men began to walk down one of the world's swankiest streets. Cotten referred to one man he spotted as having "shifty eyes." Hitchcock responded, telling Cotten that the eyes were "shifted" rather than shifty, for the purpose of observing the beautifully trim leg of a woman emerging from a parked car, who turned out to be Claudette Colbert. It did not take Cotten long to understand the rationale behind the whole exercise.

"What you're trying to say is, or rather what I'm saying you're saying is, that a murderer looks and moves just like anybody else," Cotten concluded.

"Or vice versa," Hitchcock responded.

The suave Cotten was believable in that he possessed the requisite charm to entice lonely widows, while revealing his other side with the appropriate bitterness-on-the-edge-of-rage, which he could rein in when suspicions might be aroused or opportunity in the form of a new prospective victim surfaced. Cotten as charmer was revealed in his relationship with an obviously smitten Mrs. Potter, whom he meets in Santa Rosa.

Teresa Wright served as the perfect counterpoint to the worldly, debonair, but ultimately anti-social and embittered serial killer played by Cotten. Bright and inquisitive, Wright plays the oldest of the three Newton children. All three appear to be mentally gifted and inquisitive, a contrast from their mundane, non-curious parents, portrayed by Patricia Collinge and Henry Travers. Veteran character actor Travers is widely known to film fans as the angel who descended to earth long enough to save Jimmy Stewart's life in Frank Capra's *It's a Wonderful Life*.

If the forties were kind to Joseph Cotten, the same would have to be said for Teresa Wright. With Cotten adopting an outlook of bleakness in *Shadow of a Doubt*, Wright was the perfect contrast in a role she perfected during that productive decade of her career, the sweet and sensitive girl that the husband and wife living next door prayed that their son would marry. Born in New York, Wright received her acting apprenticeship at the Wharf Theater in Provincetown, Massachusetts. By 1938, one year before she was old enough to vote, she debuted on Broadway as the lead's understudy in *Our Town*. This proved advantageous later on in that Wright made a favorable impression on playwright Thornton Wilder, who recommended her to Hitchcock for the role of young Charlie Newton.

The famous author of *Our Town* was far from alone in observing the special magic, that blend of sweetness, quiet strength, and sensitivity, that characterized Teresa Wright. Her performance in the ingénue part in *Life with Father* on Broadway in 1939 brought the young actress to the attention of Samuel Goldwyn, who signed her to a Hollywood contract. Wright quickly confirmed Goldwyn's judgment. In her first screen appearance in 1941, in the adaptation of the Lillian Hellman play *The Little Foxes*, directed by William Wyler, she was cast as the daughter of Bette Davis and launched her career with a Best Supporting Actress Oscar nomination.

If 1941 had proven a promising beginning, 1942 saw the young actress soar to even loftier heights. She played the supportive wife of Gary Cooper to elegant perfection in the biopic of baseball great Lou Gehrig, *The Pride of the Yankees*, directed by Sam Wood, receiving an Oscar nomination for Best Actress. The sagacious William Wyler recognized Wright's skills and brought her back in one of his most successful vehicles, as she played the daughter of Walter Pidgeon and Greer Garson in the pulsating war drama *Mrs. Minniver*, for which she secured an Academy statuette in the Best Supporting Actress category. After her solid triumph under Hitchcock in *Shadow of a Doubt*, Wright would receive another call from Wyler — to co-star with Fredric March, Myrna Loy and Dana Andrews in the highly celebrated drama about post–World War II civilian adjustment, the 1946 release *The Best Years of Our Lives*. Wright was compelling in yet another daughter role, this time with March and Loy as her parents. A major element of the story surrounds Wright's romance with Andrews, initially frowned upon by March. Wright proves the perfect contrast to selfish party girl Virginia Mayo, Andrews's wife. Her performance earned Wright the New York Film Critics Circle Award for Best Actress.

Wright, in later recalling her experience working with Hitchcock, cited his meticulous craftsmanship in the pre-production phase. Teresa Wright's grasp of story essence is understandable in view of the fact that she was married to two celebrated writers. She was married briefly during the forties to Niven Busch, who, following a stint at *Time*, was chief story editor at Goldwyn Productions, where he helped steer the career of studio contractee Wright.

Apropos of Hitchcock, Wright recollected: "He did such homework before he began the picture. He saw the film completely in his mind before we began — it's as if he had a little projection room in his head. When he told me the story the first time we met in his office in June 1942, we could have been sitting in a theater seeing a finished film. So during the shooting he made us feel very relaxed. His direction never came across as instruction. We felt we could trust him, and he gave us guidance and a sense of freedom. He was very calm, as if we were just plans making a contribution to something that had been completely foreseen. No one plans a film as completely as he did, and no one saw it as clearly as he did from the very start. Other directors usually let it happen when they're making it, but with him everything could be more serene, and more enjoyable."

Replete with Doubles

As noted, Hitchcock had an affinity for the use of the double, a concept employed by various Victorian writers. The perfect launching point was the complex relationship between Uncle Charlie and his young namesake niece, which was only the first (and most crucial) invocation in a story replete with doubles, as evidenced by the following breakdown:

1) Young Charlie–Uncle Charlie — This fundamental double embraces a relationship in which mutual telepathy is at work, prompting niece and uncle to be aware of each other's thoughts and emotions. The perceptive young Charlie manifested her awareness of this element when her urge to send a wire to her uncle coincides with his already having sent one to the Newtons. The more universal element of the Charlie-Charlie double is that Wright embraces light and goodness while Cotten embraces the universe at its darkest, replete with social anarchy, double dealings, and ultimately murder.

2) The crime discussion duo of Henry Travers and Hume Cronyn — Wright's father, who leads a mundane, unimaginative life working at a bank in a small town, finds it a relaxing diversion to read mystery magazines and theoretically seek the means of implementing the perfect murder. He finds a kindred spirit in next door neighbor, played by Hume Cronyn, who made his film debut in *Shadow of a Doubt*. Cronyn reads mystery magazines voraciously as an escape from a drab existence living under his mother's shadow. During one symbolically revealing conversation in the Newton dining room, Cotten sits nonchalantly, saying nothing as Travers and Cronyn unwind by engaging in friendly argument over the ideal means of killing each other. It becomes too much for the hypersensitive young Charlie, who chastises her father and neighbor for engaging in such gruesome conversation, all the while becoming increasingly suspicious of her uncle's activities. An impervious Collinge gently tells her daughter that the harmless discussion is but a means of relaxation for her father and neighbor.

3) A visit to a bar and doubles within doubles — At a time when Uncle Charlie's concern about his daughter's perceptions about him reaches a fever pitch, he takes his niece to a local bar. It is an environment in which she feels conspicuously out of place. Its name, symbolically enough, is "'Till Two." Cotten, showing a mounting inner rage bubbling ever closer to the surface, orders two double brandies.

4) Young female contrasting doubles — The young lady who serves Cotten and Wright at 'Till Two recognizes young Charlie, expressing surprise at seeing her at the bar. Whereas young Charlie represents the bright future of Santa Rosa youth, the cocktail waitress is a sad example of a life spinning aimlessly out of control. She tells young Charlie that she has been working at 'Till Two for "two weeks," embodying yet another double.

5) Pursued by two I — The film opens with Cotten being warned by his landlady, who finds him lying on his bed with clusters of bills situated next to him on the floor, that the same two men who had been asking to see him had just left. She tells him it is not a good idea to leave money lying on the floor. Once she leaves, he peers out the window and observes

the men. He is barely able to slip past them to at least temporary freedom. The opening sequence, filmed in Newark, New Jersey, sets the mood of the film, pursuer seeking pursued, revealing the unglamorous side of city life. Cotten's small, drab room was a place for a hunted man to briefly escape, after which a new option must be considered. After eluding the two men, Cotten sends the telegram to Santa Rosa revealing that the Newtons can expect a visitor.

6) Pursued by two II — After Uncle Charlie arrives in quiet Santa Rosa, hoping that the police trail will grow cold, two FBI agents appear at the Newton household. MacDonald Carey is the younger and more communicative of the pair. They originally seek information as Carey tells Patricia Collinge that the men are with a magazine and doing a series on the typical American family, of which the Newtons are a prototype. Carey's older, less smiling, more taciturn partner, Wallace Ford, on the pretext of taking a photograph of the interior of the Newton home, instead takes a picture of Cotten as he makes his entrance into the house. A wily Cotten immediately asks for the roll of film, explaining that he does not like to have his picture taken. Carey asks Ford to give the film back. Unknown to Cotten, Ford holds back the most important picture on the roll, that of him, so that Cotten receives only harmless photographs taken earlier of the Newton home. A romantic relationship ultimately blooms between Wright and Carey, but not before some rough edges are smoothed out as the federal agent overcomes Wright's earlier opposition to the investigation of her uncle after her own suspicions concerning his guilt increase.

7) Two suspects — A tactful MacDonald Carey explained to Teresa Wright at the beginning that her uncle was one of two men under investigation as the Merry Widow Murderer. One of the most dramatically revealing scenes occurs in the film after Uncle Charlie overhears crime story devotee Hume Cronyn telling fellow enthusiast Henry Travers that the Merry Widow Murderer suspect had been killed by a plane on an airport runway as he sought to elude captors. Initially a triumphant smile surfaces on Uncle Charlie's face as he hears the news standing outside the Newton residence. He contentedly announces his intention to go inside and have dinner. When he observes young Charlie standing on the sidewalk his expression of triumphal contentment quickly vanishes. It is quickly transformed into one of apprehensive concern. He knows that his shrewd niece has not only pieced together facts convincing her of his guilt, beginning with the inscription on a ring she has been given by her uncle that earlier belonged to one of his murder victims, but their no holds barred discussion in 'Till Two resulted in candid admissions on his part, culminating with a promise to leave Santa Rosa as soon as strategically possible. While he may be in the clear in the eyes of authorities, his once-

favorite niece is another matter as he plots to add her to his list of victims, setting up yet another double.

8) Two murder attempts — The duality pattern exists leading up to the film's climactic train scene, which constitutes a third attempt on the part of Uncle Charlie on young Charlie's life. The first attempt to murder young Charlie is by loosening a step on the stairway. The loose step is discovered and young Charlie is unharmed. The second attempt is straight out of the Hitchcock tradition of dutifully squeezing every drop of suspense from a scene. After observing the tendency of the Newtons' garage door to slam shut without contact, along with the corresponding difficulty encountered in opening it, the insidious criminal mind of Uncle Charlie immediately goes to work.

As Uncle Charlie and the Newtons are planning to leave for a lecture that the erudite man of the world has agreed to deliver to the Santa Rosa townsfolk, he inveigles young Charlie to start up the family car. He makes certain she cannot turn off the ignition and tightly closes the garage door. Suspense is accelerated and the moment of ultimate reckoning postponed as long as possible for dramatic effect. Seeking to enhance his prospect of success, Uncle Charlie goes back inside and decides to turn on the radio to listen to music, raising the volume until his sister inquires as to why it is so loud.

Meanwhile, young Charlie is left to choke on gas fumes. Hitchcock's ploy of extending suspense, draining every last drop of emotion from a scene, achieved devastating results when theater patrons, after Travers noticed that young Charlie was missing and the Newtons became concerned, would frequently shout "Hurry up!" when the characters began looking for her. A note of irony is sounded when Hume Cronyn, his nose always sniffing mystery as he seeks to theoretically plot the perfect murder, passes the garage and observes the exhaust fumes, quickly alerting the family. It is none other than Uncle Charlie, inwardly fuming over Cronyn's arrival and discovery, who seeks to cover his tracks by prying open the garage door and "saving" his niece. Young Charlie is by no means fooled, as revealed by the expression of tragic awareness etched on her face as she stares up at her uncle when she comes to after her near brush with death. The expression reveals more than knowledge on her part about the murder attempt; it also conveys her awareness that her increasingly desperate uncle is not finished with her.

A basic element ultimately foiling Cotten's designs is the duality of the two Charlies, increasingly enhanced as the story develops, with the killer realizing that a mental telepathy exists between uncle and niece that enables her to perceive things about him in a way that transcends his dealings with others. At the dinner table she correctly recognizes a melody as "The Merry Widow Waltz," but before she can reveal the information, Uncle Charlie deliberately spills a glass of water to prevent her from mouthing the taboo words.

When a story appears in the local newspaper about the hunt for the Merry Widow Murderer, Uncle Charlie cleverly conspires to remove the article before any of the Newton family members can read it. He does so by telling his nephew that he can perform a trick with the newspaper, turning it into a paper house. The always alert young Charlie, however, notices that an article has been ripped from the paper, prompting a frantic visit to the library. She then reads the story.

The Lurch That Saved a Life

As Uncle Charlie becomes increasingly aware of his shrewd niece's conclusions about him, aided in no small measure by his embittered monologue at 'Till Two, the suspense drama boils down to a finale reminiscent of the old formula western equation of "This town isn't big enough for both of us"—with one important modification: there is no town big enough for Uncle Charlie in view of the knowledge his niece possesses about him. As the film moves toward a suspenseful end, Uncle Charlie behaves in the manner of a "crazed animal" amid mounting suspicions of young Charlie. A major concern on her part is her mother's continuing love for her younger brother and Charlie's desire not to hurt her mother.

Ultimately deciding that he must leave Santa Rosa, Uncle Charlie explains that he has business to tend to. The relationship with his niece comes to a compelling conclusion when she follows him onto the train. The thematic threads of the film are brilliantly woven together. At the moment when young Charlie's life hangs in the balance the flashback of elegantly dressed couples dancing to the tune of Franz Lehar's "The Merry Widow Waltz," which was shown at the movie's outset and repeated when the melody was being hummed at the Newton dinner table, is played once more.

Uncle Charlie's pattern of attracting wealthy widows continues when Mrs. Poetter, who had become smitten with the suave killer, is seen entering the train, waving and smiling at him, looming vulnerably as his next victim. When the train begins pulling out of the station, Uncle Charlie clutches young Charlie, refusing to let her go. He waits for an approaching train on the opposite track to catch up with them, letting her know that she must pay the price for her knowledge, and that it will be just a little while longer before her secret will be extinguished with her. Once more Hitchcock has found a way to extend the mystery. A sudden lurch of the train causes Uncle Charlie to lose his balance and his grip on his niece, enabling her to push him directly toward the oncoming train.

The final scene reveals a somber Wright and Carey outside the church where a funeral service is being held for Uncle Charlie. The hearse bearing his body is observed proceeding slowly down the street amid a swarm of onlookers. When the scene was being shot a large contingent of Santa Rosa residents, believing

Unmasking a Serial Killer — Joseph Cotten, left, was provided with his most challenging movie role playing a serial killer of rich widows in Hitchcock's 1943 film *Shadow of a Doubt*, which the director cited as his all-time favorite film experience. Cotten's niece, played by Teresa Wright, has the same first name as the uncle she once idolized, Charlie, but has eventually figures out his true identity. In the process Wright falls in love with the FBI investigator pursuing Cotten, played by Macdonald Carey, right.

that the event was real, stopped and paid their respects. It is evident from observing Wright and Carey that they care a great deal for each other and that their relationship is only beginning. Wright concludes by sadly revealing her uncle's thoroughly negative view of the world, one he saw as sheer anarchy, concluding that, "He couldn't have been happy."

A Pleasant Experience During a Dark Period

One of the reasons Hitchcock cited *Shadow of a Doubt* as one of his favorite pictures related to the courtesies extended to the visiting film crew by the residents of Santa Rosa. Their friendliness and spirit of cooperation made the *Shadow of a Doubt* experience enjoyable as things fell into place, and one of Hollywood's greatest suspense masterpieces resulted.

The positive response came at a perfect time for Hitchcock since tragedy loomed in his native England. At a time when bombs were steadily dropping from Nazi war planes and it was impossible for him to leave to visit his native country, his mother took ill and died, adding a realistic note to the duality theme of light and darkness so brilliantly explored in the film.

In exploring the psyche of a tortured serial killer, Alfred Hitchcock entered into an area that would greatly intrigue the affluent of the movie colony following the war. Among the prominent tinsel town players who became absorbed by the subject of psychiatry in general and psychoanalysis in particular was none other than the producer who brought Hitchcock to Hollywood, David O. Selznick. It was not difficult for Selznick to interest Hitchcock in a project involving an area he too found highly absorbing.

4

Selznick and Psychiatry in
Post-War Hollywood

*Hollywood was full of neurotic people who wanted the meaning of their lives
explained to them and who had lots of money to pay for their explanations.*
— Otto Friedrich

The film industry is a profession where survivors are capable of shifting
gears with speedier tenacity than a sports car driver. Just as Hitchcock had fully
acclimated himself creatively to his new country by making a small town American film dealing with a big city Eastern invader with a propensity for killing
rich widows in *Shadow of a Doubt,* David O. Selznick had designs on putting
Hitchcock to work on a new project eons removed from a movie about small
town America.

The subject was international in scope, but with an ultimate American
flavor. In *Shadow of a Doubt* an uncomplicated Norman Rockwell small town,
Santa Rosa in Northern California, was invaded by an outward force representing an alien culture. The subject that filled the restless mind of David O. Selznick
with creative anxiety had its roots in Eastern Europe. The shifting tides of history during World War II saw many of Europe's brightest creative minds fleeing
the yoke of Hitler's Nazi tyranny. This produced a dynamic synergy, with much
of it being based in Southern California, the locus of the film industry.

It has been related how helpless Hitchcock felt during the peak period of
World War II to be unable to visit his family in besieged England. The next
project in which he would become immersed with Selznick examined the same
question that plagued him during the filming of *Shadow of a Doubt,* analyzed
from the opposite perspective. While émigrés such as Hitchcock suffered helplessly while their countries and relatives were immersed in life-threatening battles for freedom, a mine lode of some of Europe's foremost creative minds fled
when faced with Nazi advancement. While many were Jewish, seeking to avoid
the death sentence that was Holocaust, non–Jews with viewpoints incompati-

ble with Nazism were also compelled to escape or face the prospect of death. Two of the leading émigrés leaving their native Germany were Thomas Mann, the distinguished intellectual who secured the Nobel Prize for Literature in 1929, and his brother Heinrich, also a renowned author.

Whereas some of the European émigrés settled in New York City, others such as the Manns traversed westward to Los Angeles. For one thing these émigrés liked the warm, moderate climate. For another they located in an area that reminded them of home, but without the dangerous current political implications. The Mann brothers immediately became leading lights in a rapidly expanding intellectual community in and around the idyllic locale of Pacific Palisades, where they made their homes. Long after the immigration of World War II intellectuals, Pacific Palisades continues to enjoy popularity among immigrants from Germany, Austria and Switzerland. The topography is comparable to their native nations. Pacific Palisades has received much attention in more recent times for being the home of Ronald Reagan from 1952 until his election to the presidency in 1980 and is the current residence of another Hollywood actor turned California governor, Arnold Schwarzenegger.

Emigrating to America during the same period and settling in nearby Brentwood was Arnold Schoenberg, a brilliant German classical music composer. Whereas the Manns ultimately returned to Europe after the war, Schoenberg found a home in America, becoming a highly acclaimed music professor at the University of California at Los Angeles in nearby Westwood. Schoenberg's popularity at UCLA burgeoned to the point where one of the leading buildings on that large campus was named after him, Schoenberg Hall.

Bertolt Brecht, the always colorful, perpetually controversial German writer who became a committed Marxist and would ultimately emigrate to East Germany after World War II, arrived with his wife at the port of San Pedro and was driven to his new home, an apartment at 1954 Argyle Avenue in the heart of Hollywood, by Marta Feuchtwanger, the wife of the prominent Jewish émigré author from Germany, Lion Feuchtwanger, a collaborator of Brecht's. The rental was arranged by William Dieterle, who came to Hollywood before the war and achieved distinction in the thirties as a director of such films as *The Story of Louis Pasteur, The Life of Émile Zola* and *The Hunchback of Notre Dame*.

Brecht's colorful eccentricities entertained the movie colony throughout his Southern California sojourn. The Los Angeles premiere of his play *Galileo* at the Cornet Theater, starring Charles Laughton, was one of the notable local cultural events of the forties. On a different note, Brecht's appearance at a hearing before the House Un-American Activities Committee, which was investigating "Communist subversion" in the motion picture industry, resulted in a performance of dodging and weaving that was so confusing to HUAC's chairman, J. Parnell Thomas, and other members that they were happy to release the witness from further testimony, with Brecht leaving for East Germany not long thereafter.

Roosevelt Becomes Involved

The stream of refugees continued coming at a brisk pace as Nazi control accelerated throughout Europe. The fall of France in 1940 precipitated the flight of some of the nation's most gifted filmmakers, such as Parisian directors René Clair, Max Ophuls, Julien Duvivier and Jean Renoir. While many great creative intellects eventually traveled to America to avoid the oppressive Nazi boot, some attempted to remain in Europe, moving frequently, seeking to stray from harm's door.

The plight of eminent German novelist Lion Feuchtwanger served as a catalyst for direct U.S. involvement at the highest government level. Feuchtwanger was interned by the French as an enemy alien in 1939. After his release after pressure was applied by the British government, he was interned again in May 1940. As Otto Friedrich wrote in his chronicle of the period, *City of Nets: A Portrait of Hollywood in the 1940's*, "A newspaper photograph of the sickly Feuchtwanger staring out from behind barbed wire prompted his American publisher to contact President Roosevelt, who indulgently asked the State Department to provide whatever help seemed appropriate."

While the stream of some of Europe's most gifted literary minds continued in the wake of Nazi military advancement, the irony is that, given this impressive migration, David O. Selznick would take inspiration from a different talent pool — that of those analyzing the human mind. This element of the European migratory experience would result in Selznick producing and Hitchcock directing one of the most discussed films in Hollywood history.

The first four decades of the twentieth century resulted in a medical breakthrough that generated great controversy, and continues to do so in medical and social circles today. The psychotherapy revolution was launched in Vienna by a gifted innovator, Dr. Sigmund Freud, working in concert with a younger colleague, Dr. Karl Gustav Jung, until the protégé had a falling out with Freud. Psychotherapy terrified Adolf Hitler, who did not know what to make of this new area of medical science dedicated to exploring the mind. In that nothing terrified Hitler as much as the unknown, coupled with the fact that Freud was Jewish, the prominent psychiatrist, then in his eighties, quickly became a marked man.

Freud was barely able to make it out of Vienna. His departure for his new home in London at 20 Maresfield Gardens in the leafy suburb of Hampstead (his former residence is today a museum visited by thousands of people from around the world) came when he was suffering from terminal cancer. Freud was barely rescued from Nazi-occupied Vienna, being permitted to leave only after he signed a statement declaring that he had been well treated. Despite being in great pain, the remarkable Freud wit remained as he stated with irony, "I can recommend the Gestapo to anyone."

He endured at his new residence for one year, succumbing to the ravages of cancer in 1939 at the age of 83. Rapidly nearing the end of his life, Freud listened, with his doctor, Max Schur, to a radio commentator the day the war began. The optimistic message was that this would be the last of wars. As Freud lay on a couch in his garden in acute pain, Dr. Schur asked his famous patient if he believed the prediction. "Anyhow, it is my last war," Freud responded with a fatalistic reality.

The Migration of the Psychoanalysts

Freud's declining health prevented any possibility of him even considering moving to America, but plenty of his disciples in the new and burgeoning field of psychoanalysis left Europe to head across the Atlantic to a nation that was somewhat skeptical of this new European phenomenon of curing illness and generating a sense of well-being by unraveling dark clouds harboring in the mind. Hitler uprooted Freudians from their Central European nests by generating a forced dispersal into a golden exile. One authoritative account estimates the total of psychoanalysts arriving on America's shores at no less than two hundred. While most remained in New York, some ventured west to Los Angeles. Some historians have reasoned that the synergy of connecting with noted German intellectuals such as the Mann brothers, Feuchtwanger, Brecht and Schoenberg provided at least some of the catalyst for settling in the uncharted waters of Los Angeles, a city very much in constant transition and inhabited by numerous transients and fast-buck artists. Many starry-eyed optimists envisioned clicking big in the motion picture industry.

Whether they realized it in advance or not, Los Angeles was a veritable oasis of opportunity. If faith healers like Aimee Semple McPherson could find a home in Los Angeles, then so could they. McPherson had come from her native Ontario, Canada, and took advantage of a gold mine of opportunity. The Angelus Temple she had built in the Echo Park area near downtown Los Angeles seated 5,500 and was frequently filled to capacity. A spellbinding preacher, McPherson delivered a superb line whenever she passed the collection plates. "I don't want to hear the loud jangling sound of coins," she informed her parishioners. "I want to hear the soft rustle of paper."

As befitting the rootlessness and wild west nature of the Los Angeles of the thirties and forties, McPherson was a woman of great controversy. McPherson gained recognition based on an incident from 1926, in which she disappeared while swimming in the Pacific Ocean near the Venice pier. She reappeared in Los Angeles one month later, explaining that she had been kidnapped, taken hostage in the Mexican desert. Officials could prove nothing and skepticism abounded, but Los Angeles was a city where interesting stories and colorful personalities thrived. Her later marriage and divorce garnered more headlines, albeit tarnishing her image as a preacher of the gospel. Controversy continued to surround her in death as well as life. She died in 1944 while visiting Oakland for the dedication of a new Foursquare church, with the cause of death recorded as an overdose of sleeping pills.

Nathanael West was born Nathan Weinstein in New York. A sober-minded author dedicated to writing the great American novel, it was unsurprising that he found Aimee Semple McPherson an interesting character. West arrived in Hollywood and, like so many serious novelists, both despaired and failed to achieve fame as a screenwriter. He scratched out a living writing quality scripts for a string of B films made at RKO, Universal and Republic. As a respected literary figure who was a brother-in-law of famous New York author S.J. Perelman, he occupied a place at Hollywood's answer to the fabled Writer's Roundtable at New York's Algonquin Hotel. A back room at Musso and Frank Restaurant on Hollywood Boulevard near Las Palmas served as the headquarters for discussions with other frustrated novelists-turned-screenwriters from the East with a penchant for alcohol, such as William Faulkner, F. Scott Fitzgerald and John O'Hara.

West wrote novels of despair, and his personal discomfiture in the rootless city of palm trees sparked a keen-eyed interest in observing the perceived aimlessness of Hollywood. It resulted in him writing the classic novel about the film industry, *The Day of the Locust*, published in 1939. West's loneliness in the city at one point became so pronounced that after a few drinks, he took to dancing with his dog.

His life turned the corner when he found love, marrying charismatic Eileen McKenney, the leading figure in the autobiographical novel *My Sister Eileen*, which was made into a successful 1942 film starring Rosalind Russell and Janet Blair as Ruth and Eileen respectively. Just when things were looking up, after he bought a house in North Hollywood and was happy with Eileen, life then took the kind of grim turn he might have written in *Locust* or his other famous work, *Miss Lonelyhearts*, which was ultimately made into a 1958 film titled *Lonelyhearts*, starring Montgomery Clift.

After hearing about his New York writer friend and fellow Hollywood scenarist Fitzgerald dying of a heart attack in his apartment at the Laurel Arms, next door to his favorite haunt (but which he could not then afford), Sunset Boulevard's impressively exotic Garden of Allah, West cut short a hunting trip in Mexico and intended to return home for Fitzgerald's funeral. While en route to Los Angeles he pulled out hastily onto the highway in El Centro, just north of the Mexico border, and apparently did not see an approaching truck, which struck and killed him.

Irony compounded upon irony even after West's death. His brother-in-law, S.J. Perelman, came to Los Angeles to take the deceased writer back to New York for burial. Riding back with him on the same train was Sheila Graham, a stunning blonde from England who was F. Scott Fitzgerald's lover. Graham was accompanying Fitzgerald's body to the East Coast for burial, and coincidentally on the same train with Perelman, undertaking a similar task. Later she would become a syndicated Hollywood columnist writing about industry tidbits in the manner that West did in *The Day of the Locust*. Her romance with the laureate of the twenties' flapper era would become the subject of a 1959 film, *Beloved Infidel*, starring Gregory Peck and Deborah Kerr, that was based on Graham's book.

Nathanael West's death bore an ironic tinge of the bitterness advanced in his works. At the time of West's demise he had earned a grand total of $1,280 from the publication of his four novels. His happy early marriage to Eileen McKenney never had the opportunity to mature, the new house in North Hollywood had barely been lived in, and his ultimate acclaim as a great author lay in the future.

When *The Day of the Locust* arrived on film screens in 1975 it sparked an immediate controversy. Somewhere Nathanael West had to be nodding. The perfect director was there to give the film just the proper anarchistic twist that the author would surely have appreciated. Britain's iconoclastic John Schlesinger pointed the film in the same direction as two of his earlier, likewise controversial works.

With *Midnight Cowboy* (1969) Schlesinger revealed the dark underbelly of New York City, with inhabitants struggling to stay afloat, focusing on recent arrival John Voight, who turns into a male hustler, and his health-plagued friend (Dustin Hoffman), who dies on a bus before they can reach Hoffman's dream of nirvana in sunny Florida. In 1971 the controversial, always interesting Schlesinger raised more eyebrows with his depiction of restless London, his hometown, exploring the impact of the swinging sixties with *Sunday, Bloody Sunday*. The homosexual Schlesinger provided the cinema's first daringly open look at bisexuality as Murray Head gravitates with sixties' sexual nonchalance between romantic dalliances with Peter Finch and Glenda Jackson. At the film's close a philosophical Finch, who portrays a successful London doctor, delivers a calmly philosophical soliloquy summarizing his relationship with Head: "Half a loaf is better than none."

If West had been alive in the mid-seventies and could have selected the director to bring his magnum opus to the screen, he might well have selected Schlesinger. New York and London had been dissected in that order. The timing was right to turn his attention to the lotus-land with the desert setting, the city of palm trees, majestic mountains, and endless dreams that so frequently fall woefully short and turn into nightmares. Cinematographer Conrad Hall brought this adventure of the pursuers and might-have-beens to the screen with an amber hue reflecting on the anarchistic melancholia and frantic pursuits of the film's characters, while screenwriter Waldo Salt retained the fidelity of West's novel, the emphasis on chaotic hopelessness, a lonely crowd of the frustrated striving for the golden ring of success.

Ted Hackett (William Atherton) arrives in Hollywood hoping to become an art director, but develops a crush on Faye Greener (Karen Black). He seeks to generate interest in an acting career for her that is stymied in no small part by the fact that she is talent-less. Harry Greener's (Burgess Meredith) extreme cynicism is well placed in Hollywood's prevailing anarchy. Harry is a former vaudevillian turned huckster, an effortless adjustment in his case.

At first blush Homer Simpson (Donald Sutherland) might be said to be successful because he has plenty of money, but a West caveat is necessarily in order. There is a gigantic flaw. Simpson is such a social misfit that his idea of entertainment is singing the only song he knows, the national anthem. His social backwardness is underscored by a dangerous lurking rage gradually rising to the surface.

The only other would-be successful character in *The Day of the Locust* is that legend of Los Angeles, the provocative Pentecostal preacher Aimee Semple McPherson. She is known in the film as Big Sister, and exhorts her capacity throng of Angelus Temple followers to latch onto the spirit. McPherson was a natural to attract West's attention. As earlier noted, she lived and died in controversy. Big Sister is played with the non-stop proselytizing gusto of the original Los Angeles legend by one of the screen's most dynamic performers, Geraldine Page.

The major controversies flowing around the film related to two gruesome scenes depicting violent inhumanity run amok, which caused some filmgoers and critics to cry "enough." The repressed madness of Simpson erupts beneath the arc lights and surrounding maelstrom of a gala Hollywood premiere at Grauman's Chinese Theater. He goes berserk and kicks a child to death. The other scene generating protest was one depicting a cockfight. West reportedly visited such gruesome events in the then largely rural San Fernando Valley. He chronicled Hollywood with the same well-trained eyes as Somerset Maugham had the drawing rooms of aristocratic Europe.

Enter the Psychiatrists

Whether they were able to figure this out in advance or not, psychiatrists were entering lucrative environs when they set foot on Hollywood soil. The lotus land depicted with such chaotic irreverence by Nathanael West, the town where Aimee Semple McPherson surfaced as its best known member of the clergy, the city where scores arrived at the Hollywood bus station filled with hopeful dreams but who, provided they were not swallowed up in the process, generally left in disillusionment to return to their homes emerged as a promised land for doctors in that new science of the mind. The only catch was that you needed to be rich enough to afford the attention.

Ernst Simmel, a dedicated socialist who had been one of the founders of the Berlin Psychoanalytic Institute, received word early in 1933 that the Nazis were coming to get him. He left through a window and fled to Los Angeles, where he founded the Los Angeles Psychoanalytic Study Group. He welcomed distinguished professionals to his new clinic, including Otto Fenichel. Before Fenichel left his last way station of Prague he was asked what was the most pressing question confronting psychoanalytic research. "The question of whether the Nazis come to power in Vienna," Fenichel responded.

Simmel also welcomed a group of sociologists known as the Frankfurt Institute, headed by Max Horkheimer and Theodor Adorno. The Frankfurt exiles had a vision. They sought to synthesize Marx and Freud in their critique of modern society. They received foundation grants from the East and staged seminars attended by fellow German exiles, such as Bertolt Brecht and Lion Feuchtwanger, on various cultural topics, including the significance of movies and jazz.

Fenichel arrived in Los Angeles in 1938 and, while he would not be in professional practice for long, his influence would stretch beyond his own life and he would be one of the chain of catalytic agents that would ultimately result in Alfred Hitchcock's *Spellbound*. Fenichel believed that Marx and Freud both offered answers to the disaster engulfing Europe, but there was little that one lonely refugee could do. When Fenichel conducted a seminar on literature at Simmel's Psychoanalytic Study Group, one admirer commented that it was "one of the last refuges of the avant-garde period of the psychoanalytic movement before it became a commercialized specialty." The reference to commercialism was apropos in view of what was transpiring in Nathanael West's Hollywood.

Fenichel sought to interest fellow professionals in the Los Angeles area in a conference of politically minded analysts. Perhaps he would have ultimately succeeded in staging such conferences had time not cut him short. While Freud had argued fervently for the development of "lay analysts" who could spread the faith without years of medical training, the American psychoanalytic establishment insisted on it. Fenichel had earned his medical degree from the University of Vienna years before. It did not count for much in Los Angeles, so he decided to earn new credentials by interning at Cedars of Lebanon Hospital and was assigned to night duty. He was 47 and overweight. Fenichel complained of exhaustion and talked vaguely of finding a hospital that did not require night shifts. Within six months he collapsed and died of a ruptured cerebral aneurism.

While Fenichel was deprived of cashing in on a fertile new ground in psychoanalysis, others would, as interest burgeoned, particularly in the film industry, where psychological problems flowed like wine from a sprawling vineyard. "The psychoanalysts of Los Angeles didn't want to get involved in politics," Otto Friedrich explained. "They wanted to get established and make money. And in that city of cults, where, as Nathanael West had written, people preached the crusade against salt and the Aztec secret of brain-breathing, the psychoanalysts wanted respectability, medical certification."

The effort to achieve certification resulted in Fenichel's demise, but Dr. May Romm would arrive front stage center in the life of movie mogul David O.

Selznick, and a professional relationship resulted. Selznick would become so fascinated by the field that he would enthusiastically reveal to Alfred Hitchcock his desire to make a film on the subject. For numerous reasons that will be explored, Hitchcock was bullish about the prospect.

The Movie Colony and Psychoanalysis

To highly emotional people in a highly emotional business, psychoanalysis provided an opportunity to seek relief by talking over personal problems. Judy Garland, who became a star as a youngster and was saddled with the burden of making enough pictures to maintain high-level popularity and keep the MGM lion financially roaring, was sent by director Joseph Mankiewicz to see Ernst Simmel. The action came in response to the emotional young star's reaction to a floundering affair with Mankiewicz. Garland's mother reported the development to studio boss Louis B. Mayer. Mankiewicz was called into the fiery Mayer's office and the director thereafter quit MGM forever, while Garland ceased seeing Simmel.

Artie Shaw had spent much of the war leading a Navy band on hectic tours of military bases. He believed he was cracking up, and the Navy recognized a sufficient problem to provide Shaw with a medical discharge in 1944. "[A]t that point I wanted nothing more than to lie down somewhere in a hole," Shaw morbidly recollected, "and have someone shovel enough dirt over me to cover me."

As an avid reader as well as a fixture on the Hollywood scene, it was no surprise that Shaw paid a visit to the town's new psychoanalytical superstar, Dr. May Romm. He began treatments as Romm led him back through his days as young Arthur Arshawsky of the Bronx. Shaw recovered sufficiently to regain romantic feelings as he earnestly began pursuing Ava Gardner in an association that would culminate in a brief marriage. Initially Shaw decided it would be productive for him to attend sessions with Romm jointly with new love Gardner. Before this idea reached fruition, however, Shaw backed away. He decided that such joint inner reflection under the direction of the analyst might cure him of wanting to marry the beautiful actress, and so he stopped seeing Dr. Romm. In Hollywood, while psychoanalysis remained popular, analysts were subject to the results of the mood swings of patients, who were there one day and gone the next. A similar pattern would develop in Dr. Romm's treatment of Selznick.

Selznick's New Love and
the Emergence of Dr. Romm

David Selznick lived his life with such a robust gusto that a breakdown was anything but unforeseeable. His marriage to the former Irene Mayer, daughter of the man who ran the giant star factory MGM, had been marked by infidelities. A semblance of stability was nonetheless maintained, as much as possible in the household of a film titan with the mercurial manner and unpredictability of Selznick. Louis B. Mayer once remarked that if he were married to his daughter he would hit her. Irene had a cool, take charge manner when she wished to assert it, a preview of the executive leadership she would later demonstrate after her divorce from Selznick and rise to the rank of major Broadway theater producer. When a raging Selznick would remove his clothes, throw them on the floor, and stomp on them, a resolute Irene would order him to pick them up and put them away neatly.

After fifteen years of marriage, Selznick, in 1945, had fallen in love. When he sought to reveal his latest affair of the heart to Irene and plead for understanding, Selznick was astonished to learn that she was not interested. A married life that had begun in 1930, almost a decade before Selznick's major career achievement as producer of *Gone with the Wind*, resulted in the daughter of the industry's leading studio mogul having grown tired of her marriage to him.

The young actress who had sent Selznick's pulse racing was Phyllis Walker of Oklahoma City. She had been born Phyllis Isley and had married her high school sweetheart. They formed a union of aspiring thespians. Eventually both Walkers would become major Hollywood stars, but within a constrictive web of tragedy and death. After his success with *Gone with the Wind*, Selznick encountered a period of self-doubt in which he fretted that the major success of his life had been achieved as a young man and that he would never be able to equal, much less surpass it. During that interval he considered filming Hitler's *Mein Kampf* and tried to lay claim to the title. In that phase of his career Selznick, in the words of Otto Friedrich, "lived well on his stable of stars." He cast a gangly, boyishly handsome druggist's son from La Jolla, California, Gregory Peck, in A.J. Cronin's emotionally powerful *The Keys of the Kingdom*. Instead of making the movie, he sold the whole project to Fox.

Selznick, along with a number of other producers, realized a financial bonanza through highly profitable loanouts. As earlier indicated, he had been successful following this practice with the prize director of his stable, Alfred Hitchcock. On one loan of Joan Fontaine, the actress fellow Selznick contractee Hitchcock had helped propel to superstardom in *Rebecca* and *Suspicion*, Selznick collected $150,000 while the actress pocketed $30,000. Ingrid Bergman was not only beautiful and talented, which provided Selznick with an impressive shopping price, she was a performer who thrived on activity. Selznick was more than happy to oblige her industry. In one year Selznick cleared $425,000 for the actress' services, of which the Swedish beauty received $60,000.

All in the Family

Always on the alert for profitable talent, Selznick received a break via a timely tip from his brother-in-law, William Goetz, a Twentieth Century–Fox producer who ran the studio during Zanuck's service duty, and would later head Universal. The stroke of fortune was kept in the family as Goetz, who was looking for an unknown to star in *The Song of Bernadette*, sent over young Phyllis Walker, whom he had decided to rename Jennifer Jones. Twentieth's most prolific director in its history, Henry King, who had achieved fame helming thirties vehicles starring Alice Faye, Tyrone Power and Don Ameche, and who would direct the blockbuster adaptation of Somerset Maugham's international bestseller, *The Razor's Edge*, shortly after the war, had been assigned to *The Song of Bernadette*, and exclaimed after seeing Walker-turned-Jones, "This girl *is* Bernadette."

Selznick's enormous success in signing talent and parlaying it to whopping loanout profits accustomed him to assuming control at a distance while others took creative charge of the performer until he had a project of his own. It did not bother Selznick that Jennifer Jones's rise to stardom would occur at Twentieth Century–Fox in a film in which he was not involved. He was no doubt delighted to have the wily Henry King in the director's chair, in that he had guided to international stardom the three leading performers in Fox's stable, Alice Faye, Tyrone Power and Don Ameche.

In that Jones had appeared previously on screen only in several low budget Republic films, billed in every instance as Phyllis Isley, including an early John Wayne western and a Dick Tracy serial, it required little stretch for Fox to proclaim that the new star was making her screen debut. The scenario could not have worked out better for Selznick as, under King's experienced guidance, the 1943 film not only became a financial success, the 24-year-old from Oklahoma won the Academy Award as Best Actress.

Selznick proceeded to take Jones under both his professional wing and within his heart. This relationship would be more than those earlier transitory affairs in his life between producer and performer. To demonstrate the strength of his conviction to propel Jones to an enduring spot in the tinsel town star constellation, Selznick instructed former prominent model Anita Colby, whom the producer had earlier hired to help train his other actresses in proper dress and behavior, to pay close attention to his newest star.

The Meteoric Rise and Fall of Robert Walker

Often in cases of young performers marrying and seeking success in the rough-and-tumble of unpredictable Hollywood, one would excel and the other succeed to a lesser extent, if at all. Many familiar with the Ronald Reagans of the forties contended that Jane Wyman's tremendous acting success, culminating in a Best Actress Oscar for *Johnny Belinda* (1948), with her husband relegated to leads in Warner Brothers B films, was a major factor, if not the ultimate cause, of their divorce.

This would not be the case with the young Walkers. Robert's interpretive performing genius shone through like a towering beacon. The tragedy was that the star was struck down early in a potentially brilliant career. After Hitchcock's contract with Selznick had expired and he was on his own, the director would provide Robert Walker with what would prove to be his major opportunity not long before his life ended — the role of a complicated and always fascinating homicidal neurotic in *Strangers on a Train*. The film would secure a reputation among Hitchcock fans as one of the greatest of the director's career.

Robert Walker had always been unstable, but his emotional underpinnings ultimately deserted him over the prospect of losing his wife to the powerful producer of *Gone with the Wind*. The three paths would ultimately merge professionally as Selznick sought to capitalize on the success of his new love by putting her in another vehicle, but this time under the waves of his own baton. Margaret Buell Wilder had written a sentimental novel, its subject being midtown America during World War II. Selznick bought *Since You Went Away* and decided to make it his first venture into producing since *Rebecca* with Hitchcock. Newly in love, Selznick's creative juices flowed at such a feverish level that he decided he would write the screenplay as well as produce the film.

When *Since You Went Away* emerged on theater screens in 1944 its length of 172 minutes should have surprised no one accustomed to the creative gusto of Selznick, considering the benchmark against which his career would be measured, the also-lengthy *Gone with the Wind*. As Selznick sat at his typewriter and began transforming Margaret Buell Wilder's novel into a screenplay, one role continued to develop, gaining additional length and importance. It was that of the eldest daughter to the woman keeping the home fires burning while her husband was at war serving his country in the Navy. The part of the daughter naturally went to Jennifer Jones.

Selznick pulled out all stops in an effort to make the film and his rapidly rising star a blockbuster. It emerged as one of the top grossers of 1944 as Selznick brought together one of the most memorable casts in Hollywood history. To play the part of the always resolute mother he selected Claudette Colbert. Assuming the role of her platonic admirer was Selznick contractee Joseph Cotten, who portrayed a Naval officer. Cotten achieved fame as a member of Orson Welles's Mercury Theater and was not far removed from starring roles in two Welles masterpieces, *Citizen Kane* (1941) and *The Magnificent Ambersons* (1942). Playing the part of Jones's younger sister was the most enduring child star in the history of film, Shirley Temple, while roles were also assumed by such character-actor legends as Lionel Barrymore, Monty Woolley, *Gone with the Wind* Best Supporting Actress Oscar recipient Hattie McDaniel, and Agnes Moorehead.

One other casting selection led to tension that prompted Jennifer Jones to leave the set in a frightening emotional state. Robert Walker had just received rave notices starring in a comedy about a soldier in wartime, *See Here, Private Hargrove*, which propelled him to an almost equivalent footing with his wife.

Selznick signed him to play another soldier, this one the romantic interest opposite none other than his wife, then in the throes of romance with the film's producer. The scenes that spurred the film to success, those between Jones and Walker, reduced the actress to tears.

The relationship between the story's lovers had irony piled atop irony as, at a time when the Walker marriage was edging closer to the precipice of divorce, Jones was compelled to perform in an emotional farewell scene when Walker's character leaves for war. Not only was the scene written by none other than Selznick, the train station where the young lovers say their emotional goodbyes was the same one used in *Gone with the Wind*. Jones broke down in the middle of the scene and retreated tearfully to her dressing room. Selznick needed to be summoned to calm her down, then lead her back to the set to finish the emotional parting scene with Walker, the man whose marriage Selznick was in the process of destroying.

Jones's confirmation that she was suing Walker for divorce came on the heels of her greatest triumph as an actress. The divorce announcement came the day after she won the Academy Award for *The Song of Bernadette*.

Walker was devastated beyond recovery. He began drinking heavily and demonstrating mounting emotional instability just as his career was rapidly moving forward on the strength of his uniquely brilliant talent, as someone who could be a sensitive young man one moment and, as his triumph with Hitchcock in *Strangers on a Train* conveyed, a depraved killer the next. MGM officials suggested that Walker visit the Meninger Clinic.

It was while a patient at Meninger that Walker began receiving psychotherapy six days a week. While back at MGM he told another one of its promising contract players, June Allyson, "My personal life has been wrecked by David Selznick's obsession for my wife. What can you do to fight such a powerful man? My life has been hell...." The tortured actor admitted hating himself and exposing himself to blame "all my life for things I shouldn't have blamed myself for. I felt that everybody was against me, hated me...."

After Walker persuaded the Meninger staff to release him, he began drinking heavily again on his return to Hollywood. The nurse who kept house for him called Walker's psychiatrist, who arrived quickly and concluded that he needed a shot of sodium amytal. When Walker resisted, friends were summoned to control him. They held him down as the doctor prepared the injection. "Don't give it to me," Walker pleaded while friends held him. "I've been drinking. It will kill me. Please don't give me that shot."

The doctor was undeterred. He had often injected Walker with sodium amytal and believed that the shot would calm the actor down without placing him in harm's way. As friends held the squirming actor the shot was administered. A few minutes later Walker collapsed. Two hours later the 32-year-old actor was dead. An autopsy concluded that the dose had not been in any way out of the ordinary.

Selznick Meets Dr. Romm

Irene Selznick observed psychiatric trauma firsthand in her family before recommending that her husband David seek counseling. Following her mother's hysterectomy, Irene Mayer became immersed in such a prodigious fog of melancholia that she was confined for a time at Riggs Sanitarium in Stockbridge, Massachusetts.

This trauma was later followed by one involving her father. The movie mogul was told that, as a result of the "involutional melancholia" stemming from the postoperative phase of hysterectomy, Mrs. Mayer must never have sex again. Such a condition is routinely treated today by hormone therapy. Louis B. Mayer confessed to a large number of people that he did not wish to have any more conjugal relations with his wife and that the idea of considering it following the hysterectomy was repugnant to him.

Mayer, who was, according to studio gossip, spurned by some of his top female stars, eventually fell head over heels in love with a Ziegfeld Follies dancer from Texas named Jean Howard, who had just been put under contract at MGM. He would eventually propose to Howard in a setting reminiscent of one of MGM's romantic films, on a boat train in France somewhere between Le Havre and Paris. Howard later disclosed that Mayer had informed her that his wife had given her consent to a divorce. Howard had already decided to marry *another* man on her return from France, but decided, even after Mayer had stated that he would provide her with a lush premarital contract, that it would be better to explain her situation to the MGM boss after they arrived in Paris rather than amid the noisy clatter of a boat train.

Jean Howard was definitely in love at the time. The problem for the movie mogul was that her passion was for another man, a young lawyer-agent named Charlie Feldman. Mayer had no knowledge of this, but in the manner of important men of wealth, decided as a precaution to hire a detective agency to monitor the former Ziegfeld dancer for awhile.

Matters came to a noisy, chaotic, and almost deadly conclusion in Paris' George V Hotel, after Howard Strickling, Mayer's publicity chief, informed the woman Mayer hoped to marry that the movie mogul wished to see her in his suite. Feldman had come along to Paris as well and was in her company when she went to Mayer's hotel suite.

"When we went in he was white and shaking, with a large envelope in his hand," Jean Howard later related. "It was from a detective agency and told him all about Charlie and me. Suddenly he picked up a bottle of Scotch, poured out a whole glass and gulped it down. He never drank and it made him drunk. He went wild. He roared around the room and then, suddenly, made a move to throw himself out the window. The three of us needed all our strength to hold him back. We got him down on the floor, where he wept and moaned. I went straight back to New York, and Charlie and I were married."

Had Jean Howard not been accompanied by her husband-to-be Feldman and MGM publicity chief Strickling, the studio with "more stars than in the heavens" might have lost its boss that fateful day in Paris. Mayer issued orders that Charlie Feldman was never to be allowed on the MGM lot again. Meanwhile, his wife Maggie was once more in serious health difficulty. Mayer summoned psychiatrists from London and Mrs. Mayer made periodic visits back to Massachusetts to Riggs Sanitarium, but the efforts did not achieve the anticipated positive results. Maggie Mayer would spend some two-thirds of her remaining ten years at home, but, according to daughter Irene, "she could never quite pick up the threads of her life."

In the summer of 1944, just prior to his fortieth wedding anniversary, Mayer announced to his wife that he was leaving and intended to divorce her. Perhaps that knowledge and awareness prompted daughter Irene just one year later to tell David O. Selznick, "I'm leaving, the jig's up." Before that time arrived, however, after which Selznick would throw himself with even greater intensity into making a superstar of his new love, Jennifer Jones, Irene prompted her husband to seek psychiatric help. The obsessive and bizarre behavior of the producer-star maker had spun ever more out of control. According to Otto Friedrich, Selznick "drank heavily, dosed himself with Benzedrine, gambled wildly, and quarreled with everyone he knew."

A family tragedy registered devastating results when Selznick's brother Myron, a successful Hollywood agent with a serious drinking problem, died in March 1944. Selznick cloistered himself in Manhattan's Waldorf Astoria Hotel and refused to see anyone. He confided to Irene that he was "really scared" and afraid that he was "going insane."

Those professionally associated with Selznick had seen the tragedy develop, and understood its roots. His father, Lewis Selznick, one of the film industry's early moguls, had been a compulsive gambler. The gambling trait in the Selznick gene pool surfaced in David. Staff personnel noted that to Selznick, Benzedrine was consumed in a manner comparable to a sugar-craving youngster shoving Life Savers into its mouth. Hollywood's inveterate workaholic would not be confined to anything resembling a nine-to-five routine. He punished himself and those around him with exhaustive schedules. Many of those who worked under him, including his stars from *Gone with the Wind*, Clark Gable and Vivien Leigh, hated Selznick.

As to the haunting fear that made Hollywood's most famous producer petrified to leave his hotel room or entertain visitors within it, the answer was also clear to those who knew him best. Here was a man being chased by internal shadows. Those psychological shadows pertained to an overriding fear that Selznick would never be able to top the grand triumph achieved when he was but 36, *Gone with the Wind*. He told confidants that he feared that when he died the headline would reveal that he was the producer of that milestone film. Selznick feared that he had nowhere else to go, that the movie public and reviewers would compare any future work to the Civil War classic and conclude that his productive career was behind him.

Irene Selznick believed that her husband needed psychiatric help, but initially did not know where to turn. She asked Dorothy Paley, wife of the head of CBS, to recommend a psychoanalyst. Dorothy Paley recommended that Selznick see Dr. Sandor Rando, a pioneer of the psychoanalytic movement in Berlin who had immigrated to America in 1931 to head the New York Psychoanalytic Institute.

Difficulties ensued over getting Selznick to visit Dr. Rando, typical of such cases. Irene Selznick was finally able to coax her husband to see the famous doctor as she accompanied him to Rando's office. It took Dr. Rando little time to make a diagnosis in. His conclusion that the movie producer "was having a breakdown" was anything but shocking. He recommended to Irene Selznick that her husband return to Los Angeles and be treated there. There were few professional practicing analysts in the Los Angeles area then, and Irene Selznick asked Dr. Rando if he had any recommendations. The distinguished psychoanalyst recommended Dr. May Romm, and from there one of Hollywood's most memorable, as well as controversial, films would have its genesis.

Just Like Hollywood Storytelling

David Selznick quickly took to psychoanalysis sessions with Dr. Romm like a duck took to water. He enjoyed the experience of pouring out his thoughts to the famous analyst.

May Romm was part of the European intellectual migration to the United States, but unlike the wave of psychoanalysts who left their native continent in the face of Hitler's Nazi onslaught, she arrived as a young girl. She was Russian and Jewish, and was described by Selznick biographer David Thomson as "a warm, clever, funny woman who might have been David's older sister." According to Romm's daughter Dorothy, "my mother was lonely. She was looking for company."

Romm was born in Vitebsk in 1891 and came to America at the age of twelve. She took her medical degree in 1915 in Philadelphia at the Women's Medical College and practiced in Mount Vernon for twelve years. At the age of forty, inspired by the Freudian A.A. Brill, Romm decided to study psychiatry and attended New York State Psychiatric Institute. In 1938, four years after her graduation, Dr. May Romm became one of the new wave of psychoanalysts establishing a practice in Los Angeles.

Romm had a daughter but had lost her husband. On the question of why she made the move across country at the age of forty-seven, the answer was that she had lived there briefly in the twenties. Also, according to David Thomson, "She was by inclination a pioneer, and by 1938 it was already evident how many

European exiles and refugees were looking for liberty and sunshine and a chance to settle their troubled thoughts. There are always fresh crazes and new kinds of gold in Los Angeles, and in the 1940s psychiatry was one of them."

When Dr. Romm began treating Selznick, his wife Irene was shocked at how his treatment "went by leaps and bounds" as the former recluse began seeing people and poring himself back into his traditional workaholic routine. "Dr. Romm was a wise little motherly lady," Irene Selznick remembered, "and I envied David the privilege of having her to talk to and told her so. Arranging to see him every day on an emergency basis, she warned me not to let him discuss his sessions or permit him to tell me what he hadn't finished telling her. She would need my cooperation. I was delighted to share honors with her."

If Selznick experienced success and elation as a result of his meetings with Dr. Romm, it would also have to be said that the feeling was mutual. As David Thomson said, "no one ever found David less than exciting company." Thomson noted that Dr. Romm was "star-struck," a point confirmed by her daughter, who revealed, "She was impressed by movie people and she loved their sense of crisis."

David Thomson revealed insight into why the troubled mogul so eagerly adjusted to a process some patients found invasive and troubling, that of revealing one's innermost thoughts and life experiences. "To David Selznick psychoanalysis was like movies because you told stories," Thomson explained. If ever any producer in film history had a twenty-four hour penchant for story analysis and development, to the agony of those subjected to such brainstorms in the wee hours of the morning, it was David O. Selznick. Here was the producer who believed that, were he not tied up in the business end of making films, he would have been able to also fulfill writing and directing functions.

While Dr. Romm may have been initially encouraged by Selznick's producer's training enabling him to fall comfortably into the disclosure format of psychoanalytical counseling, she would learn to her chagrin that the cinematic nexus bore a decided downside as well. Selznick began treating May Romm like an employee. "He became too busy for Romm," Irene Selznick related. "He was forty minutes late, if he showed up at all. When he arrived on time, he was often unwakable through the entire session. He recounted these antics as though they were amusing.... He misinterpreted her patience as enchantment with him; in fact, he was afraid she was falling in love with him. He rang her doorbell at midnight and, standing outside, demanded to be heard. He found it unreasonable of her to refuse."

After nearly a year of putting up with the same kind of treatment that Selznick was used to displaying with employees, Dr. Romm dropped Selznick as a patient. His response was typically Selznick, manifesting megalomania. Romm was given the same regard as movie professionals with whom Selznick worked. The producer who was convinced he knew more about directing than the directors he hired, and more about writing than the scenarists who penned his films, added another area of self-proclaimed expertise. Selznick confidently told Irene that based upon his experience in analysis he now knew more about psychoanalysis than Dr. Romm, and that he could analyze her.

Convinced of his expertise in the subject and creatively fascinated, the busy mind of Selznick contacted the only individual in Hollywood who, in the words of Otto Friedrich, "could out–Selznick Selznick."

5

Hitchcock's Grand
Leap into Psychodrama

*How that woman loved to work, and how her apprehensive beauty holds the
implausibility together. The film has none of the anguish that would come to
Hitchcock's psychological thrillers in the next decade.* — David Thomson on
Ingrid Bergman's role in *Spellbound.*

When David O. Selznick spun the idea of a film on psychoanalysis to Alfred
Hitchcock, the response was immediate and electric. Hitchcock, brought up in
a puritanical world by his strict greengrocer father, found the idea thoroughly
intriguing.

A practicing Catholic who grappled as a creative force with the hobgob-
lins of death and destruction, and had achieved recent success with a film about
a deranged serial killer of rich widows, Hitchcock approached the project with
gusto. He quickly found a novel on which to base the film. The 1927 novel *The
House of Dr. Edwardes* was written by the tandem of John Leslie Palmer and
Hilary Aidan St. George Sanders, who pooled efforts under the pseudonym of
Francis Beeding.

The novel's murder mystery aspect was almost assuredly a major element
in capturing Hitchcock's interest. The same team had also collaborated on the
1931 detective novel, *Death Walks in Eastrepps. The House of Doctor Edwardes*
was set in a Swiss mental clinic and dealt with witchcraft and satanic cults.

Ben Hecht as Scenarist and Checkmate

Ben Hecht was New York born, like David O. Selznick, but made his early
mark as a writer in Chicago's newspaper world. His memoirs of that period,
Gaily, Gaily, later became the subject of a Universal film, with Beau Bridges as
a young, adventuresome Hecht in a cast bolstered by Greek Oscar-winning

96

actress Melina Mercouri. Branching out with his writing, Hecht wrote some novels that failed to attract significant notice. His play writing was another story, however, as he collaborated with Helen Hayes's husband, Charles MacArthur, and surged to fame with the 1928 Broadway comedy hit, *The Front Page*, about a subject he knew well, journalism.

Many of the world's top writers learned the discipline of their craft in journalism. As the saying went, "There is nothing to discipline a writer like deadlines." In competitive journalism one had to perform regularly with a time clock at one's back. This discipline aided Hecht. With a Broadway hit under his belt he now had a name, and when producer Herman Mankiewicz persuaded Paramount to offer Hecht a contract, Mankiewicz sent a telegram to the writer proclaiming that "millions are to be grabbed out here and your only competition is idiots."

These were the early days of the talkies when producers like Mankiewicz could not turn out pictures fast enough for studio bosses begging for more product. Even among the most disciplined journalists, Hecht stood out for his ability to swiftly and steadily produce material. According to Otto Friedrich, Hecht spent only one week writing his first script, *Underworld*, and was paid $10,000 for his effort. It also earned him a Best Screenplay Academy Award for 1927. He was credited with some sixty scripts. Hecht claimed that more than half of those efforts required less than two weeks of work. His salary reportedly rose to $10,000 per week at its zenith.

Had David Selznick been a baseball manager he would have been in constant need of relief pitchers. The constant strain would have produced sore arms. With a writer like Hecht in town, it was never a question of whether Selznick would call upon his services but when. In addition to the many scripts for which he was given credit, there were numerous others on which Hecht worked in what is now called a script doctor capacity. Amid Selznick's numerous *Gone with the Wind* production problems, including his director Victor Fleming suffering a nervous breakdown, was that of script production. Selznick called on Hecht to rewrite his most famous film after shooting had begun, paying him $3,000 per day for his salvage mission.

Selznick and Hecht would ultimately become best friends. Both men were Jewish during a period when much of European Jewry was tragically decimated in the Holocaust. Hecht took a politically active position in newspaper columns about the swift and imperative necessity to create a Jewish state, becoming a supporter of the Irgun Zvai Leumi.

In what was then Palestine, the underground organization clashed with British soldiers representing the mandatory authority set up after World War I as a means of regulating a developing problem, with Palestinians seeking to limit immigration into the country and Jews attempting to increase the flow. A leading member of the Irgun in Palestine was Menachem Begin, who would in 1977 become Israel's first prime minister from outside the traditionalistic Labor Party founded by the country's first prime minister, David Ben-Gurion.

Hecht's encouragement of Selznick to become politically active in the Jewish cause resulted in a stiff early rebuff. "I don't want to have anything to do with your cause," Selznick bluntly told his activist friend. "I'm an American and not a Jew."

The screenwriter knew his friend well enough to present him with the offer he was unlikely to refuse, the challenge of a bet. Hecht proposed that Selznick call three people in Hollywood and ask them whether they regarded Selznick as an American or a Jew. If one of the three answered "American" then Hecht would cease his efforts. If, on the other hand, all three responded that they considered Selznick a "Jew" then he would agree to support Hecht's cause.

Hecht emerged as winner, and the timing proved inopportune for Selznick, who had committed himself to funding Hecht's while having just finished paying off thousands of dollars in gambling debts. Selznick attached his name to Hecht's fundraising invitation. The effort, directed toward turning world attention to Jewish efforts to achieve a homeland in Palestine, resulted in the staging of an historical pageant about the Jewish people, written by Hecht. It was entitled *We Will Never Die* and assembled talents such as Kurt Weill, who wrote the music, Billy Rose, who produced the pageant, and Moss Hart, who directed. Paul Muni and Edward G. Robinson shared narration duties.

We Will Never Die enjoyed consecutive performances at New York's Madison Square Garden, with combined sellout crowds numbering 40,000 on a cold night in 1943. More waited in hope of a third performance. It shed light on the killings in Europe in what had not yet been defined as the Holocaust.

While Billy Rose enjoyed great success in taking the pageant on the road to major cities such as Washington, Philadelphia, Chicago, Boston and Hollywood, the pageant's appeal for a Jewish army prompted a controversy between staunch Zionists such as Hecht and more conservative Jewish organizations. This controversy resulted in the end of the tour.

When tough and seasoned film veteran Selznick approached his equally rugged and experienced friend about preparing a script about psychoanalysis, the response was immediate and positive. So many people in the post-war Hollywood world were so fascinated by psychoanalysis that they underwent it themselves. Ben Hecht fell into that class. Considering the Jewish roots of the movement with Freud and many of his followers, along with their plight in barely escaping death at the hands of the Nazis, culminating in often arduous journeys to America, it was understandable for that reason alone why Hecht's interest would initially be sparked. So Selznick had indeed found a kindred spirit.

Selznick not only wanted Hecht to write a memorable screenplay; he sought to use him as a creative checkmate as well. The person to be checked was Alfred Hitchcock. He hoped that by placing writing duties in the reliable Hecht's hands, Hitchcock could be prevented from engaging in his habit of taking a novel and changing the story to suit his own tastes.

To Hitchcock the foray into the realm of psychoanalysis as mystery solution carried a fascinating twist to his career-long duality wherein he balanced the anarchistic and evil aspects of human behavior alongside the orderly conformity of Roman Catholicism he embraced throughout his life. A side of the little boy held inside the jail cell as an exercise dreamt up by a highly disciplined father to teach young Alfred the consequences of straying from society's norms would remain with him always.

An Ensuing Psychiatric Firestorm

In that psychoanalysis generated controversy in medical circles, it was feasible to anticipate that presenting a film on the subject would evoke a comparable response. In the case of *Spellbound*, perhaps the most eminent American expert on the subject at that time entered the picture. Rather than being delighted that three of Hollywood's most famous talents, producer Selznick, director Hitchcock, and screenwriter Hecht, had gleefully coalesced to undertake the challenge of presenting psychoanalysis as a film theme, Dr. Karl Menninger, head of America's most noted facility for treating mental disorders, the Menninger Clinic in Topeka, Kansas, made his dissatisfaction clear to Selznick over story nuances being explored in *Spellbound*. It was the Menninger Clinic to which a heavily drinking, highly depressed Robert Walker had gone to secure treatment following his painful breakup with wife Jennifer Jones.

Director Joseph Mankiewicz, who got himself expelled from MGM by an irate Louis B. Mayer for talking his biggest female box office draw of the period, Judy Garland, into pursuing psychoanalysis, sent out a prompt warning to Menninger after receiving permission to bring the noted psychiatrist into the picture from his own psychoanalyst, Dr. Otto Fenichel. Mankiewicz, after he had an opportunity to examine Hecht's script, expressed alarm to Menninger at the possible damage to be sustained by the profession. Mankiewicz wrote, "The psychoanalysts at the sanitarium are without exception maladjusted men [who] take turns in making passes at [star Ingrid] Bergman, whom they constantly tease as being emotionally and sexually frigid." After forecasting that in the next few years there would be a sharp rise in films dealing with psychiatric subject matter, Mankiewicz sent out a stern warning to the eminent Kansas psychiatrist:

"I suggest to you ... that both the American Psychiatric Association and the Psychoanalytic Association consider *now* what can be done, in some way, to control — or at least temper — the presentation of their respective sciences that will be sent out to the far corners of the globe on millions of feet of film — and to prevent, if possible, the resultant disrespect and distrust that may be generated in the minds of millions of people."

The Mankiewicz letter drew an immediate response from Topeka. Menninger fired off a letter of protest to Selznick. The producer responded, detailing his previous contribution to public knowledge about psychoanalysis. He cited his *Since*

You Went Away script as his case in point, referring to "a sequence I personally conceived and wrote in the hope that it would have a value in making the American public aware of the work being done by psychiatrists to rebuild men who have been shaken by their war experiences." Menninger responded by reminding Selznick that he had evidently forgotten that he had consulted him while making the earlier film. Menninger then corrected numerous slips in the prologue to *Spellbound*.

Menninger pursued the matter beyond direct contact with Selznick. He contacted Los

Angeles friends, making his concerns about *Spellbound* known. Karl Menninger had many notable acquaintances in the area. He had spent much time in the city supervising the nascent Los Angeles Psychoanalytic Association. On one of his many trips he met his second wife. Menninger consciously cultivated Hollywood connections. He believed that the Hollywood film could provide psychoanalysis with a cultural respectability it did not then enjoy, and was delighted to assist Selznick in his *Since You Went Away* script efforts.

May Romm learned of the powerful Kansan's reservations about *Spellbound*, which prompted her to send a letter to him:

> Naturally, the question arises, why should I should have anything to do with a picture which many have interpreted as casting aspersions on psychiatry. Simply because had I not done so it would have been produced in a much more undesirable form than it is now.
>
> To give you an example, I wanted to take out the word psychoanalyst and substitute psychiatrist in regard to the leading female character, but it was impossible to accomplish this. For even what I considered improvement, I had to chew carpet.

Menninger was not mollified by the explanations of Selznick or Romm. He prevailed upon Leon Bartemeier, head of the American Psychoanalytic Association, to withdraw the promised endorsement *Spellbound* was to receive.

Selznick displayed a concern toward pacifying the psychiatric community. He had Ben Hecht, with the approval of Romm, the film's psychoanalytic consultant, write a prelude seeking to provide a cogent explanation of the positive effects of psychoanalysis:

> This movie deals with psychoanalysis, the method by which modern science treats the emotional problems of the sane.
>
> The psychoanalyst seeks only to induce the patient to talk about the hidden problems, to open the hidden doors of his mind.
>
> Once the complexes that have been disturbing the patient are uncovered and interpreted, the illness and confusion disappear ... and the evil of unreason are driven from the soul.

Walking Through Another Selznick Minefield

Alfred Hitchcock had learned long before beginning production of *Spellbound* that working with David O. Selznick was like walking through a series of minefields. With the success of *Gone with the Wind* incessantly looming, the indefatigable showman resembled the image ageless baseball pitcher Satchell Paige had in mind when he uttered the saying for which he would be remembered: "Don't look back because somebody might be gaining on you." Without looking back, the specter of *Gone with the Wind* perpetually haunted Selznick. How could he achieve an even greater success? One thing was certain, with such a great spectacle behind him, Selznick had become even more obsessed with the desire to achieve on a major scale. Looking at his output since the 1939 classic's release, and, win or lose, it would have to be said that Selznick had aimed high. One could never conceive of Selznick doing a low budget quickie for a tidy, sweat-free profit. It would be inconceivable to use the word "small" in his presence.

Hitchcock was a filmmaker of high standards, having that in common with Selznick; but as strong-willed individuals with distinct ideas of how to approach a project, clashes were seemingly inevitable. Hitchcock approached matters as a creative director while Selznick's approach was as a grandiose producer.

Spellbound was a project consumed by the kind of controversy seemingly always whirling around Selznick. The idea of combining a mystery in the Hitchcock tradition while showcasing psychoanalysis as a means of resolution put the film into a betwixt and between category. While a professional like Dr. Karl Menninger would lament that the film was not a true depiction of the profession, Hitchcock clashed with *Spellbound*'s psychiatric consultant, May Romm, over the issue of professional realism. When Romm challenged the director over a scene she believed was not professionally correct, Hitchcock responded by noting, "This is a movie and it does not have to be accurate." To Hitchcock the dramatic suspense, the tense fabric of an evolving story, was the supreme catalyst motivating his effort. This was not, after all, a documentary about psychiatry. It was a mystery intertwined with a love story.

A Superb Casting Double Play

David Selznick was noted for seeking to cast his contract players in his films, often engendering complaints from directors. Hitchcock believed that Gregory Peck was wrong for the part of John Ballantine, the tortured young amnesiac who assumes the director's position of the sanitarium Leo G. Carroll is leaving. The director found it implausible for a man who looked as youthful as Peck to be perceived as the head of such an important institution. As it turns out, he is not the man he represents himself to be, Dr. Edwardes; but the perception is important. Edwardes, more representative of a struggling young man coming to grips with himself than a successful psychiatrist, is difficult to envision as the head of such a large sanitarium, particularly in the wake of the fame he was said to have garnered as an author and lecturer in the field. A line penned by Hecht in the scene where the presumed Dr. Edwardes is meeting his new staff, along with the departing Leo G. Carroll, seeks to address the potential viewer credibility problem. "Dr. Edwardes" concedes that he appears young for his age, to which Carroll responds in a complimentary vein, noting that some people wear their years more gracefully than others, like himself.

Hitchcock entertained another misgiving about Selznick casting contract player Peck in the role. The Californian was a method actor, something the famous director found disconcerting, since the philosophy behind the system begun by the Russian Konstantin Stanislavsky emphasized performers internalizing to perceive and act out psychological motivations. Hitchcock's view emphasized camera and settings. The clash is particularly ironic since the system in which Peck was trained emphasized coming to grips with psychological forces, seemingly in synch with the film's theme.

Selznick's original intent was for Joseph Cotten, Dorothy McGuire, and Leo G. Carroll to play the leading roles. The brilliant chemistry of the resultant casting of Peck alongside glamorous Selznick player Ingrid Bergman was a major element in the film's success. The statuesque Swede initially balked at playing the role. "I won't do this movie," she declared, "because I don't believe the love story." Bergman adhered to the traditional psychiatrist's caveat of keeping one's emotions in check and never allowing them to conflict with the interactive process. Hence, if the psychiatrist were a true professional, she would not let her emotional guard down and fall in love with her patient.

After initially dropping his contractee Dorothy McGuire from consideration, Selznick made a pitch to bring Greta Garbo, the famous Swedish actress who preceded Bergman in achieving international cinematic greatness, out of a self-imposed retirement. Failing to convince Garbo to take on the part of the psychiatrist, Selznick again turned to her successor, Ingrid Bergman.

A persuasive Selznick overcame Bergman's objections. Knowing Selznick's peripatetic adventures to sound stages when his projects were being filmed, Bergman expressed delight that Hitchcock did not suffer the intrusions as willingly as she earlier surmised. "When Selznick came down to the set," Bergman recalled, "the camera suddenly stopped, and Hitchcock said the cameraman couldn't get it going again. 'I don't know what's wrong with it,' he would say. 'They're working on it, they're working on it.' And finally Selznick would leave, and miraculously the camera would start rolling again. It was his way of dealing with interference, and although I think Selznick finally guessed it was a ruse, he said nothing. I think Hitchcock was one of the few directors who could really stand up to him. Selznick then left him alone after that. They were two strong men, but I think they had great respect for each other."

Selznick might well have been suspicious, since the same technique of the malfunctioning camera was reportedly used by other wily veteran directors, such as John Ford and Howard Hawks, as a way of constructing an invisible wall between themselves and what they deemed to be intrusive producers they believed would, if permitted, potentially disrupt their creative vision.

Bergman and Peck both found a detachment in Hitchcock's directing methods. Peck was fresh from a stunning film debut in *The Keys to the Kingdom*. Hitchcock's directorial detachment concerned Selznick's brightest new star. "He really didn't give us very much direction," Peck remembered, "although I was so inexperienced I felt I needed a good deal of direction. In answer to my question about mood or expression, he would simply say that I was to drain my face of all expression and he would photograph me. I wanted more than that; the business was so new to me. But if he didn't give much direction, he did give me a case of wine when he found out I was a novice about wine. He was more than willing to improve my education in that regard.... But I had the feeling that something ailed him, and I could never understand what it might be."

As frequently occurs with brilliant directors like Hitchcock, while the actor worries that nothing is really happening, in reality the conductor has fine-tuned the orchestra so that just the desired effect is achieved. Method-trained young cinema actor Peck looked for instructional motivation, but Hitchcock's goals were being repeatedly achieved by having him drain expression, allowing the all-

Relaxing Interlude — Ingrid Bergman and Gregory Peck smile and relax with Alfred Hitchcock between takes on Selznick International's *Spellbound*. The director used his shrewd professionalism to reassure both of the film's young stars when they expressed uncertainty over their roles.

seeing eye of the camera, an instrument with which the director was so intimately familiar, to do the work. Hitchcock's sharply attuned instincts doubtlessly knew that the young actor's uncertainty worked fine on camera. After all, the character Peck was depicting in *Spellbound* was insecure, a frightened amnesiac seeking to peel away the cobwebs of uncertainty and recall his identity.

A similar incident occurred in Stanley Kubrick's breakthrough film, *The Killing* (1956), with Colleen Gray, who was concerned that her director was saying too little to her on the set when she would have appreciated more direction. She admitted later that Kubrick's distancing from her made her feel insecure at the time, after which she concluded that the person she played, the love interest of gangster Sterling Hayden, was "really insecure." In each instance, had Hitchcock and Kubrick not been convinced that the shooting was proceeding according to plan, the performers would have heard from their directors. As it was, they saw no reason to rock the boat.

Doing Their Homework and Treading a Fine Line

Selznick and Hecht shared an interest in psychoanalysis based on firsthand experience as patients, while Hitchcock was a director who was enthralled by the dark recesses of the human mind. While Selznick was ensconced in his Selznick International office in Culver City, California, a stone's throw from MGM, Hitchcock returned from London and checked into the St. Regis Hotel in midtown Manhattan.

After cabling Selznick that he would like to do a script with the prolific professional Hecht, who was then living in nearby Nyack, they began touring mental facilities in the area. They met with the chief of staff of the Hartford Retreat in Connecticut, in addition to touring other hospitals in that state as well as in New York's Westchester County. They then moved on to the psychiatric wards at Bellevue Hospital in New York City. Hecht, working from an outline Hitchcock had prepared in two nights, set to work on the script.

When circumstances dictated Hecht could work at a brisk pace, and this time he maintained an almost twenty-pages-per-day effort. "Hitchcock taught Hecht to be a cynic without even the conviction of his own cynicism," one of Hecht's chroniclers related. Hecht in his autobiography referred to the director as "the gentlemanly Alfred Hitchcock," while noting that he "gave off plots like a Roman candle." On a more somber note, the famous scenarist observed that Hitchcock was putting more into his work than he had anticipated. Hecht observed that Hitchcock was "beaming amid his nightmares."

The tense opposition the *Spellbound* project drew from Dr. Karl Menninger was symptomatic of the professional sensitivity towards the subject that Hitchcock, Selznick and Hecht had boldly tackled. Menninger, who had spent a good deal of time in California helping to establish the new profession, was fearful about a movie with massive international appeal that dealt with the subject in a negative way. The triumvirate behind the film had no desire to disparage a profession in which two of them had been personally involved as patients, and all found fascinating.

The problem was that this was an entertainment vehicle and not a documentary. It was understandable that this creative juggling act of dealing with a developing new area of medical science on the one hand, and providing entertainment for an international audience on the other, left the film's creators vulnerable to criticism from a wide number of sources.

Controversy Immediately Tackled

The Ben Hecht *Spellbound* script immediately embroils itself in the raging controversy about psychoanalysis. Rhonda Fleming was a young Selznick contractee who had been given a brief part by her producer-benefactor in *Since You Went Away*. Her one and only scene in *Spellbound* proved highly memorable, as she, playing a rebellious patient, presents the community clash over the validity of psychoanalysis. In the manner of a true screenwriting craftsman, Hecht gets his story rolling by presenting a dramatic conflict and covering ground on many fronts.

Fleming, playing troubled patient Mary Carmichael, is taken away from a card game by a male orderly who informs her that Dr. Constance Petersen, played by Bergman, wishes to see her. Disgusted over having to abandon the card game, Carmichael initially complains to the orderly, then digs her sharp claws into his arm, drawing blood. She does so after making a blatant sexual play for his affections, immediately denoting her as someone who initially fawns over men, then strikes violently. The injury leaves lines on the orderly's arm. The lines establish a theme that will be embellished in the evolution of Gregory Peck's troubled character.

When Carmichael and the orderly enter Petersen's office, the beautiful psychiatrist displays the cool distance that characterizes her professional demeanor. As soon as the orderly is dismissed, the irrepressible bearcat played by Fleming begins unleashing her fury at the doctor. She begins attacking the science of psychiatry: Hecht acknowledges the controversy from the film's outset. "This psychoanalysis is a lot of hooey!" an enraged Carmichael tells Petersen. A violent patient, she proceeds to pick up objects from a table and hurl them at the psychiatrist. The cool demeanor of Bergman's character is in further evidence as she ducks to avoid being hit, in no way becoming rattled as the still enraged Carmichael is finally led away.

A Source of Professional Discontent

The emergence of a flirtatious colleague, Doctor Fleurot, played with just the right measure of insouciance by John Emery, turned proceedings from the previous grim note of the violent and disturbed character played by Fleming to a comedic byplay that Hecht shrewdly incorporates to provide more glimpses into the character of the fascinating Dr. Constance Petersen. This is the first of several times that Fleurot teases Petersen about her unceasing professionalism and icy manner preventing her from exploring romance. He makes it abundantly clear that he is more than willing to assist her in entering this fresh dimension of experience.

Hecht has provided important details about Dr. Petersen at the film's outset and left viewers with a question mark about what the future might hold for the beautiful therapist. The major question, which is being strongly begged by her flirtatious male colleague, is whether the doctor is a workaholic iceberg or whether, under the proper circumstances, she will reveal a warmer, more romantic side. The stage is appropriately set for the arrival of Gregory Peck.

An important clash was also revealed between the cool, clinically proper, professionally curious character played by Bergman and the volatile patient played by Rhonda Fleming. When an angry Fleming shouts at Bergman about psychoanalysis being "a lot of hooey," the then-raging debate about the new science's validity is revealed. It was a debate raging in the Los Angeles of 1944, when cultural critic Theodor Adorno penned the following angry words:

"...Instead of working to gain self-awareness, the [psychoanalysis] initiates become adept at subsuming all instinctual conflicts under such conflicts as inferiority-complex, mother-fixation, extroversion, and introversion, to which they are in reality inaccessible. Terror before the abyss of the self is removed by the consciousness of being concerned with nothing so very different from arthritis or sinus trouble."

At the time Adorno was working with Max Horkheimer on the essays that were to be published fifteen years later as *The Dialectic of Enlightenment*. Adorno and Horkheimer were part of the same European immigrant wave as May Romm and artistic giants such as the Manns, Brecht, Feuchtwanger and Schoenberg. Adorno's central criticism addresses the basic point surrounding the popularity of the new system seeking approval as a science. Artistic people are used to dealing in symbols. Psychoanalysis is replete with symbols and definitions describing patterns of behavior. Adorno and other critics cautioned against using psychoanalysis as a quick fix, by pouring out secrets of the soul and receiving the same kind of therapeutic psychic release realized in a physical context by curing a headache through taking aspirin. Fleming's fury over what she deems a quack response to physical problems brings the skepticism towards the new science into *Spellbound* in a dramatic fashion.

The carefully crafted first scene also reveals an important clue concerning Dr. Murchison (Leo G. Carroll). The flirtatious Dr. Fleurot reveals to Petersen his misgivings over her being assigned the difficult Carmichael, since there is such a wide disparity between the coolly calculating professional and the troubled young woman. "Murchison must be out of his mind to assign Carmichael to you," Dr. Fleury states bluntly. At the close of the film Dr. Murchison himself is shown to be out of his mind and homicidal.

Oedipus Arrives

The initial scene, set in Dr. Petersen's office, is followed by another involving a troubled patient plagued by guilt. The Oedipus complex is introduced in the form of the guilt-plagued Garmes, played by Norman Lloyd, who in Hitchcock's *Saboteur* had played the role of the troubled Nazi spy Fry. In that earlier film Robert Cummings (as Barry Kane) pursues Fry to the Statue of Liberty in an attempt to clear himself of suspicion and implicate Fry's sinister boss, the smarmy Charles Tobin (Otto Kruger), in running a Nazi spy ring. The brilliant photography of the scene in which Kane attempts to save Fry, who ultimately tumbles to his death, is one of the most famous of Hitchcock's career. Lloyd, who prior to Hollywood achieved distinction in New York appearing with Eva Le Gallienne's company, after which he joined Orson Welles's Mercury Theatre, would eventually become an actor, director and producer on Hitchcock's long-running dramatic television series.

The scene with Lloyd further sets the stage for the introduction of amnesiac John Ballantine in the guise of Dr. Edwardes (Peck) shortly thereafter. As the coolly professional Dr. Petersen tells patient Garmes, who harbors the belief that he killed his father, "People often feel guilty for something they never did, and it usually goes back to something in their childhood. A child often wishes something terrible would happen to someone — and if something does happen to that person, the child believes he has caused it, and he grows up with a guilt complex over a sin that was only a child's bad dream."

That necessary disclosure synthesizes what occurs with Gregory Peck's character in his relationship with that of Leo G. Carroll. Dr. Murchison realizes that John Ballantine (Peck) is tormented by guilt in imagining that he committed a murder. The sinister Murchison manipulatively uses Ballantine's guilt to shift the onus of criminal suspicion onto the vulnerable young man, in the process seeking to free himself from paying the price for a murder he committed. Hitchcock, with Hecht's assistance, carries out his psychoanalytical MacGuffin by teasingly leading his audience along, providing clues for those paying close attention, all the while cloaking the mystery in a passionate love story between two appealing people whose mutual desires are shown through dramatic close-ups.

Shortly after Dr. Petersen's frank discussion with him, Garmes proves just how dangerous he is by killing a hospital orderly and then committing suicide. This is another important clue for audience members to file away. An Oedipus complex with extreme guilt is not a condition to be taken lightly. This killing potential is later dramatically exploited in the behavior of Peck's character. In one dramatically charged scene, one of the most memorable in Hitchcock arcana,

Peck's character appears to be hovering on the brink of homicide. Skilled veterans Hitchcock and Hecht set the stage early with their revelations within just a small circumference of their ultimate story compass. Examined from this standpoint, the first two scenes of *Spellbound* are highly significant for their dramatic enhancement and accompanying economy of exposition.

The exploitation of a psychological weakness displayed in *Spellbound*, with Dr. Murchison seeking to manipulate Ballantine as a cover for murder, was repeated to brilliant effect later in *Vertigo*. As will be examined in detail later, James Stewart as a police detective who took early retirement from the force due to a fear of heights that produces dizziness or vertigo, becomes an unwitting pawn in the hands of a wily Tom Helmore. The sinister villain with the polished demeanor also uses Kim Novak in his plan to find a way to carry out what he deems to be a perfect murder. As so many Hitchcock analysts point out, the director repeats some of the same basic ploys, but does so in such a clever manner that they work superbly in different settings.

Peck Arrives, Bergman's Frosty Veneer Is Punctured

Once Gregory Peck makes his arrival as Dr. Edwardes, the person selected by Dr. Murchison to replace him at Green Manors, it becomes immediately obvious that the presumed frigidity of Dr. Petersen was more perceived than real. The moment she observes the handsome, soft-spoken Peck, Bergman's eyes become alive with electricity. One penetrating close-up is all viewers need to see to know that she has found a man who definitely strikes her fancy.

When the staff members sit down together for lunch, to get acquainted with the sanitarium's new director, an element of conflict is presented. This is the established norm for a Hitchcock romantic relationship — the aura of mystery, the pursuit of romance amid a sea of conflict. Petersen learns immediately that "Dr. Edwardes" is a troubled young man when she makes some lines on a napkin during a friendly luncheon conversation. As soon as he observes the indentations she makes with her fork his face becomes riddled with tension. He delivers a harangue to Petersen about spoiling napkins and damaging sanitarium property. She does not become angry and does not appear notably surprised. Here is a thorough professional who realizes that something is wrong, which intrigues her, on top of which she is motivated by her attraction toward the sensitive and highly vulnerable newcomer.

Bergman's smitten state is disclosed in another early scene with her colleagues. The alert Dr. Fleurot, with his personal concern about Petersen's love life, observes some mustard on her nose after she has returned from an afternoon break with the new director. He guesses that the two had hot dogs at a roadside stand. "It was liverwurst," the embarrassed doctor scowls, stalking away disgustedly. The scene reveals that Petersen is indeed human, has plenty of warmth, and is sensitive about her relationship with the man who is her boss.

A Freudian Father Figure

After it is learned that the real Dr. Edwardes is missing and Peck is an impostor suspected of killing the prominent psychiatrist, he runs away and is tracked down at a New York City hotel by Dr. Petersen. With Hitchcock and Hecht determined to keep the psychoanalytical theme front row center, the opportunity emerges to make two points through the insertion of the character played by Russian stage actor Michael Chekhov, Dr. Brulov. He emerges as a father figure to Dr. Petersen with the look and demeanor of none other than Dr. Sigmund Freud. The heavy Eastern European accent and the bespectacled look, along with a goatee, makes it obvious that Hitchcock was seeking to bring the frequently discussed Viennese psychiatrist into the picture.

Chekhov's casting provides one of the most successful elements of the film. Drama was a seemingly natural field for the Leningrad-born actor and dramatic instructor, since he was related to celebrated Russian playwright Anton Chekhov. An emulator of Stanislavsky, Michael Chekhov left Russia after the 1917 Revolution to establish drama schools in London and New York. In the manner of so many stage disciplinarians, Chekhov spurned Hollywood movie offers for years. In the early forties he finally ventured west and appeared, appropriately enough, in the 1943 release, *Song of Russia*. His most prominent role by far was that of Dr. Alex Brulov in *Spellbound*. He was nominated for a Best Supporting Actor Oscar, and his success helped persuade him to remain in Hollywood. He appeared in character roles until his death in Beverly Hills in 1955.

While Brulov (Chekhov) would engage in a certain amount of professional talk with protégée Petersen in her endeavor to unlock the mysteries of amnesiac Peck's past, he straddles a fine line in avoiding potential confusion on the part of film viewers who would be put off by extended psychiatric shop talk. The Russian actor reveals a dry wit, exercising it repeatedly, in the process adding an element of comedic lightness needed to lessen the gravity of the subject matter, psychoanalysis, and the tragic plight of the truly clueless Ballantine.

When Petersen and Ballantine flee New York City she takes him by train to the Rochester clinic of Dr. Brulov. After holding two detectives at bay who are inquiring into Ballantine's whereabouts by feigning ignorance, Chekhov becomes involved in one of the two most fascinating photographic sequences of the film.

The scene occurs after Dr. Brulov has convinced surrogate daughter and professional protégée Petersen to go to bed after telling her she is understandably suffering from fatigue from all the responsibility she has undertaken, capped off by a determined effort to elude authorities seeking to find Ballantine. Peck,

More Than Professional Interest — Ingrid Bergman has developed more than just a pro-
fessional psychiatric interest toward Gregory Peck in the 1945 psychological classic
Spellbound, which was directed by Hitchcock and produced by David O. Selznick.
Looking on is Michael Chekhov, who looms large as both teacher and father figure to
Bergman.

staring at himself in the mirror, decides to leave his room and march downstairs
with his straight razor in hand. The music of composer Miklos Rozsa dramatically rises as the sensitively positioned camera of George Barnes follows him at
what we know represents a grim dramatic moment for the tortured amnesiac.

When Peck arrives downstairs we continue to see things from his viewpoint.
A clever deep focus shot reveals Dr. Brulov sitting at his desk. From Ballantine's
point of view we observe the menacing straight razor he holds tightly. Viewers
were previously apprised of the dangerous propensities of those nursing feelings
of guilt, as represented by Dr. Petersen's words to the tortured Mr. Garmes, who
ultimately took a life and eventually took his own. Now here is Ballantine standing stiffly with razor in hand, and the kindly psychiatrist sitting at his desk and
watching him from the distance.

Dr. Brulov shows his professional astuteness by remaining outwardly calm.
He casually asks Ballantine to join him for a glass of milk. The gesture gives the
doctor a chance to seize the upper hand, which he does by making certain that
his visitor's milk is heavily laced with bromide. A potential tragedy is averted as

Ballantine quickly falls into a deep sleep. The desired effect of the milk-drinking sequence was achieved by having a giant pail held in front of the camera, which photographed Chekhov in the background as the milk was poured into a trough.

Salvador Dalí's Dream Sequence

With Hitchcock's flair for artistry it is understandable that he would incorporate a dream sequence, within a film about psychoanalysis considering the value attached to this process in the writings of Freud and the professional procedures of his followers. Hitchcock saw it as an opportunity to weave a surrealistic tapestry on-screen. Influenced by Giorgio de Chirico, Hitchcock brought Salvador Dalí to Hollywood to achieve his desired effect of blending classical architecture with deep shadows.

Dalí was born and raised in the small northern Spanish town of Figueres, located near the French border. His background in architecture assisted him in developing a style that blended architectural elements with art. It provides audiences with the opportunity to observe his paintings from different perspectives; depending upon how and from where they are viewed, different elements are showcased. Dalí was very much a product of the Freudian revolution, as he used his art to reveal collages of images representative of what occurs during dreams.

One problem in hiring Dalí was that much of his work was deemed too surrealistic for use in the film sequences, and Hitchcock and Selznick used only a few of the images the Spanish master provided for *Spellbound.*

"It was a wonderful, twenty minute sequence that really belongs in a museum," Ingrid Bergman related in an interview with Donald Spoto years after *Spellbound* was made. "The idea for a major part of it was that I would become, in Gregory Peck's mind, a statue. To do this, we shot the film in the reverse way in which it would appear on the screen. They put a straw in my mouth so I could breathe, and then a statue was actually made around me. I was dressed in a draped, Grecian gown, with a crown on my head and an arrow positioned so it seemed to be through my neck. Then the cameras rolled. I was in this statue, I broke out and the action continued. We ran it backward, so it would appear as if I became a statue. It was marvelous, but someone went to Selznick and said, 'What is all this drivel?' and so they cut it. It was such a pity."

Hitchcock's recollection of the free-spirited Dalí, revealed to authors Charles Higham and Joel Greenberg some twenty-five years after *Spellbound* was filmed, was far less favorable than that of his leading lady. "I brought in Salvador Dalí to do the dream sequences, not for publicity purposes — as Selznick thought — but because I wanted to have dreams photographed vividly," Hitchcock explained. "Until then, movie dreams were always blurred, always double exposures, and misty; and dreams are not like that, they're very, very vivid. What

I wanted out of Dalí was that long perspective, that hard, clear, solid look; I wanted his sequences to be shot in the open air in bright sunlight, so they would have to stop the lens down to make it really hard in contrast. But they wouldn't do that. Dalí wanted all kinds of crazy things. He wanted Ingrid Bergman covered in ants at one point. He was really a kook."

The problem of not being able to satisfactorily achieve expectations on dream sequences would appear to have roots extending far beyond Dalí, however, relating instead to the difficulty of the challenge involved. The Hitchcock-Selznick-Hecht triumvirate might have shared an enthusiastic interest in psychoanalysis; the problem was using such a complex subject as the basis for a film that would capture and hold the audience's interest.

A professional such as Dr. Karl Menninger harbored concern that incorporating a subject that was just beginning to be understood by the public at large into a mystery drama could blur the lines between entertainment and science. In the final analysis the head of the famous Topeka clinic need not have feared anything. The resolution of *Spellbound* by the intuitive brilliance of Dr. Petersen, coupled with John Ballantine's cooperation in psychoanalysis, is akin to a parade of white rabbits being plucked from a magician's hat.

Two of the most attentive Selznick and Hitchcock chroniclers are David Thomson and Donald Spoto. While Thomson penned a lengthy biography on Selznick, appropriately entitled *Showman*, Spoto furnished both a Hitchcock biography as well as a work detailing all of his films.

Thomson related Irene Mayer Selznick's caustic view of *Spellbound*. "David was making the film *instead* of having an analysis," she bluntly stated. "He was in a terrible state and the film is a terrible piece of junk." After referring to *Spellbound* as a "collection of gimmicks," Thomson concluded that "*Spellbound* let him [Selznick] believe he was still up-to-date and in form, that he was equipped to draw material into popular entertainment. As far as analysis is concerned, the movie is a source of cliché and misunderstanding. It shows the conflict of feelings David had toward the new form of doctoring. He could not stop regarding it as the accomplice to narcissism...."

Spoto concurs with Thomson's view, delineating, as had Selznick's biographer, the clever gimmicks the wily Hitchcock had incorporated into the film. He acknowledges Hitchcock's always impressive creative resourcefulness, but credits the film's popular success to a different factor. "These touches are dandy," Spoto conceded, "but Bergman and Peck gave *Spellbound* its humanity."

A Dynamic Duo, Excellent Lighting, and a Great Composer

The special chemistry of Selznick contract players Peck and Bergman generated a successful irony in the *Spellbound* production. The concern shown by, and subsequent jousts with, the psychiatric community about filming the proper script to make the process come alive were preempted by the blend of a highly attractive young couple in love, superior lighting to invest the developing relationship with just the right scenic drama, and the presence of a great composer contributing a memorable film score.

Born in Budapest, composer Miklos Rozsa left Hungary to study music in Leipzig. A fellow Hungarian, Britain's producing giant Sir Alexander Korda, provided Rozsa with his launching pad into music score composition. If there is one element that can shrewdly augment a compelling love story, generating audience empathy, it is music, and Rozsa blossomed with a score that, by any reasonable calculation, would rank in the top five in movie history. The *Spellbound* score is one of three from great Hitchcock films in which suspense was highly intensified by mounting crescendos. The others were *The Man Who Knew Too Much* in 1956 and *Vertigo* two years later. Composer Bernard Herrmann, a frequent Hitchcock collaborator, achieved devastating results in both films.

Rozsa's stirring effort ranks with other stellar film works, such as Max Steiner's compelling "Tara's Theme" and accompanying score from *Gone with the Wind*. Another great score that immediately springs to mind when discussing impact on a memorable film is that composed by Dimitri Tiomkin for *High Noon*. The oft-repeated story in Hollywood circles tells of the film's sneak preview generating only a mild response. The Tiomkin score was then inserted, with the memorable "Do Not Forsake Me, Oh My Darling" sung by Tex Ritter, and the audience became riveted. The music coincided with the dramatic buildup as sheriff Gary Cooper took on desperados determined to kill him and take over the town for which he was responsible.

The score that Rozsa's *Spellbound* is so frequently compared to, and which also falls within the ranks of cinema classics, is that of *The Third Man*. The producer of that film was the same one who gave Rozsa his break, fellow Hungarian Alexander Korda. It was marked by the haunting zither music of Anton Karas. In that 1949 film, director Carol Reed was willing to take an innovative risk and opt for a score with one instrument that rose to peak crescendo as the drama increased. One wonders if the wily Reed could have been thinking of Rozsa's impact four years earlier with another musical instrument that registered a huge impact on audiences, the theremin. Invented by Russian engineer Leo Theremin, the electronic instrument is played by moving the hands near its two antennas.

The theremin is frequently used to generate a high tremolo effect. This made it perfect for the two kinds of scenes that characterized *Spellbound*. Rozsa's score achieved such a universal and spontaneous reaction among film viewers because of the superbly heightening crescendos used in the love scenes and at moments when it was unclear just what unstable amnesiac Gregory Peck would do. While certain critics would complain that the music was often played at excessive volume levels, the audience was enthralled, just as at the close of a stirring classical composition an audience reaches an often hypnotic state.

The use of the theremin and the raw power of the Rozsa score made the audience feel all the more for the love team of Peck and Bergman. Rozsa would secure a well-deserved Oscar for his efforts on *Spellbound* and would acquire two more statuettes during a distinguished career. He was an Oscar recipient two years later for his scoring of the 1947 dramatic classic *A Double Life*, which also resulted in an Academy Award for its leading man, Ronald Colman. Rozsa won his final of three Oscars twelve years later when he received one of the ten Oscars secured by William Wyler's 1959 classic, *Ben-Hur*.

Augmenting the romantic and mystery thematics, along with the compelling score, was the superb cinematography of George Barnes. Barnes, who received his initial break under producer Thomas Ince in the final decade of silents in 1919, had secured an Academy Award working with Hitchcock and Selznick on *Rebecca*. For *Spellbound* he supplied the same kind of shadowy hues that enhanced both suspense and romance in the earlier black and white vehicle.

Whereas suspense and romance are generally catapulted forward on the strength of a solid story constructed around tight dialogue, the element that made *Spellbound* such an astounding success with moviegoers was a successful blend of talent heightened by superb direction, along with the aforementioned elements of skillful cinematography and haunting music. As a director of incomparable instinct, Hitchcock was content with establishing the right setting and, as the circumstances warranted, basically left Peck and Bergman alone.

Ingrid Bergman provided the perfect contrast to Peck. Here is a young woman so consumed by her career that she is chided by colleagues and can display a manner so sober and mature that she often appears older than Leo G. Carroll. That initial look at Gregory Peck when they meet in the Green Manors dining room conveys the true romanticism lying beneath the mature professional veneer. When they get better acquainted during their first outing, a country walk, she symbolically sheds many years and begins giggling like a school girl, consumed by love.

More blanks are filled in concerning Bergman's character with the emergence of veteran Russian stage performer Michael Chekhov as Dr. Brulov. She is clearly more than his professional protégée; she is the daughter he never had as well. Since Bergman plays both daughter and protégée, Brulov does not mind scolding her when he feels that circumstances warrant it, but he remains dedicated to her, whatever his current frame of mind. Just as a young woman in love will often confide in her father, in Bergman's case such consultation is a quest for professional information as well as advice concerning a matter of the heart.

Spellbound integrates the resolution of a mystery with the evolution of budding love. The hypnotic appeal of Bergman and Peck in the throes of love lighten a story that could have spelled trouble in other circumstances. The mystery of ultimately determining Peck's identity as Dr. John Ballantine is resolved through a walk through the often rough patches of psychoanalysis. The film is an effort to blend psychoanalysis into the solution of a mystery. Bergman's efforts contain the essentials of formulaic professional talk, which runs the risk of slowing down the story's pace and impeding dramatic flow. This potential problem is surmounted by the appeal of the dynamic duo as they simultaneously find love while traversing the briar patch of psychoanalytical exploration.

The symbolic thread stringing together the drama is the terrifying reaction of Ballantine when he observes lines. This causes him to flair up in a rage generated by fear when Dr. Petersen uses a fork to draw lines on a napkin. Ballantine is seized by the chilling fear that he has killed someone. When Dr. Edwardes turns up missing, Ballantine is regarded as a murder suspect. Dr. Petersen's probing psychoanalysis reveals that his fear has been prompted by a slide down an apartment porch as a young man, resulting in the accidental death of his younger brother. This is the incident that has been haunting him, convincing Ballantine that he is a killer. His amnesia resulted from war traumas as a pilot. One by one the mysteries are unlocked through the diligent efforts of a woman in love, motivated by the heart as well as an uncompromising professionalism.

Tying the Loose Ends Together

The final climactic scene of *Spellbound* swiftly resolves the story at a time when it appears that much more could be in the offing. John Ballantine has just been tried and convicted of the murder of Dr. Edwardes after Dr. Petersen revealed, believing this would clear him to police that he had been on the ski slope with him prior to his death. But the deceased man's body is discovered with a gun shot wound to the head. Crushed by Ballantine's fate, and resolving to fight on for him, she returns to Green Manors and Dr. Murchison, who is back in charge.

Hecht's script induces an end through the combination of a slip on Murchison's part and the swiftly operating deductive mind of Bergman's Dr. Petersen. Dr. Murchison had revealed at the film's beginning that he had never met Dr. Edwardes. While accompanying Petersen to her quarters on the evening she arrives back at Green Manors, Carroll lets it slip that he did not know Dr. Edwardes well. With that important fact in mind, comparable to a slip made by Kim Novak that triggers James Stewart's revelation of the truth in *Vertigo*, to be later discussed, Dr. Petersen walks swiftly and resolutely into Dr. Murchison's office.

The veteran psychiatrist coolly assists her in filling in the blanks, realizing his mistake and that his colleague's "agile mind" would proceed from there to the correct conclusion that he was Dr. Edwardes's killer. The symbolism of the Dalí dream sequence is invoked to fill in the mystery's remaining blanks. Murchison despised Dr. Edwardes and had an angry verbal confrontation with him at Club 21 in New York City. He followed Edwardes and his patient, Ballantine, traumatized by war-related stress and resultant amnesia, to the ski slopes. Edwardes, as Murchison reveals, believed in solving patient traumas through liberating exercise technique. In that Ballantine is suffering from amnesia he becomes the perfect patsy for Carroll to escape detection for his murder of the famous psychiatrist he despises. Peck is selected to step into the professional shoes of the deceased.

When explanations are completed Murchison announces that the murder weapon he used to kill Dr. Edwardes, which he has removed from his desk, would be used for a second homicide, this time to silence an all-too-clever colleague. Dr. Petersen's resourceful mind goes to work as she seeks to prevent the distraught and homicidal Dr. Murchison from making her his second victim. She explains that he is too clever to kill her. His troubled condition could result in treatment and incarceration, with him being allowed to pursue his writing and research, based strictly on the killing of Dr. Edwardes. A second murder, she warns, would result in his certain execution. She reveals her intention to call the police, leaving the room and closing the door behind her.

That leaves the abandoned Dr. Murchison by himself. This is one of two memorable point-of-view sequences in the film. The other involved a disturbed amnesiac holding a razor, with the audience wondering if Ballantine will kill the kindly Dr. Brulov, played so brilliantly by Chekhov. Unlike Brulov, who puts his potential assailant to sleep with a laced drink, Dr. Petersen is compelled to use verbal resourcefulness to save her life. By pointing out the no-win situation that Dr. Murchison faces, he understands that killing her would only trigger, as she reveals, his prosecution for two murders.

The clever point-of-view camera shot with which the film concludes finds Carroll as Murchison reversing the direction of the gun. It had been pointed at Bergman, who by now has departed. Slowly he turns it around until it faces him. At that point he fires a fatal bullet at his own head. The shot was made possible by constructing a huge wooden hand holding a gun. It was mounted under the camera and turned around toward it, so that Bergman could be kept in clear focus beyond. A red explosion was hand-tinted onto the black and white image.

While reviews were mixed, *Variety* appeared to strike the note sounded by viewers of *Spellbound*, cautioning exhibitors not to "let the scientific words fool you. While an adult picture all right, beautifully played and photographed, it's still for the women patrons, containing all the suspense and characterization made to order for them."

Because of its emphasis on psychoanalysis, the film was given little exposure in small town America, but it did tremendous business in large cities domestically and internationally. *Spellbound* returned worldwide receipts of over $6 million to its distributor. Selznick used some of his profits to buy wife Irene, from whom he had separated, a diamond necklace. The film was enthusiastically received in London. On May 19, 1946, the day of the British premiere of *Spellbound*, London's Tivoli Theatre turned away a reported six thousand people.

"Even a driving rain failed to disperse the crowds," Selznick's London representative cabled his employer. A month later, playing in two theaters, *Spellbound* broke every house record. The film was the beneficiary of good timing in premiering in London during the first anniversary of Victory Week. A virtual rebirth of show business occurred at the city's historic Strand to commemorate one year since the end of World War II.

Hitchcock attended the Paris premiere of *Spellbound* in May. He then returned to the city of his birth to receive acclaim as director of one of the season's major hits.

In addition to achieving gigantic box office success, the film, despite spotty reviews (including poor ones from some of the artier periodicals), received six nominations from the Motion Picture Academy. Selznick and Hitchcock were honored in the Best Picture and Best Director categories respectively. Michael Chekhov was honored with a Best Supporting Actor nomination, while George Barnes received a nomination for Black and White Cinematography and Jack Cosgrove was nominated in the Special Effects category. The sole Oscar recipient was Miklos Rozsa for his compelling musical score. Apart from the earlier Selznick-Hitchcock collaboration *Rebecca*, none of Hitchcock's films had ever received as many Academy nominations.

Launching Another Psychological Drama

Spellbound's success prompted Selznick to step again into the same arena with director Hitchcock and writer Hecht, but with one notable difference: any attempt at story resolution through the process of psychoanalysis would be abandoned. The next Selznick team project would enable viewers to become their own analysts by appraising the behavior of the performers, who exemplified fascinating psychological personas within a strongly plotted drama. This was more in the tradition of the great gothic film that launched the Hitchcock-Selznick association, *Rebecca*, but this time the subject matter would be spy drama. While Hitchcock had handled that subject skillfully in *The 39 Steps* and *The Man Who Knew Too Much* in his London phase, the now–American-based director would increasingly inject more psychology and rely less on skilled photography and story twists. This pattern would be emphasized in some of his greatest future dramas, such as *Rope, Strangers on a Train, Psycho* and *Vertigo*.

A Perfect Vehicle for Hecht

It was earlier mentioned that Ben Hecht, Selznick's best friend in the film industry, was a strong supporter of Zionism who had written the historical pageant *We Will Never Die*. His next project, which would ultimately bear the name

Notorious and become one of Hitchcock's enduring classics, was adapted by Hecht from a 1921 *Saturday Evening Post* story by John Traintor Foote called "The Song of the Dragon." The effort resulted from a desire by Hitchcock to make a film built around a "confidence trick," in Hitchcockian parlance a highly clever MacGuffin. The result would prompt Hitchcock biographer Donald Spoto to label it as the director's "most famous MacGuffin."

Selznick assumed the role of the tough drill sergeant in analyzing the treatment and script drafts of Hitchcock and Hecht. Hitchcock sought to invest the film's leading female character, Alicia, with the brassiness of Tallulah Bankhead, the female lead of his film *Lifeboat*, which achieved fame for the novelty of staging the entire film in a sailing craft, as befitting of the title, along with the fact that future Nobel Prize recipient John Steinbeck wrote the screenplay. The tough-talking Selznick bluntly declared that the Hitchcock idea was unacceptable, and that some of the lines from the treatment were currently passé and harkened back to the work of Hecht when he combined with Charles MacArthur to write the comedy *The Front Page*. Selznick shrewdly steered the project into the same direction that he had earlier propelled *Spellbound*, toward a suspenseful drama with two magnetic performers as characters falling in love.

Another dynamic team stepped forward. After considering Greta Garbo, who turned the role down, Selznick and Hitchcock concurred that Ingrid Bergman was right for the role of the beautiful and problematical Alicia Huberman, a woman of experience. Selznick liked keeping his leading female star working as she thrived on regular activity. Hitchcock was captivated by her work in *Spellbound* and was delighted to direct her again.

Since the spy drama featured two individuals of experience who fell in love amid crosscurrents, Bergman's assignment fell into a different category than in *Spellbound*. In that case she lost her heart to a naive Gregory Peck. In *Notorious* Bergman was drawn into a nest of spies in Brazil by dashing FBI agent Devlin, played by Cary Grant. Better than a decade later, Hitchcock would cast the debonair British star in another spy thriller, *North by Northwest*, but in that film he was a wrongly pursued victim of fate, whereas in *Notorious* he was a coolly calculating pursuer of justice.

Hitchcock's Deadliest MacGuffin

Notorious was released shortly after the end of World War II. Just two years after its 1946 release Israel would be declared a new nation by its first prime minister, David Ben-Gurion. To Ben Hecht this was a burning goal fulfilled. As a staunch Zionist he sought to find a home for the Jewish war refugees who survived the Holocaust. *Notorious'* story deals with the real life tragedy of major members of Hitler's Nazi hierarchy escaping to South America after the collapse of the Third Reich. Among the Third Reich figures who escaped to South America were chief Holocaust executioner Adolf Eichmann, who migrated to Argentina, and Joseph Mengele, known as the "doctor of death," who conducted deadly and torturous experiments on Jewish prisoners. Mengele lived in Paraguay, then fled to Brazil after being detected, and died there.

In *Notorious* Claude Rains plays a prominent Nazi who escapes, along with fellow comrades, to Rio de Janeiro and assumes a major role in a spy nest dedicated to keeping the burning flame of Nazism alive, waiting for another day to fulfill deceased fuhrer Adolf Hitler's dream of world conquest. History tells of the race to produce an atomic bomb, with Albert Einstein, basically a committed pacifist, writing his famous letter to President Franklin Delano Roosevelt in 1939 warning of the necessity of constructing the deadly weapon before Hitler's scientists won the potentially destructive race. The Manhattan Project resulted, and the bomb was invented by Americans and used to shorten the war. Hitchcock and Hecht shrewdly united the themes of Nazis reuniting in Brazil, determined to ultimately triumph, along with their diligent pursuit of the devastating atomic bomb.

The wily Hitchcock, always thinking, incorporated the Nazi pursuit of the bomb in *Notorious* with the invention of his most original and ingenious MacGuffin. Just how would he tie the pursuit of the bomb to the story? Hitchcock explained to Charles Higham and Joel Greenberg that his widely known interest in fine wine directed him to his MacGuffin. His imaginativeness scored points with reviewers when *Notorious* was released. While the film deals with the pursuit of the atomic bomb by Nazis following the war, at the point when the script was being written the war was still raging and the devastating weapon had not yet been completed, much less used. Hitchcock's sole tip-off had been from writer Russell Maloney from the *New Yorker*. Maloney told Hitchcock about a place in New Mexico where men go in and are never allowed out again, it was so secret. "I guessed it was the atomic bomb," Hitchcock revealed.

According to Hitchcock: "Finally it got so wild that — being a connoisseur of wine — I came up with the idea of uranium in wine bottles. When I mentioned this to Selznick he said, 'What uranium?' I said, 'It's Uranium 235.' 'What's that?' he said. I said, 'It's the stuff they're going to make the atom bomb from.' 'What atom bomb?' 'David,' I said, 'everybody knows about this. The Germans are trying to make heavy water in Norway: this is what it's for. He said, 'I think this is the craziest thing on which to base a picture.' 'All right,' I said. 'If you don't like uranium let's make it industrial diamonds, anything you like — jewelry — I don't care.'"

Fortunately for Hitchcock and *Notorious* the director prevailed. At the time he suffered from the problem of being too far ahead of the curve. As Hitchcock and Selznick biographer Leonard J. Leff wrote, "In April 1945, a month before the military began work on deployment of the atomic bomb, two months before certain of Churchill's advisors knew of it, and three months before the Alamogordo test that demonstrated its efficacy, Hecht and Hitchcock brought uranium and atomic warfare to *Notorious*."

Being ahead of one's contemporaries can cause problems with legal authorities as well. After Ben Hecht finished the script, following an interim period when famous New York playwright Clifford Odets took on and then left the project, Hitchcock took Hecht to see leading local Los Angeles scientist Dr. Robert Millikan in his office at the California Institute of Technology. The intention of the visit was to learn more about Uranium 235 in conjunction with making an atomic bomb. The unflappable Hitchcock was determined to learn whatever was needed to make an authentic film based on an emerging reality of which the public was then unaware. The Millikan office included an imposing bust of Albert Einstein. The scientist listened as the director came directly to the point, asking, "Dr. Millikan, how big would an atom bomb be?"

Such a question, asked during the time of the top secret Manhattan Project, prompted a flabbergasted Millikan to reply, "Do you want to get arrested? Do you want to get *me* arrested?" Hitchcock's unanticipated question had taken the eminent scientist by surprise. After he caught his bearings he went into defense mode. Millikan then, according to Hitchcock, "spent an hour telling us how impossible the whole thing was." Hitchcock's prescience had repercussions. "I understand that I was watched by the FBI for three months afterwards," he explained.

Selznick Bows Out, Hal Wallis's Big Mistake

Despite Selznick's enthusiasm for the *Notorious* project, another important production compelled him to make a choice, which resulted in Hitchcock receiving his biggest break since coming to America. *Duel in the Sun* represented far more than a film to David O. Selznick. It was literally a labor of love. Not only was this intended to be the big blockbuster that would hopefully enable the highly ambitious producer to surpass, or at least match, *Gone with the Wind*, it was the vehicle meant to propel the woman he considered his artistic creation, Jennifer Jones, to meteoric heights.

Selznick's intended epic ran into significant difficulty. Problems on the New Mexico location multiplied. The rain provided difficulties, causing costly postponements, while a union strike caused more of the same. With costs steadily mounting, Selznick made a choice. As much as he was absorbed by *Notorious*, Selznick was in need of immediate money for *Duel in the Sun*. He decided to sell his interest in the Hitchcock project. The producer's decision allowed Hitchcock to sprout new wings.

Hal Wallis, along with partner Joe Hazen, expressed an interest in *Notorious*. After reading the script, however, Wallis decided to pass. While liking certain aspects of the production, his reason for declining to jump aboard related to the element that would make the film forever famous. According to partner

Hazen, "When that script was submitted to us we thought it was the goddamnedest thing on which to base a picture."

So the wily Hitchcock made a spy film involving the atomic bomb a year before it was first detonated, over the city of Hiroshima. After the war, when Joe Hazen spoke to Hitchcock about why he and Wallis had turned down the project, the director had a simple answer. "You made the same mistake as Selznick," Hitchcock explained. "You thought the story was about Uranium 235. Well, it wasn't. It was a love story."

Hitchcock's response was based on his belief that the least important part of his films was the MacGuffin, in this case Uranium 235 found in a bottle of expensive wine. In this instance, however, he was at least partially wrong. While the film was indeed, a love story, the ingenuity of including a devastating weapon of destruction that had not yet been developed for use gave the film an element of prescience. That and the uniqueness of storing the uranium in a wine bottle would generate even more talk among film historians and enthusiasts than the on-screen pyrotechnics of romantic steam-team Cary Grant and Ingrid Bergman.

When Wallis passed on the project a situation emerged that propelled both Hitchcock's career stock and motivation forward. Selznick sold *Notorious* to RKO for $800,000 and 50 percent of the profits. The man who dreaded Selznick shadowing him during production was relieved when it was stipulated that the producer abandon the scene. Stepping into his shoes as producer in a new dual capacity, for the first time since coming to America, was Alfred Hitchcock. His enthusiasm was further enhanced by RKO entering the scene. This was a family-oriented studio that did not have its own stable of stars and prided itself on making those who visited feel at home. The same type of hospitality applied to directors and producers, who were assisted while retaining their autonomy. If there was one word that Hitchcock longed to hear after perpetual creative jousting with an equally determined Selznick, it was "autonomy."

While Hitchcock might have dreaded the numerous Selznick memos and, as an individual who followed more orderly living patterns, creative discussions in the wee hours of the morning with a man who took Benzedrine to sustain his breakneck pace, with *Notorious* the director again benefited from insights provided by the man who had brought him to America. The tough drill sergeant possessed an acutely developed editorial instinct. Selznick provided sharp criticism during the earlier draft submissions by Hitchcock and Hecht. In the early going Selznick believed that too much of the Hitchcock he admired was missing. Selznick wanted more of the patented Hitchcock Roman candles in the script. Ben Hecht might have been his best friend, but that did not stop Selznick from sharply criticizing the veteran scenarist for what he often found unrealistic dialogue, just as at one point Selznick had upbraided Hitchcock by denouncing his effort to insert saucy Tallulah Bankhead–style conversation into the story for the female lead.

There was one instance, however, when the patience of Hitchcock benefited the project. At one point, with the project stalled, Cary Grant indicated that if a decision were not promptly reached that he would no longer be available for the lead role. Believing that the film might be in jeopardy, Selznick urged Hitchcock to resume shooting with his client Joseph Cotten in the lead. Hitchcock believed it was wise to wait for Grant, and the results justify his judgment.

Another Magic Love Team

Just as Selznick contract players Bergman and Peck had formed a perfect romantic team in *Spellbound*, a Cupid's arrow charisma developed with the pairing of the Swedish beauty with another dynamic leading man. In *Notorious* the diligent Hitchcock-Hecht duo weaves another screen triumph around the charismatic magic of its leads, but this time with the older, debonair Britisher Grant, who had starred with Joan Fontaine in one of Hitchcock's earlier American films, *Suspicion*. Grant plays a seasoned man of experience willing to use his charms to get what he wants from a beautiful woman like Alicia Huberman (Bergman), but finds it painful to let himself go emotionally and fall in love. In *Spellbound* Bergman's character was chided for being unemotional and too exclusively focused on her career, while in *Notorious* Alicia is frustrated by her love interest's stiffening demeanor in the wake of potential emotional commitment.

Even the name given to Grant's character is a tip-off to his cold veneer. He is called T.R. Devlin, conveying a ring of professional coldness. Alicia Huberman has, in the tragic frustration of being the daughter of an active American Nazi spy, thrown herself loosely into sexual involvement as a palliative. A clash is then presented when, after Alicia finds a man with whom she hopes she can find genuine emotional fulfillment, Devlin (unlike the many other men who instantly responded to her romantic overtures) exudes tightness and draws back.

From Grant's Viewpoint

Notorious begins with a courtroom sequence at Miami's federal courthouse as Alicia Huberman's father John is being sentenced to twenty years for treasonous activity against America on behalf of Nazi Germany. The opening notation of location and time, Miami, April 24, 1946, is a device used at the beginning of *Psycho* better than a decade later. Unrepentant, John Huberman delivers a stinging rebuke to his accusers, confidently predicting the ultimate triumph of Nazism. Bergman as Alicia is seen for the first time after the sentencing, spurning efforts by reporters to comment about her father's fate.

Hecht has hooked us initially with the dramatic courthouse scene. Now the action shifts to Alicia's Miami residence, where a party is in full swing.

Bergman's initial line speaks volumes, revealing her emotional pain: "The important drinking hasn't started yet."

A nifty Hitchcock camera device provides viewers with an impression of the male lead before his face is seen. We see the outline of Devlin's form and observe developing activity from his perspective. He is seen only from behind in darkened silhouette, while at one point Alicia serves him a drink. Devlin silently watches as a shattered Alicia seeks to drown her sorrows in alcohol. Her quest for genuine affection is displayed through succinct dialogue with the Commodore of the cruise ship on which she is slated to leave the next morning for Havana:

> COMMODORE: We'd better start breaking up, Alicia. We have to be on board at nine. One week in Havana and this whole thing about your father will have blown over.
> ALICIA: Do you love me, Commodore?
> COMMODORE: You're a very beautiful woman.
> ALICIA: I'll have another drink to appreciate that.

The brief exchange reflects the succinct professionalism of the writer, revealing much through economy of expression. It is learned that Alicia is not only eager to escape her travails through drink, but hopes that a trip to Havana will assist as well. In her question to the Commodore, Alicia Huberman reveals her quest for love. His response is noteworthy for what is unsaid. Her question concerning whether he loves her is met with a compliment about her beauty. After failing to elicit an affirmative response, she decides to have another drink to appreciate a compliment devoid of the expression she sought to hear.

When the last of the guests leave, Devlin is finally seen in full. An inebriated Alicia suggests fresh air, meaning a drive at reckless, breakneck speed. Devlin's Puritanical nature is revealed when he covers her bare midriff with his scarf on the pretext of protecting her from the cold. The audience learns of Devlin's importance after a motorcycle officer pulls Alicia over. She expects to receive a justified ticket for excessive speeding. Instead Devlin shows the officer his identification card, after which the policeman respectfully salutes and drives off. Alicia concludes that he is a policeman, angrily accusing him of being "a federal cop crashing my party" in an effort to get something on her. As a result of her father's notoriety she has been followed by many policemen. He is obliged to knock her out with a quick punch to the jaw to take over the driver's wheel and restore order.

A Clever but Crooked Perspective

Hitchcock's inventive technique of putting the viewer into the film, as had been done in the sequence at Alicia's home when Cary Grant was introduced, comes into play once more the next morning when Alicia awakens with a frightful hangover, the penalty for her all-night partying. A visually distorted point of view shot shows Alicia's spinning perspective in her morning distress. Devlin's angled image comes into view as he approaches — from an upside-down posture.

Devlin provides a glass of juice, after which he settles into the important matter at hand. He identifies himself as a federal agent and enlists her for a job. He seeks her assistance in spying on her father's associates in Rio de Janeiro. The Nazi spy nest has set up a base of operation there. As mentioned earlier, this was an actual pattern occurring at that time. The company with which the group is associated, and with whom they are carrying out scientific experiments, is I.G. Farben. The powerful pharmaceutical company's very name inspires horror in the hearts of international Jewry. It was Farben that designed the poisonous gas used by Hitler's Third Reich against Holocaust victims, so this was a subject of ultimate importance to screenwriter Ben Hecht.

Initially Alicia balks, exclaiming that she has no interest in the subject matter of Devlin's discussion. "I don't go for patriotism ... or patriots," she exclaims. Devlin knows better, playing the recording of an emotional argument she had had with her father, in which she refuses to become involved with what she calls her father's "rotten schemes" and professes her love for America.

Rather than continuing her dissolute life and taking a trip to Havana for more presumed drink and debauchery, she instead decides to accompany Devlin to Rio to undertake the job he has offered.

Part Two, a New Love
and Wooing a Nazi Scientist

The Miami getting acquainted phase and effort to recruit Alicia is followed by part two of the film, beginning on the flight to, and later focusing on the activities in, Rio. Alicia learns that her father has committed suicide in his cell by swallowing a poisonous capsule. The deadly poison is part of a recurring theme threaded throughout the film, in which destructive substances are featured. Alicia Huberman in the film's early phase is a playgirl, almost a borderline prostitute, who is using both sex and alcohol destructively. Her father commits suicide through ingesting a poisonous capsule. The Uranium 235 to be used in a bomb being designed by the Rio Nazis is contained in wine bottles. Ultimately the poison syndrome comes full circle. Her father dies from poison early in the film, while at its climax, as will be seen, Alicia falls prey to it as well.

The film's romantic conflict emerges in Rio. Alicia, feeling free of confinement, falls in love with Devlin and teases him over his fears of reciprocation. The conflict intensifies when she learns the exact nature of her assignment. The beautiful woman of previously loose morals is supposed to use her charms on a main cog in the Nazi scientific machine. Claude Rains plays Alexander Sebastian, a famous Nazi scientist who had once unsuccessfully wooed Alicia.

Alicia's pursuit of Sebastian sets off a series of conflicts. First of all, Alicia is incensed that Devlin makes no objection when his boss, played by polished veteran Louis Calhern, asks her to undertake the sensitive assignment. Devlin in turn becomes infuriated and feels betrayed by Alicia when, after she and Sebastian renew their acquaintance, the famous scientist proposes marriage to her. Each character feels betrayed by the other. Another imposing character — that of Madame Sebastian, the scientist's mother — enters the scene, providing yet another conflict within a conflict in a combustible romantic triangle.

Hitchcock pulled off a major coup when he secured the services of Russian stage great Michael Chekhov for *Spellbound,* marking the veteran performer's cinema debut. He secured a similar triumph with *Notorious* by introducing German actress Leopoldine Konstantin to the American cinema. *Notorious* was her one and only U.S. film. Konstantin reigned as one of the premier classical actresses of her day, receiving lavish praise for her European performances as Salome, Lady Macbeth and Gertrude. She is outstanding as Madame Anna Sebastian, Rains' character's mother, adding an important dimension to the film by her open clash with Alicia. While Alicia is torn by the idea of abandoning the man she loves (Devlin), to marry a man she openly does not love (Sebastian) as part of a professional assignment, Madame Sebastian expresses open displeasure and distrust toward her, believing her to be an unsuitable mate for her son.

The psychological dynamics between the characters played by Rains and Konstantin opens a dimension that Hitchcock would explore beyond *Notorious.* (Analyzing Hitchcock's work often reveals how skillfully he takes a successful story ploy and reworks it in the future.) Their on-screen relationship shows Hitchcock adding a mamma's boy dimension to *Notorious,* with the woman's obsessively critical dominance at work in the relationship. Hitchcock would successfully employ this same theme five years later in *Strangers on a Train,* as well as in his 1960 classic, *Psycho.*

Tiptoeing Around Censors

Joseph Breen, head of the powerful Breen Office, which assumed an aggressive censorship stance in sexual matters, was a force that Hitchcock (himself, like Breen, a practicing Roman Catholic) was compelled to deal with, and did effectively. Hitchcock's deft manner in finessing Breen was akin to a clever politician seeking difficult endorsements.

Screen kisses were tightly governed by the Breen Office. The rule was that a kiss could not last longer than three seconds. In a scene that begins on Alicia Huberman's balcony, Hitchcock stays within the letter of the law while manipulating in the manner of a veteran lawyer. Bergman and Grant electrified 1946 audiences with a kissing scene unlike any they had seen on film. At no point did a single kiss extend beyond the allowable three second limit, but the love scene began on the balcony overlooking Rio and ended inside the apartment.

The torrid duo would kiss for three seconds, after which Bergman and Grant would engage in breathy lover's conversation, followed by another kiss. Before the take, Bergman complained to Hitchcock that she felt awkward in her current position opposite Grant. The director shrewdly explained that, while the position might have felt awkward to the Swedish beauty, it was photographically perfect.

The wily Hitchcock remained ever aware that the always present camera and what fell within its majestic sweep ruled. Had Bergman been immersed for real in a breathy and passionate love scene with Grant she surely would have assumed a position of greater comfort. What governed a film scene was not whether the position felt awkward to a performer, but how it looked. As Hitchcock constantly reminded people, this was a movie and could be different from what would prevail in reality.

In addition to capturing two of the truly remarkable Hollywood glamour symbols, Grant and Bergman, in torrid bliss, the scene focused on the explosive sexual conflict governing their relationship. The former woman of easy virtue was seeking a permanent relationship, an idea that frightened the icy federal agent. At one point Alicia suggests that they cancel their dinner plans for the evening, a plausible ploy for a woman in the throes of romantic delight with the man she loves. "We have to eat," Devlin responds. "We can eat here," she explains. "I'll cook." Devlin has another ready response: "I thought you didn't like to cook."

The conversation becomes a cat and mouse game over whether or not they will stay in and eat or go out. The clever Hecht script spin is that the characters reverse traditional roles. In most cases it is the man who seeks to keep the woman at home, while she is wary. This time a hungering Alicia seeks to sustain the romantic flame of the moment by keeping the elusive Devlin within the confines of her apartment, while he provides reasons why they should go out. When Alicia explains that she does not like to cook, but that there is chicken in the ice box, he concerns himself with the need for plates, then with washing up afterwards. When Alicia meets every one of Devlin's dining concerns, he tries a new approach, explaining that if they are going to stay in, that he needs to telephone the hotel to see if there are any messages. This leads to some crisp and revealing dialogue:

ALICIA: Do I have to?
DEVLIN: I have to.
ALICIA: This is a very strange love affair.
DEVLIN: Why?
ALICIA: Maybe the fact that you don't love me.
DEVLIN: When I don't love you, I'll let you know.
ALICIA: You haven't said anything.
DEVLIN (kisses her): Actions speak louder than words.

Once again, what is left unsaid in screen dialogue can be as important as what is said. The elusive Devlin still finds it impossible to say the words "I love you" to a love hungry Alicia and kisses her while telling her, "Actions speak louder than words."

Psychoanalysis Without the Spellbound Albatross

Perhaps the major reason why the *Notorious* screenplay by Ben Hecht, carefully crafted with the assistance of Hitchcock, flows more smoothly than their earlier joint effort in *Spellbound* was that a major albatross was removed. In the throes of consultation with Dr. May Romm, producer David Selznick was eager to explore the fascinating realm of psychoanalysis on screen. Incorporating the act of psychoanalysis into a film as a major part of the action — while keeping the audience interested — is a difficult task, as Hitchcock had learned. In *Spellbound* the Hecht-Hitchcock team was saddled with the albatross of psychiatrist Dr. Petersen (Bergman) solving John Ballantine's (Peck) amnesia through psychoanalysis. Still, the abiding curiosity toward psychoanalysis was anything but dead within Hitchcock and Hecht following *Spellbound*. It remained alive, and could be explored in a less restrictive context in *Notorious*.

Spellbound represented a pivotal point for Hitchcock. Whereas his London phase and a good deal of his early American period emphasized his flair for utilizing surprise, action and device, *Spellbound* and *Notorious*, as back-to-back psychodramas, set a pattern that would be followed in some of Hitchcock's most enduring films which lay on a fertile horizon. This milestone had been preceded by other films in which the psychoanalytical element had been explored, including *Rebecca*, *Suspicion*, and the brilliant *Shadow of a Doubt*.

In *Notorious*, Grant's, Bergman's and Rains's characters all have great inner complexity. Their dramatic interplay provided ready-made opportunities for psychoanalysis, and audiences remained intensely focused on their every move and thought. When Madame Sebastian entered the scene, a figure outside the romantic sexual triangle but with a stranglehold on her devoted son, yet another dimension was added as she sought to draw him away from Alicia. Her warnings against involvement are followed by an "I told you so" cold fury when he learns he is married to an American agent.

MacGuffins and Roman Candles

Alfred Hitchcock would remain forever fused to his MacGuffins and Roman candles as well. The issue was one of proportion. As he matured as a filmmaker, the famous Hitchcock pyrotechnics would serve as interstitial excitement points, as lightning rods immersed in broad story processes about fascinating but often disturbed people immersed in conflict with other disturbed individuals, or those falling outside that realm who were merely caught up in the machinations of ruthless individuals and remorseless fates, victims such as those played by Farley Granger in *Strangers on a Train* and James Stewart in *Vertigo*.

The spectacular crane shot was Hitchcock's most memorable device in *Notorious*, along with the elements he included relating to the scene. Viewers follow the sweep of action as a grand party is in progress. It is reminiscent of what Hitchcock would do almost a decade later in *Rear Window*, with the voyeuristic long shot focused on James Stewart, himself playing the voyeur, peering into the windows of the adjacent apartment building and observing the activities of its occupants.

In *Notorious* the grand tease employed by Hitchcock involved the focus on the key Alicia was able to entice Sebastian into giving to her, at the behest of Devlin, who wrangled an invitation and watched as she ultimately walked toward the wine cellar. The key would hopefully unlock the mystery of what Sebastian was involved in, and so Devlin made his way to the wine cellar as well. At one point the important key, symbolic in the pursuit of unlocking the mystery of Nazi bomb exploration, drops to the floor. Alicia must retrieve it without arousing suspicion.

In *Spellbound* the letter written to Bergman by amnesiac Gregory Peck on the run fell to the floor when she was being interrogated by police officers, and was unknowingly kicked by a policeman as he was leaving. This is the "tight squeeze" device Hitchcock so effectively employed, which extended the drama as well.

This was the point in *Notorious* at which Hitchcock's spectacular MacGuffin surfaced. It certainly would not surface without another intervening Hitchcock touch. Hitchcock's trickery involved stretching out the drama, milking a scene of the last drop of suspense. When Alicia attempts to secure a bottle it drops to the floor and breaks. At that point Devlin discovers the sandy substance inside, Uranium 235.

There was no need to leave off with the breakage and the duo escaping when Hitchcock could extend the scene further. After all, as he noted, it was a love story, and with its triangular dimensions what could be more fitting than husband Sebastian surfacing as he looked for his wife?

Quick thinking agent Devlin decides to kiss Alicia and instruct her to back away, as if he were an old flame being rejected after one final effort. That was seen as a far more acceptable proposition than trying to explain about an interest in wine bottles. The scene cleverly ends with Devlin assuring Sebastian that he was rebuffed and he had nothing more to be concerned about. In actuality he had everything to be concerned about, but for an entirely different reason. His best laid scientific plans lay in imminent jeopardy.

Of Scenery and Vulnerability

Hitchcock shrewdly displays human vulnerability in dramatic settings by showing people in conflict against the backdrop of overpowering forces manifested for maximum scenic impact against large monuments. Hitchcock uses the magnificent Corcovado mountain setting and the awesome presence of the huge Christ the Redeemer statue which hovers as a permanent presence over Rio city folk below to reveal Alicia's vulnerability.

When Sebastian discovers that he is married to an American agent, his wily and icy mother, after initially rebuking him for not listening to her, hatches with her son what they consider the most effective plan under the thorny circumstances at hand. Should Sebastian's ruthless associates learn about what he is doing he will be executed, as was revealed earlier in the film when one member of the operation was promptly murdered under less serious circumstances. The decision is made to gradually poison Alicia. Her worsening illness would result in her eventually being confined to bed, after which she would expire without anyone knowing that she was a murder victim.

During the very period when Alicia falls victim to the plot she is devastated for another reason. The enigmatic Devlin, after having told his superior, Captain Paul Prescott (Louis Calhern), that he is "bored" by Rio de Janeiro, receives reassignment to Spain. The man she loves once more refuses to commit himself to her, dominated by his chilling fear of romantic permanency; Alicia meets him in a park, with Corcovado and Christ the Redeemer visible, forming a scenically intimidating backdrop. While Devlin notices that Alicia does not look well, he initially mistakenly attributes her wan look to a return to drink.

Devlin's frosty demeanor, along with her tragic plight and loss of a lover, crushes Alicia. Her vulnerability is made all the more visible against the huge backdrop of the famous mountain and statue. Human vulnerability set against imposing backdrops was used as a device by Hitchcock in numerous films. The criminal in *Blackmail*, one of the director's most important early films of his London phase, meets his death surrounded by artifacts and the imposing largesse of the British Museum. The Nazi spy played by Norman Lloyd plunges to his death from the Statue of Liberty, despite the valiant effort of Robert Cummings to save him, in *Saboteur*. As will be seen, the frustration of victim Farley Granger being pursued by psychopath Robert Walker is accented amid the imposing monuments of Washington, D.C. in *Strangers on a Train*, while *North by Northwest* captivated audiences and critics alike when pawn of fate Cary Grant fights for his life amid busts of America's famous presidents on Mount Rushmore.

While Agent Devlin could display frigidity and defy feelings propelling him toward the beautiful Alicia, the film's final scene reveals a man who has finally decided that he does love her and will even enter the enemy's lair to save her from death. Cary Grant has never mixed his traditional smoothness with devastating decisiveness in greater measure than in the memorable closing sequence of *Notorious*. He decides to rescue her by boldly walking into her bedroom and carrying her to what he hopes will be ultimate restoration of health and well-being.

Being only too painfully familiar with Devlin's past ambivalence, Alicia implores in a weak voice, "Don't ever leave me." For the first time he makes the kind of firm declaration of commitment that she has waited the entire length of their relationship to hear. "You'll never get rid of me again," Devlin emphatically declares. "I never tried to," she responds.

Alexander Sebastian, while remaining outwardly calm, is devastated by Devlin's boldness on observing him carrying the stricken Alicia downstairs. On the other hand, what can he do? The mere raising of his voice will arouse suspicion among the sinister Nazi group just one room away. When Devlin picks Alicia up and carries the extremely weak victim, who is near death, downstairs, Sebastian follows. He asks to ride along with them to the hospital. "No room, Sebastian," Devlin coldly replies, locking the door.

Once they drive off and Sebastian steps back inside, the voice of Eric Mathis (Ivan Triesault), the Nazi leader who has been suspicious of the scientist all long, delivers the final words of the film: "Alex, will you come in, please? I wish to talk to you."

Sebastian's fate is obviously sealed. Mathis has found him exceedingly expendable. As for Devlin and Alicia, as film historian Tim Dirks noted, we are unaware of whether the extremely fragile young woman survived the devastating poison attacks. While we do not know whether she lives or dies, since the film ends with a car heading for a hospital and Sebastian meeting his fate, it is clear about the direction audiences' thinking would proceed in deciding the film's end.

Notorious afforded the chance for Bergman to once more play a role in which she ends up with the man of her dreams. In *Spellbound*, it was the amnesiac she cured, played by Gregory Peck, while her complicated love interest in *Notorious*, played with just the right degree of enigmatic and frequently conflicted charm by Cary Grant, had declared that he would no longer leave her. Audiences would believe that she would recover and they would enjoy the same kind of successful culmination to their romance that characterized her relationship with Peck in *Spellbound*.

So, while Selznick labored mightily amid a turbulent constellation of conflict on the set of *Duel in the Sun*, Alfred Hitchcock, with assistance from Ben Hecht, crafted an enduring romantic suspense classic with *Notorious*.

During this period Selznick made periodic overtures to Hitchcock to extend their contract, which would expire after one more project. The project that would be selected was a novel set in England called *The Paradine Case*, based on an actual case and revolving around a tense murder trial in London's Old Bailey.

The best of intentions went wildly awry with *The Paradine Case*. To David O. Selznick the disappointment went beyond the flop that developed. Despite numerous efforts over a long period, Selznick's attempt to extend his relationship with Alfred Hitchcock failed. While Hitchcock secured his freedom and ultimately moved up the ladder of Hollywood creative status, the peripatetic, incredibly intense young producer of *Gone with the Wind* began aging fast as his career cataclysmically plummeted.

6

Hitchcock's Auteur Days
amid More Psychodrama

I still perspire when I think of the little man crawling underneath the carousel at the end of the picture because he actually did go under the machine. It couldn't be faked because it was a forward movement. — Alfred Hitchcock on the carousel scene that culminates *Strangers on a Train*

The year was 1951 and two old friends were taking a walk in the town that provided them with fame and fortune. The town was Hollywood and the strollers were David O. Selznick and his longstanding friend and sometime scenarist Ben Hecht. Selznick had aged before his time, his hair turning white and his paunch accentuating. He was in a troubled state of mind as he unburdened his thoughts to a trusted friend who would serve as a good listener.

Selznick was deeply saddened as he observed the familiar sights of the town where he had once ruled as a potentate, one of its few larger than life figures in an industry dominated by individuals striving for such lofty recognition. Selznick had become a giant as a young man, not much older than had the legendary boy genius at MGM, Irving Thalberg.

This was an industry feeling its initial pinch from that black and white box where you could watch films, news, and regular programming in your living room. Selznick's pessimism exceeded that of those simply worried about competition from the new industry of television, along with some other discomforting trends besetting the industry; he believed that the business he and Hecht loved was finished.

During that walk a deeply saddened Selznick compared Hollywood at midtwentieth century to Egypt's Sphinx and pyramids. At one time, Selznick noted, they comprised a part of a dominant and thriving civilization. Now they were stationed by themselves near Cairo, reminders of a great civilization that had long since passed from the scene. He paralleled the Sphinx and pyramids to what he saw as decaying studios and sound stages in then-present Hollywood.

The old studio system was gone, so was the star structure with which it flourished in tandem; and then there was television as well, which Selznick saw as a decidedly uprooting factor. Selznick believed that Hollywood's death resulted from the passage from the scene of individuals like himself—an innovative producer who believed in taking charge of his projects. Now that his breed had passed into the darkness of night, a breakdown had resulted that was destined to end in fatality for the industry he loved.

Selznick was correct about individuals in his category. Yes, the era of the producer as a dominating force had ended, but what he did not see was that evolution rather than extinction was in the Hollywood winds. The system had profoundly changed. Now the directors, many of whom had at one time been part of a mass production process as producers assigned projects to writers and directors with precious little time to spare before shooting commenced, were attaining increasing status in the industry power structure.

A relatively new term to Americans was coming increasingly into vogue. The term indicated status change in Hollywood. The French word auteur was one being used increasingly with respect to top ranked Hollywood directors. Directors were having their names appear before their films to symbolize the control they exerted over their product. The concept was widely accepted in European society but had numerous critics in Hollywood among the fraternity of screenwriters.

A lively discussion in the early seventies held at a Writers Guild of America meeting symbolized the differences of opinion between certain scenarists and directors. A young director whose films had made a decisive impact on the Hollywood scene asserted that "film is a director's medium." Veteran screenwriters jumped to the microphone to challenge the young director's assertion. Many other lively discussions debating the point occurred over the topic of the relative importance of directors and writers.

The saying "A picture is worth a thousand words" was never truer than when applied to film. Shrewd directors and screenwriters recognize that dialogue need not be emphasized in the cinema in the same way that it must on stage, where there is no camera to microscopically zero in on every expression and mannerism of a performer or establish ambience in such an intimate manner.

David Selznick's marriage to Irene was nearing its end. The irony was that Irene, daughter of the powerful head of MGM, would catapult from the shattered marriage into the limelight. Irene would free herself from the binding constraints of a union with a brilliant but highly problematic Hollywood genius. She would then promptly solidify herself as a dynamic presence in the same professional capacity whereby he had earned a niche, that of producing, but on the opposite coast three thousand miles away from Hollywood's cinema factories. Irene broke free and found herself soaring to the front ranks of stage producers in competitive post–World War II Broadway.

At the same pivotal point when Irene Mayer Selznick saw her marriage to mercurial David slipping away as he zealously guided the career of his discovery and love interest, Jennifer Jones, she retained sufficient feeling for him to recommend that he see Dr. May Romm. Irene became a patient of Romm's as well.

During these turbulent times Selznick had entered more of a managerial phase, disdaining film projects and concentrating on guiding the destinies of those under contract to him while making significant amounts of money by negotiating contracts with major studios for their services. His problem was hanging on to the money he made as his addictive gambling reached epidemic scales, along with his drinking and insomniac lifestyle.

Selznick finally found a project that interested him; and when he did, a series of circumstances occurred that unalterably changed Hitchcock's career. Just when the creative tension had once more increased and the strong-willed creative giants appeared ready for more lengthy jousting over another film project, Hitchcock found that he was alone and in command, and en route to establishing himself as a premier auteur, a rank he would never relinquish.

While Hitchcock enjoyed his independence in fashioning a brilliant success with *Notorious*, Selznick found himself immersed in trouble with the seemingly endless shooting of the film he hoped would stop all the talk about his achievement with *Gone with the Wind. Duel in the Sun* was meant to supplant his previous masterpiece, prompt conversation about the new Selznick magic, and propel his Pygmalion-like creation and love into the reigning ranks of superstardom.

During this period Hitchcock did some adroit fending off where his professional relationship with Selznick was concerned. Despite professional differences, Selznick was shrewd enough to recognize the benefits he had achieved artistically and remuneratively from his relationship with the director he lured from Britain to Hollywood. Hitchcock observed a tactical standoffishness when the subject of another contract was discussed. During this period observable changes occurred within Selznick that were being reported in the cinema community.

Hitchcock demonstrated signs of emerging independence from Selznick in two areas. He made trips back to his native England and began discussing a film partnership with Sidney Bernstein. On the home front, when Selznick would mention a new contract, Hitchcock would adopt increasingly more independent terms which would have undercut Selznick's producer's status.

Embarrassment surely resulted at one point when peripatetic Hollywood columnist Louella Parsons obtained a copy of one Hitchcock proposal. Parsons let Selznick's most prestigious international star, Ingrid Bergman, see it, reasoning that if the famous producer would grant such concessions to Hitchcock, perhaps she could achieve the same autonomy. The possibility of such a ripple effect through the Selznick ranks could not have set well with the former boy genius who produced *Gone with the Wind* before his fortieth birthday.

The Travails of *Duel in the Sun*

The film that provided Hitchcock with creative freedom, *Notorious*, resulted from Selznick's preoccupation with a project he hoped would accomplish the twofold purpose of erasing his inextricable link in public and professional minds with *Gone with the Wind* by crafting a new American cinema blockbuster while ultimately fulfilling his desire for success for the actress with whom he had fallen head over heels in love. Those who knew Selznick and his young contract player, Oklahoma born Jennifer Jones, cited her compliance as a reason for the producer's unflinching devotion to her career. An Ingrid Bergman might express her differences with Selznick or Hitchcock, but the youthful former Phyllis Eisley invested confidence in the legendary producer, content to let him totally guide her career.

Jones's confidence in Selznick's tutelage was understandable in view of his impressive track record. He had, after all, guided her to a Best Actress Oscar (as the youngest ever recipient) for *Song of Bernadette*, a role for which she had been plucked from the ranks of the unknowns. *Since You Went Away* also achieved notable success, with Selznick writing the screenplay as well as producing, albeit at an emotional cost to Jones, as she played heart-wrenching love scenes with the husband she had discarded Robert Walker, in favor of the producer.

Now the ever determined, eternally vigilant Selznick had his sights set on a masterpiece for the ages that would propel him into immortality along with the woman he would eventually marry. *Duel in the Sun* was adapted from a novel by Niven Busch, who had known Selznick from their boyhood days. While Busch adapted his novel to the screen, the story was gradually eviscerated as Selznick continued adding his own touches. Leonard Leff noted the trouble signs Busch observed within Selznick during that critical period of the producer's life and the impact that might have had on Hitchcock: "In the 1930s, Niven Busch recalled, Selznick had a rough attractiveness, an engaging snorting laugh, and a sense of humor; he turned 'heavy and bloated' in the 1940s, his jokes more cruel, at others' expense. Hitchcock apparently sensed the difference, perhaps even stalled in signing his contract for that reason."

All the same, Leff revealed, there remained a side of Selznick that was helpful to Hitchcock. Leff credited Selznick with assisting Hitchcock in the first stage of what eventuated in a masterpiece with *Notorious*. "Yet Selznick remained an extraordinary editor," Leff wrote. "He read the *Notorious* first draft, criticized the occasionally precipitous story turns or mediocre treatment of certain plot points, and scribbled double question marks and triple exclamation marks in the margins."

The Public Broadcasting System documentary dealing with the relationship between Hitchcock and Selznick focused on the element that those who knew Selznick attributed to his feverish devotion to *Duel in the Sun*. Beyond the aforementioned reasons, there was the fact that his erotic passion for Jennifer

Jones transformed Selznick, a man in his forties, into a young man in the first blush of love. A searing eroticism emerged on-screen in the relationship between Jones and fellow Selznick contract player Gregory Peck. The scenes were particularly daring at that juncture of cinema history considering the sturdy influence of Joseph Breen.

Sexual tension exploded on the screen in the relationship between cowboy Peck and half-caste Indian Jones. Peck's persona was a rarity in that the actor Selznick discovered was known throughout his career as a smooth nice guy who conquers effortlessly. His memorable breakthrough role in *Spellbound* found him as the same intelligent and sensitive man he would portray in his mature screen incarnation.

Duel in the Sun marked a career aberration for sophisticated nice guy Peck as he portrayed a merciless westerner who would just as soon shoot down an enemy as look at him. It was Charles Bickford, his on-screen rival for Jones's affection and the man Peck's villainous character ultimately gunned down, who ironically demonstrated the values and fundamental decency of the tall, dark-haired, engaging star who won the hearts of audiences.

As Selznick approached the project with a tenacious singleness of purpose, the perfectionism that had always dwelled within him reached new heights of unencumbered zeal. He began quarreling with director King Vidor, a respected veteran whose first major triumph, *Our Daily Bread*, came during the silent era. Selznick zealously rewrote scenes. Location filming in the hot Arizona desert sun resulted in tempers and budgetary expenditures concurrently rising like the mercury in the thermometer.

The frequent creative jousting matches between Selznick and Vidor reached a volcanic climax, at which point the veteran director announced he was quitting. In a manner replete with the kind of drama that could have been etched on screen, Selznick, actors, and crew members watched as King Vidor stalked angrily toward one of the limousines in service for the film's major personnel. Vidor stepped inside and closed the door. Selznick and entourage watched as the limousine made its way down the dusty road, stirring up a rising cloud in its wake as it headed to Tucson, where production personnel were staying. The rising dust symbolized a type of makeshift smoke reflective of a highly troubled project immersed in chaotic conflict.

When Victor Fleming walked off the similarly turbulent set of *Gone with the Wind* it was Selznick who took over the film's directorial reins. He did the same with *Duel in the Sun*. Once the shooting was completed, a massive project awaited Selznick as he presided over the editing process. An incredible 26 hours of film had been shot. It was ultimately reduced to a rough cut of 4 hours.

When a thoroughly exhausted Selznick finished the entire process, he hoped that the film would be greeted with the same acclaim as had *Gone with the Wind* upon its release. Instead he was lacerated by critics, and his hopes for large, impressed audiences also evaporated.

Selznick's film was denounced for what critics saw as excesses, particularly in the area where he had hoped to showcase Jennifer Jones. For using a sledge-hammer rather than subtle approach to the on-screen relationship between Jones and Peck, the producer was sharply criticized. Ensuing years have taken some of the edge off of the stinging criticism doled out in 1946. Gradually the film's length was whittled down to a little more than two hours.

While the film's spectacular color shots have been recently praised, critics continue to denounce *Duel in the Sun* for its bizarre ending, a desert shootout marked by love-hate implications in which Jones and Peck's characters alternately fire deadly shots at one another, then end up kissing passionately in each other's arms as they share their last moments of life together. For Selznick biographer David Thomson the producer's motivation behind such an ending and the project itself was crystal clear.

Selznick had interlinked his passions toward Jennifer Jones to his desire for another blockbuster on the level of *Gone with the Wind*. The movie's two most passionate scenes, both featuring Peck, involved Jones's raw sexuality: a rape scene and the film's frenzied conclusion in which their searing love-hate relationship results in the death of both characters. Selznick had been so concerned that the right level of sensuality be maintained that he had long discussions with film composer Dimitri Tiomkin to insure the proper mood. As David Thomson summarized, "He [Selznick] had made it [*Duel in the Sun*] Pearl's story [Jones's character].... *Duel in the Sun* is still precariously pitched between the awesome and the ridiculous. But time has not tamed it. David was crazy and in love. *Duel* is truer than all his love letters. He was mad about Jennifer, and the feeling will show forever."

The Giants' Final Project

The relationship between film giants Hitchcock and Selznick had commenced with *Rebecca*, which had received Best Film honors from the Academy, but their last collaboration was destined to end with a sour whimper rather than a ceremonial bang. Hitchcock began with soaring spirits for two reasons; he would be returning home to London, scene of his early triumphs, and the subject was one that intrigued the perpetual sharply honed dramatic instincts within him.

The Paradine Case was a courtroom drama that made Hitchcock harken back to his youth, when he fantasized about becoming a successful barrister arguing a case to a jury before a packed courtroom at London's famed Old Bailey. The film centered on the dilemma faced by Britain's most famous courtroom advocate as he finds himself falling madly in love with the woman he is defending for the crime of murdering her husband.

The film was based on a 1933 novel of the same title by Robert Hichens, formerly an associate of Oscar Wilde. According to Hitchcock historian Ken Mogg, "Hichens based the novel on two sensational murder cases. The first was that of Madame Fahmy, an attractive Frenchwoman who in 1923 was acquitted by a British jury after she'd shot and killed her husband, an Egyptian prince, at London's Savoy Hotel. At the trial, it was suggested that the prince had been intimate with his male secretary. The fact that Madame Fahmy herself seems to have been a woman of loose morals wasn't revealed to the jury—her famous advocate Edward Marshall Hall saw to that."

The other murder case to which Mogg alluded involved Florence Maybrick, a young American woman found guilty of poisoning her English husband in Liverpool in 1889. "The Maybricks lived comfortably at 'Battlecrease House,'" Mogg wrote. "But the husband seems to have had a violent disposition, probably the result of his chronic hypochondria. It's also likely that he discovered that his wife was having an affair with a man named Brierly. Mrs. Maybrick eventually went to prison for fifteen years."

The ponderous five hundred page novel that resulted centers on Ingrid Paradine, a beautiful but enigmatic Danish woman accused of poisoning her blind husband, Colonel Paradine, a ruthless war hero. Malcolm Keane, a middle-aged lawyer known for grandstanding before juries, takes her case, believing her to be innocent. Despite being happily married, the prominent courtroom lawyer becomes enraptured with his beautiful client and falls in love with her.

Keane ultimately learns that Ingrid Paradine has engaged in a liaison with her husband's manservant. He grows jealous, but his resolve increases to secure freedom for Mrs. Paradine by blaming the valet for the murder. The opportunistic defendant uses her attorney's affections toward her to enhance her defense. The case is ultimately referred to the wily and unctuous Judge Horfield. After perjured testimony wins Ingrid Paradine an acquittal, Keane finds his career in shambles and returns to Gay, his wife.

According to Leonard Leff, "*The Paradine Case* may have begun to fall apart with the hiring of the screenwriter." In the spring of 1946 Hitchcock convinced Selznick not only to hire Scottish physician-turned-playwright James Bridie, but to allow him to complete an unsupervised first draft. "Hitchcock remained blind to his [Bridie's] weaknesses," Leff revealed. "The director needed someone with a strong grasp of dramaturgy, which Selznick had formerly provided. Yet Bridie cared little about structure. Asked about illogical twists or slack motivation, the Scot would respond, 'What does it matter?'"

Demonstrating his desire to achieve an international blockbuster as well as universal attention, Selznick aimed high in seeking the services of Greta Garbo to play Mrs. Paradine. The Swedish beauty had been retired from the screen for the past five years following her last effort, *Two-Faced Woman*, a 1941 comedy flop directed by George Cukor in which Melvyn Douglas co-starred. Selznick was rebuffed, a harbinger of future casting problems that would plague the production. According to Hitchcock, Garbo turned the part down immediately because novelist Robert Hichens had described the woman he based his character on as "working in a barber's shop in Stockholm." Hitchcock related that the Swedish legend "was also infuriated at being offered the part of a murderess."

After being rejected by the top former Swedish leading lady of film, Selznick logically turned next to Sweden's current leading lady, Ingrid Bergman, though their relationship had, in the words of Leonard Leff, "become as knotty and sensitive as the Selznick-Hitchcock relationship." While Bergman had formerly called Selznick "my father" and "my second husband," the honeymoon had ended. According to Bergman's husband, Peter Lindstrom, the Swedish beauty "disliked Selznick for several reasons. He kept her out of work when she wanted to work. He wanted to prolong her contract against her will. He refused to let her appear on radio. When he sold her services to other studios, he never gave her an increase in salary, though even despite the wartime labor law, he could have found a way to give her more money. She had firmly decided not to make another contract with him."

Finally, buoyed by the prospect of launching a new star as well as bolstering his opportunities to do business in Italy, Selznick decided to sign Alida Valli to a contract. The actress was well known in her native Italy, and, after expressing satisfaction with the test he ordered, Selznick, despite Valli's poor English, was willing to offer her the lead. For a time his plans remained in abeyance due to the unfavorable publicity generated in Italy and elsewhere by the announcement that Bergman was leaving Selznick's employ, but the lure of Hollywood beckoned, and the dark-haired European beauty cast aside any reluctance and agreed to play Mrs. Paradine.

David Selznick's effort to obtain his first choice for the male lead of London barrister Keane was unsuccessful. He sought Laurence Olivier, reasoning that the great Shakespearean actor could provide the proper internalization for the role of an obsessive lawyer with conflicted emotions. Olivier was unavailable, and for a time Maurice Evans was considered. Despite the fact he looked like something less than the glamorized image of the emotionally torn attorney, Selznick reasoned that a wig and a good cameraman could work wonders, in addition to which Maddalena Paradine loves her valet Latour, not the man defending her in the Old Bailey.

As so frequently occurred with Selznick, his ultimate instinct was to go with an actor from his own client roster, Gregory Peck. One common point existed between Peck as the lead in *The Paradine Case* and *Spellbound*—in each instance he was younger than the character he would be playing. In *Spellbound* Peck's youthful naiveté blended into the aura of mystery-cum-psychodrama at the film's apex. His part in *The Paradine Case* provided no such positive opportunity. Despite graying his hair, Peck exuded the look of an idealistic young lawyer rather than the emotionally torn veteran of the London trial wars the script called for.

An attempt to develop a British accent also proved a problem. In an effort to adopt a suitable accent, Peck listened to speeches of British Prime Minister Anthony Eden, whose elegant Oxford tones provided the kind of mellifluous sounds befitting a smooth-talking veteran courtroom advocate. Despite making a valiant effort, the accent never seemed comfortable for Peck. As a result, he assumed the role of an Englishman while maintaining his normal American accent. This would be one of many points that critics would cite in attacking the film's credibility.

As for Hitchcock, he was not enamored of the choices of either Peck or Valli. In Peck's case he believed that the part should have gone to a Britisher, such as Ronald Colman or Olivier. As for Valli, Hitchcock stated that as Mrs. Paradine the Italian beauty "wasn't really what I wanted. She was too impassive and didn't know her English too well, which is a tremendous handicap to an actress."

A major casting blunder that would dominate critical opinion involved the pivotal role of Latour, the valet with whom Mrs. Paradine falls in love. Selznick's choice was disputed by Hitchcock, and circumstances corroborate the director's judgment. Selznick chose a handsome and dashing French leading man not that well known at the time to American audiences, Louis Jourdan.

Hitchcock told Charles Higham and Joel Greenberg that Selznick's casting of Jourdan was "the biggest casting mistake of all [in the film]." He called Jourdan a "pretty-pretty boy" and stated, "It [the role of Latour] should have been a man like Robert Newton, because the whole point about the lawyer falling in love with the murderess was to realize the degradation of falling for a woman who'd had as one of her lovers a manure-smelling groom."

The Jourdan casting embodied a tragic mistake on the part of Selznick, a talent promoter who doubtlessly saw in the young actor's finely chiseled good looks and dapper elegance the makings of an international superstar. While such an insight was accurate, the problem stemmed from the fact that casting Jourdan in that particular role was as disconcertingly off-base as casting Parisian boulevard habitué Maurice Chavelier as Jack the Ripper. In short, it was casting that, as Hitchcock accurately noted, defied credibility. The closest Jourdan could credibly come to fulfilling the expectations of the Latour role would be that of a gigolo, which he played convincingly in the 1964 release *The V.I.P.s*, as the man seeking to take Elizabeth Taylor away from husband Richard Burton.

Another casting choice that caused problems of a different dimension was Charles Laughton. "Negative acting is what I want most," Hitchcock said in 1947, "the ability to express words by doing nothing. That is the hardest thing on screen — to do nothing well — and that is what I demand." According to Leonard Leff, "The sluggish progress of *The Paradine Case* resulted in large part from problems with actors — none more so than Charles Laughton."

The role of Horfield, the judge presiding over the Paradine trial, called for a thoroughly unpleasant but clever man with elements of sadism and lechery in his character. It appeared to be the type of role that a brilliant character actor like Laughton could successfully play, but rather than perform the role of the complex jurist by emphasizing his subtlety, another approach was taken. "A Laughton picture is one long battle from start to finish — Laughton versus Laughton," Hitchcock ruminated. "He frets and strains and argues continuously with himself." Laughton achieved big laughs with his exaggerated facial expressions and gestures.

One casting decision that received Hitchcock's wholehearted approval was that of Ann Todd as the aristocratically polished wife of barrister Keane. The elegantly beautiful Todd had risen to international stardom opposite James Mason in the recently released *The Seventh Veil*. Selznick's signing her for the role of Peck's wife in *The Paradine Case* represented good timing, though it resulted in an unexpected problem. Todd looked and acted every bit the part of the supportive wife of a wealthy and professionally successful British barrister. The problem arose when Todd's natural fit into the part contrasted glaringly with Peck's, who uncomfortably appeared like a young American mid-level professional on the rise, despite the effort to make him look older and more mature with the addition of gray hair.

Selznick attempted to pull out all the stops to achieve a film classic, as he also cast venerable character performers Ethel Barrymore, Leo G. Carroll, and Charles Coburn. Barrymore, who played Laughton's wife, secured the film's only Academy Award nomination (for Best Supporting Actress). Carroll had performed twice before on the Selznick-Hitchcock team — in *Rebecca* and as the psychopathic killer who attempted to frame Gregory Peck in *Spellbound* — and would appear more than a decade later in *North by Northwest*.

The impressive cast of some of the brightest stars in the cinema constellation gave the impression on screen of pulling in disparate directions simultaneously. In such instances one immediately looks to the script for ways out of the morass, but the same problem plaguing *Duel in the Sun* was transported from the Arizona desert to London sound stages. In order to rescue a script and corresponding story from meandering dangerously, a resolute Selznick took charge.

The irony for Hitchcock was that this was the occasion when Selznick, hoping to sign the director to a new contract, provided him with the greatest amount of autonomy in all of the films on which they worked, with the notable exception of *Notorious*. Hitchcock bided his time and headed for the door at the first propitious opportunity, after he had completed his contractual obligation and provided Selznick with a very rough cut. It was done without the dramatic conflict of the parting of the ways with King Vidor on the set of *Duel in the Sun*, but every bit as decisively. Selznick's response was the same in each case as he attempted to pull the production together by constantly rewriting the script and taking charge of directing responsibilities.

The film was destined to sink or swim on the strength of the Old Bailey trial sequences. While bringing together such a talented array of screen presences would provide dramatic sparks, an anarchistic uncertainty prevailed in the critical scenes where the fate of Mrs. Paradine is being decided. The badly miscast Peck appears to be searching for motivation.

Negative acting had worked superbly in Peck's role as the sensitive and naive young doctor searching for his identity as an amnesiac in *Spellbound*, but in his role as barrister Anthony Keane a clear cut and determined demeanor needed to be established as he attempted in midstream to switch from an attorney seeking to demonstrate Mrs. Paradine's innocence to someone vindictively prosecuting his rival for his client's affections.

While criticisms were launched at Laughton's voracious scene chewing, he could not be faulted for one dilemma posed in the film, for which there was no logical answer. Laughton plays a hard-nosed, no-nonsense, experienced judge in command of his courtroom. When Keane becomes emotionally overwhelmed by circumstances as he realizes that Mrs. Paradine loves Latour, he switches from his role of defense counsel to vigilant prosecutor. During this period, with his fiery-eyed demeanor, he overwhelms Horfield's determination to maintain discipline. Horfield incredulously becomes Keane's supplicant as the aroused attorney demands procedural leeway and the judge repeatedly succumbs. Histrionics overwhelm proportion and reality, making it easy to see why a shrewd Hitchcock bailed out at the first opportunity once his contractual commitment had been completed.

While *The Paradine Case* nosedived at the box office and critics pointed out its numerous dramatic excesses and credulity problems, as time elapsed, harsh viewpoints apparently softened. As noted, Selznick assembled a brilliant ensemble of players who brought natural dynamism to the screen. The film was brilliantly photographed. Lee Garmes had been one of the cinematographers Selznick used on *Gone with the Wind*, though uncredited. Garmes was also cinematographer on Selznick's *Since You Went Away*. Recent viewers have sometimes been inclined to ignore the histrionics and lack of believability and observe instead an interesting, well mounted tableau on screen, dominated by fascinating personalities. *The Paradine Case* reveals that with a team as professional and creatively dynamic as Alfred Hitchcock and David Selznick, a sense of style can engage viewers despite a panoply of difficulties. Even what might be considered a bomb under other circumstances attains an entertaining level of style in such talented hands. Hitchcock and Selznick were incapable of doing anything conventional, so that even when the overall product was off form a gloss and style remain.

When Hitchcock departed from London after completing his obligation on *The Paradine Case* the partnership with Selznick ended. The wily Hitchcock recognized that their careers were headed in different directions. Though Hitchcock had been born in the final year of the nineteenth century and Selznick in 1902, Hitchcock was seen as a filmmaker in his prime while the younger producer was someone whose productive career was behind him.

The perception of Selznick in contrast with Hitchcock stemmed only in part from the toll of the producer's physical and emotional problems. There was another force at work: the changing dynamic of the film industry. In the film industry emerging following World War II the director assumed increasing importance. The prestigious French magazine *Cahiers du Cinema* saluted the auteur, a high-powered director whose name appeared above a film's title. Hitchcock assiduously involved himself in every aspect of a script's development. The David Selznick who took the walk in Hollywood in 1951 with his old friend and frequent working colleague Ben Hecht failed to observe the passing of the guard, and instead, seeing his own career sinking, issued the gloomy pronouncement that Hollywood's cinema temples stood as ruins, reminders of a bygone period.

Following the failure of *The Paradine Case* Selznick would produce one more blockbuster, the internationally acclaimed *The Third Man*, but as the American coproducer working with Britain's reigning production giant, Alexander Korda. The film was shot on location in Vienna while interiors were filmed at Sheperton Studios outside London. When Selznick broke with Hitchcock, the only other director in England who held comparable high-level international status was Carol Reed. While Selznick provided a steady flow of his memos from America, Reed was able to assume creative control and the brilliant 1949 film noir classic was steered to completion in his capable hands.

It is fortunate that some of the points for which Selznick lobbied were not implemented. Two of his contract players, Joseph Cotten and Alida Valli, assumed the leading male and female roles. The Graham Greene script depicted Holly Martins (Cotten) as a bungling American hack western writer out of his depth in racket-torn post-war Vienna as he attempted to resolve the alleged murder of his old friend, played by Orson Welles. Selznick at one point protested that Greene's depiction of Martins as a bungling innocent could be seen and interpreted as anti–American, jeopardizing the film's U.S. box office. Martins comes across as someone indeed out of his depth, but a foreigner of his station, irrespective of national identity, would be at the same disadvantage in the labyrinthian Vienna underworld.

The complaint leveled by Selznick concerning his Italian discovery Alida Valli stemmed from his concern for style. He wanted the glamorous Italian to be showcased in more elegant attire befitting her international star status. Reed kept her attire simple, which in no way detracted from her natural beauty. The director's decision to dress Valli simply was consistent with the location and period. The Greene script notes the impact on rationing when Valli, cast as comedy actress Anna Schmidt, while meeting Martins backstage following a performance, expresses delight when he declines an offer of a drink. She explains that she can sell the full bottle of whisky with which she had been gifted by a fan. Schmidt cuts their meeting short by explaining that she is expected to turn the lights off promptly following performances.

Guy Hamilton, who would later gain fame as a director of some of Sean Connery's major James Bond hits, including *Goldfinger*, was beginning his career as an assistant director on the film. Hamilton cited another Selznick complaint that was fortunately not addressed. When Orson Welles was considered for the role of the enigmatic racketeer Harry Lime, presumed dead until he appears in the last third of the film, Selznick was not pleased. "Selznick thought that Orson Welles's name would prove to be a disaster in places like the American Midwest," Hamilton explained. Yet Welles captivated audiences with his performance.

Welles would harbor one major regret from his otherwise successful role in *The Third Man*. Korda gave him a salary option: a flat fee arrangement or a lesser amount and a percentage. Welles chose the former and deeply regretted it. "The film was a success in America but in Europe it was like the *Sound of Music*," Welles lamented. "I could have made a fortune."

Selznick produced two more films following *The Third Man*, neither of which succeeded. The 1950 British release *The Wild Heart* was co-financed by Korda and starred Selznick's wife Jennifer Jones. Seven years later an adaptation of Ernest Hemingway's *A Farewell to Arms*, which had been previously adapted in 1932 as a version starring Gary Cooper and Helen Hayes, appeared, with Jones starring opposite Rock Hudson. The film's final scene represented a symbolic goodbye to giant Selznick's screen career, as a forlorn Lt. Henry (Hudson), following the death of Catharine Barkley (Jones), copes with his sad loss by walking alone down the street of a small Italian town.

As for Hitchcock, his career would regain earlier firepower as he revisited an area of success that he had traversed with Selznick, that of exploring psychological roots. He would tap the roots of madness with two creative endeavors that would not be fully appreciated by the film community until later.

Exploring Madness Again

Spellbound had been a rousing international success, and it focused on a subject that inspired Hitchcock's creativity, the psychology of madness. Now on his own, the captain of his own cinematic ship, Hitchcock would be able to explore madness as a creative filmmaker, unfettered by the restraints Selznick had imposed on *Spellbound* to achieve verisimilitude. Hitchcock, free as the proverbial bird, could explore madness on his own creative terms.

When *Rope* was shown recently on American Movie Classics it was introduced by cerebral blonde beauty Sharon Stone, who revealed that the 1948 Hitchcock film was her personal favorite. It was understandable why someone like Stone, who blends intellectual prowess with performer's creativity, would find the film fascinating. *Rope* sailed over many heads when it initially appeared and would ultimately gain praise and respect in the film community over the passage of time, in the manner of two later Hitchcock efforts, *Strangers on a Train* and *Vertigo*.

Rope, loosely based on the 1924 Leopold-Loeb thrill killing of Bobby Franks, features two college students with superiority complexes that match their undiminished ruthlessness in the manner of the aforementioned Chicago University true-life murderers. A thinly disguised version of the Leopold-Loeb case would be brought to the screen in 1959 by director Richard Fleischer as *Compulsion*, an adaptation of the novel by Meyer Levin, who had been a Chicago University student at the time of the tragedy. Levin knew perpetrators Nathan Leopold and Richard Loeb and covered the tragedy for the school paper.

The 1959 film, in which Dean Stockwell and Bradford Dillman starred as the young killers, focused strongly on the issue of crime and punishment, with Orson Welles playing with consummate fidelity the lawyer who defended Leopold and Loeb, famed Chicagoan Clarence Darrow. The issue of whether or not America should maintain the death penalty was key to the film's climactic scene. It was a cinematic depiction of one of the most famous summations in criminal law annals, with Darrow arguing to spare the lives of Leopold and Loeb.

The thematic distinction between Hitchcock's 1948 film and the Fleischer drama eleven years later could well have stemmed from the priorities of the respective periods. The death penalty was a burning issue in the late fifties, a period when Caryl Chessman, California's "red light bandit," who would spend twelve years on death row before his 1960 execution, became a national celebrity. He chronicled his earlier life of crime and detailed his death row period in a gripping biography he smuggled out of San Quentin Prison, which became an immediate bestseller, *Cell 22455 Death Row.*

Rope reflected the compelling moral issues of the recent post–World War II period. The war had a profound impact on Hitchcock, who, as noted earlier, felt helpless and was saddened by the fact that as his countrymen and family members battled for survival against Hitler's mighty air force, the Luftwaffe, in the Battle of Britain, he remained an ocean away in America.

A supreme irony stems from the source of a great intellectual influence on the sinister Leopold-Loeb team circa 1924. Both of them were Jewish, and a formative influence for them at that juncture was the controversial German philosopher Friedrich Nietzsche. Convinced of their superior intellects, Leopold and Loeb were fascinated by Nietzsche's beliefs concerning the nurturing of supermen within society. Adolf Hitler also developed a similar fascination, and in so doing linked Nietzsche's superman beliefs to those of Plato's Republic, applying the thinking ruthlessly in the anticipated pursuit of eliminating those the German dictator believed "unfit" to live in the kind of society led by a "super race" of Germans. Jews were singled out as Holocaust victims, along with Slavs, Gypsies, homosexuals and the mentally challenged.

While Richard Fleischer's *Compulsion* focused on the issue of the death penalty, Hitchcock in *Rope* focused on madness from the standpoint of genius-level intellects embracing nihilistic superiority. Hume Cronyn, the Canadian character actor who made his film debut as the next door neighbor to the Newton family in Hitchcock's *Shadow of a Doubt*, adapted the film from a Patrick Hamilton stage play.

In *Doubt*, Joseph Cotten's character of Charles Oakley is filled with venomous rage toward rich widows in particular and society in general. In a tense barroom conversation with his niece who had idolized him, Oakley mocks her idealism and faith in humanity, imploring her to face what he sees as reality. He refers to civilization as a "pig sty."

The brilliant and amoral young college students in *Rope* mock society as being woefully deficient when compared to their self-perceived stratospheric intellectuality. They engage in a thrill killing of a vulnerable fellow student and then orchestrate a ritual to tease presumably vulnerable human beings they see as distinctly beneath their level.

Once more Hitchcock would walk on the daring side regarding the tough morality code established by Joseph Breen. Homosexuality would be approached. In *Rope*, as in the case of the real Leopold and Loeb, the perpetrators were lovers. The attachment was there to be discerned by the alert viewer through the subtle nuances emerging from the tight bond they forged in the film.

The two young actors chosen for the parts would gain prominence in the film noir world by starring in two of the most daringly original presentations of the genre, with one of the future films being directed by Hitchcock. The director chose John Dall for the role of the controlling partner Brandon Shaw. A New York native, Dall attracted notice on Broadway in *Dear Ruth* and was brought to Hollywood on the strength of his attention-garnering effort.

As with many promising young cinema performers, Dall secured seasoning at the famous Pasadena Playhouse. He then scored a breakthrough while still in his twenties by garnering a Best Supporting Actor Oscar nomination playing a young Welsh coal miner in *The Corn Is Green*. He played the alter ego of the Welsh playwright Emlyn Williams, whose work was being adapted to the screen.

For Dall, whose early good fortune went unsustained, with him ultimately dying of a heart attack in 1970 at the age of 52, the aforementioned *The Corn Is Green* and *Rope* would serve as hallmarks of his career, but they are not the films that have caused his reputation to rise in the last few years. Dall's recent popularity stems from *Gun Crazy*, a film that has been called one of the greatest low budget movies in screen history. It has revived interest in Dall better than thirty years after his death.

Director Joseph Lewis has recently been saluted for his low budget craftsmanship on the film that starred Dall with sexy British blonde actress Peggy Cummins in 1949, one year after the release of *Rope*. The film was said to be a loose adaptation of the activities of Depression-era bank robbers Clyde Barrow and Bonnie Parker.

In *Gun Crazy* Dall's character, Bart Tare, is poles apart psychologically from his role in *Rope* as a crime-instigating sociopath with a superiority complex. Peggy Cummins joins the ranks of the great *femmes fatale* as a seductive young woman, Annie Laurie Starr, who shares Tare's passion for guns. Their motivations are markedly different, however, as Tare approaches guns from an aesthetic standpoint, enjoying the feats he can achieve for their own sake, having drifted into the fascination during a lonely youth. Starr, on the other hand, realizes that firearm expertise can achieve a fortune if exploited in a particular fashion.

The young, introverted Tare falls helplessly in love with the shrewdly controlling Starr, who propels him into a spiraling world of crime. *Gun Crazy* provides one of the more original seduction scenes in film. Tare and Starr meet in a shooting competition in which her sensuous expressions and body language achieve their desired effect. While Tare wins the battle — namely, the shooting competition — Starr prevails in the larger psychological war. She ultimately convinces him to enter the world of crime with her, as holdup artists, a brief career that ends with their destruction.

Granger as "The Young and Vulnerable"

Farley Granger, who played the role of Philip Morgan, John Dall's vulnerable follower in *Rope*, later in his career appeared as a regular on the popular television soap opera *One Life to Live*. His meteoric rise to stardom as a young performer is worthy of a soap opera title of its own, a spin-off of the long running *The Young and the Restless*, which, in Farley Granger's case, could be called *The Young and the Vulnerable*.

Alfred Hitchcock concluded that Granger might be just the performer he was seeking when he observed him in a sneak preview of *They Live by Night*, the film that provided him with the role of his life. Granger catapulted to stardom in his early twenties. Born in 1925, Granger was noticed in a Los Angeles little theater production by a talent scout. He was promptly signed by Samuel Goldwyn and received plaudits for playing a Russian youth in Lewis Milestone's 1943 film *The North Star*, starring Anne Baxter and Dana Andrews. After war service, the slender, dark-haired Granger, who exuded a look of brooding, vulnerable youth, received a career break at RKO when director Nicholas Ray, "the laureate of night," cast him opposite another image of vulnerable youth, Goldwyn contractee Cathy O'Donnell, in *They Live by Night*. In the film, Granger becomes a pawn of fate, as does equally vulnerable Cathy O'Donnell, after they meet, fall in love, and marry.

By signing Granger for *Rope*, Hitchcock may have been a factor in helping propel *They Live by Night* to the level of recognition it deserved. RKO head Dore Schary was almost certainly influenced by a British connection to release Nicholas Ray's haunting film after it had gathered dust in the studio vaults for one year. The film was released in Britain, with successful results, while Hitchcock provided exposure for the noir drama's male star Granger with the debut of *Rope* in

1948. The chain of circumstances continued, this time to Hitchcock's future benefit. Hitchcock tapped proven vulnerable leading male victim Granger for *Strangers on a Train*.

In the world of Hitchcock it was wise to establish a casting roadmap to determine what the Master was thinking. Once he found a player who fit a particular type, and the dramatic theme being approached was utilized again, that same individual could be used as well. Hitchcock found a way to tailor the natural talent of America's "Mr. Nice Guy" and "Man Next Door" James Stewart for multiple projects. A homespun suburban Pennsylvanian, albeit with an engineering degree from Ivy League Princeton University, Stewart won the prestigious New York Film Critics Circle honor for Best Actor as an idealistic young senator bucking a corrupt political machine led by Jim Taylor (Edward Arnold), in Frank Capra's 1939 blockbuster, *Mr. Smith Goes to Washington*. One year later he secured the only Oscar of his lengthy career in the Best Actor category for the 1940 George Cukor comedy *The Philadelphia Story*, playing a likable reporter opposite Katharine Hepburn and Cary Grant. In 1946 he played an idealistic banker who saves a small rural Pennsylvania town, very much like his own hometown of Indiana, Pennsylvania, from the greedy clutches of Mr. Potter (Lionel Barrymore) in *It's a Wonderful Life*.

Alfred Hitchcock found the perfect vehicle for the cinema's "nice guy neighbor" in a story built around two ruthless murderers. *Rope* was the first time Hitchcock called on Stewart's services. The two screen legends also teamed up on three of Hitchcock's most brilliant creative efforts, *Rear Window*, *The Man Who Knew Too Much* and *Vertigo*.

The strategic value of casting likable Stewart as Professor Rupert Cadell in a role far removed from the Capra-esque traditional American values films is the sharp dramatic contrast to be drawn between Stewart and the partnership of John Dall and Farley Granger. Hitchcock had Stewart gray his hair in *Rope* to contrast with the youthful killers he had impressed with his intellect as their college professor. It was from Cadell that they heard lectures on Nietzsche's philosophy. While Cadell was delivering lectures endowing students with intellectual grist, Shaw and follower Morgan put into practice some of the most remorseless elements of the German philosopher's teachings by engaging in a thrill killing of fellow student Kenneth Lawrence, played by Douglas Dick, whom they considered to be pathetically expendable.

Hitchcock put the principle of making the camera the star and revealing element in the first scene of the 1951 film noir classic, *Strangers on a Train*. Two men with luggage are shown entering a train station en route to a train, on which they will meet for the first time. The two shots of the film's main characters reveals an enormous contrast between them.

Robert Walker as Bruno Antony wears flashy sporting attire and moves with an energetic strut. Farley Granger as Guy Haines, while equally youthful and lithe (he is a top athlete), sports attire and a demeanor markedly different from that of the man he will soon meet, and shortly regret having met. Haines's attire is modest and unassuming. The same would have to be said of his walk, which is one of purposeful nonchalance, the walk of someone in no particular hurry and in no pursuit of a stellar destiny.

During a critical period in 1950, when Hitchcock was mulling over his next project, the master of mystery was enduring a fate akin to a ballplayer in a slump. Hitchcock was looking for a hit. The director's last four films had met with box office ennui. The first and last of the string, *The Paradine Case* and *Stage Fright*, had been shot in England, while *Rope* and *Under Capricorn* completed the quartet.

Seeking to end the slump and secure a success, Hitchcock was understandably intrigued by Patricia Highsmith's novel, *Strangers on a Train*. As Donald Spoto commented, "The most reflective passages of Highsmith's novel could have been taken from a Hitchcock diary (had there been one)." Highsmith proved to be a kindred creative spirit with Hitchcock in exploring that gold mine of the duality of nature, the world of contrasts: "Nothing could be without its opposite that was bound up with it.... Each was what the other had not chosen to be, the cast-off self, what he thought he hated but perhaps in reality loved ... there was that duality permeating nature.... Two people in each person. There's also a person exactly the opposite of you, like the unseen part of you, somewhere in the world, and he waits in ambush."

This was familiar language for Hitchcock. He had his agent negotiate in secret for the rights to the novel. By keeping his identity hidden, Hitchcock was able to purchase the rights for $7,500, which made him happy and displeased Patricia Highsmith. He then completed a treatment with Whitfield Cook, who had assisted him on dialogue for *Stage Fright*. The initial response after completing the treatment might well have prompted Hitchcock to wonder if his slump was continuing. "I remember when I was working on *Strangers on a Train*," Hitchcock recollected. "I couldn't find anyone to work on it with me. They all felt my first draft was so flat and factual that they couldn't see one iota of quality in it. Yet the whole film was there visually."

Chandler Returns to the Scene

While noir and mystery master Raymond Chandler, so pervasive a fixture on the Hollywood landscape during the forties and early fifties, would eventually become involved in the project, Hitchcock initially submitted his treatment to Chandler's forerunner in the hard-boiled detective school, Dashiell Hammett. Again Hitchcock may have wondered if destiny was against him, as the Hammett prospect immediately fell through. According to Donald Spoto, "[T]he meetings with Hammett were unaccountably sabotaged, apparently through nothing more mysterious than a secretary's carelessness."

After the Hammett debacle, Raymond Chandler entered the scene when

Finlay McDermid, story editor at Warner Brothers, welcomed him to the fold at a salary of $2,500 a week. Hitchcock and Chandler held the mutual admiration and abiding curiosity toward one another that frequently surrounded creative genius. Each was an acknowledged virtuoso of suspenseful mystery. Although born in Chicago, Chandler, like Hitchcock, spent his formative years in London. From all evidence they were at the outset delighted to work with each other. In the beginning their collaboration revealed greater collegiality and promise than Chandler's earlier stormy relationship with Billy Wilder on *Double Indemnity* at Paramount. Eventually, despite their differences, the team of Wilder and Chandler finished their joint effort, while Hitchcock and the great detective novelist did not.

By the time that Chandler had been signed to a contract by Warner Brothers and begun working on the project, Hitchcock and treatment co-author Cook had already made some important changes from the Highsmith book. Whereas the Guy Haines character in the novel is a rising young architect, he becomes a tennis player in the film. The change reflects Hitchcock's constant preoccupation with the camera. Tennis denotes action, providing Hitchcock with the opportunity to film cinematic sequences of briskly paced action on a tennis court.

Hitchcock filmed scenes of Davis Cup match play between the United States and Australia at Forest Hills, New York. The match involving Haines, which forms a dramatic high point of the picture, was filmed in California in 97 degree temperatures. Tennis pro Jack Cushingham coached Granger on technique as well as playing the part of his opponent in the film. Hitchcock endured the discomfort without once removing his jacket.

Another fundamental departure from the Highsmith novel involved another major story concern for Hitchcock, that of duality, contrasting elements. Whereas the novel presents activity spread throughout the country, the film focuses on the nation's capital, Washington, D.C., with Forest Hills another significant location, along with the small Pennsylvania town of Guy Haines's roots. In addition to changing the name of the psychotic killer played by Robert Walker from Charles Bruno to Bruno Antony, the father of the woman Haines hopes to marry after divorcing his faithless wife is a prominent United States Senator rather than a millionaire, as he is in the novel.

The changes underscore duality and contrast in several respects. Bruno Antony represents anarchy while living in an Arlington mansion with his parents, as somber and dark as it is vast. Washington as the seat of the U.S. Congress, as well as the presidency, represents the effort to establish order in society. Distinguished British character actor Leo G. Carroll as Senator Morton is the proper antidote to Walker's cunning but reckless, charming but sociopathic Bruno Antony.

Forest Hills, along with the world of competitive amateur tennis, represents the monied social set into which Guy Haines seeks to enter, and where his fiancée Ann Morton, played by Ruth Roman, is comfortably ensconced as the daughter of a prominent senator. Antony demonstrates his familiarity with that world by engaging in easy cocktail banter with the Forest Hills set, infuriating Haines, an uncomfortable outsider seeking to adjust to a new life.

The small Pennsylvania town where Haines was born and raised, Metcalf, conceivably a Santa Rosa of the East, represents a dark cloud to the socially ambitious young tennis player, since his wife, who initially sought a divorce after shamelessly philandering, has second thoughts as she observes him climbing the Washington social ladder. Another contrast is represented in the difference between Washington's vastness and importance and the small town roots from which Haines is seeking to escape.

Chandler detested working in a studio atmosphere, doubtlessly reflecting back to his stormy relationship with Billy Wilder when they co-scripted *Double Indemnity*, and had moved from Hollywood to the quiet and scenic San Diego suburb of La Jolla. Chandler's contract with Warner Brothers allowed him to work at home, so Hitchcock traveled to the writer's residence, being transported by limousine. Despite their differences, Chandler credited Hitchcock with arguing pleasantly. Chandler expressed his hatred for "these god-awful jabber sessions which seem to be an inevitable though painful part of the picture business."

While disdaining studio work, Chandler soon began to resent what he saw as intrusions into his domesticity, becoming disagreeable and sarcastic. One day, while waiting at his front door for Hitchcock to emerge from his limousine, Chandler commented acidly to his secretary, "Look at that fat bastard trying to get out of his car!" The secretary expressed concern that the director might hear the disparaging remark. "What do I care?" Chandler replied.

Chandler and Plausibility

Despite difficulties, Chandler completed a first treatment in which he transformed an introspective novel into a suitable film vehicle. According to Chandler biographer Frank MacShane, the detective author changed the story in a fundamental way by tackling what he deemed to be a major issue, plausibility. He did not feel the audience would believe that Guy would murder Bruno's father.

The Highsmith novel moves from one phase, where Bruno successfully carries out the murder of Guy's wife, to another, in which Guy is pressured by threat of blackmail to reciprocate by killing Bruno's father. The character of the fundamentally decent Guy is maintained, as well as a sense of plausibility. In the Chandler version Guy only pretends for Bruno's sake that he will carry out the prospective "bargain" conceived by the psychotic. In reality he is stringing Bruno along while planning instead to visit the Antony estate to tell Bruno's father that his son needs medical attention.

The Hitchcock-Chandler relationship suffered from two brilliant creative minds looking at a story from differing perspectives, Chandler's as a detective writer striving for verisimilitude and logical expression, and Hitchcock's as a director seeking to merge fast-paced action with innovative ways of putting an all-revealing camera to the best possible use. As Hitchcock later put it, "Our collaboration was not very happy. After a while I had to give up working with him. Sometimes when we were trying to get the idea for a scene, I would offer him a suggestion. Instead of giving it some thought, he would remark to me, very discontentedly, 'If you can go it alone, why the hell do you need me?' He refused to work with me as director."

Chandler's discontent stemmed from the fact that Hitchcock, unlike some directors who delegated sole script responsibility or afforded virtual autonomy to writers, sought close collaboration with scenarists, delivering steady input into finished shooting scripts. His organized storyboard concept envisioned a film as a series of scenes consisting of sharply focused cinematic images blending with character action and story development.

Shadow of a Doubt would culminate in a train scene, *Saboteur* would feature a nail-biting scene atop the Statue of Liberty, and *Strangers on a Train* featured a grand climax involving a runaway merry-go-round at an amusement park. With the survival of the two main characters hanging in the balance, Hitchcock worked out his story's visual elements well in advance and incorporated them into the script. Chandler regarded such important considerations in the eyes of the director as intrusions strait-jacketing his creative flow. It was a case of two strong wills embracing varying theories being ultimately unable to creatively coalesce their fecund talents.

Doubles Upon Doubles,
Contrasts Upon Contrasts

The Hitchcock propensity for developing the theme of the duality of nature, manifestly embodied in *Shadow of a Doubt*, was again revealed in *Strangers on a Train* as doubles compounded upon doubles and contrasts upon contrasts were unleashed. The director who focused our attention by making us wonder when he would make his sole appearance on camera provoked our imaginations and insights by challenging us to unravel the patterns of doubles and pairs. "Isn't it a fascinating design?" Hitchcock asked proudly. "You could study it forever."

After having cited the basic doubles elements used to dramatic effect in *Shadow of a Doubt*, it would be equally instructive to use the same approach with *Strangers on a Train*:

1) Good vs. evil — In *Shadow of a Doubt* an uncle and niece, both named Charlie, were so much alike in a psychical context that they eerily knew each other's thoughts; on the other hand, they exemplified great contrasts

in that the uncle was a serial killer of wealthy widows and represented the darkness of society, wherein his niece was an optimist typifying the decent side of human existence. Farley Granger and Robert Walker as Guy Haines and Bruno Antony in *Strangers on a Train* have certain outward similarities which contrast with their sweeping internal differences. Antony is a glib, pompous showoff and unashamedly amoral. Haines's shy awkwardness is the starting point of his troubles with Antony due to his failure to brush him off in the manner that a more assertive man would have.

2) The social equation — Walker and Granger's characters are both part of the District of Columbia social scene, with the cocky Antony having been born into great wealth and more than willing to crash any social gathering he wishes to attend, while Haines is the outsider from a small Pennsylvania town attempting to move up the social ladder. When Antony shows up at a party hosted by Senator Morton and makes small talk at Forest Hills with Anne Morton and her sister, among others, Granger is apprehensive for two reasons: he fears exposure by Antony for a murder the psychopath is convinced he committed for Haines and with his approval, Antony's madness, coupled with his explanation that he knows Haines is embarrassing and socially damaging to the young climber.

3) Two sisters — Ruth Roman as Anne Morton has a sister (Barbara) who speaks with decisive candor about her distrust and dislike of Haines's wife. Playing the role of Barbara, with just the right dash of panache, is Hitchcock's daughter Patricia. Was there nepotism involved? The story behind her casting represents another significant double within the initial double of her onscreen sister status.

4) Two young women with eyeglasses — Patricia Hitchcock, who had previous acting experience on the Broadway stage, found out about the role of Barbara Morton not from the film's director, who happened to be her father, but her agent. She was informed that there was a juicy role in her father's upcoming film. Hitchcock interviewed her as he would any other actress, did a screen test, and concluded that she might be right for the role. As Donald Spoto pointed out, "She was more than right, as it turned out: she provided the perfect semi-comic counterpoint to the studied seriousness of the other players." An important element of Patricia Hitchcock's role was her physical similarity to Laura Elliot, who played the role of Miriam, the non-obliging wife of Guy Haines. They both wore eyeglasses, leading to yet another double within a double.

5) Two murder victims with eyeglasses — After Antony has carried out what he sees as his part of the bargain in a binding double murder contract with Haines, strangling Miriam outside the tunnel of love at an amusement park, he stares into Barbara Morton's eyes while carrying out an

experiment on strangling with a Washington matron at the party hosted by the Senator. As he places his fingers around the older woman's neck, Antony observes Barbara standing nearby. Her physical similarity to Miriam (Laura Elliot), accented by her glasses, prompts him to symbolically strangle Guy Haines's wife a second time as he tightens his grip and almost strangles another victim, this time by proxy, before he is pulled off and order is restored.

6) Two boyfriends of victim — When Antony eerily follows murder-victim-to-be Miriam Haines in the amusement park, she is with two boyfriends. A determined flirt, Miriam makes periodic eye contact with Antony through which she encourages his attention. The eeriness of the scene stems from the cross purposes at work. Already receiving the attention of two local male escorts, Miriam is pleased by further attention from a well dressed, well built, handsome stranger following her. The coldly calculating manner in which the prospective killer stalks his prey is reminiscent of a lithe tiger anticipating an impending jungle kill. When Elliot leaves her two male escorts, Antony deceptively makes it appear that he is ready to kiss her, when instead he strangles her.

7) Two women discussing murder technique — Hitchcock has taken a page from the relationship between the neighbors played by Henry Travers and Hume Cronyn in *Shadow of a Doubt* by having two older women in *Strangers on a Train* discuss theoretical ways of committing the perfect murder. Bruno Antony delights in joining the discussion and, as earlier mentioned, conducts an experiment with one woman, in which she is almost strangled when he stares fixedly at Barbara Morton and mistakes her for Miriam, seeking to kill Guy Haines's wife a second time.

8) Two influential fathers — Two important men, who live near one another in Washington but do not know each other, are important figures in the drama. They make their opinions, backed by much experience, known as they represent different sides in the story. A concerned Leo G. Carroll as Senator Morton provides Guy Haines with advice on how to deal with the tragedy of his wife's murder and the ongoing difficulties with Antony. As Anne Morton's devoted father, the senator realizes only too well the political repercussions from which he could suffer if the murder investigation of the wife of his prospective son-in-law develops into a full blown scandal. The senator is also concerned about the overall well-being of his daughter. As for Jonathan Hale, in the role of Bruno Antony's father, an open clash has developed in which he recognizes the importance of his unbalanced son receiving immediate medical attention. Mrs. Antony, played by Marion Lorne, is a doting mother who refuses to believe anything negative about her son. In that respect she is out of touch with reality in the same way as Emma Newton in *Shadow of a Doubt*, who can see only good in her younger brother, Charlie. As

will be later explored, Lorne's character is far more out of touch than that of Collinge.

8) Two pairs of detectives — When Guy Haines becomes a murder suspect he is staked out by the District of Columbia police. A conflict emerges as the easygoing Hennessey (Robert Gist), Haines's main tail, sympathizes with and likes the tennis player, believing him to be an innocent man victimized by circumstances. Hennessey's hard-nosed partner, Hammond, believes otherwise, articulating his suspicions to Hennessey. Hammond becomes all the more convinced when, after finishing a grueling match at Forest Hills, Haines gives them the slip and heads toward Grand Central Station. After they follow him to the station an anxious Hammond, learning that Haines is returning to his Pennsylvania home town, is eager to continue the pursuit. Hennessey, the cooler, senior member of the duo, concludes that a sharp turn has been taken. His detective's instincts tell him that the fast-paced action on Haines's part reveals that the mystery will soon be resolved. Rather than pursue Haines, Hennessey concludes that it is better to telephone the local police at the tennis player's home town. After he does so, two new policemen enter the scene, following the case to its conclusion at the same amusement park where Mrs. Haines was murdered by Bruno Antony.

9) Two Hitchcocks — In a celebrated, never to be repeated double, father and daughter appear in the same film. Patricia Hitchcock invests her role as Anne Morton's sister with shrewdness and humorous gusto. The director makes that singular appearance for which he was noted as a man carrying a double bass fiddle, which he wrestles with as he boards the train on which the first meeting between Haines and Antony occurs.

10) Amusement park doubles activity — The doubles theme is enhanced by the appearance of two little boys during the two visits to the amusement park. There were also two elderly men at the carousel. The two pairs could symbolically represent the innocence of youth contrasted with the skeptical sagacity of advanced experience. As for the trips themselves, one resulted in a brutal murder, the lone killing in the film, while the other resolved the mystery and resulted in the vindication of suspect Haines, along with the demise of the real killer, his antagonistic shadow, Antony.

11) Opening doubles — Baton-master Hitchcock opens the action with a series of doubles. There are two men, and the camera shows two pairs of feet. There are two sets of train rails that cross twice. The crossing pattern is extended when, as Haines and Antony sit in the club car of the train, their crossed feet accidentally touch under a table. Antony also orders a pair of double scotches.

Fast Story Pacing,
Slowing Down for Suspense

The judicious Hitchcock mix of a rapidly paced story with an appropriate slowing down and attentive scrutiny to enhancing the drama prevailed in *Strangers on a Train*. When Raymond Chandler was taken off the project he was replaced by Czenzi Ormonde, who became involved when her frequent collaborator, Ben Hecht, was immersed in other projects. Chandler, after receiving a copy of the final script months later, lamented that "Hitchcock succeeded in removing almost every trace of my writing from it." The finished product bore the names of Chandler and Ormonde, in that order.

The concern registered by Chandler that Granger's character not be made to appear in any way involved or supportive of the killing of his wife is deftly handled in the finished script by having Bruno Antony be the active partner in the conversation, with Haines (Granger), step by step, being pushed out of his initial passivity. Antony, who initiates the conversation by asking if he is the famous tennis player Guy Haines, immediately astounds his new acquaintance by revealing how much he knows about him. Not only does Antony know about Haines's on-court prowess, he demonstrates acute awareness of his social life, specifically his courting of Morton, which makes Haines feel awkward. While Haines seeks to wiggle free of the conversation, Antony displays bulldog assertiveness to the point where the tennis player ultimately agrees to have lunch with him in his compartment.

Antony expresses an admiration for Haines in that he is a person capable of doing things, contrasting Haines's status with a bleak self-analysis in which he reveals that he had been expelled from no less than three colleges. The irony is that, whereas Haines is solid and much more focused, resulting in his formidable athletic achievements, he is less personally assertive, whereas the tenacious Antony is capable of worming his way into any situation.

The awkward meeting ends when Haines, expressing relief, departs the train for a meeting with his wife in Metcalf, the town where she works and in which they both grew up. Before he makes his exit a highly assertive Antony, explaining that he knows about Haines's domestic difficulties, recommends that two problems can be resolved by striking a bargain. He would like to see his father gone so he could control the family fortune, and Haines would be better off with his troublesome wife removed from the picture.

A Deadly Proposal

Bruno Antony's proposal is that he kill Haines's wife and Haines eliminate his father. Antony sees this as a stroke of genius since each man's problem can be eliminated while authorities would be stymied because neither man would be considered a suspect in killing a complete stranger with nothing to tie either individual to the killings.

Rather than argue vehemently against the proposal, Haines makes the error of responding to Antony as one would a mental patient. He tells him he has a great idea and quickly makes his departure, convinced he is dealing with a lunatic engaging in wildly speculative thinking.

Haines does not realize it, but he has mistakenly left his cigarette lighter containing his initials behind. A resourceful Antony will later use the lighter to attempt to frame Haines for the murder of his wife, laying the groundwork for one of the most chillingly dramatic sequences ever filmed by Hitchcock, along with the finale when the murderer dies and Haines's innocence is established.

As earlier indicated, Bruno Antony's dogged pursuit of Mrs. Haines at the amusement park establishes his cold-blooded ruthlessness. The killing sequence is highly inventive, again invoking Hitchcock's camera ingenuity. With Miriam Haines temporarily free of her two male admirers, Antony slowly leans forward, prompting her to think he is about to kiss her. Instead his hands thrust forward and he strangles her with brutal efficiency. When he makes initial contact her glasses fall to the grass and the murder is witnessed through the glasses themselves, symbolically representing imagery of the killer's distorted outlook.

The drama enters a new phase when Antony telephones Haines, informing him that he has carried out his end of their bargain. Now it is his turn to reciprocate by killing the senior Mr. Antony. A terrified Haines realizes too late that Antony was anything but the merely talkative, mildly disturbed individual he imagined him to be. Not only is Antony pushing him to carry out his end of what the killer considers a binding mutual obligation, Haines knows that a dark cloud of suspicion hangs over him since, during his brief Metcalf stopover, he engaged in an irate shouting match with his wife in a listening room at the record store where she worked.

Haines's dilemma, as well as the major story thread, is graphically evoked in a transition sequence. Not long after his argument with his wife ends, Haines becomes furious anew in a telephone conversation with Anne Morton, and he blurts out, "I could strangle her!" The quick transition finds Bruno Antony, lounging in his robe at the Arlington mansion, having his hands manicured by his dutiful mother. The symbolism is plain enough: Whereas Haines's statement is figurative, the rantings of an angry man, the focus on Walker's hands reveals that he can and will carry out such a misdeed without losing his temper or becoming ruffled in the slightest.

Extending the Dramatic Sequences

The familiar Hitchcock technique of wringing every last drop of suspense from a scene, in his words, "playing the audience like an organ," was utilized in

Strangers on a Train to fullest advantage. This Hitchcock technique came to the attention of critics and audiences during the director's English phase with the 1936 release *Sabotage*, starring Sylvia Sidney, Oscar Homolka, and John Loder. The sinister spy played by Homolka provides a harmless and thoroughly likable boy with a time bomb, which, instead of destroying the intended target, detonates inside a crowded bus, killing all inside, including the boy and the puppy he had befriended.

While the audience hears the incessant ticking of the time bomb, the camera cuts to a clock, informing all of the moment at hand. Every bit of suspense was wrung from that scene, reminiscent of the failed attempt to kill Young Charlie (Teresa Wright) in *Shadow of a Doubt*, when she lies in the garage overcome by gas fumes as audience members shouted "Hurry!"

In *Strangers on a Train* Hitchcock is provided with an opportunity to wring every last bit of suspense from a scene after Antony has contacted Haines by mail and provided him with a diagram of the second floor of the Arlington mansion, revealing where his father's bedroom is located and providing a key. Antony follows up his correspondence by telephoning Haines, who accents the mystery by indicating he will carry out the plan.

While audiences question whether Haines has, in his desperation to flee from the web the wily and tenacious Antony has constructed, decided to become a killer, Hitchcock extends the suspense. Haines opens the door and enters a large, gloomy house draped in ominous shadows. The long staircase he climbs enhances suspense, as does the potential obstacle thrust in his path, the family dog standing near the bedroom he intends to enter. The question of whether the dog will present a fierce obstacle is resolved when it greets Haines as a friend, licking his hand. From there the next step is opening the door and entering the bedroom of Bruno Antony's father.

Granger's true motivation is revealed when he enters the dark room and, believing he is addressing Mr. Antony, indicates his concern that his son is troubled and needs immediate medical attention. A surprise twist occurs when, in place of Mr. Antony, it turns out that son Bruno is in his room, and his father is away. The crazed Bruno harangues Haines for lacking the conviction to go through with what he still refers to as "their plan," after which the stunned and angry tennis player strikes Bruno. A coldly calculating Bruno warns Haines that he will pay for resisting and ultimately striking him.

As Haines prepares to play an important tennis match at Forest Hills, Bruno notifies him by telephone that he has his lighter, and with it the opportunity to plant evidence directly implicating him in the murder of his wife. This disclosure sets into motion an elaborate double chase sequence as Haines, known as a patient, methodical tennis player, is forced to abandon his regular style and play with supreme aggressiveness, since time is his enemy, knowing that Antony will plant his cigarette lighter where it will do him the most harm — in the grassy area where his wife's body was found at the amusement park.

The tennis match sequence enabled Hitchcock to use the camera to capture blazing court action, with the ulterior motive of prompting the audience to wonder if Haines can complete his match in time to reach the Pennsylvania amusement park before Bruno achieves his objective. As the newly aggressive Haines jumps quickly on top and steps up the pace of play, the radio commentator expresses surprise at his tactical change.

As Haines and Jack Cushingham are shown sweating under a grueling sun in tense competition, a new problem surfaces for the man determined to avoid being framed for his wife's murder. The commentator excitedly reports the determined comeback of Cushingham. While it looked at the outset as if Granger would win easily, Cushingham's comeback had placed him squarely back into the competition. Again the dramatic focus is on the time delay, that by being closely pressed the match is taking longer than Haines had hoped, providing Antony with an advantage.

Identifying with the Killer

A Hitchcock ploy of teasing his audience into identifying with, if not rooting for, the killer was invoked when, while Haines battles his opponent, the action abruptly shifts to Antony arriving in Pennsylvania. Before he can reach the amusement park, however, an accident occurs. He drops the cigarette lighter through a grill and into a sewer. He reaches down into the small opening but is not quite able to reach the lighter, whereupon he desperately seeks help, explaining that the lighter is a valuable family heirloom.

The mounting tension is closely observed by a camera shifting from street to ground level. As the determined efforts to regain the lighter persist, an all-seeing camera toys with the audience's emotions, tantalizing those caught up in the drama to root for the killer. When a smiling Bruno regains his lost evidentiary jewel he smiles triumphantly while bystanders applaud, adding a note of irony in that they are unwittingly encouraging, even aiding and abetting, a killer intent on framing an innocent man for the crime he himself committed.

The action then shifts back to the tennis court, where Haines finally wins after a long and tenacious struggle. He uses Barbara Morton to distract Officer Hennessey, who fancies her, to make his break and reach Grand Central Station.

A Runaway Merry-Go-Round Finale

Considering that this was a film notable for its use of thematic doubles and contrasts, it was appropriate for *Strangers on a Train* to conclude with a mind-numbing conflict within a conflict. The battle for possession of the cigarette lighter, the drama's evidentiary key through which guilt and innocence are resolved, takes place on the merry-go-round of the amusement park. When the merry-go-round's operator suffers a heart attack, all goes awry as it spins out of control. Amid shrieks and the chaos of children being rescued, Antony and Haines battle from sitting positions on wooden horses. Haines simultaneously fights with Antony while attempting to aid a terrified youngster. The sequence, which would be compared to Hitchcock's famous shower scene in *Psycho* for technical virtuosity, involved an intricate pattern revealing Hitchcock's mathematical, optical, and engineering skills. As Hitchcock explained:

This was a most complicated sequence. For rear projection shooting there was a screen and behind it an enormous projector throwing an image on the screen. On the studio floor there was a narrow white line right in line with the projector lens and the lens of the camera had to be right on that white line. The camera was not photographing the screen and what was on it, it was photographing the light in certain colors; therefore the camera lens had to be level and in line with the projector lens. Many of the shots on the merry-go-round were low camera setups. Therefore you can imagine the problem. The projector had to be put up on a high platform, pointing down, and the screen had to be exactly at right angles to the level-line from the lens. All the shots took nearly half a day to line up for each setup. We had to change the projector every time the angle changed.

Robert Burks, who had been a special effects photographer at Warner Brothers, began a lengthy collaboration with Hitchcock as cinematographer on *Strangers on a Train*. Burks, whose extensive special effects background proved helpful in the challenging merry-go-round sequence, would serve as cameraman for every Hitchcock film from 1950 to 1964, with the exception of *Psycho*.

When the carousel finally breaks down there is a massive explosion. Screams are heard while bodies and machine parts fly. To achieve this dramatic effect Hitchcock took a toy carousel and photographed it being blown up by a small charge of explosives. The film was then enlarged and projected on a vast screen. Actors were strategically placed around and in front of it, creating the effect of a mob of bystanders intermingled with plaster horses and hysterical passengers in a state of great confusion. The effort to achieve order amid the reigning chaos can be said, once more, to symbolize Hitchcock's fascination with duality, juxtaposing the cruel and anarchistic side of nature with that of orderliness and human decency.

Given the potential of such a spine-tingling dramatic climax, Hitchcock could not resist the opportunity to once more delay the moment of resolution. An amusement park worker is compelled to crawl slowly beneath the runaway carousel, creeping slowly underneath it to finally shut off the power and bring it to a screeching halt. In true Hitchcock fashion, every slow, difficult movement was photographed. Another clever touch had the veteran amusement park employee pausing briefly to blow his nose.

Antony is thrown violently from the merry-go-round. Haines implores him to tell the truth during his final moments of life. But he remains consistent to his character, insisting that he will not lie to save Haines. At the moment of death his clenched hand, which tenaciously held the cigarette lighter, falls open, demonstrating to the policemen standing by that the tennis player was a victim rather than a killer.

A Grand Finale

The virtuoso effort provided by Robert Walker in what was his final completed film marked an eminent U-turn in a career in which he had excelled playing the likable boy next door, as in *The Clock* (as Judy Garland's love interest), along with *Since You Went Away* and *See Here, Private Hargrove*. Walker invested the unforgettable psychopath Bruno Antony with the proper mix of outrageous gall and brutal inner torment.

If Hitchcock were capable of playing film audiences like a Wurlitzer, the same could be said in the adroitness with which he finessed censors. Just as he had carefully fine-tuned the lesbian nuances of Judith Anderson's Mrs. Danvers in *Rebecca* to hold the censors at bay, he accomplished a similar feat with *Strangers on a Train*. Walker and Hitchcock worked out an elaborate series of subtle gestures in the film concerning the movie's sub-theme of homosexual courtship. Antony's fondness for Haines was demonstrated as Hitchcock once more walked the tightrope around censorial difficulties.

Farley Granger provided just the right note of frustration and victimization as the unceasing target of Bruno Antony. One unforgettable scene showed a rattled Haines explaining his plight to Senator Morton and his daughters in the living room of the Morton residence. His lament about Antony's persistence is underscored with photographic poignance when his pursuer's presence is eerily revealed with the appropriate amount of foreboding shadows as Antony stares at the Morton residence, calmly smoking a cigarette and looking doggedly menacing. Marion Lorne as Mrs. Antony is also convincing, contrasting sharply with her husband, who sees his son's problems clearly. When Anne Morton visits her, attempting to convince the doting mother that her son needs medical attention, she dismisses Morton's concerns with a whimsicality reminiscent of Billy Burke.

A revealing moment in the film occurs when Mrs. Antony proudly displays a portrait she has just finished. Bruno thinks it resembles his father, while Mrs. Antony explains that it was supposed to be a portrait of St. Francis. The camera closes in on a hodgepodge monstrosity resembling a gargoyle.

A brilliant photographic sequence offering the patented Hitchcock duality occurs when Bruno Antony is observed smoking a cigarette at the Jefferson Memorial. The monument dedicated to the great patriot who drafted the Declaration of Independence — is in contrast to the ominous presence of a killer personifying anarchy.

The Hitchcock Persona

A Warner Brothers press release dated November 30, 1950, described a disturbing incident involving Hitchcock and his daughter Patricia. The publicity department release described an occasion on which Pat had begged for a ride on a Ferris wheel. When she reached the uppermost point in the ride, Hitchcock ordered the Ferris wheel stopped and all lights shut off. With the area enveloped in total darkness the director left and turned his attention to a scene in a far corner of the amusement park while she became hysterical with fear. An hour later Hitchcock ordered the carriage containing a trembling Pat to be lowered.

The incident was noted by Donald Spoto, serving as an example supporting his thesis that the great director, rather than just seeking to tell clever stories, used his films to project his own troubled inner duality. Hitchcock's ploy is reminiscent of one of the defining occurrences of the director's life, when his father, to teach his young son a lesson, had him held in the darkness of a dank jail cell.

Hitchcock's warm, generous nature contrasted with another behavioral element characterized by cold withdrawal was said by Spoto to typify the Master's persona. Many creative geniuses are noted for marked dissimilarities from average individuals. The Freudian viewpoint associates creative endeavor with a desire on the part of the individual to unburden oneself psychologically by revealing tormented inner longings.

Charles Bennett was a frequent collaborator of Hitchcock's during the director's London phase. Bennett's scripts for Hitchcock were all written during the filmmaker's British period, save one, *Foreign Correspondent*. Their collaboration essentially ended when Hitchcock moved to the U.S. One Bennett script, *The Man Who Knew Too Much*, which he had penned in England, was remade as a 1956 release starring James Stewart and Doris Day. Bennett's personal reminiscences of Hitchcock, with whom he remained friends during their respective American phases, are akin to the man of duality described by Donald Spoto. In addition to the aforementioned films, Bennett collaborated with Hitchcock on *The 39 Steps*, *The Secret Agent*, *Sabotage*, and *The Girl Was Young*. "At my original meetings with him, I found him a very congenial, little fat man," Bennett revealed during an interview in the Eighties. "It was only when I got to know him better that I got to know the darker side of him, the sadistic side — which did come out in his pictures, as you must have noticed over the years."

Bennett and his wife and Mr. and Mrs. Hitchcock spent many Christmas seasons together at the fashionable Swiss ski resort of St. Moritz. "I would ski while Hitch sat in the Palace Hotel and wouldn't come out at all," Bennett recalled. "This big fat man, and he would just sit, look out the window." Bennett's reference to Hitchcock's obesity reflects on what some observers believed lay at the root of his troubles — being an intrinsic part of a glamour business and directing some of the world's most beautiful women, while harboring feelings of inferiority regarding his own appearance.

The mysterious side of Hitchcock's nature was manifested in Bennett's recollection of a meeting with the director at a cocktail party hosted by actor Brian Aherne at his Malibu home. Bennett remembered chatting amiably for about an hour with Hitchcock. The next day a case of expensive champagne arrived from the director, along with a note saying, "From that stupid man, Hitchcock." Bennett immediately called him, asking him what he meant by his strange remark. "That's what you called me, isn't it?" Hitchcock replied. "You passed me and said to everybody, 'There's that stupid man.'" A puzzled Bennett responded, "When did I say that? We were talking by the fire for an hour." Hitchcock insisted that the conversation never took place. "He couldn't remember any of it," Bennett related.

As for *Strangers on a Train*, while Hitchcock expressed certain misgivings about the film, he was overruled in the best way, by an enthusiastic public that flocked to the theaters and broke the director's slump, as the major success he sought was realized. The master director was back on track.

7

Voyeurism as High Art

I was feeling very creative at the time. The batteries were well charged.
— Alfred Hitchcock on the period when he made *Rear Window*

A young writer of 33 had an opportunity for a major breakthrough. John Michael Hayes had, as they say in the film industry, "paid his dues." The Worcester, Massachusetts, native, like many, came to Hollywood following World War II in hopes of grabbing the brass ring of success.

Hayes learned his craft by proving himself a fast and efficient scriptwriter, gaining success and recognition on radio by turning out quality scripts in the then-burgeoning mystery field. Eventually he received the opportunity to write film scripts, but the early efforts were in low-budget B terrain. Hayes began with the 1952 release *Red Ball Express*. The following year three more films were released in which Hayes had functioned as scenarist, *War Arrow*, *Thunder Bay* and *Torch Song*. The last two films marked Hayes as a writer on the rise in that *Thunder Bay* had James Stewart as its star and was directed by the highly regarded Anthony Mann, and *Torch Song* marked the return to MGM, following a period at Warner Brothers, of Joan Crawford.

It was Hayes's good fortune that he and Alfred Hitchcock were represented by the same agency, the highly influential Music Corporation of America. When Hitchcock, a noted radio mystery enthusiast who had heard about Hayes, mentioned his name in connection with a new project, he was told that they were both represented by the same agency.

A meeting was planned. Given Hitchcock's flair for gourmet dining and drama, a simple meeting in MCA's office could never match a dinner engagement in the Polo Lounge of the Beverly Hills Hotel. Hayes was told that the project of interest to Hitchcock was a novella by New York hard-boiled mystery writer Cornell Woolrich called *Rear Window*. Realizing what an assignment to write a script for the Master could do for his career, Hayes boned up like an eager student determined to please a distinguished professor, practically memorizing the story prior to the Friday night meeting.

Hayes arrived at the Beverly Hills Hotel at 8:30 for his dinner meeting with Hitchcock. When thirty minutes passed without Hitchcock appearing, Hayes grew nervous. A light drinker, he nonetheless felt the need for something strong to steady his nerves, so he went to the bar and ordered a martini. When more time passed, his nervousness intensifying, Hayes ordered another martini.

When 9:30 arrived a downcast Hayes concluded that Hitchcock would not appear. As he began walking despondently toward the parking lot Hayes observed a taxi pull up in front of the hotel. He then saw Hitchcock alight. Hayes rushed up to the cab, and Hitchcock, thinking the young author was an autograph seeker, told him that there was no time for such activity since he had an important meeting to attend. Hayes then identified himself and the two men went into the hotel. Hitchcock never apologized for being late. As they seated themselves, the most topsy turvy evening in the career of John Michael Hayes began.

Hitchcock was eager to drink, and Hayes, not wanting to appear unsociable, did not desire to cross him. "I like a man who drinks," Hitchcock enthused. When Hayes professed a preference for martinis, avoiding a switch from what he consumed earlier to ease his troubled nerves, Hitchcock was again delighted, ordering double martinis along with hors d'oeuvres. Hayes, feeling increasingly tipsy, hoped he would not get sick.

Hitchcock next ordered a bottle of wine, at which point it was time to move on from hors d'oeuvres to Dover sole with a rare white wine. Hitchcock poured a large glass of wine for Hayes while extolling its virtues. Hayes, struggling in an increasing fog, slowly sipped, attempting to demonstrate appreciation.

Hayes, who had diligently prepared for a discussion of *Rear Window*, might as well have saved himself the trouble. What Hayes had assumed would be topic number one was never mentioned. As they moved under Hitchcock's gourmet direction to the next course, which was steak, the director approached the subject of film. He asked if Hayes had seen any of his movies. Hayes replied that he had, wondering if there was a particular film he wished him to discuss.

Hitchcock recommended *Shadow of a Doubt*. As fate would have it, Hayes was confident that he had seen the film more times than its director. As an Army projectionist it was his responsibility to show *Shadow of a Doubt* to his fellow soldiers. As a result he knew the film backwards, forwards and sideways. His tongue loosened by imbibing more alcohol than he was accustomed to, Hayes then proceeded to detail what he liked, as well as what he disliked, about the Master's films. At one point a now loquacious Hayes told Hitchcock that he thought of the scene in *The 39 Steps* where Robert Donat's life was spared when the bullet was thwarted by the Bible in his overcoat pocket as "corny."

While Hayes expressed his opinion of Hitchcock's films the director said nothing, continuing to avidly eat and drink. At the meal's conclusion Hitchcock ordered dessert to be brought with a concoction of brandy and drambuie. Hitchcock devoted the same meticulousness to eating and drinking that he did to crafting a great film.

When Hitchcock brought the meeting to a close by announcing it was time to leave, Hayes offered to drive him home, but the director instead opted for a taxi. Hayes was more than a little concerned over the fact that *Rear Window*, the potential future project for collaboration, was never once mentioned.

Hayes drove over the Santa Monica Mountains north back to his home in the East San Fernando Valley in Burbank. His wife Mel asked anxiously, "Well, how did it go?" The writer then detailed what he was convinced was his horrible plight. "Well, we had one of the great feasts of all time," Hayes began, "but I am through, not only with Alfred Hitchcock, but maybe forever in this town. I'd better start thinking of a new profession. Because I analyzed his pictures, and I analyzed them like a reviewer, critically."

The writer had an entire weekend to sadly reflect on all that he perceived had gone wrong in his Polo Lounge meeting with Hitchcock. On Monday morning MCA agent Arthur Park phoned with good news concerning the meeting.

"You're in," Park assured. "Hitchcock loved you. You start work tomorrow. Report to Warner Brothers, where he's preparing *Dial M for Murder*."

"Are you sure you have the right John Michael Hayes?" the stunned writer sputtered in disbelief.

"Why?" Now agent Park was perplexed.

"We never talked about *Rear Window* or anything," Hayes explained.

"You're fine," Park confidently assured.

Hayes arrived at Warners the next day and the two men had their first discussion about *Rear Window*. It took a year before John Michael Hayes worked up the requisite nerve to ask Hitchcock about the interview, which he believed he had miserably flunked.

"Well, let me tell you what happened," Hitchcock responded. "I went to a cocktail party at Jules Stein's house [the founder of MCA]. That's why I was late. You know, I was dieting and I had several drinks. I remember meeting you and going in to eat, but I don't remember anything after that. But you talked a lot, and on the assumption that a man who talks a lot has something to say, I hired you. But don't forget, if I didn't like you, two weeks later I could have let you go."

After two weeks Hitchcock was far removed from letting Hayes go. The two would creatively collaborate on four films before their association ended during a productive period when Hitchcock overcame a box office slump and pushed his career into the high-level commercial ranks. The 115-page treatment that Hayes completed on *Rear Window* was considered so ideal by Paramount, the studio that ultimately became involved in the project, that it was used as a model for writers on how to achieve perfection in crafting such a work.

One fascinating note of irony about *Rear Window* is how Hitchcock moved back into the financially productive cinema ranks by following the familiar adage of "Know thyself." *Rear Window* is the film that more than any other made by the famous director in his entire career reflects the director himself.

Hitchcock as Hitchcock

James Stewart in his lead role as L.B. Jefferies in *Rear Window* served as close to a Hitchcock surrogate as would be viewed on screen. Hitchcock biographer Donald Spoto referred to Stewart as serving "as Hitchcock's chair-bound alter ego, a photographer whose mobility is limited by a hip-to-toe plaster cast." The wheelchair to which Stewart was confined for the entire length of the film could be said to resemble a director's chair. While he begins by using binoculars as a spying device on neighbors, he ultimately opts for a deep focus camera lens, which he uses in his profession as a daring international photographer.

The voyeuristic side of Hitchcock extends to spying on an entire collection of neighbors he sees through the perspective of the apartment building where he resides. One of them is a shapely ballet dancer about whom he provides an additional note of delicious enthusiasm. In the world of Stewart-Hitchcock lives unfold and names are provided for the ensemble unwittingly parading for the laid-up photographer's benefit.

Blending Old and New Technology

Rear Window initially appeared in the February 1942 issue of *Dime Detective* under Cornell Woolrich's pseudonym of William Irish. The short story then bore the title "It Had to Be Murder" and, in the manner of detective magazine potboilers, was intended to generate a creative pull by using the mystery device to transform readers into helpless page turners. Applied to the screen, does this not sound like the technique of Alfred Hitchcock? In the case of this story the ultimate surprise occurs on the final page when readers then learn what was wrong with the first-person narrator, that he was laid up with his leg in a cast.

The most recent incarnation of the novella before Hitchcock entered the scene was a story treatment written by successful Broadway stage director Joshua Logan. After having directed two major Broadway musical successes with *Annie Get Your Gun* and *Mister Roberts*, he hoped that perhaps the Cornell Woolrich story would provide a ticket to Hollywood and an entry into film directing ranks. Had Logan been successful in that endeavor, he might well have starred James Stewart in the same role, since, in their young and struggling New York days, he had shared an apartment with the actor, as well as Henry Fonda.

The John Michael Hayes treatment, written with substantial creative input from Hitchcock, retained the basic element of Lars Thorwald killing his wife, with the apartment-bound Jefferies discovering it, which Logan adapted into his treatment. In the film, however, the male lead becomes a fiercely independent and daring photographer, while in the Broadway director's treatment he was a sportswriter.

Logan made one major adaptation in his treatment that Hayes and Hitchcock would incorporate into the finalized film script, the inclusion of a girlfriend for the male lead, someone he called Trink. In the Woolrich work, which ultimately became *Rear Window* when it was reprinted in a 1944 collection entitled *After Dinner Story*, the two characters with whom Jeffries interacts are an African American houseman named Sam and a homicide detective named Boyne.

Hitchcock was an experienced filmmaker who combined the best of the old and the new technology. During the filming of *Rear Window* he must have thought back to his youthful London days. After a trip to Berlin, where he observed the way that German masters such as Murnau, Lang and Pabst used the camera, he was creatively fortified to begin his own quest for cinema immortality. In those days before dialogue, inventive filmmakers utilized busy cameras to keep audiences entertained, since they were not privy to conversation.

Rear Window, with its emphasis on wheelchair-bound Jefferies' voyeurism, was in many ways a throwback to those early days, as the characters the intrigued photographer watches with close attention are frequently seen but not heard. If they are engaged in dialogue the audience does not hear it. Hitchcock has created his own virtual village with numerous stories spinning simultaneously, reminiscent of his busy, all-seeing camera's eye from his silent days.

In order to understand the use of the new technology it is important to ascertain when the film was made. *Rear Window* was a product of the early fifties and was released in 1954. David Selznick was far from the only leading Hollywood film figure running scared in the fifties. What movie people referred to sarcastically as "that ugly box with the black and white pictures," by others as television, had made a chilling impact within the cinema capital. Hitchcock was certainly aware of the current trend. All he needed for a reminder was his last film prior to *Rear Window*, his adaptation of the suspense thriller written by Frederick Knott that had wowed audiences on Broadway and in London's West End, *Dial M for Murder*. The drama revolved around a triangle in which Margot Wendice (Grace Kelly) is seeing Mark Halliday (Robert Cummings). Her husband, a former tennis professional played by Ray Milland, is in financial arrears and proposes to have her killed by an old acquaintance to acquire her share of vast family wealth. It was shot in the 3-D process, one of Hollywood's new innovations devised to compete with television. It proved to be a fad with a short life span.

While disdaining some of the cheaper trickery of 3-D, such as knives and bats lunging toward audience patrons wearing the glasses required to view the product, Hitchcock reached into his bag of tricks to generate effects commensurate with the fad's demands. The problem came when 3-D's short life ended and Hitchcock was stuck with a product he would have molded in a different manner had the film been made in the traditional manner. While the film was anything but a success, there was one plus resulting from *Dial M for Murder*, Hitchcock's association with Grace Kelly and his use of her in two subsequent triumphs, *Rear Window* and *To Catch a Thief*.

Hitchcock was mindful of current pressures and demands that filmmakers provide high entertainment value to coax a new generation of television addicts back into theaters, product they could not see with the black and white restrictions of small boxes in their living rooms. He used the most glossy technicolor available for his latest creation.

Voyeurism in Hitchcock Village

Hitchcock, aided by the superb writing craftsmanship of John Michael Hayes, offered a story about a man in deep frustration over his physical plight who, as a result of his forced temporary invalid status, has his schedule thrown into disarray. Cornell Woolrich's lead character and narrator reveals that he is accustomed to regular physical activity. In his sedentary state he is plagued by bouts of insomnia. The insomnia, coupled with boredom, provides the ideal catalyst for voyeurism. Hitchcock and Hayes doubtlessly saw this possibility immediately. Here is a restless man filling in time, and during that period he stumbles upon a murder by observing the suspicious activity of its perpetrator.

Alfred Hitchcock always saw story development through the eye of a camera, making it difficult to work with a hard-boiled mystery wordsmith like Raymond Chandler. John Michael Hayes was more conducive to collaboration since he had an initial grounding in radio mystery, and later television and film.

Together the Hitchcock-Hayes team created a village of their own. They created Hitchcock Village, in which James Stewart resides as sidelined daring international photographer L.B. Jefferies (changed from "Hal Jeffries" in the Woolrich story). In the film version he is known as Jeff. By making Jefferies a photographer who uses his long focus lens to study what is going on in the apartment building across the courtyard, the movie's lead character becomes the perfect Hitchcock surrogate with trusty camera in hand, an adult Puck discovering what fools mortals can truly be. A discerning viewer will envision Hitchcock chuckling all the way.

Suffering insomniac Jefferies invents names for his ensemble of characters as we see his village assume increasing importance in his life of new adventure, this time lived from a sedentary position rather than from the dangerous professional photographer's posture he generally assumes.

In the opening scene Hitchcock uses the camera as what John Ford termed an information booth by panning to pictures Jefferies has taken, including *Life* magazine covers. The one photograph of particular importance is an Indianapolis race car smash-up. An ensuing call from Jefferies' editor reveals that the photographer broke his leg getting too close to the dangerous accident and was forced to pay a severe price that could have been even worse, costing him his life.

Hitchcock's village was constructed on one confined set built at Paramount

Studios. It consisted of a courtyard and 32 apartments, 12 of which were completely furnished. The building was a replica of one in New York's Greenwich Village. The address of Thorwald's apartment is described as 125 West Ninth Street, which doesn't actually exist, since West Ninth Street ends at what out-of-towners call Avenue of the Americas but New Yorkers commonly refer to as Sixth Avenue.

From that point West Ninth is called Christopher Street. In 1953, when *Rear Window* was being filmed, moviemakers were compelled to refrain from using actual street addresses for murder sites. Standing at 125 Christopher Street, at the corner of Hudson Street, is the building that inspired the design of the Thorwald apartment.

A courtyard separates that building from Jeff's, which is on Tenth Street, just east of Hudson. Hitchcock, as always, meticulously did his homework. When the police are summoned at a point when Jefferies realizes that Thorwald knows who he is, where he is, and what he is up to, they arrive promptly, led by Jeff's old friend Lieutenant Tom Doyle. The Sixth Precinct of the New York City Police Department is situated on Tenth Street, directly across the street from Jeff's apartment.

Another point that squares with reality is the brisk business activity at the Albert Hotel, which has since been converted to apartments. The old Albert Hotel stood at Tenth Street and University Place, a short walk away.

The People of Hitchcock Village

The people of the Hitchcock Village living in the courtyard apartments that seize L.B. Jefferies' imagination are the kind of fascinating mix one might expect to encounter in the colorful Greenwich Village section of Manhattan, known for diversity and artistry. Some of the more prominent characters bear names provided by Jefferies as he views their activities, sometimes with high-powered binoculars and on other occasions with his long focus camera lens. One prominent occupant, played by Georgine Darcy, is christened by Jeff with the name of Miss Torso. An energetic ballet dancer, she moves briskly through her paces by day as Jefferies eagerly watches, while at night she spends much of her time fighting off the advances of male admirers who flock to her apartment.

Miss Lonelyhearts, played by Judith Evelyn, is the polar opposite of Miss Torso, as the name indicates. She is a lonely woman who appears to be in her early forties. She drinks, takes pills, and fantasizes by acting out romantic dates alone in the privacy of her apartment.

The Songwriter, played by Ross Bagdassarian, is determined to finish the song he hopes will make him famous by landing him on the nation's popular hit charts. It is a romantic ballad, and he can be seen pecking at his piano even as he mops his floor. His tragic and lonely side is revealed early one morning when he stumbles into his apartment, drunk, and falls down. He and Miss Torso are the apartment building's leading entertainers. As the songwriter nears the completion of the work he hopes will establish him, he proudly plays his selection on the piano before a group of people.

On one occasion Alfred Hitchcock surfaces. He tunes the Songwriter's clock while also turning his head at one point and casting an anxious eye at Bagdassarian playing his piano. Knowing Hitchcock, there was plenty of intended symbolism in the choice and manner in which he made his traditionally brief and celebrated appearance. He emerged as a Puck in his own right by reminding theater patrons of the importance of time, as well as the fascinating aspect of it spent in observation. Nobody could observe like Alfred Hitchcock.

The Newlyweds offer hope for a new beginning. They surface appropriately at the beginning of the film, full of smiles and loving optimism as they are shown their new apartment by their landlord.

Naturally, a contrasting couple would have to be present, and it consists of the pivotal characters of Lars Thorwald and his wife Anna, played respectively by Raymond Burr and Irene Winston. Anna lies bedridden and demonstrates unhappiness toward her grim-faced husband, who, at one point after a brief conversational exchange, frowns, gestures with a disgusted sweep of the hand and walks away.

Sara Berner and Frank Cady, as the couple above the Thorwalds, spend their nights sleeping on the fire escape outside their apartment. Their actions reveal that a ferocious heat wave has descended upon Manhattan, which is also evidenced by the beads of sweat on Jeff's brow and provides another explanation, along with his sedentary plight, as to why he is unable to sleep during regular hours.

Bess Flowers plays a woman with a poodle and has an integral role in the drama, despite having precious little time on screen. When her poodle dies, Jefferies is stirred to a new level of suspicion concerning Lars Thorwald, as will be revealed later.

"Miss Hearing Aid" and "Bird Woman," played by Jesslyn Fax and Iphigenie Castiglioni, are also among the interesting mix of characters watched by the laid-up photographer. Then there is also a cluster of shapely young women who periodically sunbathe on the roof. Their appearance triggers that same expression of interest revealed on the photographer's face when the shapely Miss Torso commences her vigorous dance routines.

This is a film offering two levels of activity, activity performed by those who watch and by those who *are* watched, with discussions constantly occurring in Jeff's apartment about what is going on and what it all means. Hitchcock's Village is a microcosm of life, with four individuals dominating the voyeuristic action. The superlative casting assists Hitchcock and Hayes in making their points in the most effective and efficient manner.

Jimmy Stewart, America's Guy Next Door

Whether a James Stewart film was set in small-town America or a large city, the essence of the man and his rock-ribbed human values remained intact. While America may have been a land in flux, James Stewart remained one of its unbending constants.

It was anything but a surprise that two of Stewart's most recognizable and popular earlier roles, films made when he was in his thirties, were in movies directed by the fervent mainstay of traditional American values, Frank Capra: *Mr. Smith Goes to Washington* (1939) and the actor's favorite, *It's a Wonderful Life* (1946).

What made his roles in two of Frank Capra's most legendary films so archetypally Stewart were the quintessential portrait of the decent small-town American male, and the basic heroism and achievements to which hard working, good, often underestimated individuals are capable of rising under the right circumstances. This link to the common man was what made the *New York Times* refer to Stewart in the headline of its obituary following his July 2, 1997, demise as "Actor and American Icon." One paragraph from the *Times* article captured the essence of Stewart:

"The lanky actor with unruly hair and an ungainly stride had a boyish grin and an engaging manner. The Stewart way of speaking — laconic, with a hesitant, nasal drawl — is instantly recognizable by virtually every American. His early screen image, like his personal life, epitomized a Middle American ideal in a confusing, sophisticated world."

Stewart's performance as the small-town Pennsylvania banker George Bailey in *It's a Wonderful Life* made a profound impact on the occupant of the White House at the time, Missouri's Harry Truman, also noted for his common touch. President Truman paid Stewart the ultimate compliment after viewing the film: "If Bess and I had a son, we'd want him to be just like Jimmy Stewart."

The genius of Stewart lay in the subtlety of his performances, making his work look so easy that it was difficult to believe he was acting at all. Critic Vincent Canby of the *New York Times* in 1990 hailed Stewart as a great behavioral actor who absorbed each role to coincide with his own persona. Canby noted that "This he does with such simplicity and ease that, for many years, the initial response was to say that what he does isn't acting, followed up by the damp, desperate criticism that he is always the same."

An Early Oscar and Ultimate Character Integration

The Stewart roles of the thirties and forties were tailored to reflect a frequently shy and often restless young man eager to explore the truth and succeed in life. As he moved into the fifties a more mature Stewart tackled more worldly and complex roles. Through the transition the basic Stewart persona remained, however, the essential common man of quiet strength and dignity seeking truth.

The characteristic difference was his added maturity, and with it, a less naive, more worldly demeanor. It was characteristic of his career and the turn it took that Stewart received a Best Actor Academy Award and a New York Film Critics honor early in his career, and garnered another New York Film Critics Best Actor honor and a Venice Film Festival accolade for a memorable role from his mature phase.

Stewart won a New York Film Critics Best Actor honor for his glittering triumph as the idealistic young senator Jefferson Smith fighting corruption within the political system in *Mr. Smith Goes to Washington.* One year later he garnered Best Actor Oscar laurels for his sensitive role as a plainspoken reporter talking sense to headstrong Katharine Hepburn in the 1940 comedy hit, *The Philadelphia Story.* It was befitting that Stewart won by playing the down-to-earth man of common sense capable of breaking down the facade of Eastern United States upper crust society, as represented by Hepburn. In 1959, the veteran Stewart secured New York Film Critics and Venice Film Festival top acting laurels for portraying a homespun country lawyer who secures the acquittal of murder suspect Ben Gazzara in Otto Preminger's *Anatomy of a Murder.*

Aided by a Master's Touch

Any performer, no matter how good, requires challenging vehicles to develop his or her talents to their zenith. The lanky leading man found a willing benefactor in one of the screen's premier directors of suspense films, Alfred Hitchcock. Possessing an astute eye for talent and story potential, Hitchcock recognized that Stewart had the persona and raw talent to enhance the director's carefully constructed suspense vehicles. Hitchcock was a master of ambiguity, with a penchant for depicting average citizens caught up in complicated webs of uncertainty, and confronting mysterious forces and circumstances.

With victims confronted by circumstances beyond their control, they are forced to use every possible resource to scale heights never previously imagined. In that Stewart was Hollywood's representative example of the common man coming to grips with external forces, America's kindly "guy next door," Hitchcock realized the benefit of tapping the actor's potential for confronting challenges in the manner of an average individual pressed to new heights by necessity, demonstrating all the while his human vulnerabilities.

Stewart's value to Hitchcock as America's Everyman, everybody's friendly next door neighbor, bears recollection to the meeting the director had with Joseph Cotten when the Virginia country gentleman was worried over how he should play a serial killer of rich widow in *Shadow of a Doubt.* Hitchcock sought to assuage Cotten's doubts by having the actor watch men walk down a busy Beverly Hills street. Hitchcock assured Cotten that there was no prototype for a killer; he could resemble any of the men Cotten observed.

By casting Stewart in a string of mystery thrillers, Hitchcock provided the suspenseful element of having the likable next door neighbor facing countless physical and psychological disasters. As noted, in their first film together, *Rope*, Stewart, playing a cerebral college philosophy professor, must contend with the shock of discovering that two of his brilliant students and admirers, played by John Dall and Farley Granger, have proudly killed a vulnerable classmate they believed was unfit to live.

When Stewart and Hitchcock reunited, the Master had a fresh challenge for the actor. In *Rear Window* Stewart portrays a photographer so daring that he would place himself too close to harm's way and almost lose his life in the process. He is a man who has survived jungles and revolutions throughout the world, but is confronted by one dilemma at home that has him thoroughly frightened. He meets a beautiful woman who falls in love with him and wants to marry her. The conflict shrewdly generated by Hitchcock is that she is "too perfect"!

While Stewart, as daring photographer and perpetual man of action L.B. Jefferies, can handle the occasional dictator who contemplates throwing him in jail for getting too close to thorny political situations, not to mention having to survive by eating creatures most ordinary citizens would be frightened to even look at, he becomes tongue-tied in the presence of fashion model Lisa Fremont, played by Grace Kelly. This initial conflict is cleverly extrapolated into the Hitchcock Village lying beyond the courtyard. The frightened photographer who sits wheelchair bound sees himself in many of the human dramas unfolding among the apartment dwellers he observes.

So Perfect She Became a Princess

The casting choice of Kelly could not have been more perfect for the woman who leaves Stewart's character sputtering. When she was provided with a copy of the script of *Rear Window* the future princess was confronted with a dilemma. Another distinguished director wanted her, so she had to weigh the Hitchcock offer against one presenting a great dramatic challenge. Budd Schulberg, the son of Paramount Studios executive B.P. Schulberg, who soared to success as a young man with the runaway best-selling novel *What Makes Sammy Run?*, had worked with director Elia Kazan with the same diligence that Joseph Michael Hayes applied in concert with Hitchcock.

For their current project Kazan and Schulberg developed the theme of mob corruption dominating New York longshoremen. The story was entitled *On the Waterfront*, and accepting that role afforded certain advantages for Grace Kelly. For one thing, the Philadelphia blonde beauty would be able to do a film in her then hometown of New York, replete with its authentic waterfront settings. The other consideration was artistic, with the tremendous impact that Kazan and his leading man from *A Streetcar Named Desire*, Marlon Brando, were making on the aesthetic scene.

On the Waterfront would ultimately win eight Oscars, including Best Picture, while Kazan beat out Alfred Hitchcock, who was nominated for *Rear Window*, in the Best Director category. As for the role intended for Kelly, that of Brando's love interest, the blonde actress who made her film debut, Eva Marie Saint, secured an Academy Award in the Best Supporting Actress category.

Hollywood is a town where fate twists in strange ways. While Kelly would ultimately forsake a role that could have secured her an Oscar statuette for Best Supporting Actress, she would deliver a thank you speech on the same night that Eva Marie Saint was honored. Grace Kelly would win in the Best Actress category for the one and only role in which she did not essentially play herself, the symbol of sophisticated glamor.

In the adaptation of the Broadway drama written by Clifford Odets and directed by George Seaton, *The Country Girl*, she played a wife seeking to save her guilt-ridden and alcohol-prone husband. It was a role far removed from Kelly's glamorous image. Kelly was deliberately outfitted in frumpy looking clothes. Her hairstyle was austere. Edith Head, known for accenting the glamor of beautiful women like Grace Kelly on screen, was called upon to complete the reverse assignment of making the dazzling former Manhattan cover girl look less appealing for a role commensurate with somber character acting.

Kelly plays the wife of a tortured actor making a Broadway comeback who continues to feel guilt over the tragic death by automobile accident of his son and turns heavily to drink. Bing Crosby turned in one of his finest efforts playing the actor, while William Holden performed the part of the play's director with sensitivity and care.

Kelly won her Oscar for a role in which, deliberately stripped of her glamour, she plays a character who is not what she initially appears to be. Holden, in the film's earlier stages, clashes with a woman he finds tyrannical and suffocating. As more is revealed about her relationship with problematical and guilt-ridden husband Crosby, however, Holden's initial opposition and dislike is replace by empathy and respect for a woman who is doing her utmost to help her husband survive.

The name of Hitchcock's former cinematic partner, the peripatetic David O. Selznick, surfaced in Kelly's active pursuit of the role that would result in her winning an Oscar. A man with keen instincts when it came to storylines, Selznick believed that the film based on the play by Broadway achiever Clifford Odets, who achieved fame with Depression dramas *Waiting for Lefty* and *Golden Boy*, provided a brilliant dramatic opportunity for the actress fortunate enough to be cast in the lead role. Selznick lobbied hard. Using his considerable Hollywood influence, he moved his wife Jennifer Jones into the front runner's position, at which point fate intervened, the kind that seemed to incessantly plague the colorful producer in the post-war period.

William Perlberg and George Seaton, the producers of *The Country Girl*, were working on their previous Paramount film, *The Bridges at Toko-Ri*, a Korean

War drama which also starred Grace Kelly and William Holden, and was directed by Mark Robson. The call came from Selznick in early 1954 revealing that his wife was pregnant. Perlberg and Seaton were well into the making of *Toko-Ri* at the time of Selznick's call and but three weeks away from starting on *The Country Girl*. "George and I don't tear our hair out," Perlberg later recalled, speaking in the present. "We just look at each other. We're both thinking the same thing at the same time — Grace Kelly."

While Grace Kelly in *The Country Girl* undertook a challenge by playing a character and physical type far removed from her own persona, the role she accepted in *Rear Window* represented Kelly playing herself, right down to the cover girl element. The Philadelphia girl was a high level achiever who soared in real life to the front ranks of New York's competitive modeling world, just like the character she plays in the film, Lisa Fremont.

Grace Kelly was trained to be a winner by a father who was a self-made man and a legend in his own time in Philadelphia. Grace's biographer Robert Lacey called Jack Kelly "one of the city's more remarkable and charismatic sons." Lacey describes the rags to riches climb of Jack Kelly in one paragraph:

> Born in 1890, one of a sprawling Irish Catholic family of ten children living in the poor, immigrant quarter of East Falls, Philadelphia, Jack Kelly had earned his first wages as a bricklayer. Then he started his own contracting firm, Kelly for Brickwork, and, by dint of charm, hard work, and the right connections, he managed to build the business into the largest construction enterprise on the East Coast. Kelly for Brickwork had a hand in everything from the classical pillars of Philadelphia's Thirteenth Street Station to Radio City Music Hall in New York. Jack Kelly became a millionaire.

Dynamic achiever Jack Kelly also won distinction in a challenging athletic competition. In his spare time he was an oarsman who became a champion in the solitary rowing event of the single sculls. Robert Lacey described the event as "eight minutes or more of self-imposed torture propelling a fragile wooden shell through 2,000 meters of water," and his athletic feats marked Kelly as a local hero.

Kelly's road to riches was assisted by his activities in the Philadelphia Democratic Party. In 1935, when his daughter was five years old, Jack Kelly ran for mayor in the then Republican stronghold. While losing by a respectable margin of 40,000 votes out of 700,000 cast, Kelly assisted President Franklin Delano Roosevelt and his Democratic organization by making significant inroads into a key city that became, and continues to be, a party stronghold. Kelly's assistance in bringing Philadelphia into the expanding FDR urban strategy orbit brought dividends for the construction entrepreneur as major federal contracts were granted to Kelly for Brickwork.

While Grace Kelly benefited from being the daughter of a successful businessman with political connections, vaulting into society in a manner befitting her starring role in *High Society* (1956), in which she played opposite *Country*

Girl co-star Bing Crosby, her career choice of acting more closely resembled the path taken by her father Jack's older brother.

Uncle George Kelly lived just around the corner from Grace's New York City residence. Outside Philadelphia George was better known in many circles than her father. In 1926 George Kelly won the Pulitzer Prize for *Craig's Wife*, a morality play about a woman who marries for status. Four of George Kelly's plays were made into movies that starred such cinema luminaries as Spencer Tracy, Joan Crawford and Will Rogers. His satirical comedy *The Torch-Bearers*, concerning the backstage misadventures of an amateur dramatic company, has been — and still is — frequently revived.

The Model for Lisa Fremont

Two women served as models for Lisa Fremont: one was the wife of screenwriter John Michael Hayes — Mel, and the other was New York legend Anita Colby, a model turned beauty expert.

Anita Colby earned the nickname "the Face" in the mid–1930s when she was the nation's foremost magazine cover and hat model. At one time she was the highest paid model in America. In addition to her beauty, Colby also possessed a superior intellect. She became a top executive in the advertising department of *Harper's Bazaar*. Colby's astute business sense earned her the position in the forties as Feminine Director of Selznick Studio. Many of the leading ladies under contract to Selznick, including such influential Hitchcock stars as Joan Fontaine and Ingrid Bergman, attended what amounted to Colby's one woman finishing school. Hitchcock may have been aware of the ironic fact that Stewart had once been romantically linked to Colby, who reportedly turned down a marriage proposal from the actor. In 1949 Stewart ended one of Hollywood's more celebrated bachelor statuses by marrying former model Gloria Hatrick McLean, who lived in Larchmont, a bedroom community outside New York City. Gloria Stewart was cut from the same elegant cloth as *Rear Window*'s Manhattan fashion model Lisa Fremont and real life's Anita Colby.

One key scene in *Rear Window* involves a daring Lisa Fremont, in order to gain precious information about Lars Thorwald, the film's suspected killer, invading his apartment. This occurs after L.B. Jefferies has tricked Thorwald into leaving via a phone call proposing that the two men discuss blackmail terms at the hotel across the street. The scene is significant in that now it is Lisa, the woman Jefferies regards as too perfect for him, who is behaving in the daring manner of the photographer.

At that moment Jefferies realizes just how much the beautiful model means to him. Hayes's wife Mel was also a beautiful blonde model, and the scene in which Jeff realizes how much Lisa means to him was drawn from his own relationship with Mel prior to their marriage:

In the case of Jimmy Stewart ... when Lisa was in danger, he suddenly realized how much she meant to him, and that if anything happened to her, my God, life was worthless. That came out of my life. Before my wife and I were married, we decided to delay our marriage until I was more successful. We got into an automobile accident, and she was thrown out of the car and onto the highway, amongst broken glass and metal and everything. But in the brief moment when I saw her rolling down the highway before I was knocked unconscious against the windshield, I said, "Oh, my God. If anything happens to her, my life won't be worth anything." And I decided I was not going to wait another minute if we ever lived through this thing.

Hayes dreaded the prospect of what he considered might be a dull scene in which the photographer's realization prompts him to give in and admit that she is right and that they should get together. Hayes finally concluded, "...we never had to have it." As Hayes noted, "When she was in danger, you looked at his face and knew instantly that he valued her more than anything. So when I came to figure out how we were going to write that scene, I said, 'The automobile accident.' He saw her and thought maybe it's the last he'd ever see of her, because this man is capable of killing and cutting her up. Mel was capable of having died rolling down the highway, or being terribly injured for life, and so I said, 'We don't have to say anything.' When I went out and picked up my wife, that was it, we weren't going to be separated again. So when I came to that scene, I drew on my experience for emotion."

Thelma Ritter as Greek Chorus

A third instance of casting perfection after Stewart and Kelly occurred with the selection of saucy character performer Thelma Ritter in the role of Stella McCaffery, an insurance company nurse who visits the injured photographer daily to massage his back and relieve his pain from being confined to a wheelchair. "I like a character like that to act as a Greek chorus," Hayes related, "to tell us what might happen and to go for comic relief. Because you can't have unrestrained suspense all the time. You have to give your audience a chance to laugh and catch their breath and get set for the next scary thing that's going to happen. You can't keep them on a level of fright and suspense through an entire picture.... I told Hitch that we'd need a character of this sort to unite the audience with laughter, right from the beginning."

The Greek chorus character had been used by Hayes in his screenplay for *Torch Song*, the film that marked Joan Crawford's return to MGM after she had bolted from the studio of so many of her triumphs to go to Warner Brothers. Crawford's character is a successful but lonely Broadway stage star seeking love, which she ultimately finds with blind pianist Michael Wilding. Her character is complemented by the shrewd common sense witticisms displayed by her mother, played by Marjorie Rambeau, who earned a Best Supporting Actress Oscar nomination for her effort. In Hayes' next Hitchcock screenplay, in which French Riviera settings and the glamor of stars Grace Kelly and Cary Grant were fully utilized, Jessie Royce Landis, as the mother of the spoiled rich girl played by Kelly, makes witty comments about her daughter's wealth and her pursuit of the debonair male star.

Hitchcock was imaginative enough to recognize the creative validity of Hayes's point. What was then needed was to find the right performer. It would have been inconceivable for Hitchcock to have seen Joseph Mankiewicz's witty film about the backstage machinations of the Broadway drama scene, the celebrated 1950 release *All About Eve*, and not come away impressed by the shrewd characterization and acerbic wit displayed in the script. Mankiewicz was one of the true auteurs of the period who both wrote and directed, and it was easy to envision Alfred Hitchcock sitting in a theater with a broad smile on his face when Ritter, Bette Davis or George Sanders delivered dialogue lined with razor blades.

Mankiewicz recognized Thelma Ritter's inimitable talent for seeing situations in their broadest dimension and delivering pearls of wisdom in succinct and biting fashion. Mankiewicz put Ritter's unique touch to work in *A Letter to Three Wives* and then cast her as the all-knowing Birdie Coonan, Bette Davis's maid, one year later in *All About Eve*. Ritter served as Greek chorus and was the lone person in the cast who immediately saw through the opportunistic Eve Harrington, played by Anne Baxter.

Thelma Ritter is able to revisit familiar Greek chorus territory in *Rear Window*. As soon as she arrives she puts a key element of the drama in perspective. When she observes Jefferies staring beyond the courtyard into the apartments lying beyond, Ritter crisply comments that there is a New York law against Peeping Toms. As she begins rubbing Stewart down she tells him bluntly that any man who would not marry the dazzling Lisa Fremont (Grace Kelly) would have to be crazy. The plainspoken performer seeks to allay Jefferies' fears about long term commitment by referring to her own marriage, and how the relationship has managed to survive problems. At one point she even comments that marriages launched "under the gun" frequently turn out to be enduring.

In keeping with the traditional omniscience of the Greek chorus Stella at one point causes Fremont to wince when she surmises that the presumed murder victim's body parts are probably "floating in the East River." She might have jolted the model with her comment, but it is later proven accurate.

Keeping an Investigation Among Friends

Frequent leading man Wendell Corey proved ideal as Detective Tom Boyle, playing the role with a casualness that blended into solid character interaction with Stewart. The casual air plays well as Jefferies and Fremont are able to speak with candor and without fear of censure, an element that pervades many investigations, particularly when the subject is murder. It is clearly established that

Jefferies and Boyle are the best of friends, and that their relationship extended to a period when closeness was demanded in pursuit of survival. Boyle was pilot and Jefferies photographer in the Army Air Force on World War II aerial reconnaissance missions.

When Jefferies called his friend, who by then was a crack New York City detective, to come over and listen to his theory about how the man across the courtyard killed his wife, the photographer is much freer in stating his case. Boyle, in turn, feels less constrained when it comes to telling his friend, over brandy, why he finds his amateur sleuthing less than compelling.

A Deliberate Allusion to Selznick?

Any discussion of Raymond Burr, cast in the role of ruthless wife killer Lars Thorwald, involves David O. Selznick. A recent documentary about the Hitchcock-Selznick professional relationship revealed the producer as a possible character inspiration. The dour, bespectacled, white-haired and overweight image of killer Lars Thorwald as played by Raymond Burr bore a definite resemblance to David Selznick during the period when the film was made. The question has accordingly arisen as to whether Hitchcock, an inveterate practical joker, was parodying Selznick with the close physical resemblance of Burr's Lars Thorwald.

Burr has very few lines in the film, but his expressions tell the story as Jefferies and later Lisa Fremont observe his actions. *Rear Window* capped a cornerstone of the first phase of Raymond Burr's career as a heavy. Burr possessed a baleful stare that came in handy when the occasion warranted, as in *Rear Window* or *A Place in the Sun* (1951), when he portrayed the cold and ruthless district attorney determined to send George Eastman (Montgomery Clift) to a speedy execution by convincing a jury that he killed Alice Tripp (Shelley Winters).

In a film released one year before *Rear Window* Raymond Burr performed the role of a character who engaged in the same conduct as Miss Lonelyhearts. In Fritz Lang's *The Blue Gardenia* Burr plays the part of an insincere Don Juan heel, artist Harry Prebble, who hopes that sketching young women will lead to amour. Norah Larkin (Anne Baxter) intends to spend her birthday dinner in make-believe romantic fantasy at her apartment after her roommates, played by Ann Sothern and Jeff Donnell, have gone out. She places a picture of her high school sweetheart, then serving in Korea, on the dining room table and opens a bottle of champagne. With delight Norah opens the last letter that he sent her, which she has saved for the special occasion.

Her best laid plans go awry when she opens the letter and reads the contents, which are provided by a male voiceover for dramatic effect. He tells her about being wounded in the Korean War and being shipped to Tokyo for treatment, where he fell in love with his nurse. He reveals their intention to marry.

Norah Larkin's make-believe interlude is reminiscent of Miss Lonelyhearts looking so hard for love that she drinks wine with and speaks to an imaginary attentive male at her dining room table. Could Hitchcock and/or Hayes have been influenced by the earlier film? The question becomes increasingly significant in view of the fact that a tearful Norah is interrupted after reading the letter by the ring of the telephone. The person on the other end of the line is Raymond Burr's character, Harry Prebble. The wolfish artist thinks he is talking to Crystal (Ann Sothern), who has gone out on a date with her former husband. Rather than explaining to Prebble that he has the wrong party, Norah, in her lonely despair, agrees to join him for dinner at the popular Hollywood Polynesian restaurant, the Blue Gardenia.

Prebble pounces on the opportunity with alacrity. He tells Norah when he orders the special house drink that it contains little alcohol, after having earlier instructed the waiter to see that the Polynesian specialties are robust. The film turns on the uncomfortable moments when a very drunk Norah sobers up enough at Prebble's apartment to realize his motives and fight him off, collapsing into deep sleep thereafter. She finds him lying dead after awakening. Norah then steals off into the night in morbid fear, leaving her shoes behind in her rattled haste.

Baxter's character ultimately becomes the subject of a vast Los Angeles hunt orchestrated by sensation-seeking newspaper columnist Casey Mayo (Richard Conte), who is destined to eventually become her love interest. Mayo stirs up interest by christening Norah with the exotic name of the Blue Gardenia suspect.

Long after Burr leaves the scene he remains within the audience's consciousness, until Norah is eventually cleared of all suspicion and the real killer is found, the result of conscientious detective work by journalist Mayo. The film was directed by Fritz Lang, one of the German directors that a young Alfred Hitchcock closely studied on his productive trip to Berlin. Burr made such a fascinating heavy in Lang's film that his role in it could well have motivated Hitchcock's selection of him as the killer in *Rear Window*. While in *The Blue Gardenia* Burr played a smarmy but highly extroverted artist perpetually delivering romantic pitches to the women he draws, in *Rear Window* he is a brooding man who is scarcely heard but observed carefully from a distance. Burr as Lars Thorwald looks troubled, something Jefferies and Fremont observe.

Raymond Burr, who so closely resembled David Selznick, would just three years later catapult out of the ranks of film heavies and into the realm of the heroic through the instrument the producer of *Gone with the Wind* believed would be the ruin of cinema: television. Series creator Erle Stanley Gardner handpicked the Canadian actor to star in the hugely successful *Perry Mason* mystery series. The former heavy, who had been so smarmy in *The Blue Gardenia* and menacing in *Rear Window*, displayed the charmed expertise of the righteous defense attorney in the long-running television series.

The Romantic Element

The additional element propelling *Rear Window* beyond the ranks of a cleverly done suspense story involving murder is the added psychological dimension of romance. Fearless photographer L.B. Jefferies is frightened by the presence of a woman who is, in his words, "too perfect." After spending the day with some of Manhattan's social elite, Lisa has stopped at the 21 Club not only for lunch, but to order dinner for her shut-in photographer boyfriend. It is served in the apartment by the uniformed 21 waiter who brought it. After the lobster dinner has been consumed and Lisa asks Jeff how he liked it, he replies with a dejected sigh that it was "perfect"—just like Lisa.

The psychology of the romantic element has antecedent roots in several Hitchcock films. *The 39 Steps*, the important film from Hitchcock's London phase, included an adversarial relationship between another cool and highly glamorous blonde of the Grace Kelly mold, Madeleine Carroll, and Robert Donat.

Hitchcock's lone comedy effort, *Mr. and Mrs. Smith*, bore an even closer thematic resemblance to the Stewart-Kelly romantic uncertainties. In the 1941 RKO release Robert Montgomery and Carole Lombard, in a turbulent marital relationship reminiscent of the comedies of Howard Hawks, learn that, due to a legal technicality, they are not officially wed. The expected element of conflict then surfaces in the person of Jeff Custer (Gene Raymond), who provides competition for no-longer-husband Montgomery and begins seriously wooing Lombard. In a variance of the plot element later surfacing in *Rear Window*, David Smith (Robert Montgomery) seeks to use the alleged "perfection" of competing suitor Custer against him. Smith counters his competition by pointing out that, whereas he is a regular guy with normal imperfections, lawyer Custer, with his Harvard pedigree and status as a former All-American football player, is a poor bet for a lasting relationship. As a means of enhancing the comedic element, the presumably superior Custer demonstrates appropriate stiffness.

The Stewart-Kelly relationship also bears certain thematic similarities to that of the dynamic superstar combo of Cary Grant and Ingrid Bergman in *Notorious*. In *Notorious* the male in the relationship also has cold feet, though in that film his fear of commitment, not a sense of inadequacy, plagues the troubled relationship. Clearly, Hitchcock found conflicts between men and women in love, but struggling to get together, a useful and important plot device.

Miss Torso as Thematic Focal Point

A clever twist of the *Rear Window* script Hitchcock worked on so diligently with the highly talented John Michael Hayes involves a woman who has no dialogue, other than that unheard while spoken in her apartment. Georgine Darcy appears as the shapely dancer an attentive Jefferies names Miss Torso. Viewers are able to recognize the dilemma of a conflicted Jefferies through comparing and contrasting his reactions toward Miss Torso and the glamorous and aristocratic Lisa Fremont, who is pressing for a marital commitment from the psychologically beleaguered photographer.

The voyeur in Jefferies enables him to react to Miss Torso, given the benefit of distance, in contrast to Lisa Fremont, who stands a few feet away. One evening when Miss Torso holds court before a group of breathless male admirers in her apartment, Lisa Fremont confidently tells the fascinated photographer that Miss Torso is not romantically interested in any of the men in the room. When the photographer commends her on her intuition, Lisa ruefully replies that she would gladly trade her female intuition for an evening in his apartment.

The psychological dynamics exposing the inner dilemma of Jefferies is further revealed when Lisa, realizing that she is in competition with Miss Torso, comes prepared to stay for the night. The Manhattan model changes into ravishing bedroom attire. The facial beauty and captivating figure of Lisa would be expected to send any male heart racing, but a trapped Jefferies leaves his mind and interest focused on the woman across the courtyard. Lisa realizes that Jefferies can readily identify with the men in the room admiring Miss Torso, since he does not know her and a potential marital attachment is not confronting him. At one point she becomes frustrated and draws the curtains shut. She then emphatically exclaims, "The show's over for tonight."

A Police Detective and Miss Torso

An element of humor is supplied when Jeff's old Army Air Force friend Tom Doyle is sipping a brandy and discussing concerns about jewelry salesman Lars Thorwald as a potential murderer. At one point he demonstrates his own natural voyeuristic inclinations as he watches the seductively proportioned Miss Torso dance gracefully around her apartment.

James Stewart demonstrates his endearing propensities as a relaxed actor when, seeing Detective Doyle's interest in observing activity at the apartment across the courtyard, he asks matter-of-factly, "How's your wife, Tom?" Wendell Corey delivers a superb response, returning to the matter at hand while refusing to be baited by his old friend. Both performers play the moment low key. Therein lies its comedic value, as we learn that Stewart is not the only voyeur around.

Stewart and the Clever Microcosm

In the manner of a brilliantly crafted silent film, the busy camera of Robert Burks, one of the industry's finest cinematographers, kept its focus on the activities occurring across the courtyard. The events closely observed by Jefferies represent differing aspects of where his future might lie. His concern over whether he should take the matrimonial step with the elegant Lisa Fremont is accented by events he sees transpiring in the apartments across the courtyard. How much unfolding activity represents a preview of what lies ahead for Stewart's character?

There is the case of the Newlyweds, who have just moved in to one of the apartments. Jefferies naturally wonders about their early adjustment phase and whether it will presage his own future with Fremont. In the case of Lars Thorwald, the man Jefferies becomes increasingly convinced is a murderer, his bedridden blonde wife with whom he fought bears some resemblance to Lisa. Given Hitchcock's attention to detail, this similarity almost certainly was by design rather than a coincidence.

The preoccupation with watching the graceful steps of seductively attired Miss Torso enables Jefferies to let his male hormones react while he maintains a safe distance. The beautiful and available woman at hand, Lisa Fremont, seeks a commitment, whereas it costs him nothing to lust after Miss Torso.

A notable potential for apprehension resides within the characters of Miss Lonelyhearts and the Songwriter. With savvy nurse Stella (Thelma Ritter) observing, Miss Lonelyhearts, after a traumatic episode in which she chased a young man out of her apartment when he sought to make love to her, has apparently given up her romantic hope of finding a Prince Charming to sweep her off her feet. Stella notes she is contemplating a potentially suicidal dose of pills.

In one of the most creatively inventive scenes of the film, Miss Lonelyhearts listens to the sounds of the piano being played by the Songwriter as he continues working on the ballad he hopes will eventually become a hit record. The song has a romantic ring. The result is that the romantic side of Miss Lonelyhearts, feeling an infusion of optimism after listening to the song in progress, puts her pills aside. The conclusion to be drawn is that a potential suicide has been thwarted as the romantic instincts of Miss Lonelyhearts are again awakened, and with them the urge to live.

Close observer Jefferies has seen the lonely desperation evidenced by the Songwriter and Miss Lonelyhearts at different points. In the former case there was the time when he came home drunk and morose, while the latter presented tears and a potential suicide attempt frustrated in the nick of time by a melodic piano. Seeing these activities makes Jefferies fully aware of another potentiality for himself, that of becoming a lonely man who has spurned the opportunity to marry the dashing fashion model.

It is obvious that Fremont, one of Manhattan's brightest and most attractive women, and a celebrated star of the city's upper social circles, is far from devoid of opportunities. Jefferies knows that if he does not take advantage of the situation soon he risks losing one of the city's most eligible young women. Early in the film, when Jefferies is conversing with his boss and telling him about his reluctance to marry, he is cautioned about the possibility of becoming a "lonely old man."

Bing Crosby and Hitchcock Humor

The wily Hitchcock uses a ballad crooned by the number one song plugger in movie history, Bing Crosby, to add a touch of humor to *Rear Window*. An apartment dweller plays a tenderly sung Crosby ballad called "To See You Is to Love You," and the words are loaded with meaning in the psychological framework of the film. After all, Thelma Ritter, as the film's Greek chorus, made an earlier reference to the New York law against Peeping Toms. Now Crosby, utilizing the appropriate romantic tone, sings, "...to know you at all is to know you by heart ... I'll see you in the same old dream." Jefferies, in his shut-in status, has become immersed in a world of fantasy. Lisa Fremont, as a practical realist, seeks to bring him out of it while he retreats to an erotic world starring Miss Torso. If Jefferies had the voice of Crosby, one wonders whether he would be singing the flowing words of the ballad to Miss Torso, the neighborhood fantasy woman busily fending off the advances of numerous men.

Kelly as a Woman of Adventure

The team of Hayes and Hitchcock crafted a story that contains layer upon layer of psychological nuances. Early in the film Jefferies, feeling pressured by Fremont to commit himself to marriage, delivers a laundry list of unpleasantries to demonstrate how hideous life could be traveling with him on photographic assignments to distant points of the world. He is telling Lisa that he could not imagine her adjusting to circumstances in which she would not be perfectly attired and elegantly coiffed, not to mention dealing with the absences of quality food and lodging in a world devoid of comfort.

At a key moment toward the end of the picture Lisa jolts Jefferies to a new level of awareness. In her anxiety to solve the case and prove that Thorwald is the killer that she, Jefferies and Stella believe him to be, Lisa climbs up the fire escape and sneaks into the salesman's apartment while he is gone. Jefferies not only has to eat his words concerning the elegant and sophisticated Lisa Fremont, who is now showing her daring side, he realizes after Thorwald returns and finds the beautiful blonde intruder how much she means to him. After Lisa is grabbed by the returning Thorwald, Stewart, realizing that the model's life is under imminent threat, telephones the police station. Even though the visit will ultimately result in Lisa being carted off to jail for breaking and entering, police intervention saves her from becoming the ruthless killer's latest victim.

Now that the story had been carried to that point and audiences were breathlessly hooked, the question remained of how to bring the drama to a conclusion. To do so a clever ploy is utilized, one that employs two elements of the story — the attempt to solve a murder, entwined with the romantic element of Lisa Fremont seeking a marital commitment from Jefferies.

Aware that Jefferies is watching her from his apartment while the police, having answered Jefferies' call, are in Thorwald's apartment, Lisa engages in communication that inadvertently puts the photographer's life at immediate risk. In her quick search for evidence prior to Thorwald's arrival Lisa found his wife's wedding ring. As the killer stands next to her, and with the police in sight, she shows Jefferies the ring — which she has placed on her finger, symbolizing her matrimonial desire.

A stirring close-up reveals the bespectacled killer's reaction as he notices Lisa making eye contact with Jefferies. The killer then becomes aware of who is pursuing him so relentlessly. As soon as Lisa is hauled away to jail, to be bailed out shortly thereafter under the supervising presence of Jefferies' longtime pal Doyle, Thorwald makes his move.

In the typical Hitchcock fashion of maximizing suspense, a wide-eyed Jefferies sits in the darkness as he hears the sound of footsteps moving slowly but surely up the stairs toward his apartment. When Thorwald realizes that what Jefferies knows can lead to his execution or life-long imprisonment, he moves menacingly toward him. One of the more original confrontations between a killer and intended victim has Jefferies, bound to his wheelchair, fighting back by using his camera as a weapon, using quick flashing light to prevent Thorwald from killing him.

Although he eventually falls through the window in his struggle with Thorwald and lands on the ground below, Jefferies avoids death. Meanwhile, Detective Doyle has arrived with the recently released Lisa Fremont and his fellow officers to apprehend Thorwald.

Tying the Threads Together

Once the killer is apprehended and confesses to murdering his wife, the steady camera of Robert Burks moves from apartment to apartment in a denouement that ties the various threads of the story together. As for the newlyweds, there is already trouble on the horizon as the wife is heard lamenting that her husband has quit his job, and had she known he would take such a step, she would never have married him.

The message that life marches inexorably onward is conveyed with a quick stop at the former Thorwald apartment. Already a crew has arrived to paint the walls, after which another tenant or tenants will arrive, hopefully unaware of the murder that occurred in the unit.

As for the adventures of Miss Torso, a swift resolution occurs. A bespectacled soldier arrives in uniform with duffel bag in hand. Miss Torso throws herself into his arms and welcomes him home. Her Prince Charming has arrived after fulfilling his duties to Uncle Sam, and intuitive Lisa Fremont is presumably proven correct in her earlier analysis when, after observing an apartment filled with men, she announced confidently to Jefferies that Miss Torso was not romantically interested in any of them.

The stories of Miss Lonelyhearts and the Songwriter are superbly integrated. It will be recalled that listening to the romantic sounds from the Songwriter's work in progress prompted Miss Lonelyhearts to decline taking the pills that were presumably intended to end her life. The man whose music provided hope in the midst of suicidal gloom is seen talking to her in his apartment. Their smiles and seeming contentment indicate that love is in bloom. He then plays for her on his phonograph the song he hopes will become America's next major hit. It is appropriately titled "Lisa."

The action then shifts to Jefferies. He is sleeping, his legs propped up in front of him, both of them now in casts, indicating the price paid for the fall from the window during his struggle with Thorwald. Finally, the beautiful Lisa Fremont is seen. She is reading a book about the Himalayas, conjuring up images of a dutiful young wife making a commitment to her husband's lifestyle. A moment passes and we see ambivalence within Lisa. When she sees that Jeff is fast asleep she picks up a copy of the latest *Harper's Bazaar*.

Hitchcock's grand cinema soufflé brought him the financial hit he sought, along with artistic recognition. Hitchcock received an Oscar nomination for Best Director, while John Michael Hayes, Robert Burks and Loren L. Ryder were also nominated in the Screenplay, Cinematography and Sound categories.

On to the Riviera and Romance with a Prince

Now that Hitchcock had scored a solid box office smash during a difficult period when television was cutting substantially into film profits, it was far from unexpected for him to roll the dice again with the bright young scenarist who had constructed such a brilliant screenplay with *Rear Window*. The scene of *To Catch a Thief*, their next collaboration, and the spot to put down the camera and let Robert Burks engage in his superb cinematic craftsmanship, was a location called by many the most beautiful and majestically scenic spots on earth — the French Riviera.

With the dividends rolling in from *Rear Window*, a grateful Paramount Studios was happy to unleash the A-team and spend what was needed to help ensure another Hitchcock box office bonanza. Glamorous Grace Kelly was back again, providing Edith Head with an opportunity to design dresses fit for Kelly's role as a young heiress. Head secured one of her 40 Academy Award nominations in Costume Design for this effort, to go along with her 8 Oscars. Kelly's romantic interest would be played by the dashing Cary Grant, who had previously starred opposite Ingrid Bergman in one of Hitchcock's biggest hits, *Notorious*, and before that alongside Joan Fontaine and her Oscar-winning performance in *Suspicion*.

The Greek chorus element that Hayes successfully incorporated into *Rear Window* returned; this time the performer doling out the pearls of wisdom was Jesse Royce Landis, as an heiress who jokes about her vast wealth and speaks practically about her beautiful daughter. From the time she sets eyes on John Robie (Grant), the worldly-wise and practical Jessie Stevens (Landis) deems him a perfect man for her daughter. She reasons that he possesses the maturity necessary to forge a successful romantic relationship with her rich and spoiled daughter.

To Catch a Thief was adapted to the screen by Hayes from a novel by David Dodge. Cary Grant plays John Robie, a French Resistance World War II hero and daring jewelry thief who swears that he has retired from heisting to live a life of quiet luxury at his villa overlooking Cannes and the Mediterranean. Local police authorities doubt that he has really retired from his earlier career when a spate of jewel robberies occur in the area. Insisting that he has nothing to do with the latest crime spree, Robie agrees to use his expertise to help locate the actual perpetrator or perpetrators of the crimes. His support is enlisted by Hitchcock regular John Williams, who had played the lead Scotland Yard detective in Paramount's *Dial M for Murder*. In *To Catch a Thief* veteran British character performer Williams plays H.H. Hughson, a Lloyds of London insurance investigator with a strong pecuniary interest in bringing the jewel thefts to a stop, and who believes that Robie, as a former inside operator, is the man possessing the expertise to help him crack the case.

The magnificent scenery and elegant setting of the Grand Casino in Monte Carlo, where the mystery is resolved and the thief apprehended in the midst of an elegant costume party, provide the perfect opportunities for cinematographer Robert Burks to fill the screen with dazzling technicolor imagery. While Burks failed to secure an Academy Award after being nominated for *Rear Window*, he won the Oscar for this 1955 release. Burks worked with Hitchcock on 12 of his films and would probably have remained as a mainstay through the rest of the director's career had it not been for a fire that engulfed his Los Angeles home in 1968, costing the cinematographer his life, along with his wife's.

To Catch a Thief embodied considerably lighter fare than the psychological gem *Rear Window*, but the combination of elements, beginning with majestic settings and a true "steam team" in attractive leads Kelly and Grant, provided more delight for happy Paramount stockholders. The Academy also registered robust artistic approval. In addition to the Oscar won by Burks for Cinematography and the nomination Head received for Costume Design, *To Catch a Thief* also secured a nomination in the Best Color Art Direction category for the team of Arthur Krams, Art Pereira, J. McMillan Johnson and Sam Comer.

The good news for Hitchcock was that he had another hit with the scenic Riviera-set classic. The bad news was that he lost one of his most elegant and celebrated leading ladies, one of the dazzling parade of blondes with which he had become inextricably linked. After starring in three fifties Hitchcock films for Paramount, the last two of which were among the director's biggest hits, Grace Kelly would leave the cinema scene while at the peak of her beauty and drawing power.

One fateful afternoon the dazzling film star met 31-year-old bachelor Prince Rainier of the Principality of Monaco at the Hotel de Paris, situated next door to the Monte Carlo Casino that played a dominant location role in *To Catch a Thief*. It was the beginning of a courtship that resulted in Kelly leaving Hollywood to become a princess of a glittering principality where the world's super rich lived and congregated. While Hitchcock would periodically tempt Princess Grace to return to the screen during her Los Angeles visits, when she stayed with the Hitchcocks at their Bellagio Road residence, she would resist all entreaties. To the end, Hitchcock longed to put her in front of the cameras again.

The Hitchcock-Hayes team continued through two more films. The first was a more modest, lower budget effort, *The Trouble with Harry*, starring Edmund Gwenn, John Forsythe and Shirley MacLaine, that was filmed on location in Vermont. The final Hitchcock-Hayes pairing resulted in another Paramount technicolor box office bonanza.

Once More, in Glossy Technicolor

The Man Who Knew Too Much was one of 1956's most popular productions. It was a remake of a Hitchcock London film released in 1934. Always mindful of the impact of television, Hitchcock and Paramount provided abundant glossy color to showcase fascinating Morocco and London locations. In that the film concerned the abduction of a youngster of vacationing Americans who would inadvertently become caught up in international political intrigue, no one would better serve story interests than Mr. Typical American James Stewart in the role of Ben McKenna, an Indianapolis doctor. The casting decision for the role of his wife was also a master stroke — the Warner Brothers blonde who dominated in the most-popular-star category during the fifties, Doris Day, who was seen as every bit as traditional an American woman as Stewart was perceived as a traditional American male.

The story begins with the McKennas touring Morocco on an extended holiday after the doctor has attended a Paris medical conference, an element that tags him as an outstanding individual in his profession. His pedigree is further enhanced when we learn that his lovely blonde wife Jo, played by an always effervescent Doris Day, has given up a successful career as a Broadway musical star to marry and settle down in Indianapolis. The clear deduction to draw is that this desirable and talented lady would not have abandoned her career for anyone other than a man she believed was a conspicuous winner.

This story has a real ebb and flow, with a quick transition at the beginning. The script by Hayes begins with the McKennas of Indianapolis immersed in success, but even at that point there is a duality that is represented through humor. His professional enrichment as a doctor results from tending to the pain and suffering of others. This point is made humorously in a dialogue exchange between the couple as Jo McKenna mentions that Mrs. Campbell's gall stone have paid for their three days in North Africa; Bill Edwards's tonsils have provided the money to buy her new dress, purchased in Paris; Johnny Matthews's appendix has paid for the doctor's new suit, while the boat trip to Europe stemmed from multiple births and Mrs. Morgan's hives. The journey home was underwritten by Herbie Taylor's ulcers and Alida Markle's asthma.

Soon Dr. Ben McKenna's prosperous world is shattered as he is instantly transported into a world that he had been previously able to observe and deal with at a professional distance. One dramatic event makes Ben and Jo McKenna realize how quickly circumstances turn. Hitchcock, as the wily adult Puck once more, displays through his art life's tug of war between tranquil order and dangerous uncertainty, using the experiences of an American family many would envy.

A Success on Any Level

The beauty of Hitchcock's remake of his 1934 black and white suspense story is that it can be appreciated on both a pure entertainment and a psychological level. Filmgoers can readily identify with and eagerly root for two loving parents determined to rescue their kidnapped young son. On that level *The Man Who Knew Too Much* carries the kind of visceral entertainment value of the old Saturday afternoon serials, with the hero speeding to rescue the lovely and innocent young heroine from the clutches of the villain. The psychological element allows Hitchcock, in his Puck guise, to dramatically display life's uncertainties and the constant tug of war between good and evil. This presentation of conflict cleverly extends to the middle-aged husband and wife abductors, with the man rigorously committed to the plan at hand and the woman becoming increasingly disenchanted as she grows emotionally attached to the young kidnap victim.

Alfred Hitchcock delivered a comparative summary of the 1934 and 1956 versions of *The Man Who Knew Too Much* when he succinctly concluded, "Let's say that the first version was the work of a talented amateur and the second was made by a professional." The final of four collaborations between Hitchcock and John Michael Hayes combined some of the same elements that made *To Catch a Thief* a winner, including superb color combined with virtuoso cinematographer Robert Burks' fascinating location shooting (this time in North Africa and London).

The character played by Stewart, along with the story line, has antecedents in other Hitchcock films. He becomes caught up in a web of international intrigue revolving around an attempted assassination of a European head of state. His involvement in intrigue he knows nothing about, purely as a victim of circumstances, is reminiscent of Robert Donat in *The 39 Steps* and, as we will observe later, Cary Grant in *North by Northwest*.

The film demonstrates how quickly the fickle hand of fate can disrupt lives operating in a positive pattern and spin them into a web of tragedy. Inherent in this element is that McKenna, thought to be a confident man on top of life, realizes how helpless he can become with one intervening event.

The kidnapping of young Hank McKenna, played by Christopher Olsen, results from a misunderstanding. The reason why French intelligence agent Louis Bernard (Daniel Gelin) makes contact with the McKennas on a tour bus is that he wrongly believes that they are the tourist couple involved in a plot to assassinate a European head of state. This misunderstanding becomes twofold when, as a result of mistakenly coming into contact with Bernard, young Hank McKenna is apprehended by the couple sought by the intelligence agent, because they now fear what Stewart might know. It is imperative therefore to intimidate the McKennas into silence until the murder plot can be carried out.

The intrigue intensifies when Agent Bernard, who is finally aware of the real identities of the plot perpetrators, is stabbed to death and dies in Dr. McKenna's arms. The link that carries the mystery to its next phase is the clue he is able to whisper to the doctor before death, the name of Ambrose Chappell in London.

When the McKennas arrive in London, determined to find their kidnapped son, Hayes and Hitchcock deftly lighten the suspense when it appears that the audience might become overloaded. A contingent of Jo McKenna's fans are on hand at their Heathrow Airport arrival with placards welcoming her to London. This event provides a twofold purpose, relieving some story tension while reminding her husband and the audience that this was a woman who gave up a successful career to become a wife and mother. Indeed, when the McKennas were in their pre-kidnapping halcyon vacation state Jo was discussing with her husband the prospect of a brother or sister for young Hank.

When the couple arrives at their hotel the fame of Doris Day's character is further underlined by the arrival of friends she had made on the London theatrical scene. Veteran British character star Alan Mowbray, along with future leading lady Carolyn Jones and Hilary Brooke, are used for comedic effect to lighten the plot. The McKennas are determined to both treat her friends politely and not burden them by revealing their current tragedy. They simultaneously focus on their efforts to locate their son and achieve his release. At one point Jo's show business friends are left alone in the fashionable hotel suite for hours as the mystery intensifies and the couple closes in on the criminal gang that abducted their son.

A Scene of Graphic Symbolism

While Jo entertains her friends, her husband finds the name Ambrose Chappell in the London telephone directory. Londoner Mowbray is able to tell him that the location he seeks is in the nearby Bayswater section. Stewart then walks to the address in hopes of finding his son. Instead he encounters unexpected danger.

In Donald Spoto's analysis of this craftily made Hitchcock film he notes how Stewart, who stood at 6'4", had his size emphasized in close-ups provided by Robert Burks. This demonstrated psychologically how Stewart was seemingly in charge of things, standing well above the crowd; but, in the Hitchcock representation of duality, events can sharply reduce him to a seemingly smaller, less awesome player in the flow of life's events. A scene that strikingly shows this contrast is that in which Stewart visits the taxidermy shop of Ambrose Chappell.

The noted Hitchcock flair for extending drama to keep audiences alert and on edge is revealed when the troubled Dr. Ben McKenna asks to see Ambrose Chappell. The man with whom he initially speaks, and who he walked past on the street moments earlier, realizes he does not know the American and concludes that he must want to talk to his father.

A tense McKenna receives quick confirmation from the man that he is indeed Ambrose Chappell Senior and has been for 73 years. Having received confirmation in his mind that he is talking with the man who holds the power of life and death over his son, McKenna, who towers over the two Chappells and the other employees in the shop, demands that Chappell give him back his son, reaching out and grabbing the elderly man by the neck.

Pandemonium reigns as the towering McKenna shrieks with increasing desperation while the younger Chappell and other employees, all of whom are male, seek to exert control over the situation. We see the fickle hand of fate transform a tranquil taxidermy shop operated by two seemingly gentle and polite father and son proprietors in West London's Bayswater district into a state of panic. It was the kind of quick, disruptive event that the McKennas experienced when their son was kidnapped.

The brilliantly filmed close-ups of Robert Burks tell us much about the circumstances of life. While Ben McKenna towers above the other men, they soon surround and contain him. This scene is one of the most brilliantly conceived of Hitchcock's career, as visuality and psychology merge. At one point, as the men wrestle with McKenna and seek to subdue him until the police can arrive, the man who has now become the victim moves toward a stuffed lion.

The old expression "head in the lion's mouth" becomes reality when McKenna's is propelled briefly into that position during the intense struggle. The doctor's position represents symbolically how abruptly events can turn and how an individual can figuratively end up with his or her head in the lion's mouth.

The clever ploy of having the struggle occur in a taxidermy shop in which Stewart can graphically and symbolically be devoured by a hungry lion was one that Hitchcock would include in his popular 1960 release *Psycho*. In that film Anthony Perkins is fascinated by stuffed birds, which hang from the walls of the Bates Motel he runs. In *Psycho*, as well as *The Man Who Knew Too Much* four years earlier, the symbolism is clear — the struggle between life and death in a turbulent world, a struggle that wily film craftsman Hitchcock understands.

Ben McKenna's Sudden Realization

The dramatic scene at the taxidermy shop run by the Chappells contains a clear and sudden point of demarcation. Initially we see a determined man who is a frustrated victim and seeks justice. The existential reality is that his tremendous energy, coupled with determination to seek resolution in a righteous cause, turns against him. The fury and determination result in the innocent Chappells and their employees concluding that their unexpected visitor is a dangerous psycho who needs to be immediately incarcerated in the interest of society.

Ben McKenna might have been gasping and immersed in physical struggle, but the mind that the Chappells and their employees are convinced has abandoned him is very much intact. In a millisecond viewers can observe the change as he comes to the sudden realization that he has made a mistake, that the Chappells know nothing about his son, and that they are convinced that he is mad and are intent on handing him over to the police.

With that sudden shift, McKenna realizes that his role has changed. He was the determined and vigilant investigator intent on prying the truth out of Ambrose Chappell concerning the whereabouts of young Hank. Now he is in a position in which he is unable to extricate himself from the control of others, namely the taxidermists convinced they are serving the best interest of society. He will have plenty of explaining to do to the London police, not to mention the fact that precious time will be lost, which he knows could spell the difference between life and death for the son he loves.

Eventually, after much struggle and unsuccessful verbal protests that a mistake has been made, McKenna is able to pry himself loose and make a quick escape from the taxidermy shop. The sharply honed Hayes script then makes a turn toward what, after much struggle and uncertainty, will lead to a happy ending and the release of young Ben into the arms of his loving parents.

A Place, Not a Person

The determined husband and wife team of Stewart and Day ultimately conclude that "Ambrose Chappell" is a place — a chapel — and not a person. It is in fact a dreary looking would-be place of worship whose pastor and principal figure is involved in foreign intrigue and murder. The dour team of Mr. and Mrs. Drayton are themselves figures of conflict, with the husband, played by Bernard Miles, and his wife, portrayed by Brenda de Banzie, ultimately tugging in different directions. In addition to Mrs. Drayton being a nicer person appalled by her husband's involvement in assassination plots for profit, another element enters into the picture as well, one that ultimately prompts her to cast her lot with the McKennas and step away from the sordid interests of her opportunistic husband.

A strong maternal element weighs on Mrs. Drayton as she becomes attached to Christopher Olsen. It is easy to see how this could occur. Here is a woman who is apparently childless. She is married to a man hypocritical enough to take people's money by pretending to be a sincere man of God, and ruthless enough to become involved in an international murder plot. Her maternal instincts draw her to the young man who has been kidnapped as she envisions him as a son she might have had but never did.

The strong family element of a man seeking to both get his son back and assist his wife who is emotionally devastated at the prospect of losing her only child is combined with the wife of a provocateur developing a bond with a kidnapped youngster she realizes under different circumstances could have been her own son. *The Man Who Knew Too Much* could ultimately be called a film about family values. It evokes memories of Hitchcock's comment when Hal Wallis told him that he had declined producing *Notorious* due to the spy element and development of the atomic bomb. Hitchcock's response was that *Notorious* was actually a love story.

To play the key roles of the Draytons, Hitchcock used his superb casting instincts to hire two British performers with long and impressive resumes. Bernard Miles was a man of many accomplishments who, after graduating from Pembrooke College at Oxford University, taught school before entering films as a bit player in 1933. He became a regular in the films of Michael Powell and Emeric Pressburger before graduating to larger roles. In 1942 Miles had a starring role in the most impressive film ever made about the British Navy, *In Which We Serve*, which was co-directed by the celebrated tandem of David Lean and Noel Coward. The 1947 comedy about British bird watchers, *Tawny Pippit*, in which he starred and also co-wrote and co-produced, resulted in Miles receiving a Best Actor nomination by the New York Film Critics Circle. That same year Miles was also nominated by the same group in the Best Actor category for his work in two adaptations of Charles Dickens novels, *Great Expectations* and *Nicholas Nickleby*.

Miles's 1950 film, *Chance of a Lifetime*, in which he starred alongside his wife, Josephine Wilson, as well as produced, directed, and co-wrote, was a comedy about labor management in a British industrial town. Three major distributors rejected it before it was finally picked up by British Lion at the behest of the government. The film went on to secure Best Film honors at the British Academy Awards. Miles, along with Josephine Wilson, founded the Mermaid Theatre in the atmospheric Old City of London on the bank of the Thames. He was knighted in 1969 and given a life peerage ten years later. For the rest of his life he answered to the names of both Lord Bernard Miles and Baron Bernard.

Brenda de Banzie had an interesting and varied British acting background as well. She made her stage debut in 1935 but did not appear in films until well into her thirties. She made her bow in the 1951 suspense drama *The Long Dark Hall*, starring Rex Harrison and his wife Lilli Palmer. Her biggest film success came three years later as Charles Laughton's industrious daughter in David Lean's *Hobson's Choice*. She also appeared as the long-suffering wife of Laurence Olivier in both the stage and film versions of *The Entertainer*, based on the highly successful John Osborne drama and directed in both venues by Tony Richardson.

Making a Point Through Music

Just as Hitchcock had made a point through music by playing Bing Crosby's ballad "To See You Is to Love You" in *Rear Window*, in *The Man Who Knew Too Much* a song is introduced that not only captured the lone Oscar for the film, it could well serve as a Hitchcock theme song for all of his movies that illuminate the dramatic tug of war between good and evil, which he saw as reflective of the human race.

Jay Livingstone and Ray Evans wrote "Whatever Will Be," which is also referred to as "Que Sera Sera," and had the perfect performer in Doris Day to sing it. Day left Ohio and forged a successful career as a band singer with Les Brown and his Band of Renown before clicking in films and achieving numerous star popularity awards at Warner Brothers. One of her earliest triumphs, which gave her a chance to combine her dramatic as well as singing talents, came at Warners for its biggest director of the period, Michael Curtiz, who had directed *Casablanca* (1942) and *Mildred Pierce* (1947). Starring alongside another up and coming talent, Kirk Douglas, Day played the mercurial trumpet player's band singer who, as a woman of wholesome values, ultimately reforms him and wins his heart in a romantic triangle that included cold high society dilettante Lauren Bacall.

The fifties were the peak decade for Doris Day. *The Man Who Knew Too Much* is considered one of her milestone films, while "Whatever Will Be" ranks high among her hit songs. Aided by exposure in a major Hitchcock triumph, the song catapulted to the top of the sales chart. After her Hitchcock hit Day rounded out the fifties with solid triumphs in the film adaptation of the Broadway musical hit *The Pajama Game* in 1957, opposite John Raitt, and one year later in *Teacher's Pet*, with Clark Gable. Day culminated her most productive decade by starring in her most successful comedy pairing with Rock Hudson at Universal — *Pillow Talk*.

It is highly probable that Doris Day had in mind her major dramatic performance in *The Man Who Knew Too Much* when she launched the sixties by appearing in a challenging dramatic role without song in the familiar London setting of her earlier success, as she starred opposite Rex Harrison in *Midnight Lace*. It is virtually certain as well that producer Ross Hunter, who turned out the successful Day comedies with Hudson, was also well aware of the earlier hit in a similar role and was confident that lightning would strike twice, which it did, as she turned in a stirring performance playing another woman immersed in tragedy. In the earlier film she had been concerned about her son's life, while in the 1960 release the life she sought to save was her own, as husband Harrison conspires with lover Natasha Parry, who masquerades as Day's best friend, to kill her for her wealth at a time when his business is in a state of collapse.

Sung in Disparate Situations

Hitchcock never would have achieved international success without superb creative instincts. Having a tune ultimately headed for an Oscar sung twice by Day in key contrasting situations again illustrated Hitchcock's use of duality. On the first occasion the world was a bright place for the McKennas. Dr. McKenna had just finished participating in an important international medical conference in Paris. Now the successful family was vacationing in exotic Morocco, seeing the world. As Day sings the song to young Hank while he lay in bed following an eventful day, "Whatever Will Be" connotes limitless horizons.

On the second occasion it is employed as an inventive strategy to save Hank McKenna's life. As she sings at a consulate reception after saving a head of state's life through her warning shout at an Albert Hall concert, sparing him from an intended fatal bullet fired by a professional assassin, she correctly perceives that her son is being held somewhere in the gigantic mansion. She sings "Whatever Will Be" in a loud voice, hoping young Hank will hear her and sing along with her, revealing his whereabouts. He does so, with the cooperation of Mrs. Drayton, who is anxious to see the boy she has come to love reunited with his mother and father.

A Defining Moment for a Hitchcock Scholar

The Man Who Knew Too Much holds significant meaning for Ken Mogg. Seeing the film the first time represented the defining moment for the Australian film historian, who remembers the evening when he became intrigued by Hitchcock's rare cinematic genius. The result was a keen interest coupled with ambitious research efforts leading ultimately to the creation of the foremost Internet website dealing with Hitchcock's films, called, appropriately enough, "The MacGuffin Web Page" (a fertile exchange for the serious Hitchcock scholars who meet there). The Melbourne film historian also wrote one of the definitive books on the famous director, *The Alfred Hitchcock Story*, published in 1999. "My book has only one authentic edition," Mogg informed, "the U.K. edition from Titan Books of London. The U.S. edition is a travesty of the original." The book contains a foreword by Janet Leigh, whose role in *Psycho* will later be explored within the context of the film.

"Hitchcock was a rhetorician who tried to include rather than exclude," Mogg explained. "Precisely that feeling of rare pleasure is what has always intrigued me about Hitchcock's films, and which I find epitomized in the Albert Hall scene of *The Man Who Knew Too Much*."

Mogg recalled how the film became a defining moment for him. "*The Man Who Knew Too Much* was probably the first Hitchcock film I ever saw," Mogg said. "I remember the occasion well. It was at a local scout hall one night in the late 1950s, and the film was shown on 16mm to a group of parents and kids. At that time, the Elvis Presley phenomenon had just arrived, exciting some of my fellow teenagers rather more than it did me. But on the night when we watched *The Man Who Knew Too Much*, everyone was excited! There was only one projector, I remember, which meant that there were three reel-breaks. At each break, the whole audience was audibly impatient for the film to resume. And the Albert Hall scene, with its attempted assassination and 'Storm Cloud Cantata' greatly affected me. Analyzing its elements today, including the words of the cantata, about restless Nature, and how the scene functions 'pantheistically' in a film showing diverse faiths and lifestyles, I believe it epitomizes Hitchcock's 'pure cinema' and what life-death matters are at stake for us as we watch Hitchcock's melodramas."

A Dickens Connection

Mogg noted that he had "nearly always been a film teacher or film scholar," with the exception of a "lost decade" in the eighties, and has closely followed critical debates in major movie journals such as *Sight and Sound* and *Cahiers du Cinema*. He has read extensively and professes a love for English literature. "When I read Dickens's *Bleak House*, I sensed at once that Hitchcock had been there before me," Mogg related. "I was surely right. Donald Spoto says 'it seems to have engraved itself on Hitchcock's memory.' What the French film critics singled out as a key Hitchcockian motif— transference of guilt from one character to another — is everywhere to be seen in that dream-like Dickens novel."

The MacGuffin website began as an offshoot of the MacGuffin journal, which is officially the newsletter of a Hitchcock Special Interest Group of Australian Mensa that Mogg initiated at the end of 1990. According to Mogg, "the website began in late 1995 or early 1996." He professed "happy memories" of those early days on the web. Two Hitchcock historians who have contributed generously to the site are Dan Auiler, author of *Vertigo* and *Hitchcock's Notebooks*, and Dr. Nandor Bokor, a physicist who helped translate French director Francois Truffaut's *Hitchcock* into Hungarian.

Another Stellar Musical Contribution

The famous scene in which Jo McKenna saves the life of the visiting head of state targeted by an assassin's bullet marked the second use of music to great effect by Hitchcock. His duality theme was once more apparent, represented by the classical "Storm Cloud Cantata," written by Arthur Benjamin and D.B. Wyndham-Lewis, and performed by the London Symphony Orchestra to the accompaniment of the Covent Garden Choir, with soloist Barbara Hewitt. As Ken Mogg observed, the selection appropriately set the mood of the film, as the brooding and the beautiful intermingled. Magnificent sounds reverberating through the majestic Albert Hall, and its richly historic West London setting across the street from Hyde Park, denoted triumphal beauty mingled with a sad reality.

Playing himself as guest conductor of the London Symphony Orchestra was frequent Hitchcock collaborator Bernard Herrmann. His brooding yet hauntingly beautiful score for the next Hitchcock film to be analyzed is among the greatest ever written. It blended into a profound psychodrama exploring voyeurism in unique circumstances. *Vertigo*, which Ken Mogg cites as the most frequent choice of Hitchcock's best by those who have studied his career, provided the greatest acting challenge for James Stewart, making his final appearance for the Master.

8

Hopelessly in Love with a Woman Who Never Was

It's too late. There's no bringing her back.—James Stewart to Kim Novak about the fictitious Madeleine Elster in *Vertigo*.

James Stewart's bona fides as America's friendly neighbor provided suspense master Alfred Hitchcock, with his strong psychological sense, an opportunity to manipulate circumstances and create a universal response. If James Stewart could be thoroughly overwhelmed by an unpredictable and relentless fate, then so could any of us.

In the 1958 release *Vertigo,* Stewart's character is made vulnerable via a physical affliction, which is reminiscent of *Rear Window.* In *Rear Window* he plunges into the life of a voyeur and solves a murder. In *Vertigo* Stewart plays a San Francisco police detective considered so steady and precise in his work that he is called "reliable Ferguson." He takes early retirement for medical reasons after developing vertigo, or dizziness, when confronted by heights. The discovery is made when he and a uniformed officer are chasing a criminal suspect over rooftops in the heart of San Francisco. Ferguson carries with him the painful emotional scar of his fellow officer falling to his death after extending a hand to him in an attempt to save Ferguson's life. "What a time to find out I had it [vertigo]!" Ferguson tells Marjorie Wood (Barbara Bel Geddes), his old friend and onetime fiancée from his college days at the University of California at Berkeley.

Hitchcock might have achieved his greatest coup in *Vertigo* by once more tap dancing around the censorial Breen Office. There were stern strictures in place about wrongdoers ultimately paying for their crimes. Femmes fatales such as those played by Barbara Stanwyck, Jane Greer and Claire Trevor generally ended up, if not convicted and sent to prison for their murderous misdeeds, gunned down. The same applied to hardened criminals such as those played by James Cagney and Edward G. Robinson.

In *Vertigo*, Tom Helmore as Gavin Elster is a master manipulator with enough diabolical skill to make Sherlock Holmes's nemesis, the infamous Professor Moriarity, turn green with envy. He applies the Svengali touch in his dealings with his mistress, Judy Barton, played by Kim Novak, in the manner of George Bernard Shaw's Professor Henry Higgins in his relationship with Covent Garden flower girl Eliza Doolittle, but with an added sinister touch. Novak impersonates Elster's wife Madeleine in a plot designed to make a murder appear as suicide.

Kim Novak, in her role as Madeleine Elster, not only dyes her hair blonde and wears the garments of a woman of wealth, she learns to speak in the manner of an aristocrat. The success of her effort is manifested by Detective Ferguson falling madly in love with her. Elster pulls the strings and his plan succeeds. He uses Ferguson's credibility as a man with a solid record as a police officer to convince authorities that the death of the real Madeleine was a tragic suicide and devoid of any criminal conduct.

Hitchcock once more had his way with the Breen Office, since Gavin Elster emerges as one of the most cleverly ruthless murderers to ever appear on film. Viewers need to fill in the blanks to recognize how truly unpitying he is, someone who ultimately cares about nobody but himself. On screen he behaves as a perfect gentleman. As a result of his skillful machinations, at film's end the real Madeleine Elster and Judy Barton are both dead, while John Ferguson is so totally broken that many analysts believe that he would be expected to commit suicide.

There is nothing revealed in the film indicating that Svengali Elster paid any penalty for the murder he committed and lives he destroyed. The evidence points in the opposite direction. At the end of the inquest concerning his wife's death Elster tells a thoroughly devastated Ferguson that he intends to go away, probably to Europe, and expects never to return to America. He leaves a wealthy man who inherited his wife's impressive estate.

Fourth Time the Charm

In the case of the Stewart-Hitchcock collaboration, their fourth and final effort proved to be the charm, the crowning masterpiece of their association. Just as Stewart's personal favorite, *It's a Wonderful Life*, failed to achieve immediate commercial success, so too did *Vertigo*, released two years after *The Man Who Knew Too Much*. *Vertigo* is now considered one of the all-time great suspense classics, a psychological thriller containing so many sophisticated plot and character nuances that it requires numerous viewings to sufficiently appreciate its multi-dimensionality.

Perhaps the reason why so many film historians have concluded that *Vertigo* was Hitchcock's crowning triumph is the recognition that, in the career of an imaginative director noted for tantalizing the minds of audiences and presenting multi-tiered mystery entertainments, the 1958 classic was the largest extension of his labyrinthian creative intellect. Never before had Hitchcock dumped as many plot twists and psychological nuances into the collective laps of the audiences he loved to tease and titillate. So many events and character patterns are left for audiences to figure out on their own.

The basic plot structure contains the following elements:

1) A sincere and dedicated police officer, played by Stewart, discovers that he suffers from acrophobia, fear of heights, which brings on dizziness, or vertigo, while he and a colleague are chasing a criminal suspect scurrying from building to building above downtown San Francisco. In the process of this chase Stewart's partner plunges to his death while attempting to rescue Stewart, who clings for dear life to the edge of a building.

2) After resigning from the police force, and now haunted by the image of his partner tumbling to his death (along with his failure to act due to his acrophobia-vertigo difficulties), Stewart is enlisted by an old college friend to undertake a private detective assignment that involves following a woman he describes as his wife. The woman is reportedly possessed by the spirit of a relative from the nineteenth century who committed suicide at the identical age of the alleged wife.

3) The old friend talks Stewart into taking the assignment, despite Stewart's initial misgivings, after which the retired detective, having followed the beautiful blonde to various settings, such as an art museum and an old hotel, jumps into San Francisco Bay to rescue her from an apparent suicide attempt.

4) Stewart's character falls deeply in love with the hauntingly mysterious and ethereal blonde, portrayed by Kim Novak. At the point of another apparent suicide attempt Stewart fails to help the woman he loves as she runs frantically up a flight of stairs toward the bell tower of a building at a mission some one hundred miles from San Francisco, where she has driven, presumably in one of her possessed states. She plunges to her death as he painfully gropes along, nearly paralyzed by his fear of heights and corresponding dizziness.

5) His apparent failure to save the beautiful blonde he deeply loved throws Ferguson into a catatonic state, resulting in temporary institutionalization. During that period he is totally uncommunicative, staring blankly into space.

6) On his release, Ferguson dejectedly walks the streets of the city. On one such excursion he observes a brunette woman who reminds him of the deceased blonde for whom he longs. He follows her to the hotel where she lives, begging her to have dinner with him.

7) It is revealed to the audience — but not to Ferguson — that the brunette is actually the blonde who apparently committed suicide. She contem-

plates leaving the city immediately, but decides to stay due to her love for Ferguson. Ferguson then seeks to remake the "new" woman into his "old" love, buying her clothes to match, along with inducing a hair change to the blonde color to which he had grown accustomed.

8) A clash ensues as Judy Barton recognizes the inevitable. As the changeover becomes more complete, the moment of truth when her true identity will be revealed comes ever closer. All the while, a doggedly determined Ferguson presides over change upon change.

9) When Barton mistakenly wears a locket owned by the "dead" woman, Ferguson becomes a man possessed to learn the truth. They drive to the mission where the earlier tragedy occurred. He angrily pulls her up the steps leading to the bell tower, discovering that, in his agitated state, his fear of heights has left him and he can easily transport himself up the stairs.

10) An angrily determined Ferguson pressures Barton to reveal the murder plot in which she was involved. She no sooner completes her confession than a nun surfaces in the beckoning darkness to ring the mission bells. A startled Barton accidentally falls from the bell tower to her death.

A Concert and a Picture Gallery

Hitchcock's tour de force displays the combined artistry of an art film and a chilling suspense drama within the same vehicle. The first half of the film, in addition to presenting ever-mounting suspense, contains aspects of a musical concert and a picture gallery, in which Hitchcock's camera's eye trains on the fascinating sights of San Francisco, while a haunting musical score reminds viewers of the inherent dangers lurking behind a picturesque facade.

The uniqueness of an experienced filmmaker pulling out all stops becomes evident from the opening credits. The eerily haunting musical score of Bernard Herrmann coincides with a large close-up of an expressionless woman's face, then her lips, followed by her frightened eyes darting left and right. A close-up of her right eye results in the screen becoming dominated by the color red. The title of the film emerges from the center of the woman's pupil.

Hitchcock instantly captures the attention of his audience with a fascinating action sequence set against the backdrop of San Francisco by night. Amid the shining lights below a chase sequence between an escaping criminal suspect and a pursuing uniformed police officer unfolds. The lifelong love affair between Hitchcock and the movie camera was never more apparent than in the exquisitely etched photographic pictorial of San Francisco and surrounding environs woven by the director in conjunction with cinematographer Robert Burks. As the chase continues, the slender image of plainclothes detective John Ferguson

Love in Bloom — A meeting with Kim Novak in front of James Stewart's apartment occurs at the outset of his rising passion for the elegant blonde falsely representing herself as Mrs. Gavin Elster in *Vertigo*. The scenic backdrop of San Francisco is representative of Alfred Hitchcock's penchant for using the camera to visually entertain filmgoers.

(Stewart) emerges from the shadows. He fails to negotiate the leap that the fleeing suspect and his uniformed partner had just completed. His life hangs by his fingernails as he tenaciously grips a gutter pipe. When his partner abandons his pursuit of the fugitive to save Ferguson's life he falls forward and plunges to his death.

Fill in the Blanks

The screenplay by Alec Coppel and Samuel Taylor, adapted from the French novel *D'Entre les Morts* by Pierre Boileau and Thomas Narcejac, adopts the Hitchcock technique of leaving a great deal to the audience's imagination. The riveting opening sequence set on a tall building high above an exciting and picturesque American city is a classic illustration of a scene in which the public is invited to fill in the blanks. Rouben Mamoulian had crafted such a scene at the end of *Queen Christina*, in which he instructed photogenic marvel Greta Garbo to let her face assume the pose of a mask, allowing the audience to fill in the blanks.

The gripping opening sequence ends with the death of the officer, and the scene shifts to the apartment of Stewart's old friend from his college days, Midge Wood, played by Barbara Bel Geddes. The audience is not furnished with even the faintest clue as to how John "Scottie" Ferguson extricated himself from his frightening situation.

Ferguson immediately discusses with Wood, to whom he was briefly engaged during their college days, his acrophobia, and how it prompted him to resign from the San Francisco Police. A touch of dramatic irony becomes immediately evident. Wood, a shrewd lady of great common sense who makes a good living designing brassiere advertisements, has a comfortable apartment with a picturesque view of the sprawling city many floors below. Their relationship provides continuity for Ferguson as Wood is someone with whom he can discuss the tragic problem confronting him, which has profoundly altered his life. As he talks about his problem, he does so from the perspective of a great height. The very fact that he lives in San Francisco, America's most notable city of dramatic upsweeps, a hilly panorama, enhances the irony of the height-plagued John "Scottie" Ferguson's situation all the more.

Ferguson develops enough confidence from discussing his problem with old pal Midge that he decides to engage in an experiment designed to demonstrate at least a developing improvement of his acrophobia. He begins with a small stool and is pleased with his progress. His next effort produces a different response as he experiments with a taller kitchen step-chair. This time he breaks into a deep sweat and faints into Midge's comforting arms. His reaction is made all the more dramatically intimate by the sweeping and picturesque view out of Midge's window of the city spread out so hauntingly far below, a clinging reminder of the nightmarish evening when Scottie's partner plummeted to his death.

The Meeting with Elster

It is with a high measure of curiosity that retired detective Ferguson responds to a request from an old college friend he has not seen since the war, Gavin Elster, played with adroit sophistication by Tom Helmore. Once more there is the reminder of Ferguson's problem, as evidenced by the view of San Francisco far below from the window of Elster's large and impressive office in the Mission District of the Embarcadero. This is the area where the great shipping offices are situated. Elster fills his old college friend in on what has transpired in his life since they last met. Elster married into the shipping business, explaining, "My wife's family is all gone. Someone has to look after her interests." Despite his enormous success as a shipping magnate, a touch of sadness surfaces in Elster's voice as he mourns regretfully the enormous changes in San

Francisco and that he could not have been a part of the city's exciting bygone days.

Gavin Elster demonstrates concern for Ferguson, revealing that he had read about the rooftop tragedy and his vertigo. With probing sensitivity Elster discusses the problem with his old college friend:

ELSTER: Is it a permanent physical disability?

FERGUSON: No, no. It just means that I can't climb stairs that are too steep or go to high places like the top of the Mark [Hopkins Hotel]. But there are plenty of street level bars in this town. I never married. I don't see much of the old college gang. I'm a retired detective and you're in the shipbuilding business.

A common sense Scot possessing traditional virtues, Ferguson is rocked on his heels when the articulate, highly sophisticated Elster asks him: "Do you believe that someone out of the past, someone dead, can enter and take possession of a living being?" When the former detective responds emphatically in the negative, Elster jolts him anew when he explains that his wife Madeleine is operating under the possessive control of Carlotta Valdes, a woman who had died one hundred years earlier in San Francisco. What compounds the gravity of an already frustrating ordeal, Gavin Elster explains, is that Valdes died at the age of 26, the precise age of Madeleine. He harbors a grave apprehension that Mrs. Elster will commit suicide to fulfill her role as a possessed double of the deceased.

Elster implores his college friend to help him out, knowing that the retired detective's days are now free. Elster reveals that Madeleine is taking long drives, then not remembering what occurred. Before going to see doctors, the suggestion of the practical Ferguson, Elster explains that he would like to learn more about how his wife is actually spending her days. Once more a reluctant Ferguson seeks to decline, explaining that Elster would be better served by hiring a private detective agency, that the type of work being offered is out of his line, and that he is reluctant to get involved in such a bizarre case in the first place. The shipping magnate explains how important it is to have a trusted old friend involved in such a delicate assignment, finally prevailing upon a still highly reluctant Ferguson to at least go to Ernie's Restaurant that night and catch a glimpse of his wife dining with him. Ferguson's agreement to do so seals his fate.

Stewart Meets Novak

Obsession, the grist of suspense, comes into play when Ferguson sets eyes on the mysterious Madeleine Elster for the first time. Hitchcock's mastery of the camera was never in greater evidence than in the dialogue-free scene when the retired police detective observes Madeleine from the darkened bar section of Ernie's Restaurant while he sips a drink. He observes Elster dining with

Madeleine, a statuesque, beautiful blonde, watching in rapt fascination as they leave together presumably to attend an opera performance.

When the detective decides to accept the case and track the hauntingly beautiful blonde, one of the truly interesting love teams is formed, the homespun, practical James Stewart and the mysterious blonde Kim Novak. It is from such contrasts, the pairing of opposites, that fascinating drama evolves. The demented Bruno Antony (Robert Walker), for instance, had an overpowering fascination with Farley Granger's character in *Strangers on a Train* that found him following virtually every move the tennis player made.

It can be said that James Stewart, in the films that made him famous, was conveying the same screen image with minor variations, adjustments linked to age and experience. In earlier roles when he played the solid homespun man of common virtues it was with greater nervous energy and less certainty, as befitting a younger man. This was the Stewart emerging as Jefferson Smith in *Mr. Smith Goes to Washington*. It almost certainly was no coincidence that Jefferson, the first name of Senator Smith in the film, was the last name of the man who drafted the Declaration of Independence.

The fervent determination to locate the truth, which Ferguson demonstrates once he goes to work for Gavin Elster, reflects the same degree of zeal displayed by Jefferson Smith while righting political wrongs two decades earlier in *Mr. Smith Goes to Washington*, the difference between the two characters being the methodical maturity the older retired detective evidences, as opposed to the nervous energy and righteous indignation summoned by Capra's homespun American hero. In Stewart's other Capra triumph, *It's a Wonderful Life*, banker George Bailey fights for the interests of the common citizen of his small Pennsylvania town against the economic bullying of the local financial magnate played by Lionel Barrymore. The chief difference between Stewart's two Capra film roles and *Vertigo* is the desperate uncertainty confronting former police detective John Ferguson in analyzing apparently strange psychical forces dominating Madeleine, the mysterious and beautiful blonde by whom he is totally captivated.

The psychological forces represented by Stewart's commonsense police detective overwhelmed by events he never believed possible interacting with Novak's mysterious blonde provide the perfect opposites necessary to enhance dramatic tension. Novak's role is a familiar one, with variations, in the Hitchcock cinema lexicon — the legendary "cool blonde" with whom the British director became so closely identified. In this case the woman of mystery who is later discovered to be a controlled object in the hands of a Machiavellian puppet master.

The cool blonde phenomenon began in Hitchcock's British phase with Madeleine Carroll, the elegant actress appearing opposite Robert Donat in *The 39 Steps*. Considering Hitchcock's penchant for symbolism, it is entirely possible that Novak's name during the first half of *Vertigo*, Madeleine, was drawn from the actual name of the woman identified as Hitchcock's first cool blonde. Grace Kelly and Eva Marie Saint were discernible cool blonde types in three films preceding *Vertigo*. The future Princess Grace starred in *Rear Window* opposite Stewart, as well as *Dial M for Murder* and *To Catch a Thief*, while Eva Marie Saint starred in *North by Northwest*. Tippi Hedren performed in that capacity in two sixties Hitchcock releases, *The Birds* and *Marnie*. Hedren's role in *Marnie* had been earlier offered to the by-then Princess Grace of Monaco, who turned it down.

Hitchcock was said to have an obsession of his own in his close psychological involvement with the leading ladies in his films. He chose blondes possessing sophisticated beauty, creating dramatic tension by injecting a contrast between desirability and aloofness. This presented problems for the leading men, such as Donat, Grant and Stewart, who pursued them. Despite her youthful naiveté, such an aloofness and air of mystery also surrounded Joan Fontaine in her epic role opposite Olivier in *Rebecca*. It was by design rather than accident that Fontaine's maiden name was never revealed, and that she was known on screen strictly as Mrs. De Winter.

A Man in a Quandary

Ferguson, at a time he is seeking to fully come to grips with his acrophobia and vertigo, plunges headlong into the pursuit of a woman so mysterious that obsession takes hold of him early in the investigation. She provides, with her ethereal aura of unattainability, both an ultimate challenge and frustration for Scottie Ferguson.

The fictitious Madeleine is the opposite of the witty, homespun, and thoroughly reliable Midge, played with the appropriate measure of casualness by skilled former Broadway star Barbara Bel Geddes. Midge is a pleasure to be with, and Ferguson can relax in her presence in a manner that he never could with the mysterious Madeleine, but it must also be remembered that his college engagement to the brassiere advertisement designer lasted only three weeks.

The practical Scot longed to have quiescent fires raging within him liberated, and his pursuit of the elusive Madeleine sees a long dormant characteristic, an element of the man hovering in the background, robustly surface. It arises, however, in a manner consistent with a man obsessed by fantasy and illusion rather than a passion predicated on a foundation of reality. This is demonstrated in the second half of the film, when Ferguson, confronted with the flesh and blood Judy, who longs to be accepted for herself, becomes rattled and retreats back into the realm of fantasy and illusion represented by Madeleine Elster.

Hitchcock's artistic triumph in *Vertigo* is characteristic of two of his more celebrated films, *Rebecca* and *North by Northwest*. All three movies brilliantly integrated two major production elements: a series of riveting scenic sequences

Madeleine or Judy?— James Stewart as retired police detective John Ferguson, in Alfred Hitchcock's brilliant 1958 psychological classic *Vertigo*, is left in a quandary as he falls in love with Madeleine Elster, the fictitious creation of a diabolical criminal. Kim Novak handles dual roles, an impersonation of the elegant blonde Elster and her real persona as Judy Barton, a department store sales clerk and lover of the sinister Gavin Elster, who involves Barton in his nefarious scheme. Because the film is divided into distinct halves, Novak essentially plays two completely dfferent characters.

taking advantage of photogenic settings, and stories built around the mystique of mysterious cool blondes.

The sharp delineations separating fact from fantasy in Ferguson's pursuit of Madeleine are reflective of French literature and drama. One can see the shadowy presences of Camus and Sartre as Stewart seeks to come to grips with his feelings for Novak, and to understand the forces governing them, an age-old conflict where fantasy and illusion collide with the tough world of reality that comprised the terrain which the practical-minded detective formerly occupied.

The first half of the movie features the colorful settings of an art gallery in which the rich scenic tapestry of San Francisco and surrounding environs are emphasized while the overpowering score of Bernard Herrmann reveals the eerie tension existing beneath the beautiful and often tranquil settings. Herrmann, one of the most technically daring of all film composers, launched his career with a blast as he received an Oscar nomination for Best Musical Score for a Dramatic Picture in 1941 for *Citizen Kane*. He was beaten out for the statuette by the talented young composer of *All That Money Can Buy*, who also happened to be Bernard Herrmann. He holds a unique Academy distinction for receiving two Oscar nominations in both his first and last years of Academy consideration. In 1976, following his death the previous year, Herrmann was posthumously nominated for Best Original Score for *Obsession* and *Taxi Driver*.

As John "Scottie" Ferguson, Stewart manifested the two qualities that endeared him to audiences throughout his career: the hard working, sincere, decent, uncomplicated typical American; and the fervent man of determination who, when presented with a challenge, will pursue truth to its ultimate conclusion.

The blonde, statuesque Novak played a woman of mystery with convincing believability. The mystique was also symbolic of the young actress who, as Marilyn Novak from Chicago, a Los Angeles City College student, dancer and model, rose meteorically to cinematic heights when Columbia studio boss Harry Cohn decided it was time to groom a new female star for the Gower Street dream factory to follow in the footsteps of his longstanding number one leading lady, Rita Hayworth. As a man whose finger was always on the public pulse, Cohn also recognized that Novak, with her blonde hair, creamy rich skin, and voluptuous figure, could be commercially packaged as a taller version of Marilyn Monroe.

The Chicagoan's breakthrough film was *Picnic*, an adaptation of a Pulitzer Prize–winning William Inge play by Daniel Taradash, an Oscar-winning screenwriter. The film was directed by one of Broadway's most successful post–World War II directors, Joshua Logan. Cohn surrounded Novak with a stellar cast consisting of William Holden, Rosalind Russell, Arthur O'Connell, Cliff Robertson and Susan Strassberg. One year after Novak's successful 1956 starring debut, Cohn, in a move tinged with irony, cast his new blonde star as one of two love interests for Frank Sinatra in the musical, *Pal Joey*. Novak's competing love interest for Sinatra's affections was Cohn's first big female discovery, Rita Hayworth.

When Cohn agreed to loan his new star to Universal and Hitchcock for *Vertigo*, he shrewdly insisted that a reciprocal arrangement be instituted in which Stewart would do a film for Columbia. Recognizing the successful chemistry of Stewart and Novak, Cohn recast them in the highly successful *Bell, Book and Candle*.

Kim Novak received the opportunity to star in *Vertigo* due to the pregnancy of Hitchcock's first choice, Vera Miles, who had starred opposite Henry Fonda in *The Wrong Man*, the Hitchcock film that immediately preceded *Vertigo*. Hitchcock expressed a measure of dissatisfaction with Novak's performance. "What fascinated me was the idea that Jimmy Stewart was trying to turn the girl into someone she once had to play as part of a murder plot and is later trying not to be," Hitchcock exclaimed, "and I'm not sure Kim Novak had the ability to put this across."

Hitchcock's perspective may have been colored by the fact that the director and Ms. Novak were said to be less than personal admirers of each other at the time. What was needed in the challenging dual role portrayed by Novak was a young actress who could believably demonstrate naiveté in the face of a confrontation between the past and the present, with the issue being forced by the man she loved, and who hoped she could make him forget earlier sordid events in which she played a major role. Samuel Taylor, who wrote the *Vertigo* script with Alec Coppel, endorsed what Hitchcock biographer Donald Spoto termed the "majority opinion": "If we'd had a brilliant actress who really created two distinctly different people, it would not have been as good. She seemed so naive in the part, and that was good. She was always believable. There was no 'art' about it, and that's why it worked so very well." Her co-star Stewart endorsed her performance, as well as Hitchcock's direction: "Kim was wonderful — and it was all Hitch's doing." The admiration was mutual between the film's leading performers, as the glamorous Novak termed Stewart "the sexiest man who played opposite me in 30 years."

The Screen's Most Unlikely Villain

Vertigo tapped the imagination as few films ever could. What made the movie such a unique experience was the manner in which viewers were compelled to fill in blanks to fully appreciate the story and its psychologically challenging cast of characters. While much has been written about great villains of the screen, Tom Helmore in his fascinating portrayal of Gavin Elster is not likely to appear on short lists of scoundrels compiled by film historians and interested viewers. The reason for his omission is that, unless one scrutinizes his character and fills in blanks, it is difficult to conceive of him as a villain at all, much less the cold, highly intelligent, calculating killer and master manipulator of lives that he turned out to be.

While cinema annals include killers and human manipulators of sophistication, with Clifton Webb's Waldo Lydecker in *Laura* notably among them, these individuals exude superiority complexes and convey contempt for humanity, which they perceive as existing many sociological notches below themselves. Lydecker's Park Avenue world was not the most conspicuous milieu from which a cold-blooded killer would emerge, but at least he was nasty and disagreeable.

Gavin Elster's consistent on-screen chivalric manner was Arthurian. In each scene with Ferguson he displays courtesy and compassion toward his old college friend. When Stewart, in their first meeting, exhibits his Scottish and police detective's common sense in suggesting psychological help for Madeleine Elster, and perhaps even for Gavin, after being told of seemingly supernatural events unfolding in their lives, the wealthy shipping magnate takes the sharply critical comment in calm stride. He admits that his account appears highly strange. His now sympathetic college friend then apologizes for sounding "rough."

Elster's quiet sensitivity and gentlemanly demeanor win over the skeptical former police detective so that his earlier resistance is overcome and he agrees to take on the assignment of monitoring the presumed Madeleine's behavior. Elster's softspoken, gentlemanly manner bespeaks of a nobly aristocratic Ronald Colman rather than a sinister and manipulative killer.

The choice of Tom Helmore to play the cleverly sinister Gavin Elster stemmed from Hitchcock's penchant to use performers who had worked with him previously. Helmore was a product of Hitchcock's London days. The London-born actor, like Hitchcock, later moved to America. His link to Hitchcock extended back to the 1927 release *The Ring*, in which he was cast as a challenger to the hero. He later made two brief appearances as a young officer in *Secret Agent* (1936).

Just prior to the time that Hitchcock cast Helmore as Gavin Elster in *Vertigo* the actor was appearing in the role of master manipulator Professor Henry Higgins in *My Fair Lady*, the musical version of George Bernard Shaw's *Pygmalion*. Considering the fact that Gavin Elster was a sinister and homicidal version of Higgins it may well be that Hitchcock made a connection and decided to hire the London actor who had performed in two of his pre–Hollywood films.

When Ferguson receives scorching criticism from the coroner at the inquest surrounding Madeleine's death, the first person to comfort him and extend an offer of assistance is Elster. When he tells Scottie of his need to leave San Francisco and relocate far away, perhaps Europe, his statement is plausible in that he told his old friend at their meeting in his office that he was tired of the city and was sorry he could not have been a part of what he deemed a more exciting period of its history a century earlier. With this dissatisfaction compounded greatly by the memory of his wife's death, Elster is able to convey the precise impression he wishes — that of a man running away from a painful period of his life and disenchanted with his longtime home town.

Much has been said about James Stewart portraying a Pygmalion-like figure in the second half of the film as he attempts to remake Judy into the departed Madeleine, but since Madeleine was a creature of Elster's invention and molding, the ultimate Pygmalion is Elster. Scottie's ferocious anger at the end of the film is understandable in view of his realization that he was seeking to restructure Elster's creation. Scottie was also manipulated by Elster to respond to a person and situation that never existed, a contrivance that totally reshaped his life, which thereafter took the form of a maniacal quest to retrieve a fantasy existence.

By using both John Ferguson and his mistress, Judy Barton, to serve his evil ends by supplying him with what he deemed to be an iron clad explanation for the real Madeleine Elster's death, the devious Elster, in addition to killing his wife, brutally transformed the lives of his two psychological victims. At each turn he was ruthlessly shrewd, a master of calculation. Elster married into a wealthy shipping family, then plotted to dispose of his wife. As Judy noted when she filled in missing blanks for an angry and rattled Scottie, she was selected due to her physical resemblance to Madeleine Elster. The plot was enhanced by the fact that Madeleine Elster seldom came into the city, living in the country outside San Francisco.

Ferguson was seen as the ideal choice to lend credibility to Elster's plot due to his twin afflictions of acrophobia and vertigo, rendering him unable to climb steps when a woman, the real Madeleine, was to be pushed by Elster from the mission bell tower. Scottie's imagination was gripped by the theory, initially dismissed by him, that Judy, portraying Madeleine, was under possession of the spirit of Carlotta Valdes. Here the brilliant calculator Elster researched the period of San Francisco's history, the middle of the nineteenth century, which he told Scottie at their first meeting intrigued him much more than the present, weaving facts from the tragic biography of Carlotta Valdes into a brilliant scenario of his own construction.

Unlike traditional films, which would have provided audiences with at least a brief window into the mind of Gavin Elster, *Vertigo* presented him solely in the guise that he maintained when John "Scottie" Ferguson encountered him. Never was he revealed as anything other than the aristocrat of unimpeachable civility that he appeared to be. The sinister cleverness of the character played by Tom Helmore was that it would be difficult for audiences to envision the Elster depicted in *Vertigo* shouting at anyone, much less killing his wife.

Filling in Blanks

The audience was invited to fill in many blanks by the Hitchcock script. As previously mentioned, the first such instance occurred at the film's outset, the result of the swift transition between Detective Ferguson's dangling from his fingertips from the edge of a building, and the next scene in which we see him conversing in the apartment of his friend Midge. We have no idea how Ferguson surmounted his ordeal as he dangled at death's door moments after his colleague, a uniformed officer, had fallen from the same building onto the street far below.

Another blank-filling situation emerged from Ferguson's early pursuit of Judy Barton posing as Madeleine Elster. The persistent detective followed her to the old McKittrick Hotel on Eddy Street, which we later learn was once the residence of Carlotta Valdes. He speaks with the desk clerk, played by Ellen Corby. While confirming that a "nice young woman" who signed the register as Carlotta Valdes had taken the room, Corby insists that she has not been there that day.

Initially reluctant to answer questions from Ferguson, explaining that guests are entitled to their privacy, the clerk relents only when he shows her his official police badge. Convinced that he saw Barton inside the hotel, he asks to see her room. Corby openly declares the mission a foolish one, insistent that the young blonde woman had never been there. She then opens the door and they discover that the room is indeed empty.

Just what did happen? Was Ferguson seeing things? If not, and Barton, posing as Elster, was actually there, what happened to her? Was Corby's character an active part of the Gavin Elster team? It would be a shrewd ploy to convince Ferguson that something mystical was really afoot. The theory would gain plausibility if Ferguson began doubting himself by believing that what he thought he saw within the confines of the McKittrick Hotel was some form of an illusion. Was a spirit present? Had Elster discovered yet another way to plague his old college friend's mind as he sought to use him to unwittingly help him avoid a murder charge? Paying off the hotel worker and having her insist that the young woman had not visited her room that day would be a skillful ploy by the manipulative mastermind. We can speculate, but the story never reveals what happened. Again, we are invited to fill in the blanks.

Answers Through Voyeurism

A notable trait shared by Stewart's characters in *Rear Window* and *Vertigo* was a pervasive voyeurism. In the earlier film the activity commenced due to Stewart being wheel-chair bound, and in the latter the incidents arose from Stewart's recruitment by a former college classmate seeking to use him in a brilliant murder plot. While Stewart in *Rear Window* as a voyeur paid frequent attention to Miss Torso across the courtyard, not fearing the need for commitment from her in the way that it loomed in his relationship with Grace Kelly, in *Vertigo* he falls desperately in love with Kim Novak's fictitious version of Madeleine Elster. The desperation stems from his belief, following a cleverly scripted campaign by Gavin Elster, that the false Madeleine is a woman dealing with unexplained forces beyond her control.

The Machiavellian ploy to seal the deal and hook the vulnerable John Ferguson comes in the form of a fake suicide attempt, as the presumed Madeleine Elster leaps fully clothed into San Francisco Bay, only to be quickly rescued by the detective. We then see Judy Barton playing Madeleine Elster awakening in Ferguson's bedroom at his apartment near Coit Tower. A question emerges: How did the beautiful blonde get there? While the intervening events are not explained, promoting more filling in of the story by the viewer, it could be logically inferred that Ferguson undressed the woman in her unconscious state, dressed her in pajamas, then tucked her into bed until she awakened much later in the darkness of evening.

Filling in a Final Blank

In addition to filling in blanks to determine the full measure of Gavin Elster's sinister opportunism, reflection is needed to determine how Scottie would ultimately react to the third in a string of tragic deaths he encountered, beginning with his police partner, extending to the murder of the real Madeleine Elster, and culminating with the accidental death of Judy Barton at a moment of peak distress after Ferguson became aware of the conspiracy.

The obvious possibility would be that of suicide in the wake of a string of tragedies. Scottie had suffered a calamitous breakdown earlier after Madeleine's death, believing her to be the woman he loved. Another plausible response would result in a furious retired policeman pursuing Elster, perhaps even to Europe or wherever the brilliantly devious killer had gone. Another possibility is a permanent breakdown on Ferguson's part following Judy's death.

Possibilities abound in analyzing *Vertigo*. As Hitchcock pointed out, to trade a brief moment of surprise and shock for continuing analysis and second guessing is a good bargain. *Vertigo* demonstrates the soundness of the suspense master's theory more than any other film in his long career.

The film's ending, as mentioned earlier, was one more instance of Hitchcock dancing around the Breen Office's censorship code. It was not until the early seventies that it became acceptable to have wrongdoers march into the sunset unpunished, as occurred with the brilliant international drug syndicate head in *The French Connection*, the celebrated 1971 film directed by William Friedkin. Gene Hackman won a Best Actor Oscar portraying New York detective Popeye Doyle, who became obsessed with apprehending drug syndicate mastermind Fernando Rey, who escaped to Marseille with his stash. Audiences found the psychological give and take absorbing, as the film also garnered Academy Awards for Best Picture, Best Direction for Friedkin and Best Adapted Screenplay for Ernest Tidyman.

Four years later the less heralded sequel, *The French Connection II*, which was directed by John Frankenheimer, carried the story forward to Hackman's pursuit of Rey to Marseille, where he obtained revenge by killing him. In the end, though it required a second film, the drug kingpin paid the ultimate price.

Many filmgoers who analyzed *Vertigo* wondered what might have happened to the brilliantly sinister yet gentlemanly Gavin Elster. Hitchcock was not among them. Once a project was completed Hitchcock believed it was time to move on. Gavin Elster was in the past and new projects beckoned. When Hitchcock was asked about what might have ultimately happened to Elster his response was comparable to that of avant garde Nobel Prize–winning playwright Samuel Beckett when asked whether the unseen Godot eventually appeared in the heavily symbolic *Waiting for Godot*. "Damned if I know," Beckett was said to have responded. Raymond Chandler reportedly gave the same answer when asked by director Howard Hawks and scenarist William Faulkner about who killed the chauffeur in Chandler's detective novel that they were adapting to the screen, *The Big Sleep*.

Creative geniuses have a way of moving on after they have made their points, and Hitchcock definitely fit into that pattern. It was left for film historians and sophisticated cinema aficionados to debate topics such as what might have happened to Elster or the tragic, badly used John Ferguson.

Two Films and Two Roles in One

Much discussion has arisen about *Vertigo* being two divisible films of equal length. Some moviegoers believed that the film had ended when the real Madeleine Elster met her death. Kim Novak shifted gears abruptly in the film's second half and moved from portraying a well dressed, elegant and polished aristocrat wife, albeit hugely troubled, from San Francisco's upper class to an insecure, unpolished department store clerk who had moved to California recently from Kansas and lived in a cheap hotel next door to her place of employment. In a pivotal dramatic point of the film, after Ferguson has followed her to her room at the Empire Hotel subsequent to seeing her on the street, she agrees to have dinner with him and asks for an hour to prepare herself. Through voice-over we learn that the added time is merely a pretext to allow her to clear out of California and hopefully put a great deal of distance between herself and the Elster tragedy. We are provided with the contents of the note she is preparing for the forlorn Ferguson.

Because Judy Barton realizes that she deeply loves the detective she so badly fooled, the note is torn up and the young woman makes a decision predicated on dangerous uncertainty. She will meet Ferguson for dinner. This leaves a second half pregnant with possibilities for suspense and rife with psychological nuances.

Some viewers of the film wondered if it would have been better for Hitchcock to pursue another strategy, such as building to a surprise twist at the end of the film, a device used in so many suspense vehicles. The question was asked: "Why didn't Hitchcock keep his audience totally in the dark and reveal the Barton-Elster conspiracy at the end?"

Hitchcock had a ready answer. He believed that waiting until the end of the film to reveal that the Kim Novak in the second part of the picture and the elegant blonde in the first half, were one and the same would be an unacceptable tradeoff. By taking that approach he would have been discarding the psychological character exploration that made *Vertigo* unique, as well as one of the most cinematically dazzling movies ever made. Hitchcock did not believe in trading the kind of psychological character interaction found in the second half of *Vertigo* for one moment of surprise at the film's finale.

A Second, Less Successful Makeover

A significant key to understanding the clever psychological nuances of *Vertigo* involves a tortured admission made by Ferguson in the traumatic final scene after he explodes and goes to pieces under the realization that he was used as a tool by the wily Elster and that the woman he loved was a manufactured artificial creation. Referring to Elster, an out of control Stewart concedes, "He made you over just like I did, only better." This statement is important to understanding the flow of events. Ferguson was unknowingly remaking Judy Barton without understanding the dynamics of the situation, that the woman he fell hopelessly in love with had been made over previously. The conflict in the relationship arose because Barton did not encounter two Fergusons, only one, and was in love with him.

The dichotomy stems from their first encounter, after the rescue of the fictitious Madeleine from her presumed suicide attempt in San Francisco Bay. The practical, no nonsense detective is charmed off of his feet by the poised, thoroughly aristocratic demeanor of Barton, playing her role perfectly for Elster's benefit. She is ultimately caught off guard emotionally and falls in love with the detective, who thinks that he is in love with the real woman and not a glossy imitation created by a wily Svengali.

When Barton, playing Madeleine Elster, awakens from what Ferguson was meant to believe was a trance, she captivates him in their first conversation in his living room. Anxious to learn more about her, as well as the affliction which he presumes she suffers from, he resorts to a form of police interrogation to learn as much as he can about the blonde. He is told that he is direct in his questioning. The detective tells her apologetically that he did not mean to be rude. "You're not rude," the dazzling blonde explains, "you're merely direct."

The manner in which the trained blonde responds to the questions of a shrewd and educated man who has made his living interrogating people is impressive, befitting of the elegant aristocrat she is depicting. This elegant demeanor is a factor in bowling Ferguson over emotionally, making him vulnerable to Elster as an unwitting dupe in the murder design.

Barton as Barton

Even in the early stages of Ferguson's wooing of Barton the central question is there: Can he love Barton as herself? The following dialogue is revealing in terms of each character's development in the psychological flow of events:

> FERGUSON: We could just see a lot of each other.
> BARTON: Why? Because I remind you of her? That's not very complimentary. And nothing else?
> FERGUSON: No.
> BARTON: That's not very complimentary, either.

When Ferguson takes her to the swanky department store Ransohoff's to try on clothes, a clash arises. Barton, seeking to retain her identity, expresses preferences for certain dresses, but a stoutly determined, to the point of obsession,

John Ferguson knows precisely what he wants. His recollection of a year-old dress design astounds the saleswoman, who exclaims, "The gentleman certainly knows what he wants." Nothing short of what the fictitious Madeleine Elster wore will placate Ferguson.

There is no compromise whatever in the obsessive Ferguson. Gradually, every ounce of resistance within Judy Barton drains away as, in her anxiety to win Ferguson's heart, she reluctantly agrees to what becomes a total makeover.

It is no easy transformation, however. After Ferguson has decided what clothes she will wear and her red hair is dyed blonde, Barton still desperately seeks to retain a semblance of individuality. When she returns from Ransohoff's to an eagerly anticipating Ferguson, he immediately notices one deviation from the Elster redux game plan. As an attempt to retain at least a sliver of individuality, Judy, rather than have her now blonde hair done up in a bun, allows it to flow freely. When a concerned Ferguson protests, she explains that the style did not work when the beauticians tried it. An adamant Ferguson then removes that last vestige of individuality a smothered Judy Barton attempted to maintain.

A brief dialogue exchange records the moment when Judy Barton surrenders herself to a man of obsession seeking to restore her to a previous existence she knew to be artificial, not to mention criminal:

BARTON: If I let you change me, will that do it? If I do what you tell me, will you love me?
FERGUSON: Yes—yes.
BARTON: All right, then, I'll do it. I don't care anymore about me.

The specter of Gavin Elster hovers over the relationship of the psychologically devastated Judy and Scottie at all times. The only thing Ferguson definitely knows is that he must continue his effort to resurrect Madeleine Elster as he thought he knew her. At one point Judy asks him pointedly if all the makeover efforts will ultimately do any good. Ferguson, looking baffled and forlorn, honestly replies, "I don't know." He explains that the only thing about which he is certain is that he must seek to transform Judy back into the Madeleine Elster figure he previously knew. The irony is that Elster, by then presumably in Europe or another foreign setting, is still the influential force in a troubled relationship. His efforts were so convincing to Ferguson that the former detective cannot release the image of his fictitious fantasy.

The Haunting Mission Dolores

One of the most haunting and artistically affecting elements of *Vertigo* is the incorporation of the historic Mission Dolores, both scenically and storywise. Not only does Mission Dolores play an integral role in viewers' understanding important elements of *Vertigo*, in a broader context its thematic invocation reveals an important element of Hitchcock's thinking in his mature veteran's phase of filmmaking, which will be explored later.

Ken Mogg traveled from his Australian home to California in 1975. It was no surprise that the dedicated Hitchcock historian made a stop at Mission Dolores. He explains the thematic significance of the historic Northern California site within *Vertigo*:

> The Mission Dolores — originally called the Mission San Francisco de Asis — was founded in 1776, the same year as the city to which it eventually gave its name. That's why, when early in the film Scottie trails Madeleine there, and watches her walk around, we take the hint that her story concerns the city itself. Like Scottie, we soon become intrigued, fascinated. At this early stage, too, the film is already building a motif whereby Madeleine repeatedly leads Scottie from places of glare and busyness — the city streets — to pockets of shade and stillness, where time seems suspended. More than just a life-death thing, whose obvious referent is Madeleine's dream in which she's walking down a corridor into darkness, it's as if she were somehow promising him an answer to nothing less than what used to be called "the world riddle."

The Mission Dolores and its link to the past reflects a past-and-present duality addressed by Hitchcock through the finely honed script crafted by Samuel Taylor and Alec Coppel. "When you enter the little church tucked away in a side street, you instantly feel the stillness the film conveys," Ken Mogg observed. "On the whole, it's a benign feeling. As a booklet I obtained there notes: 'Within the silent walls of the old mission, time seems to have stopped.' The booklet adds that the interior of the church 'differs little from its earliest appearance. Decorated redwood ceiling beams are just as created by Indian workmen.' There's a slightly sinister note to that, if you care to so interpret the use of Indian labor, but the film doesn't stress it."

Mogg praises the mastery of Robert Burks' camera in the cemetery scene where Madeleine goes directly through the church to the cemetery alongside, with Scottie following at a distance. "By adroit use of lenses and camera placement, Robert Burks managed to transform the spot into a haunting maze-garden," Mogg related. "Watching the film, you understand how Scottie feels lost as he tries to fathom the truth about Madeleine and her Spanish ancestor who is supposedly buried here. In fact, the real cemetery is much smaller than it looks in the film. Scottie could hardly have spied on Madeleine without her seeing him. Also, contra the impression the film gives, most of the cemetery's plots are neglected, the gravestones crumbling or overturned. An asphalt yard at the back is visible as you walk around, or was in 1975."

A Key Point Raised by the Villain

A key point that would arise in subsequent films during Hitchcock's mature phase was raised in *Vertigo* by the film's villain, Gavin Elster. In his first meeting with John Ferguson, when he is seeking to enlist him as a pawn in his sinister enterprise, the suave and sophisticated Elster laments the passage of time and what he perceives as a San Francisco that is a worse place than what the city's forebears handed over to subsequent generations.

On one level Elster's mourning establishes an important precedent for the moment after the inquest into his wife's death, when he tells Ferguson that he is journeying far away from San Francisco and will probably never return. Some of his reasoning is naturally meant to relate to the tragedy of his wife's death, but he had also told his old college friend during their reunion in his plush Embarcadero office that the current San Francisco was a keen disappointment compared to what he plainly saw as a prouder period of accomplishment from one century earlier.

This consciousness of the passage of time and how the current generation rates alongside its predecessors was addressed in the scene when Scottie takes Madeleine into the scenic redwood forest that is one of Northern California's rich natural treasures. The thick ancient redwood tree that had been cut open and put on display, with its written historical chronology of events, provides viewers with awareness of the passage of time and the events that have shaped human destiny, subtly pressing the Hitchcockian duality of the past measured against the present, of whether humankind his progressed or regressed.

The Experts on Vertigo

It may have taken a few years before the public began responding to *Vertigo* in a manner befitting the film's quality, but those who carefully evaluate the medium never had any doubts. The film offered brilliance at every level, from the superb photography to the color, along with the labyrinthian psychological nuances that kept viewers engaged until the film's end.

The opinions of two experts bear scrutiny. Ken Mogg has devoted decades to the study of Hitchcock's work, taught courses on his films, wrote one of the most influential books detailing the director's work, *The Alfred Hitchcock Story*, and operates the leading Internet website devoted to the study of the Master. "*Vertigo* continues to be esteemed as the top Hitchcock film by most people," Mogg commented. "In Melbourne, where I live, it's always being mentioned and featured in film courses at universities and in repertory cinema programs. Currently, a musical-physical theatre show called 'Phobia' is running here, and claims inspiration from *Vertigo*."

Donald Spoto is one of the most knowledgeable figures regarding Hitchcock's career. He wrote two books about the famous director. *The Dark Side of Genius* was a highly acclaimed biography, while *The Art of Alfred Hitchcock: Fifty Years of His Motion Pictures* provided analyses of his films. Not only did Spoto meticulously research his books, he also had the opportunity to interview Hitchcock many times and discuss his films with the famous director in detail.

In *The Art of Alfred Hitchcock*, Spoto's chapter on *Vertigo* is by far the longest of the book. By comparison, *Shadow of a Doubt* and *Strangers on a Train*, two of Hitchcock's most thought-provoking works, each receive much briefer treatment. Early in the chapter Spoto refers to "what this author considers Alfred Hitchcock's greatest masterpiece, *Vertigo*."

Vertigo met with a tepid reception when it was released, and only later received the critical accolades it merits. A complex, multi-layered suspense story requires careful concentration and more than one viewing to be anywhere close to fully appreciated. A shrewd, sophisticated masterpiece requires a great deal of time and concentration. David Lean directed notable masterpieces. The British master explained that he took three years to produce his great spectacles, such as *Lawrence of Arabia* and *Doctor Zhivago*, with one year devoted to each of three categories: script writing, filming and editing. If great creative geniuses require so much time and careful attention, often to the point of cloistered obsession, then what chance does even an intelligent and perceptive viewer have to definitively grasp such a movie with one viewing, sometimes after a tough day on the job?

Of all the films to appear on screen, *Vertigo* stands in the forefront as demanding the closest of scrutiny, the kind that comes from repeated viewings, to be fully appreciated. The case of *Vertigo*'s belated recognition as the classic that it is harkens back to Herman Melville, whose masterwork, *Moby Dick*, generally considered the greatest novel ever written by an American, was published in 1851 when he was 32. Years later, financially unsuccessful, Melville took a job in New York City as district inspector of customs. He reportedly walked the streets of the city in a state of melancholia over a life he considered a failure after he had written one of a handful of universally recognized international literary classics. It was not until after Melville's death in 1891 that *Moby Dick* became appreciated as a work of towering genius.

While it would require time for *Vertigo* to be fully appreciated, Hitchcock promptly returned to the drawing boards and developed a project using time tested formulas that resulted in a commercial and artistic triumph. To bolster the likelihood of success he cast a British leading man who had been closely linked to past Hitchcock box office winners, while essentially adapting a blueprint for success from his London period to the glossy color and wide screen technology of the late fifties.

The Triumph of North by Northwest

Hitchcock explained how the triumphal 1959 release *North by Northwest* materialized. "*North by Northwest* grew out of an idea I had for doing a story called *The Wreck of the Mary Deare*," Hitchcock said. "MGM owned *The Wreck of the Mary Deare*, so I sat down with Ernest Lehman — he was under contract to Metro — and, after about a month, we gave up. But I still owed Metro a picture. Now it so happened that a New York journalist had given me an idea about an ordinary businessman being mistaken for a decoy spy. I took that and, with Ernie Lehman, worked up the whole thing. It took about a year to write."

While a creator such as Hitchcock might be apolitical, that individual's sensitive attunement to what is occurring in contemporary society can leave one with a finished product heavily laced with political content. *North by Northwest* presented in biting form an America and a world immersed in Cold War intrigue and ruthless ambiguity in which people on both sides were served up as sacrificial lambs.

A World of Anarchistic Cynicism

In *North by Northwest*, Hitchcock, employing comedic technique and utilizing colorful location shooting, pulls out all stops in using his photographic bag of tricks, those Roman candles, to provide a film that is both long on entertainment and thematically rich (for those looking for more than sheer movie enjoyment). As a means of enhancing international box office success, Hitchcock cast Cary Grant in the role of Thornhill, a man trapped in the claws of fate.

North by Northwest was made and released during the latter phase of the second term of President Dwight D. Eisenhower, when the Cold War was in full swing, with the United States and rival Soviet Union utilizing the most sophisticated spy techniques. In addition to Cold War tensions, the American spirit during the conformity-ridden fifties was plagued with a hypocritical win-at-all-costs commercialism that flew in the face of pretenses of homespun morality. This was the period of payola, when songs were plugged over the airwaves in exchange for financial favors. A number of highly publicized quiz show scandals kept America enthralled as additional facts were released, and there was sharp criticism registered against commercial television and the outlandish claims made by advertisers. (This was a period when Listerine Antiseptic was advertised as containing such a potent germ killing capability that taking it would prevent the common cold. Eventually the Food and Drug Administration compelled the company to stop making this unproven claim.)

The Advertising Man as Main Character

A product of his times, Hitchcock was well aware of the television scandals and stinging criticisms of a society steeped in vapid commercialism. In the intellectual sphere, Harvard academic Vance Packard examined Madison Avenue's significant influence on society in his 1957 non-fiction best seller, *The Hidden*

Persuaders. Three years later Packard explored the subject of planned obsolescence in *The Waste Makers*. Hitchcock and Lehman seized on a popular theme and integrated it into the fabric of a film about a man being chased by evil spies in a case of mistaken identity.

During a period when muckrakers like Vance Packard were denouncing the influence of Madison Avenue on Americans, Hitchcock and Lehman made an interesting choice regarding the profession of Roger O. Thornhill, Cary Grant's character in the film. He was a New York advertising man, making a handsome living on Madison Avenue. Grant did not even attempt to disguise the fact that he perpetuated myths.

Early on, the Lehman script reveals Thornhill as a vapid man with nary a concern for reality. Advertising executive Thornhill has given orders to his secretary, Maggie (Doreen Lang), to arrange his love life. It is rush hour on Madison Avenue and, amid much congestion, Thornhill convinces a man preparing to enter to taxi to give it up by lying about his secretary being sick. When Maggie expresses misgivings about Thornhill's deceptive ploy, his response is revealing: "Maggie, you ought to know that in the world of advertising there's no such thing as a lie — there's only the expedient of exaggeration."

The Lehman Touch

Hitchcock hooked up with the right screenwriter at the opportune moment in securing Ernest Lehman's services for *North by Northwest*. Hitchcock loved sharp and biting dialogue, and Lehman was an expert at creating it.

A good example of the Lehman wit, which bore a decided resemblance to that possessed by Hitchcock, was revealed on press preview night in the offices of Hecht-Hill-Lancaster following a screening of the corrosive film noir drama *Sweet Smell of Success*. Lehman had been the sole writer at the outset, but became ill and was advised by his doctor to avoid tension and recover in an appropriate setting. So while Lehman recuperated in exotic Tahiti, the writing reins were turned over to the highly capable Clifford Odets to steer the project to completion.

Burt Lancaster starred as a ruthless newspaper columnist said to have been modeled on Walter Winchell. At the preview party he looked at Lehman and registered anger that was more than likely at least partly theatrical.

"You walked out on us," Lancaster exclaimed. "I oughta punch you in the nose."

"Go ahead," Lehman quickly responded, "I need the money."

The Lehman one-liner is reflective of what appeared in *Sweet Smell of Success*, which was released in 1957, just one year before Lehman went to work with Hitchcock to craft the script for *North by Northwest*.

In *Sweet Smell of Success* Lancaster delivered one of his most memorable performances, as did Tony Curtis in his role of a publicity man so devoid of principle that Lancaster at one point stares at him and sneers, "I didn't know that anyone could stoop so low." At another point Lancaster tells Curtis, regarding an ambitious U.S. senator with presidential aspirations, "My big toe would make a better president." Early one morning Lancaster steps out from his apartment and, glaring at an empty street, exclaims, "I love this dirty town!" This is the closest to an optimistic point made in the film, which was referred to by Tony Curtis as "a feel bad movie."

Sweet Smell of Success was destined to experience the same early fate as *Vertigo*. It was such an initial box office loser that British director Alexander MacKendrick, who brilliantly captured New York opportunism at its most ruthless, was fired from his next assignment by short-sighted producers who cited the enormous flop he had just directed.

The big difference between the Lehman script for *Sweet Smell of Success* and what ironically turned out to be his next assignment, *North by Northwest*, where his corrosive wit could once more be put on display for film audiences, was motivation. The 1957 release was decidedly noir in approach, with black and white cinematography that brought out the city by night.

The Casting of Grant

North by Northwest put Grant's breezy British charm on display. His Thornhill character, while lacking a certain kind of substance, displayed a devil-may-care charm, whereas Lancaster played an egomaniacal tyrant who used his power of the pen to destroy.

Sweet Smell of Success, in the manner of *Vertigo*, compelled viewers to probe into a gray netherworld of psychological nuances. In the case of *North by Northwest*, Hitchcock's excellent use of Roman candles, playing off of Grant's charm, kept the story moving in an entertaining fashion so that a viewer did not have to dig into the psychological meanings Lehman and Hitchcock deposited throughout the film in order to appreciate it. In the manner of another Hitchcock technicolor success of the fifties, *The Man Who Knew Too Much*, this was an entertaining vehicle to be appreciated at any level.

North by Northwest marked Grant's third time before the cameras in a Hitchcock film, the predecessors being *Suspicion* and *Notorious*. Born Archibald Alexander Leach in Bristol, he escaped his impoverished roots in the South England town by joining an acrobatic troupe, where he blossomed into a tightrope walker. He made his way across the Atlantic, where his sleekly athletic form and dark good looks provided him with an opportunity to work in Broadway musicals.

The British performer was ultimately signed to a contract by Paramount. It was said that he was named Cary Grant as a means of inverting the letters "GC" of Paramount's leading male star, Gary Cooper. While Grant was playing

Pinkerton in a non-musical version of *Madame Butterfly*, a role that had been rejected by Cooper (feeling that Pinkerton's dastardly character might alienate his female fans), an event occurred that catapulted Grant into an accelerated orbit as a leading man.

Mae West was riding high on the Paramount lot as she parlayed her risqué humor, which was considered highly provocative at the time and had prompted problems with censors during her career on stage, into solid film dividends. West, whose box office prowess kept Paramount out of the bankruptcy courts during the darkest days of the Great Depression, was a genius at self-promotion. An account of her first meeting with Cary Grant was frequently repeated by her and, according to West biographer Maurice Leonard, was "never denied" by Grant, "at least not too vehemently." Reportedly, West observed Grant getting out of his car while she was walking across the lot with Paramount Studios head Emanuel Cohen and, impressed by the strikingly good looks of the tall, 28-year-old actor, gasped, "Who's that?" Cohen reportedly told her that he was a bit actor and no one to be concerned about. She reportedly insisted on being introduced, and, after their first brief meeting, West reportedly told Cohen, "If he can talk, I'll take him."

Grant had actually moved up to the ranks of playing a lead in a Paramount film by then, but Mae West was decidedly impressed by him and told Emanuel Cohen that she wanted him to star in her next film. When Paramount's studio head revealed that Grant was assigned to *Madame Butterfly*, she remained adamant, and so Cohen, through rescheduling, made Grant available after completing *Madame Butterfly*.

Cary Grant proved such a perfect comedic foil for the star with the mastery of the double entendre that, after he had starred opposite West in *She Done Him Wrong* (1933), Paramount reunited the comedy team in *I'm No Angel* (1934). While Grant would move from that comedy phase to star in many dramatic films, and would earn his two Best Actor Oscar nominations for solid dramatic roles in *Penny Serenade* (1941) and *None but the Lonely Heart* (1944), a major portion of his lengthy career was consumed by comedy.

A 1940 release provided Grant with an opportunity that would be resurrected in various guises from that point forward. The same year that a major Grant triumph, *The Philadelphia Story*, directed by George Cukor, was released, in which he appeared with James Stewart and Katharine Hepburn, Grant appeared in a madcap comedy that provided him with effective latitude. The Howard Hawks screwball comedy, *His Girl Friday*, provided Grant with an opportunity to display his charm and sense of humor in a manner that many thought of as delightfully going "over the top."

His Girl Friday, based on the Broadway comedy hit *The Front Page*, written by Ben Hecht and Charles MacArthur, found Grant playing fun loving reporter Hildy Johnson in a film much like Hitchcock's sole effort in the comedy field, *Mr. and Mrs. Smith*. Grant tries to win back his ex-wife, played by

Rosalind Russell, who, in pursuit of stability, is engaged to marry rich, stiff, and stodgy Ralph Bellamy—the same plot of Hitchcock's film starring Robert Montgomery and Carole Lombard, with Gene Raymond serving as the stiffly formal foil.

His Girl Friday gave Grant an opportunity to develop a unique form of comedy. Bolstered by his interesting British accent, Grant delivered lines with racehorse rapidity. His ability to dispense rapid-fire dialogue was repeated in various segments of many films, including the Frank Capra 1944 comedy *Arsenic and Old Lace* (which also starred Priscilla Lane). The shotgun comedy delivery became such a trademark that even in his leisure time, when he hosted parties at his home far away from the cameras, Grant enjoyed excelling at a party game in which guests recited tongue twisting lines in rapid-fire fashion. The host's mastery of the art made him a formidable competitor.

While Grant's role in *North by Northwest* did not call for him to go "over the top" in the manner that he did in madcap comedy, the comedic satire found in the film was such that Hitchcock was anxious to invoke certain aspects of Grant's fast-talking demeanor. Grant was, after all, playing an advertising man living by his wits in a world of illusion. He repeatedly talks himself out of jams throughout the film.

Hitchcock Stew

With the collection of shrewd cinematic tricks Hitchcock kept in his bag, retrieving them at appropriate intervals, he in many ways resembled a chef. *North by Northwest* is a discernible example of chef Hitchcock blending ingredients to provide a savory stew for cinema patrons.

Just as the remake of *The Man Who Knew Too Much* was an example of how Hitchcock had benefited from experience and technological advancements, *North by Northwest* bears a comparable kinship to *The 39 Steps*. Cary Grant steps into the shoes occupied by Robert Donat in the earlier 1935 black and white production. In the earlier film the foreign enemy that seeks to kill Richard Hannay (Donat) is nameless, but knowledge of the then-current world scene clearly equated it with Nazi Germany. *North by Northwest* was filmed and released during an active phase of the Cold War, and it was just as evident that the alien force, represented by Phillip Vandamm (James Mason), seeking to kill Thornhill was the Soviet Union.

The 1935 and 1959 films also showcased two of Hitchcock's more notable blondes pitted in conflict with the male leads. In *The 39 Steps* Pamela (Madeleine Carroll) turns in Hannay to authorities and initially believes the propaganda line that he is a dangerous man who killed a woman in his Portland Place apartment. Finally she learns that Hannay's protests of innocence are true, and ultimately the former adversaries become romantically involved.

Eva Marie Saint, the blonde Eve Kendall in *North by Northwest*, engages in a conflict-laden relationship with Roger Thornhill, but with an additional twist distinguishing it from the association between Donat and Carroll in *The 39 Steps*. Thornhill is romanced by Kendall and then doubts her sincerity, believing she is working for the enemy who seeks to destroy him. He ultimately learns that she has become the mistress of ruthless master spy Vandamm in order to bring down his enterprise, and that she actually works for the U.S. government.

Grant and the Notorious Connection

Hitchcock presents the relationship between Thornhill and Kendall in a similar fashion as that seen between the British star and Ingrid Bergman in *Notorious*. In that foreign intrigue film built around a unique love relationship it was Grant playing a federal agent with a frigidity towards personal relations commitments who hands Alicia Huberman (Bergman), who loves him deeply, over to the enemy Nazis and the man who yearns for her, played deftly by Claude Rains. In *North by Northwest*, conversely, Grant's character is emotionally crushed when he believes that Eve Kendall has double-crossed him and plans to turn him over to Phillip Vandamm.

While Grant in *North by Northwest* is an innocent victim of circumstance in the manner of Robert Donat in *The 39 Steps*, he is less of a babe in the woods than the main character of the 1935 film. Though unaware of the machinations of the international spy forces with which he deals, the older and more experienced Thornhill has a glibness developed from his advertising experience that assists him when trouble arises.

The vulnerable position of Eva Marie Saint as mistress to the suave master spy played by James Mason is reminiscent of victim Alicia Huberman after she marries Alexander Sebastian (Claude Rains), another suave Hitchcock villain, in *Notorious*. Rains's sophisticated villain is also reminiscent of Gavin Elster in *Vertigo* and the control he exudes over Judy Barton.

Eva Marie Saint's opportunity to play opposite Grant in one of her greatest starring roles came about because of a choice made by Hitchcock at an earlier point in her career. It will be recalled that when Grace Kelly opted to play a dazzling New York fashion model in *Rear Window* and was compelled to reject a choice role in Elia Kazan's *On the Waterfront*, the New Jersey–born newcomer Saint took the part, and secured a Best Supporting Actress Oscar for her performance.

Hitchcock's Suave Villains

The smooth and dapper Yorkshire actor James Mason was a superb casting choice. Mason was sufficiently acidic and acerbic to invest his role of Phillip

Vandamm with credibility. His role harkens back to other suave villains who appeared in Hitchcock suspense vehicles. In *The 39 Steps* Robert Donat's nemesis was the man with the missing finger who shoots him but fails to kill his victim when his shot is blocked by a Bible resting in Donat's overcoat pocket. In *Saboteur* Robert Cummings is pursued by the troops of suave Nazi ringleader Otto Kruger. Joseph Cotten was charming and debonair when he was not killing wealthy widows as a serial murderer in *Shadow of a Doubt*. Mother-dominated Nazi spy Claude Rains was the suave villain who vies with Cary Grant for Ingrid Bergman in *Notorious*, then poisons her when he discovers that she is working for America. Robert Walker had his suave moments when his insanity was held at bay in *Strangers on a Train*. Then there was Tom Helmore exerting Svengali-like powers over Kim Novak in *Vertigo*.

In moving from *Vertigo* to *North by Northwest*, Hitchcock sustained the element of duplicity, of things not being what they seem, reflecting the murkiness of a Cold War atmosphere dominated by spying on the international front and Madison Avenue marketing on the domestic scene, with network television deeply involved in corrupt game show activity.

In the case of Thornhill of *North by Northwest* we have a man caught up in an advertising world based on hype who is adept at spinning webs to the point where he is devoid of any real identity. He is never seen in his own home, is always on the run wearing the same suit, and has a seeming penchant for the most inhospitable environments. He concedes that his middle initial "O" stands for nothing, then further states, "It's my trademark — ROT." This is the team of Hitchcock and Lehman at its most biting. The initials for the name Roger O. Thornhill, "ROT," relates in its basic definition to decompose, morally corrupt and degenerate.

Kaplan and Madeleine

Vertigo and *North by Northwest* have plots held together by the existence of fictional entities. In *Vertigo* Tom Helmore creates in Kim Novak a fictitious Madeleine Elster as an integral part of his plot to kill his wife. In *North by Northwest* veteran Hitchcock performer Leo G. Carroll, playing a U.S. intelligence agent, has created a fictitious operative named George Kaplan. This is the individual Phillip Vandamm and his entourage believe they are pursuing in the person of Roger Thornhill. The dramatic irony results from the fact that Thornhill is very much of an enigma in his own right.

Anarchy amid Symbols

In Hitchcock's initial foray into sound, the 1929 release *Blackmail*, he introduced a recurring element used in key situations of certain films, that of the contrast between anarchy and functional social disharmony on the one side, and the enduring symbols of structured society on the other. The film's blackmailer, the symbol of social disharmony, plunges to his death in the British Museum by lowering himself on a rope past an enormous Egyptian god's head, which was actually a miniature enlarged by a trick process shot. To make the scene even more cinematically and dramatically effective, the blackmailer shatters glass in his death descent.

The memorable climax of Hitchcock's 1942 release *Saboteur* occurs when Robert Cummings attempts to save his Nazi-spy nemesis, played by a Hitchcock repertory favorite, Norman Lloyd, after he has sought refuge on America's leading symbol of freedom, the Statue of Liberty. This is a classic illustration of Hitchcock's biting social irony, what with a symbol of internal subversion seeking to impose foreign totalitarianism through Nazism seeking refuge on the nation's symbol of freedom.

While a less spectacular shot, the image of Robert Walker smoking a cigarette in shadowy darkness at the Jefferson Memorial in *Strangers on a Train* provides another stark contrast representing order versus anarchy. The symbolism is further accented by the fact that Guy Haines's prospective father in law, played by Leo G. Carroll, is a prominent U.S. senator, and much of the film is set in Washington, D.C.

North by Northwest included an ambitious undertaking involving a treasured American symbol on the order of *Saboteur*'s climactic sequence. This time Hitchcock set his sights on Mount Rushmore and the busts of U.S. presidents. The famous memorial is the perfect resolution point for the battle pitting master spy Vandamm and his forces against Roger Thornhill, who by that time has formed a team with Eve Kendall and is battling to preserve America's interests. Hitchcock, known for his naughtiness, stated, "I wanted Cary Grant to slide down Lincoln's nose and hide in the nostril. Then Grant has a sneezing fit." Conventional wisdom and the censors got Hitchcock's attention on the point of not engaging in actions that viewers could perceive as mocking or diminishing the significance of one of our nation's great presidents, but the Mount Rushmore memorial sequence provided a capstone to a film deep in symbolism. If a conflict with a Nazi spy could culminate at the Statue of Liberty, as it did in *Saboteur*, then a confrontation with Soviet agents would be appropriate for Mount Rushmore.

Mason and Crew

With an emphasis on moral ambiguity and a society in conflict, as emerged in *North by Northwest*, James Mason was the perfect choice for chief spy. The Yorkshireman from Huddersfield had successfully tackled roles of troubled intellectuals and offbeat rebels during his career. Here was an actor in perpetual search of a challenge. After impressing as an embittered, emotionally troubled musician who fell in love with cousin Ann Todd in *The Seventh Veil* in 1946, one year later he appeared in what he termed his favorite role under the man Mason called his favorite director, Carol Reed, in *Odd Man Out*. Using authentic Belfast locations, the film, superbly directed by Reed, encompassed the final day in the life of an Irish Republican Army stalwart who robs a bank with compatriots and is shot in the process, gradually dying.

As for playing a spy, Hitchcock was certainly well aware of Mason's role in the 1952 Joseph Mankiewicz film *5 Fingers*. Based on a true story, Mason serves as the valet to the British ambassador to Ankara, Turkey, during World War II. Known by the code name of Cicero, Mason's character sells British state secrets to the Nazis, not from ideological conviction, but because they offered him the best price. The British government ultimately decided that trying him would result in harm, and so he was allowed to go free, with the loyal agent who had led the effort to track him down (Michael Rennie) fuming helplessly. The real Cicero penned a memoir that sold to Hollywood and inspired a U.S. television series in 1959, the difference being that the antihero element was scratched and the Mason character became a loyal agent.

Sandwiched between *5 Fingers* in the early fifties and *North by Northwest* at the end of that decade, Mason became so attracted to a challenging project that he produced as well as starred in *Bigger Than Life*, which was directed by Nicholas Ray immediately following his classic dealing with troubled teens, *Rebel Without a Cause*. In the 1956 brooding drama *Bigger Than Life* Mason plays a school teacher with a potentially life threatening disease who, in an effort to give himself every chance of surviving, takes a drug new to the market, cortisone, with damaging results. Mason becomes a Jekyll and Hyde figure who turns from a mild-mannered teacher to someone with homicidal tendencies until being restored to normal at the film's conclusion. This was a hard-hitting film that disturbed many with its view of a man under the influence of medication. While it failed at the box office, discerning moviegoers recognized its raw power as well as the fact that Mason was a daring leading man who loved taking chances.

Hitchcock provided his take on Mason's character in an interview with Charles Higham and Joel Greenberg. "James Mason was the heavy," Hitchcock acknowledged, "but I didn't just want him behaving villainously. I wanted him to be polite, but not so polite that he wasn't sufficiently menacing. So I divided the character into three: gave him a secretary who *looked* menacing and a third man who was brutal." Adam Williams portrayed the secretary while Martin Landau, who rose to fame along with his then wife Barbara Bain in the sixties on the popular television series *Mission: Impossible*, was cast in the role of the sadist carrying out Vandamm's dirtiest assignments.

From Cyclone to Crop Dusting

A few years ago I did a survey in the Los Angeles area concerning the popularity of stars and films. I was told that the photograph standing decisively in first place among all film shots was that of Cary Grant running for his life as a crop dusting plane pursued overhead. While it is true that a combination of forces would tend to enhance such a still's popularity, such as a blend of a superstar (Grant) and a popular director (Hitchcock) in a commercially successful film, there was another factor involved. Film fans appreciated the uniqueness of the scene, one of the most truly creative ever seen. To the kind of film enthusiast who ardently collects movie stills it is understandable that something signifying a rare moment of cinema footage would be most appreciated. The more films one has seen, the more the crop dusting scene would stand out as one of a kind.

Just how did this scene come into being? That was an understandable question asked by John Brady in an interview from his book, *The Craft of the Screenwriter*, which included Ernest Lehman and a number of other highly memorable scenarists, including Neil Simon and Paddy Chayevsky. Lehman told Brady that the crop dusting scene idea stemmed from a discussion in the study of Hitchcock's home. Its genesis was a discussion held about different ways for the spy contingent headed by Phillip Vandamm to attempt to kill Roger Thornhill once he arrived in Chicago. Lehman recalled how Hitchcock became fascinated by the idea of a cyclone menacing Grant from the sky.

"Hitch, that's not good," Lehman responded.

"Oh, that would be wonderful," Hitchcock said. "It's easy to do."

"Yeah, but *they're* trying to kill him," Lehman said. "How are *they* going to work up a cyclone?"

While the idea appealed to the fertile creative mind of Hitchcock, which operated like a camera's eye, logic was on Ernest Lehman's side. The spies were not invested with supernatural powers, and the ability to conjure up a cyclone to destroy Cary Grant strained credulity, despite its scenic potential. The cyclone served as a catalyst to the creative minds of Hitchcock and Lehman. As Lehman noted, "somewhere during that afternoon, the cyclone in the sky became the crop-duster plane. Before the day ended, Hitch and I were acting out the entire sequence. The plane making its passes, Grant seeing the cornfield, ducking into the cornfield, the various passes of the plane with a gun; then he sees a car, he tries to wave it down, it ignores him, and he races into the cornfield. Crop-dusting poison is going to drive him out. He sees a diesel truck.... The next day I went to my office and wrote it [the scene], naturally with the greatest of ease. I had already seen it all."

Grant Waits for Godot?

The crop dusting scene holds significance for more than its visual elements. Hitchcock historian Ken Mogg made a perceptive connection between the scene and Samuel Beckett's riveting and highly unconventional play, *Waiting for Godot,* which was performed initially in 1953, just six years before *North by Northwest* debuted. The play delineates the vapidness of life as seen through the eyes of two tramps waiting for Godot, who never appears.

In the case of the crop dusting scene, Hitchcock exercised his propensity for milking the maximum dramatic tension from a scene. This characteristic was noted by Lehman. "It's amazing ... how he [Hitchcock] could manipulate an audience," Lehman explained.

"Most directors would have had maybe one or two cars whiz by," Lehman noted, "and figure that that was about all an audience could tolerate. But Hitchcock knew better than that. He had a car come from one direction, zoom by and disappear in the distance; then he had a car come from the *other* direction, and zoom by and disappear in the distance; and then *another* long interval of silence with nothing happening; and then a truck came by and merely blew dust all over Cary Grant and disappeared in the distance. And still nothing had really happened. Hitch knew how to milk that sequence in a way that no other director would have known how to do, or would have had the guts to do. There was an awful lot of ominous *nothing* going on for a long time before the stranger appeared on the other side of the road. That was just one aspect of Hitchcock's unique style."

Hitchcock's Explanation

Hitchcock's explanation for the famous crop dusting scene was his desire to avoid what he considered a clichéd situation:

> The crop-dusting scene, staged out near Bakersfield here [one hundred miles from Los Angeles], was an example of avoiding the cliché. In ordinary circumstances, if they're going to put a man on the spot, they make him stand under a street lamp on a corner at night. The cobbles are washed away by the recent rain. A black cat slithers along the wall. Somebody peers from behind a curtain. A black limousine goes by and — boom, boom, boom! — that's the cliché.

So I said: I won't do it that way. I'll make it in bright sunshine, without a tree or a house in sight. Thus the audience are worked up by much more: they know the man's put on the spot, but they're mystified as to where it's coming from. I had him waiting and waiting. Then a car pulled up, a man got out, approached our hero and said, "That's funny." "What is?" "There's a crop-duster over there dusting a place where there are no crops." And with that he hops a bus and is off. Sure enough the plane then dives on our hero [Cary Grant] and attacks him: no cliché.

North by Northwest embodied the Hitchcock style at its glossiest. Cary Grant would be secured for the same million dollar figure for which the director signed on as box office insurance, while the most advanced color technology would be utilized to help ensure a steady cash register jingle. Interesting locations were selected, beginning with Mount Rushmore, for Robert Burks to employ his camera.

The MGM production secured three Academy Award nominations. Ernest Lehman received a Best Original Screenplay nomination in his first effort outside the adaptation category. George Tomasini received a Best Editing nomination, while a team of five was nominated for Best Art Direction. While being bypassed by the Academy, Hitchcock was nominated for Best Director by the Directors Guild of America.

If *North by Northwest* represented commercial entertainment at its zenith, coupled with brilliant technical expertise, Hitchcock's next project choice, which was essentially devoid of expensive frills, was made in black and white, contained no expensive names, and was shot on a short schedule, was a step in another direction. Less was expected of this film, which launched Hitchcock into the sixties, but today it stands as his most recognizable work and its popularity shows no sign of ebbing.

9

A Low-Budget
Horror Jackpot

*You could never have shot that under TV conditions — seven days' work for
45 seconds' screen time! TV work is nine minutes a day. Unfortunately,
feature filmmakers are attuned to a minute and a half a day.* — Alfred Hitchcock
describing the shower scene in *Psycho*.

As the 1960s dawned, Alfred Hitchcock, born in the final year of the nineteenth century, moved into his early sixties. He had ended the 1950s with two
expensive technicolor films, *Vertigo* and *North by Northwest*. When he announced
that his first project that would debut in 1960 was a black and white low-budget
effort in which costs would be diminished by using his own television crew there
was considerably less enthusiasm in Hollywood than greeted news of the two
aforementioned glossy vehicles.

The conventional wisdom that a lower budget equates to lower expectations missed the mark. Hitchcock was, after all, a director associated with cost
effectiveness who was sharply on his game in less expensive black and white
movies. *Psycho*, which debuted in 1960, became the Master's most memorable
effort. It endures as a popular monument at two Universal Studios theme parks
on both U.S. coasts.

In Orlando, Florida, one of the most popular regular attractions at the Universal theme park is the recreation of what has become the most famous scene
in film history. The shower scene in which Marion Crane (Janet Leigh) is stabbed
to death is meticulously recreated, with a member of the audience selected to
go backstage, be made up, then return to play the role of Norman Bates (Anthony
Perkins), dressed as his mother, stabbing Crane to death. The irony is that neither Leigh nor Perkins were involved in the key scene — their characters were
represented by stand-ins. Despite not being directly involved in the murder
scene, Janet Leigh later revealed that she never showered again, but instead took
baths from that point forward.

Some three thousand miles away, at the venue where the film was shot, visitors to the tour at Universal Studios get the opportunity to see the most widely discussed house in cinema annals. The Victorian Bates home is observable in all its gothic ghoulish splendor, the structure immediately identifiable due to its association with *Psycho* and the bizarre personality that inhabited it.

Spawning a Cottage Industry

Hitchcock achieved such a breakthrough with *Psycho* that it ultimately became much more than a singular film success. *Psycho*'s enormous popularity begat a cottage industry in what quickly became a burgeoning horror film field. Noted horror film director William Castle was quick off the blocks in delivering a slasher film released in 1961, *Homicidal*, that provided his take on *Psycho*, with accompanying box office success.

A spate of slasher films would eventually flood the market. While Hitchcock might have been the horror master model behind these inferior products, it would have to be said that seeking to imitate a film craftsman and accomplishing comparable results are distinctly different propositions. While many of Hitchcock's imitators provided nothing more than exploitative violence, *Psycho*, as seen on a broader level, is a complex study of society and its numerous contradictions and hypocrisies, including forays into the world of violence.

Taking Dead Aim at Puritanism

The earlier expressed view of Hitchcock as Shakespeare's Puck in maturity attains its most convincing explication in a thorough analysis of *Psycho*. Hitchcock was again spectacularly on his mark as what was termed the "uptight fifties," accented by the corrupt superficialities of Madison Avenue advertising and television game show rigging, was passing from the scene, and the sixties, marked by sexual experimentation, drug experimentation, hippies, love-ins, and rock concerts (reaching its zenith at Woodstock), was dawning.

Hitchcock as a sensitive filmmaker had his finger constantly on the public pulse, and *Psycho*, with careful study, stands as a critique of the fifties, as well as a conscientious predictor of how a period predicated on inhibition, or, worse yet, its false pretense, would be fundamentally challenged. It would be followed by a period in which pent-up sensations held in check would be explored, and a Cold War, in which adversaries came perilously close to nuclear conflict, would have its fundamental premises challenged. The challengers were many of the same youthful forces who challenged the same status quo thinking present in the sexual sphere.

Hitchcock Legend Become Tourist Site — A prominent and popular stop on the Universal City Studio Tour is the Victorian house where macabre murderer Norman Bates, played by Anthony Perkins, resided in *Psycho*. The low budget film achieved soaring success beyond even Hitchcock's expectations and is now his best-known work.

Teasing Viewer Voyeurism

Hitchcock is into his puckish naughtiness at the film's outset. He begins with a documentary approach, showing us the skyline of Phoenix, Arizona. He flashes the name of the city on the screen, followed by the date and time of Friday, December the Eleventh, Two Forty-three P.M.

The director as Puck then surfaces as the camera ever so slowly pans toward a building, which turns out to be the kind of rundown hotel where people meet for clandestine affairs. The camera closes in on an open window. Hitchcock the voyeur is at work, and his interested viewers follow attentively as the camera takes us inside that small window opening and into a hotel room where Janet Leigh, attired in slip and bra, sits in bed after a sexual interlude with John Gavin, who is barefoot and wearing trousers, but is shirtless. By having viewers enter the room in the manner described, Hitchcock is seemingly chuckling at his audience and exclaiming with his impish grin, "Well now, when all is said and done we're all voyeurs, now aren't we?"

Hitchcock was back on the scene challenging the censors, who served as his perpetual jousting partners. Not only was Janet Leigh in her undergarments, but convention was defied by the positioning of her feet. To be conventionally safe a woman in bed was supposed to have her feet in contact with the floor, indicating that she was sitting on it rather than, well, otherwise engaged. Leigh's feet were not touching the floor.

A Struggling Couple

The images of Leigh and Gavin, playing Marion Crane and Sam Loomis, in what is obviously postcoital conversation can easily deceive viewers into initially believing that their lives were in much better shape than was the case. While an allowance can be made for meeting in a dreary hotel that would never appear on anyone's 5-star list, upon looking at such a striking young couple engaged in an intimate relationship the initial conclusion might be that they are fortunate and have life's circumstances pulling in their direction.

The spare and lean dialogue from Joseph Stefano's script offers a scene in which the couple is presented as swimming in a murky sea of grim doubt and facing futures of foreboding uncertainty. Indeed, the very love scene we as Hitchcock's dutiful voyeurs just missed, rather than holding tender meaning to Marion Crane, instead catapults an issue into the forefront that she feels compelled to immediately discuss with Sam Loomis. While Loomis is prepared to luxuriate in the aftermath of a romantic afternoon interlude with his lovely girlfriend, the cross-purpose dialogue reveals a troubled psyche on part:

SAM: You never did eat your lunch, did you?

MARION: I'd better get back to the office. These extended lunch hours give my boss excess acid.

SAM: Why don't you call your boss and tell him you're taking the rest of the afternoon off? It's Friday anyway — and hot.

MARION: What do I do with my free afternoon? Walk you to the airport?

SAM: Well, you could laze around here a while longer.

The reference to spending additional time in a seedy hotel room, even with a handsome, broad-shouldered hunk, is insufficient for the young lady. Sam Loomis's reference to lazing around longer in those confines provides the catalyst the frustrated and trapped young woman needs to lay her concerns squarely on the table. She wants much more than to be a woman visiting hotels in search of romantic fulfillment.

MARION: Checking out time is 3 P.M. Hotels of this sort are interested in you when you come in, but not when your time is up. Oh Sam, I hate having to be with you in a place like this.

SAM: Married couples deliberately spend an occasional night in a cheap hotel.

The irony of this phase of the first and ultimately only dialogue exchange in the film between Sam and Marion is that he is the person who has brought up the very subject that is foremost on the young woman's mind — marriage. Sam finally exclaims, "You sure talk like a girl who's been married." Actually the opposite is true, she has not been married and believes she is at an age and stage of her life when it is time to do so and have a child. Marion stops Sam short by proclaiming with serious and straightforward meaning, "Sam, this is the last time."

When a startled Sam asks for an explanation, Marion explains that she will no longer conduct a backdoor affair with clandestine lunchtime meetings in seedy hotels. She explains that they can see one another respectably. Sam then explains his problematical financial affairs as the reason why he has not pursued her matrimonially. He runs a hardware store in the small California town of Fairvale and sleeps in small quarters behind it. His ex-wife, who lives comfortably in another country, receives his monthly checks. Sam gives every appearance of being a decent but financially strapped man who hates to reveal the unpleasant details of his troubled life to the woman he loves. The subject turns bluntly to Marion's plans and her concurrent desire for a marriage and family:

SAM: A couple years and my debts will be paid off. If she remarries, the alimony stops.
MARION: I haven't even been married once yet.
SAM: Yeah, but when you do, you'll swing.
MARION: Oh Sam, let's get married! (They kiss and embrace.)
SAM: Yeah. And live with me in a storeroom behind a hardware store in Fairvale? We'll have lots of laughs. I'll tell you what. When I send my ex-wife her alimony, you can lick the stamps.
MARION: I'll lick the stamps.
SAM: Marion, you want to cut this off, go out and find somebody available?
MARION: I'm thinking of it.
SAM: How could you even think a thing like that?

Once more the spare and lean dialogue from Joseph Stefano's script reveals much with few words. Sam reveals himself to be far more than a run of the mill man looking for responsibility-free romance with an attractive woman. As she emphasizes her desire for marriage he explains his difficulties. He does not back away from the relationship when she explains the need for a fresh set of ground rules. Sam does, however, explain his troubled economic circumstances, not an easy task since he is anything but proud of them. Marion, to her credit, does not back away as some women would, but summarizes her wishes for a fresh start with him when she exclaims in reference to sending his ex-wife monthly alimony checks, "I'll lick the stamps."

Sam then displays his concern for Marion as a person, disrupting any notions audience members might hold about him being an opportunist out for a good time with no strings attached. His concern for Marion prompts him to blurt out the words that perhaps it is time for her to go out and find an available and substantial marital type. When she responds, "I'm thinking of it," he promptly rejoins, "How could you even think a thing like that?" While he was concerned about Marion's future well-being, it hurt him to hear her agree to the suggestion that she find someone else to replace him in her affections. Sam clearly wants to stay with her.

Hitchcock's Ominous Presence

The opening hotel scene reveals much in a brief period. The same can be said for the second scene, which lays the groundwork for the remainder of the film. We see what happens when Marion Crane returns to the office. As she open the door and prepares to step inside the building Alfred Hitchcock is seen wearing the kind of white ten-gallon hat popular with so many Arizonans as he casually stands on the sidewalk and stares straight ahead. Given Hitchcock's legendary sense of humor, he no doubt expects us to appreciate the humor of this Cockney-accented Britisher wearing a cowboy hat.

There is something significant in Hitchcock's appearance at that moment in time. He stands as a mature and omniscient Puck in front of the building into which the story's main tragic victim enters, only to have her life change. The turn of events will ultimately cost secretary Marion Crane her life.

When Marion steps inside, the scene begins in seemingly innocuous fashion, so characteristic of a Hitchcock "lull before the storm" moment. Marion begins conversing with the other secretary in the office, played by none other than Hitchcock's daughter Patricia, who supplies the audience with comic relief while at the same time making some points about social duplicity. Marion has marriage and commitment very much on her mind after her tense conversation with Sam following their sexual interlude.

Patricia's character, Caroline, is recently married. When Marion, apparently feeling tense from her blunt conversation with Sam, complains of a headache and needing an aspirin, Caroline offers her a tranquilizer instead, which leads to a story. She tells Marion about her nagging mother's suggestion that her doctor prescribe tranquilizers for her wedding day. This insertion into the Stefano script was surely Hitchcock tweaking the public on its uptight fifties fears about sex and the loss of virginity on the wedding night. Also, during the late fifties, prior to the drug experimentation era of the hippies and flower children, tranquilizers became highly popular with people seeking to cope with stress.

Flirtation and Temptation

Marion's conversation with Caroline is interrupted by the appearance of her boss, George Lowery, played by Vaughan Taylor. A sharp contrast is immediately detectable between his no-nonsense business demeanor and the flamboyance of the man he is with, Tom Cassidy (Frank Albertson), who wears a suit, a ten-gallon hat, and is mischievously drunk. Lowery is embarrassed when Cassidy explains in front of the two secretaries that he intends to imbibe some more from the bottle that the straight-laced-appearing boss keeps in his office, a detail Taylor would prefer to keep secret, as his facial reaction reveals.

Lowery's expression makes it plain that he would prefer that Cassidy and his alcoholic extroversion be kept between them in the privacy of his office, but after seeing Marion the recalcitrant client will have none of it. He moves into a quick flirtation as Lowery stands stiffly by, reflecting more awkwardness with each passing moment, and this is without knowing what will ultimately arise from the interlude. Cassidy moves boldly to the forefront, sitting on Leigh's desk as he regales her with conversation.

Cassidy tells Marion about the $40,000 he has stashed in a paper sack, which will buy the wedding present he is bestowing on his 18-year-old daughter—a new home. Marion appears amused, a beautiful woman used to male advances. In Cassidy's case he is probably emboldened by the alcohol he has consumed; drink often loosens the tongue. Cassidy sounds like a high roller swimming in money. He boasts that his daughter has never experienced an unhappy day in her 18 years and explains the impact of his money on her life, as well as his own. "You know what I do about unhappiness? I buy it off." As Marion listens, he elaborates: "Now, that, that's not buying happiness. That's just buying off unhappiness. I never carry more than I can afford to lose."

As Marion Crane listens to high roller Cassidy as he sits on the edge of her desk and talks casually about his money, the expression of attentive amusement masks what she must be thinking. Hitchcock once more engages in his game with viewers of letting them fill in the blanks. Could temptation be rearing its ugly head when he speaks casually about leaving the entire amount in cash? Marion's cautious-looking boss, Mr. Lowery, immediately suggests a check transaction, but a devil-may-care Cassidy waves him off. The wealthy oil man is more interested in quenching his thirst with more liquor.

It is ultimately decided that the money be banked, and since Marion has complained about a headache and has told her boss that she plans to spend the weekend "in bed," Mr. Lowery leaves the sack containing $40,000 in cash for her to deposit before going to her apartment to get some rest.

Marion is shown stopping for a traffic signal. She has not deposited the money, and the guilty look on her face indicates that temptation is taking possession of her. Mr. Lowery crosses the street in front of her with Cassidy, who does not notice her, walking beside him. Initially her boss nods, but as he takes several more steps he looks back, his expression one of baffled concern, that of someone sensing that something is wrong.

Marion's expression reflects troubled anxiety. Here is another example of Hitchcock as a classic filmmaker realizing that the cinema presents an advantage over an oral form of storytelling in that frequently silence and allowing expressions and silent actions to delineate what is occurring can be the most effective means of conveying a point. The silent exchange of expressions between troubled and tempted employee and surprised boss proved far more dramatic in this instance than any scene in which Mr. Lowery sees her and asks, "Marion, what are you doing here?"

Emphasis on Silent Temptation

Hitchcock has set the stage for more viewer voyeurism, this time invading a troubled young woman's psyche as she wrestles with the demon of temptation. The voyeurism extends again to the sexual realm when she reaches the bedroom of her apartment and slips out of her dress. There is a difference between the color of her slip and the one we saw in the film's opening scene in the shabby hotel room. In the black and white context of a film in which stark and naked human activity is stressed and corresponding psyches explored, Marion's slip and bra are now black.

The color change provides a major clue from Hitchcock and Stefano that the troubled secretary has reached a decision. The forces of temptation have triumphed. This point is further manifested when Marion Crane empties the contents of the bag on the bed, the same spot where she told Mr. Lowery she would be spending the weekend. Her sister is away in Tucson to do "some buying" so she is very much alone, preparing to take a fateful step. Filling in the blanks becomes even easier when a suitcase is observed next to her.

The preceding scenes were laid out so simply that it is easy to underestimate all that has been revealed in the story in such a brief period of time, the kind of narrow compass storytelling successfully employed only by the masters. It all becomes clear in retrospect. Here was a young lady who had never been married and was concerned about entering that world at a time when she still has her youth and attractiveness. That revealing line when she tells Sam she would be happy to "lick the stamps" of the envelopes containing the alimony checks that he can barely afford to pay, as long as their relationship can be properly solidified, takes on a darker resonance now that a certain envelope lay on her bed, an instrument for lovemaking as well as sleep.

The envelope contains $40,000. How casually Cassidy boasted about his wealth in his semi-drunken flirtatious state. He told her about buying off unhappiness, not knowing just how desperate Marion was to escape the strait-jacketed emotional confines she shares with her lover Sam. What a difference that amount of money could make to them! If Cassidy had that much wealth would he really miss $40,000? Such were the temptations troubling the psyche of the secretary in the silence of her bedroom on a Friday afternoon.

Marion Steps into the
Shoes of Youngster Hitchcock

"*Psycho* all came from Robert Bloch's book," Hitchcock explained in an interview with Charles Higham and Joel Greenberg. "The scriptwriter, Joseph Stefano—a radio writer, he'd been recommended to me by my agents, MCA—contributed dialogue mostly, no ideas."

The Bloch novel was adapted from a true case involving a serial killer. Hitchcock spun the story in a direction with which he was intimately familiar. Once more he retrogressed back to the frightening day when as a young boy his father taught him a lesson about doing wrong by having him, with the cooperation of local authorities, spend some time in jail. He described this incident, which was terrifying to the young man, in many subsequent interviews. In *Psycho* the audience serve as voyeurs to Marion's troubled psyche as she leaves Phoenix on a Friday afternoon, with an envelope containing $40,000 her only companion.

In *Vertigo*, released just two years before *Psycho*, Hitchcock revealed the criminal mind par excellence via Tom Helmore's brilliant performance as Gavin Elster. Here was a criminal mind so cunning that each time he spoke the villain oozed charm and sophistication. In *Psycho* Hitchcock's escaping embezzler heading west with forty grand is to the criminal element what Peter Sellers's side-splitting Inspector Clousseau is to police investigation.

It is clear from the outset that Marion is far out of her element as a would-be criminal and feels much of what the youngster Hitchcock felt when he had misbehaved as a boy—guilt, and plenty of it. In fact, when Marion's actions are evaluated they appear so conspicuous that, had the film been made by a director of lesser reputation, reviewers would poke holes in the plot and conclude that an amateur was at work. They would reason that such conspicuous conduct was not credible to film audiences. In Hitchcock's case critics and historians know about his meticulous concern for detail, meaning that Janet Leigh as Marion Crane was behaving in a manner the Master, in concert with scriptwriter Stefano, deemed appropriate under the circumstances.

A case in point that could under other circumstances raise red flags is the decision Marion makes after driving all night. She takes the conspicuously inept step of pulling off to the side of a remote desert highway for some much-needed sleep. Had she applied any thought, Marion should have realized that no one would link her to criminal activity until Monday morning, and so she had a window of opportunity over the course of the weekend. The prudent move would be to stop at a motel and get up early the next morning fully rested. The idea of stopping at the side of the road to sleep was a dangerous one since such terrain is patrolled by state highway patrolmen. By no coincidence, Marion is awakened when an officer taps on her window as she lies sprawled out on the front seat of her car.

Entering the scene is Mort Mills, portraying the patrolman, who wakes Marion up with his window tapping. The tall, lean character actor would, from that point forward, be known as the highway patrolman who pursued Janet Leigh's character in *Psycho*, just as Leigh would thereafter be linked to the famous shower stabbing scene as the victim of a psychotic Norman Bates. Leigh as Marion Crane never once pursues the prudent course of someone escaping the wheels of justice. The highway patrolman immediately tells her that there are plenty of motels in the area, inquiring why she chose to sleep in her car. "I didn't intend to sleep all night," she responds. "I just pulled over. Have I broken any laws?"

Marion's colloquy with the highway patrolman reveals her as a poster girl for a police training film revealing suspicious criminal behavior. As is so often the case with guilty behavior, it is not even so much what she says as how she articulates it. The prudent strategy would be to reflect a cool and polite calm, tamping any fires of suspicion in the process, but that is not Marion. She responds with a brittle impatience, the rattled indignance of someone who is eager to get away from the officer. This naturally increases his suspicion. When he begins questioning her, Marion's tart abruptness increases:

> HIGHWAY Patrolman: Is anything wrong?
> MARION: Of course not. Am I acting as if there's something wrong?
> HIGHWAY PATROLMAN: Frankly, yes.
> MARION: Please, I'd like to go.
> HIGHWAY PATROLMAN: Well, is there?
> MARION: Is there what? I've told you there's nothing wrong, except that I'm in a hurry and you're taking up my time.

Marion has made another cardinal error in citizen-police relations. Rather than smilingly complying and making minimal comment, increasing the chance of a quick resolution while hopefully eliminating suspicion, Marion's behavior is likely to increase misgiving while irritating the highway patrolman. Had her demeanor been cooperative rather than combative he would perhaps have let her go with a warning about sleeping beside the road. As a result of her suspicious and argumentative behavior, Marion is compelled to provide identification. Also, after she is allowed to leave, the highway patrolman's suspicion has been aroused to the point that he decides to follow behind her. He becomes a frightening sight to the rattled Marion in her rear view mirror.

Ingenious Irony and California Charlie's Quick Sale

One of the most inventively masterful uses of dialogue is to display irony in a manner to convey one meaning when a listener anticipates another, leading to misunderstanding. It is a technique used only rarely because of the difficulty of achieving such an effect. The technique was used to brilliant effect after Marion drives off the main road once she reaches California and into what is apparently the first town of any size in the Golden State.

Marion arrives at a used car dealership run by a smooth talking and affable owner-salesman who calls himself California Charlie, played by John Anderson. He greets her with a smile. His initial comment jolts her, increasing her already rattled state.

> CALIFORNIA CHARLIE: I'm in no mood for trouble.
> MARION (rattled): What?
> CALIFORNIA CHARLIE: There's an old saying. The first customer of the day is always the most trouble.

The playful reference to "trouble" jolts both Marion and the audience.

If carefully constructed irony is difficult for a writer to accomplish, then irony upon irony is probably doubly difficult. Hitchcock and scriptwriter Joseph Stefano attained double irony when the salesman sees his comment about the first customer of the day quickly refuted in a manner that stuns him.

Once more the rattled Marion Crane engages in suspicious behavior. Now that she has crossed the state line into California she has decided that a change of cars and license plates will make her less vulnerable. She startles California Charlie with her rattled, and impatient demeanor and by exhibiting a pattern of hurriedness. At one point the startled salesman stammers, "Why, this is the first time the customer ever high-pressured the salesman!"

While Marion's stop is intended to thwart authorities, who should show up across the street to view the transaction but the pursuing highway patrolman. Marion is asked if she wants to take the car she has selected for a test run, the usual procedure for a car purchaser. Once more the rattled woman on the run invites suspicion with her comment. "Can't we just settle this?" she asks. "Is there anything so terribly wrong about making a decision and wanting to hurry? Do you think I've stolen my car?"

Once more the Inspector Clousseau of criminal activity has spoken. What would arouse suspicion faster on the part of the salesman she hopes will suspect nothing than to ask him if he thinks her car has been stolen? Even from across the street the omnipresent highway patrolman can observe how rattled Marion is from her body language, along with the contrasting demeanor of California Charlie, who could not help but notice the reversal of form as the customer pressures the salesman.

Another moment of irony is achieved when Marion begins to drive away in the used car she has just purchased. One of California Charlie's garage mechanics races onto the scene, shouting "Hey!" at an anxiously departing Marion. When she slams on her brakes the mechanic explains that she has forgotten her luggage.

After retrieving her luggage the nervous woman can then depart. In retrospect one wonders just how much worse she could have played her hand in attempting to represent herself as a person passing through town under assumed normal circumstances who wishes to trade her used car for a newer model.

A Hitchcock Principle of Reversal?

In regards to one of the most famous scenes of his career, that of Cary Grant being pursued in a vacant field by a crop duster, Hitchcock pointed out that he had sought to reverse the normal circumstances of such a cloak-and-dagger scenario by having the victim pursued by a sinister and determined criminal force not through the expected dark, rain-slick streets, but through a sunny, dusty cornfield. Could Hitchcock have had the same principle of reversal in mind with Janet Leigh as Marion Crane? Was Hitchcock making a mental contrast separating Marion from the master criminal who comported himself in seemingly effortless manner as a smooth gentleman — namely, the suave Gavin Elster from *Vertigo*?

If this dualism can be accepted for discussion purposes then another point surfaces in the mind of a discerning behavioral analyst. Tom Helmore as the unforgettable Gavin Elster behaves as a super-smooth criminal because, no matter what his surface demeanor indicates, he is treading in comfortable water. This Professor Moriarity–style criminal genius is so comfortable in that environment that he makes no waves at all.

Contrast the wily criminal mastermind of *Vertigo* with a thoroughly blundering Janet Leigh as Marion Crane and the conclusion can easily be reached that Hitchcock the moralist is revealing the significant point that a basically honest and upstanding citizen from the community might well behave in the manner of the would-be embezzler for the opposite reason than would a Gavin Elster type. If Elster represents the worst at its best, then Marion represents the best at its worst.

Marion Crane's guilty discomfort over the act of running away with the stolen $40,000 has turned a seemingly intelligent woman into a conspicuous bungler as she makes wrong decisions and generates suspicion. She is every bit as uncomfortable in her current surroundings as suave professional Gavin Elster was comfortable in the criminal milieu. Marion Crane's demeanor reveals that she has a conscience, whereas Elster was not bothered by what under the circumstances can prove to be a great deficiency.

Raymond Durgnat, who wrote a lengthy analytical book about *Psycho*, titled *A Long Hard Look at Psycho*, made a sound observation about the casting of Janet Leigh in the female lead. Durgnat revealed that international superstar Lana Turner was considered for the role of Marion Crane. He concluded that Janet Leigh, as a relative newcomer lacking the star status of Lana Turner (who had received the MGM star treatment from the late thirties on and by then had been a big name internationally for better than two decades) was a better choice for this unique film.

When Hitchcock selected stars such as James Stewart, Cary Grant, Grace Kelly and Doris Day for major vehicles during his productive middle-to-end-of-fifties period these individuals stepped into the shoes of characters similar to the basic personalities and character demeanors with which audiences had become familiar. In the case of *Psycho* the female star is brutally killed 45 minutes into the film. Previously the entire film rests on her shoulders as the team of Hitchcock and Stefano turn the audience into voyeurs peering into the rattled and indecisive world of Marion Crane as she stands at a crossroad in her life.

As Durgnat notes, there is a distinct advantage in having the character with whom the audience becomes so familiar, sharing the innermost secrets of her life, be a woman with whom they are just becoming acquainted. Hiring a veteran glamorous superstar such as Lana Turner circa 1960 carries expectations based on better than two decades of viewing her on screen. With Turner there was an audience familiarity as well as expectation level that did not apply to Janet Leigh, who, after appearing in the 1949 MGM hit *Little Women*, was basically known for starring with husband Tony Curtis in three films, *Houdini* (1953), *The Vikings* (1958) and *Who Was That Lady?*, released the same year as *Psycho*.

There was another irregular element to Leigh's starring role in *Psycho* in addition to the anomaly of being killed off so early having to carry the film and heighten viewer curiosity through the unconventional means of bits and spurts. It is one thing to carry scenes through brilliant dialogue and notable emoting. In Leigh's case the challenge was to carry interest through a series of freak events in which much of the time she was anything but her best and feeling high levels of discomfort. She begins by laying down the law to her lover in the uncomfortable surroundings of a cheap hotel following a lunchtime tryst. She then hears out a drunken and boastful Tom Cassidy as he brags about his money while flirting with her, at one point suggesting that a headache or case of the blues can readily be cured by a quick trip to Las Vegas. It takes little imagination to conclude that Cassidy had himself in mind as a weekend Prince Charming to make her feel better in the gambling city.

Through bizarre circumstances Marion finds herself bearing $40,000 in cash due to the stubbornness of Cassidy in declining to follow the sage advice of Marion's boss. Her discussion with Sam Loomis following their sexual interlude was all about money and the difficult circumstances he was in due to its absence in his life. Here was the man in her life sadly strapped for funds just as she was hoping he would marry her. Here she was with $40,000 in cash belonging to a wealthy oil magnate whose breezy attitude toward the subject leads her to believe that the green stuff practically grows on trees. The $40,000 quickly becomes a hot potato in her hands, but nonetheless a potential elixir to heal difficulties in her life with Sam.

When Marion took to the road and headed west toward California, the rattled demeanor exhibited called for truly unconventional acting by Leigh. Mannerisms and body language revealed her circumstances in larger measure than dialogue.

An Existential Ending?

Janet Leigh as Marion Crane might have finally shaken Highway Patrolman Mort Mills once she left California Charlie's car lot, but shaking her own tormented psyche was another matter. A clever series of stream of consciousness monologues disrupts the tortured young woman's concentration as she drives on a highway in the darkness in what quickly turns into heavy rain.

After initially imagining a conversation occurring the same day, Saturday, following her purchase of the car between California Charlie and the Highway Patrolman, she then listens to speculative conversation on Monday morning at the office where she works concerning her failure to appear. The most revealing conversation occurs between her boss Mr. Lowery and Cassidy. Cassidy, in his typically earthy language, exclaims, "Well, I ain't about to kiss off $40,000. I'll get it back and if any of it's missing, I'll replace it with her fine soft flesh."

The imagined comment dovetails with Marion's fate after stopping that evening at what would ultimately become the most famous name for a fictitious inn of its kind, the Bates Motel. Marion's brutal demise occurs in the wake of a series of coalescing circumstances that make her appear to be the victim of a cruel and merciless fate reminiscent of an existentialist drama written by Jean Paul Sartre or Albert Camus.

The flashing commentaries that disturb Marion as she drives through a heavy rain might well be the ultimate catalyst prompting her to leave the main road. When the rain becomes so intense that she believes it is wise to stop for the evening she happens to notice the neon light for the Bates Motel. This is where the "fine soft flesh" will be extracted in a most brutal fashion.

As explained by Norman Bates (Anthony Perkins), the smaller road onto which Marion has wandered was once the main highway. During the fifties the National Highway Act was passed, creating a system that greatly aided commercial interstate commerce by shortening time routes for truck drivers. As one drives through America today signs are regularly observable bearing the name of President Dwight D. Eisenhower. His name appears throughout the modernized highway structure that took shape through enabling legislation during Eisenhower's presidency.

The Eisenhower Highway Act wrought changes throughout America. A notable change occurred on Route 66, which was saluted in song with a hit record by Nat "King" Cole and a popular American television series starring Martin Milner and George Maharis. A large part of commercial America, particularly smaller towns where income was generated through lodging and restaurants accommodating travelers, was promptly changed. It was easier to reach major destinations, and those who stopped along the way did so at new hotels and motels and dined at new restaurants built to conform to changing times.

Businesses such as the Bates Motel suffered enormously. When Marion Crane accidentally left the main road in the driving rainstorm she journeyed from the new, enhanced modern technology and a rapidly developing national highway system to the old. It all happened as a result of veering off course.

Another point arises early in Marion Crane's meeting with the tragically conflicted Norman Bates that makes her loom like a victim of fate in a Sartre or Camus story, a fact that's revealed in conversation with the motel proprietor. When Marion mentions having dinner Bates explains that there is a diner just 15 miles away in Fairvale. Marion expresses surprise over learning that she is that close to her destination. Judging from her tone of surprise it appears that, had she known she was so close to the town where her lover Sam Loomis lives, she would have ventured for what would have been less than another half hour to reach her destination. Since she has reached her destination for the evening, however, Marion accepts her fate and agrees to have a modest supper prepared by the innkeeper himself.

Had it not been for the merging of the aforementioned elements Marion would never have stayed at the Bates Motel and become the ultimate victim of the tormented innkeeper. Another element must also be added to the foregoing mix of events. Mort Mills as the vigilant Highway Patrolman was immediately suspicious of Marion, an easy deduction based on her rattled and impatient behavior. If he had been able to piece together any kind of solid evidence to corroborate his suspicion then he would have arrested Marion, which means she would have spent an evening in a local jail and never met psychopathic killer Norman Bates.

Robert Walker and Rooting for the Criminal

While there are broad differences between Tom Helmore as criminal genius Gavin Elster in *Vertigo* and excessively cumbersome, perpetually rattled embezzler Janet Leigh as Marion Crane in *Psycho*, an interesting comparison can be made to one of the most dramatic phases of *Strangers on a Train* when the psychotic killer played by Robert Walker seeks to frame Farley Granger's Guy Haines for murdering his wife. The brilliant chase sequence, in which Haines races through a tennis match to beat Bruno Antony to the amusement park where Haines's wife was killed before the killer can plant a piece of incriminating evidence can be thematically compared to Janet Leigh's predicament in *Psycho*.

It has been noted that the wily Hitchcock is teasing viewers into rooting for the criminal as Antony drops the incriminating cigarette lighter into a manhole, then, with assistance, is able to retrieve the important item. The question emerges as to whether Hitchcock, through letting viewers observe the torment of Janet Leigh as a woman in love with a man who is financially strapped, is engaging in a similarly teasing pattern.

Hitchcock lets us see how unfairly the dice can roll in life. Sam Loomis can use a financial break, and so can Marion Crane, strongly desiring marriage and a family and believing that time is running out on her. She meets flirtatious braggadocio Tom Cassidy in her boss' office immediately after her tense conversation with Sam. The wealthy oil man waves the huge chunk of money at the secretary with carefree abandon.

The question must surely emerge in the minds of viewers, just as it does with Marion Crane: Will Cassidy be strapped if he loses $40,000? What injury will he possibly incur? On the other hand, what will $40,000 mean to Marion and Sam? It would provide them with a new lease on life, enable them to marry, and extricate Sam from financial burdens relating to his previous marriage.

If the aforementioned details provide motivation for viewers to root for the criminal, in this case secretary Marion, then other elements can be included as well. Whereas psycho killer Bruno Antony had a smooth side when it came to criminal behavior, and was plotting diabolically to implicate Guy Haines for the murder he himself has committed, Janet Leigh plays a rational and intelligent young woman who becomes overwhelmed by the overpowering temptation during a trying period of her life. Her discomfiture in adopting a new criminal role causes her to behave in a guilty fashion. In so doing, viewers can be easily tempted to root for her to succeed in her endeavor and see her turn her life dramatically around by stealing money from a wealthy oil man.

Enter Anthony Perkins

The novel *Psycho*, from which Joseph Stefano adapted the screenplay, was written by Wisconsin resident and author Robert Bloch, who adapted the story from the ghoulish antics of Ed Gein, who lived a lonely life near a tiny Wisconsin hamlet. A man given to mumbling, he was presumed by the few people aware of him to be feeble-minded. In 1957 his house was found to be crammed with female bodies and body parts. He sat in chairs made of human bones and wore apparel made of women's skins. Along with being the catalyst for Bloch's Norman Bates, Ed Gein also inspired *The Texas Chainsaw Massacre*.

Norman Bates, the character sculpted in fiction from Gein by Robert Bloch, emerged in print as fat and fortyish, a soft, bookish, timid creature. The fictional Norman created by Bloch understands Freudian theory and that the Oedipus complex is his problem.

The Norman Bates character seen in the film *Psycho* is yet another example of the casting genius of Alfred Hitchcock. Rather than seek an actor to fulfill the requisites of Norman Bates found in Bloch's novel, he instead opted for a totally different physical and chronological type. This maneuver would make a dramatic difference.

Paramount had not been enthusiastic when Hitchcock approached them with the *Psycho* project. Despite what film historians now think of *Vertigo*, this was the period in the immediate wake of its then financial flop status, and Hitchcock was told he would have to function with a smaller budget, black and white film stock, and no international star of the stature of James Stewart or Cary Grant. Working with writer Joseph Stefano was a means of remaining within a "leaner and hopefully meaner" budget since he, like Hitchcock, was under contract to MCA. By no coincidence so too were Janet Leigh and John Gavin.

Stefano at one point in the early going lamented to Hitchcock that he disliked the character of Norman Bates. "I really couldn't get involved with a man in his forties who's a drunk and peeps through holes," Stefano complained. "The other problem was that there was this other horrendous murder of a stranger I didn't care about either. I just kept talking to him in the vein, 'I wish I knew this girl. I wish Norman were somebody else.'"

"How would you feel if Norman were played by Anthony Perkins?" Hitchcock asked.

"Now you're talking," Stefano enthused. "I suddenly saw a tender young man you could feel incredibly sorry for. I could really rope in an audience with someone like him."

With Hitchcock needing to toe the mark budget-wise for Paramount, there were glowing considerations for hiring Perkins apart from aesthetics. Perkins was also an MCA client. In addition, Hitchcock was aware that Perkins owed Paramount a film under an old contract for $40,000. This figure represents the exact amount that Janet Leigh embezzles from her boss in the film. It stood in stark contrast to the $450,000, plus 10 percent of the gross over $8 million, that Cary Grant had received to star in *North by Northwest*.

Stefano had a personal awareness of Anthony Perkins through having been hired at Twentieth Century–Fox to adapt a J.R. Salamanca novel, *The Lost Country*, for the rising young actor. It was eventually made two years later as *Wild in the Country* with Elvis Presley starring and Clifford Odets scripting.

Perkins was delighted to work with a legendary director like Hitchcock, believing it could provide his career with a jump start, and accepted the role of Norman Bates before he had an opportunity to read the script. Hitchcock had seen Perkins in the pivotal film of the early phase of his career, *Fear Strikes Out*.

"He always cast from seeing the actors in other films," Perkins explained. "He couldn't subject any of them to the ritual reading, or even the meeting in his office was too tender for him to contemplate. He never auditioned, he never screen-tested actors for major roles or even minor roles. He chose them always from other performances, which I think is rather a unique quality. I've never known another director to have the confidence in himself to do that. By the time I was in his office, I'd already got the part. So the getting of the job step was one I didn't have a chance to strive for."

From Daddy's Boy to Mamma's Boy

The Perkins film that Hitchcock viewed and, considering his offering of the *Psycho* role, was favorably impressed by was the 1957 Paramount release *Fear Strikes Out*. This was the first starring role for Perkins as well as the initial film directed by Robert Mulligan. Whereas in playing Norman Bates, Perkins was following an old Hitchcock tradition of playing mamma's boys, such as Claude Rains in *Notorious* and Robert Walker in *Strangers on a Train*, his career breakthrough role in *Fear Strikes Out* revolved around an intense young man eager to please his highly demanding father.

Fear Strikes Out was a film adaptation based on the autobiography of major league baseball star Jim Piersall. The Piersall story had previously been produced as a highly acclaimed television drama in 1956 starring Tab Hunter. In the film version Perkins plays opposite prominent character actor Karl Malden, who received an Oscar as Best Supporting Actor playing Mitch, the more refined and sensitive pal to Marlon Brando's Stanley Kowalski an Elia Kazan's *A Streetcar Named Desire* (1951).

Perkins as Piersall was groomed from early boyhood in Waterbury, Connecticut, by his demanding father to play for New England's revered American League baseball team, the Boston Red Sox. His father's dream, which he seeks to live out, is for Piersall to become starting center fielder for the Red Sox. The elder Piersall performed as a minor league baseball player who always longed for the top rung. Malden accordingly tells Piersall, who works out vigorously daily under his tutelage, "We're going for the big leagues!"

The dream appears to be on track when Piersall is signed as a free agent by the Red Sox in 1949. A point of conflict ensues, however, with the opening of the 1952 season. Amid the tremendous pressure of seeking to live up to his father's high expectations, Piersall eventually suffers a nervous breakdown and is confined to a mental institution. He ultimately recognizes that he sought major league baseball success not for himself but to live up to his father's expectations. Piersall then returned to baseball and enjoyed a successful career, after which he gained distinction as a baseball commentator. Perkins was a performer noted for living a role, investing every measure of physical and psychological energy into performing activities.

If Anthony Perkins caught Hitchcock's attention playing a daddy's boy, his own life provided the grist for empathizing with the mamma's boy existence of Norman Bates in *Psycho*. Perkins was the son of distinguished Broadway actor Osgood Perkins, who had graduated from Harvard and found a niche in the theater. Osgood discovered that he was going to become a father in 1932 while rehearsing to perform in *Foreign Affairs* on Broadway. Osgood was so cognizant of his son following in his father's dramatic footsteps that he chose the name of Anthony because it contained seven letters as did Perkins, and would therefore look symmetrical on a marquee.

The elder Perkins was delighted to have a young son to follow him into the profession, but their association was destined to be tragically short-lived. A performer used to working with the top available talent, it was no surprise when Gertrude Lawrence signed on opposite him in the lead role of the Washington, D.C. pre–Broadway tryout of *Susan and God*, which in 1940 became a film starring Joan Crawford and Fredric March. Perkins played the role of the estranged alcoholic husband of Lawrence.

After opening night on September 20, 1937, Osgood Perkins remarked to co-star Lawrence, "Thank God, we'll never have to go through that again." To Gertrude Lawrence, one of the stage legends of London's West End and Broadway, the statement did not appear to be foreboding, and she took it as nothing more than an actor expressing delight at completing an opening night production. Lawrence later took careful note of Perkins's post-performance comment. "He said later that he had never been so nervous at a premiere in his life," Lawrence revealed. "He complained of heartburn, and said his throat was hurting him, and that he had pain in his arms. That was all the intimation we had that he was desperately ill."

Osgood Perkins walked back to the Willard Hotel, where he was staying, with his wife. He died of a heart attack in his room the next morning at the age of 45. A true thespian to the end, according to the obituary in the *New York Times*, Perkins's final words were, "I like that role. I hope the play never closes."

Anthony Perkins could understandably relate to the *Psycho* role with which he would become so closely associated. As Norman Bates he confided to Marion Crane, the woman he would soon brutally murder, about his mother: "She had to raise me all by myself after my father died. I was only five, and it must have been quite a strain for her." Perkins was five when his father died.

In the final minutes of the film Simon Oakland, portraying the psychiatrist Dr. Richmond, explains how Norman Bates became a sharply conflicted schizoid and ultimately a serial killer: "Now he was already dangerously disturbed—had been ever since his father died. His mother was a clinging, demanding woman, and for years the two of them lived as if there was no one else in the world."

Tony Perkins would avoid the psychosis of Norman Bates, but the aforementioned comments rang true where his life was concerned. While his father was an Ivy Leaguer with a Harvard degree, Tony developed his skills at Columbia. In terms of how Perkins saw himself, his biographer, Ronald Bergan, wrote, "Tony, though as harmless and hinged as Norman was harmful and unhinged, claimed to have suffered from the classic Oedipus complex symptoms, which his years in psychotherapy helped him confront. Using the language offered by his shrink sessions, Tony confessed, 'I loved my father but I also wanted him dead so I could have my mother to myself.'"

Ronald Bergan went on to note in his revealing biography of the actor, *Anthony Perkins: A Haunted Life*, that the performer's Oedipus complex revelation was expounded with variations in several interviews that he gave to the press in the late seventies. Bergan wrote that the revelations were made "when he was feeling more secure, enveloped as he was in a reassuring marriage. True or not, he had certainly begun to believe it."

Words uttered by Simon Oakland's Dr. Richmond at the end of the film regarding the psychopathic innkeeper's mother contained a familiar ring where Perkins was concerned. Perkins's own background surely weighed heavily as Oakland commented on Norman Bates's mother, "She is so undependable ... she has moments of true affection and moments of love for Norman. He's not always on his guard about what betrayal or horror she's going to come up with next, because she suckers him into being tender and sweet with her."

According to Tony's own disclosures, his mother was constantly touching and caressing him. "She didn't mean any harm," Perkins explained, "but she clearly channeled all the feelings she had for my father onto me. We were more like lovers than mother and son."

Perkins and Leigh in Perfect Synch

Anthony Perkins and Janet Leigh shared an important career niche in that *Psycho* would become the milestone film for which each performer would be remembered. The recognition was attributable in no small measure to the luminous naturalness achieved by each performer in the long scene prior to the brutal death of Marion Crane.

Previously Marion Crane was observed as a rattled individual who could do little other than generate suspicion from the time that she decided to abscond from Phoenix with the stolen $40,000. Now that she has decided to return to Phoenix with the remaining money, and has even calculated how much she will owe after spending some of the funds, notably for her automobile trade-in for a better vehicle, a discernible tranquility has come over her.

In addition to making such a key decision, Marion has overheard the presumed voice of Norman's mother berating him for inviting his motel guest to their house for dinner. Leigh is impressive at conveying empathy while at the same time making it clear that she feels no physical attraction for Perkins. Marion takes on the role of a big sister trying to help a young man trapped in a tragic situation. We know that she went to work and enabled her younger sister, played by Vera Miles, to obtain a college education.

When Marion frankly tells Norman that she would never allow anyone to talk to her in the manner that she heard his mother speak to him, the appearance of school boy naiveté shifts to a new demeanor as his body stiffens and he becomes highly defensive. He lets her know that he could never leave his mother and that a mother, after all, is a son's best friend. As mentioned earlier, this scene produced natural empathy within Perkins considering his own life and disclosures made through the years in interviews concerning his real-life mother.

Despite her best intentions, Marion, in seeking to help Norman, eventually upsets him by explaining the importance of freeing himself from the suffocating specter of his mother. When the suggestion is made that the mother could be confined somewhere, Norman Bates becomes rattled in the same manner as Marion had earlier in the film. His expression is both angry and defensive as he erupts, "You mean an institution? A madhouse? People always call a madhouse 'someplace,' don't they? Put her in 'someplace.'"

After Marion apologizes, explaining that she did not mean to sound "uncaring," Norman then describes what mental institutions look like. He then delivers a line that impacts significantly on the film's climax when he exclaims, "But she's harmless! She's as harmless as one of those stuffed birds!"

The statement about the stuffed birds is loaded with meaning. Once more Hitchcock has repackaged a concept from an earlier film. One of the most dramatic scenes of the 1956 remake of *The Man Who Knew Too Much* involved James Stewart invading the taxidermy shop run by Ambrose Chappell Senior

Shy but Dangerous—Janet Leigh as Marion Crane is a guest at the motel of Norman Bates, played by Anthony Perkins, who exudes a boyish shyness. This is the lull before the savage storm—the shower sequence in which the psychopathic killer takes Marion's life in *Psycho*.

and Junior in the mistaken belief that they are involved in the kidnapping of his young son. The shop filled with stuffed animals represents a symbolic dualism between life and death, in this case through preserving dead creatures in the same shape and manner as when they were alive. The preserved creatures take on the appearance of being alive, representing the duality of appearance and reality along with that of the living and the dead.

After Norman has explained that he cannot have Marion as his dinner guest in his house, something she knows from overhearing the loud ranting of someone she believes to be Mrs. Bates, he is able to convince her to share a modest supper of sandwiches and milk in his motel office. Norman smiles boyishly as he comments about the stuffed birds present in the office. He tells about his taxidermy hobby and then laughs at the double entendre when he teases Marion that she "eats like a bird."

Tim Dirks, in his analysis of *Psycho* on his Internet website The Greatest Films, makes an interesting point about the slang meaning of bird. In British slang it is used to refer to a woman. In that Hitchcock grew up in London he was undoubtedly aware of this fact. Six years later an entire international film world would become familiar with the meaning when Michael Caine starred as a womanizing Cockney in the 1966 hit *Alfie*.

The reference to birds is significant regarding the film's leading female character. Marion's last name is Crane, which is a type of tall wading bird resembling the heron.

Norman's comment will be seen as irony-loaded when it is ultimately learned that the mother the schizoid son sought to keep alive really was as harmless as a bird, since she was, after all, dead. The suddenly tense conversation includes the following dialogue, which is reminiscent of another famous Hitchcock character from one of his personal favorites:

> MARION: I am sorry. I only felt — it seems she's hurting you.
> NORMAN (bitterly): People always mean well. They cluck their thick tongues and shake their heads and suggest oh-so-very-delicately. (Returns to affable side.) Of course, I've suggested it myself, but I hate to even think about it. She needs me. It's not as if she were a maniac, a raving thing. She just goes a little mad sometimes. We all go a little mad sometimes. Haven't you?

Uncle Charlie and Voyeurism

The first part of Norman's dialogue, delivered with succinct bitterness, is a shorter version of commentary delivered by another psychotic serial killer from one of Hitchcock's favorite films — Uncle Charlie, played convincingly by Joseph Cotten in *Shadow of a Doubt*. In the manner of Perkins as Norman Bates, Uncle Charlie shifted personalities swiftly, and was able to exude a charming enough demeanor to capture the hearts of the rich widows he then ruthlessly killed. In his angry tirade delivered to Teresa Wright, who plays the niece who once idolized him, Uncle Charlie referred to the world as foul and rotten, calling it at one point a "pig sty."

Anthony Perkins's Norman Bates character never espoused such extreme sentiments in his conversation with Janet Leigh, but it must be remembered that he was also much younger than Uncle Charlie, whose bitterness assuredly increased with passing years. Perkins is able to shift moods quickly as he, following his brief negative remarks, returns to affability. The exchange with Marion lays the groundwork for all that will follow, as the then hidden side of Bates' persona is revealed by the film's conclusion.

Marion Crane, intent on making things right, is anxious to get an early start on her return trip to Phoenix, and so her conversation with Norman Bates ends. His voyeuristic side is then evidenced when his attractive guest, now in her room, begins to disrobe. He removes a painting from the wall of an adjoining room, revealing a jagged peep hole. Norman is able to view Marion in her bra and slip. The picture that serves as a covering for the peep hole is laden with significance. It is a replica of *Susanna and the Elders*, and shows a nude being assaulted by two male satyrs.

A Scene for All Seasons

After Bates views Marion, the stage is set for the scene for all seasons, the most famous single scene in film history. While it is true that the famous fire sequence of *Gone with the Wind* has also gained great fame, and the film was released twenty-one years before *Psycho*, as a continuing sequence it was longer than one scene. What provides the shower sequence with such devastating impact is that, through brilliant use of technology, the viewer is taken by surprise and sees an event that will last forever in the human consciousness but in actual screen time encompasses only 45 seconds.

"The shower-room stabbing sequence took seven days to shoot, although it was only 45 seconds long on the screen," Hitchcock explained. "I did it with heads of Janet Leigh, a nude — a girl in full figure — and the woman doing the stabbing. I shot a lot of the nude in slow motion because I had to have her breast covered by an arm at the crucial moment; it was speeded up for the final film. There were actually 78 cuts, 78 little pieces of film, used in those 45 seconds. The prop department made me a very nice pink rubber torso filled with tubed blood which shot out whenever you stabbed it, but I didn't use it."

Hitchcock went on to discuss the making of *Psycho* within the circumference of economy, an interesting element of the film. The movie's box office success combined with a pruned down budget has been long cited as an example by filmmakers, movie historians, and critics of camaraderie and expertise compensating for an absence of budgetary freedom.

"The picture took about 36 days to make, including retakes," Hitchcock said. "I used my TV film unit because of speed and because I wanted to make it for a price. I only slowed up when I came to something cinematic, like the shower scene. You could never have shot that under TV conditions — seven days' work for 45 seconds' screen time! TV work *is* nine minutes *a day*. Unfortunately, feature film-makers are attuned to a minute and a half a day. There are very few feature cameramen — unless they're *passé* or semi-retired — who'll bother with TV."

Hitchcock used the Revue Studios portion of the Universal lot to shoot *Psycho*. This was where MCA client Hitchcock shot his popular *Alfred Hitchcock Presents* television series. While he used his television unit, as he explained, the director employed his regular editor, George Tomasini. The inclusion of Tomasini in the otherwise low-budget strategy was surely linked to the challenge of the shower scene and later shocking stairway murder sequence with Martin Balsam portraying private detective Milton Arbogast.

Universal received an added benefit that was unanticipated at the time from having *Psycho* shot there. Just as Universal's Orlando theme park has its tribute to Hitchcock and *Psycho*, in Universal City, California, the old Norman Bates home has been maintained and remains a staple of the regular tour that has attracted millions from around the world.

Spinning into Part Two

Psycho shares one notable structural element with *Vertigo*. Each film is divisible into two distinct parts. Part one of *Vertigo* ended with the traumatization of Scottie Ferguson after the apparent suicide death of Kim Novak in the first of her two roles in the film. Part one of *Psycho* ends with the brutal slaying of Janet Leigh, portraying Marion Crane, 45 minutes into the film. Leigh was so unforgettably vulnerable in her role of distraught secretary Crane, who wanted marriage and a family before time and opportunity completely passed her by, that audiences had the opportunity to empathize with her uncomfortable feelings in the role of an embezzler and feel gratification when she decided to pursue the decent path of returning to Phoenix with the $40,000 she had taken. Just after she had decided to take that important step her life was tragically snuffed out by a knife-wielding assailant.

Part two of *Vertigo* featured the recovery of Ferguson from his catatonic state of depression and an opportunity to remold a woman he thought to be someone other than the false Madeleine Elster, with whom the retired detective had fallen hopelessly in love. The dramatic tension sprang from the audience's awareness that the department store sales clerk Judy Barton was the same woman her lover, the scheming Gavin Elster, manipulated in a plot to kill his wife, the real Madeleine.

Part two of *Psycho* furnishes a different dynamic. The story revolves around who killed Marion and the detective hired by an insurance company to investigate her disappearance, Milton Arbogast. While one could classify the last 75 minutes of *Psycho* as a "who done it," we will see that this was a term disputed by Hitchcock. During the extended effort to unravel circumstances leading to Marion's disappearance, her sister, played by Vera Miles, teams up with the man viewers learn ultimately intended to marry the secretary, Sam Loomis, played by John Gavin.

Rooting for the Killer I and II?

Anthony Perkins had every reason to empathize with certain elements of the complex and fascinating character he played. As a serious actor with extensive technical training, a performer known for throwing heart and soul into a film, the sensitive Perkins recognized the career challenge and value of playing Norman Bates, not to mention the salient fact of the film being directed by Alfred Hitchcock.

Hitchcock recognized artistic dedication and developed a high regard for the young actor. Hitchcock, as in the case of Carol Reed in appreciating the brilliant improvisation of Orson Welles in *The Third Man*, did not let his ego stand in the way of his crafting the finest film possible on the tightest of budgets. He was happy to accept a suggestion made by Perkins that enriched his character psychologically. Perkins recognized the arrested development of Norman Bates, and suggested to Hitchcock that Bates's character could be visually enhanced if he munched candy corn, revealing to screen viewers his juvenile side.

When Bates carries out his swift cleanup campaign after discovering the body of Marion in the shower, his expression and fidgety manner resemble those of an immature boy eager to avoid trouble. His immaturity, coupled with a marked Puritanism, was revealed earlier when he showed Marion the unit where she believed she would spend the night. As he showed her the room he pointed nervously toward the bathroom, never mouthing the word. It is up to Janet Leigh to say, "the bathroom."

After tidying up, with the audience believing that it was a case of an immature and thoroughly dutiful son seeking to avoid trouble after the deadly act of his knife-wielding mother, Bates stuffs the body of the dead woman into the trunk of the car she recently purchased from California Charlie. He drives it to a nearby swamp and, after exiting, watches the car slowly disappear. The folded newspaper in which Marion had wrapped almost $40,000 in cash slowly disappears along with the car.

Norman watches in the darkness, munching on candy corn. The slow manner in which the automobile sinks little by little into the swamp is a classic illustration of Hitchcock's penchant for milking every precious second of drama from a scene. It is reminiscent of the scene from *Strangers on a Train* when Bruno Antony receives help in attempting to retrieve the vital cigarette lighter from the manhole into which it dropped.

With the incident, the sinking of Marion's car, and later the disappearance of Milton Arbogast's car after the insurance investigator is killed, the Hitchcock tease is in ample evidence. In all of the aforementioned cases the director wrings every potential moment of suspense from the scenes while also teasing viewers by daring them to root for the enemy. The camera's eye allows filmgoers to step into the shoes of individuals seeking to escape criminal responsibility.

Within a Narrow Compass

One area demonstrating cinema genius is the ability to reveal a great deal within a narrow compass. The crucial scene in which *Psycho* spins into its next phase is delivered with such swift simplicity that a viewer can absorb it and think that nothing special has been accomplished. This is a reaction that can occur regularly in this remarkable film, and the pivotal scene in Sam Loomis's hardware store in Fairvale serves as a definitive example.

On the issue of whether or not Sam's intentions toward Marion were honorable, that question is immediately answered as viewers get to read the honest and sincere letter he has written and intends to send to the woman he hopes to marry. He explains his concern over not being able to provide for her the kind of affluent lifestyle he would prefer, and mentions the tiny back room where he is writing the letter, which serves as his residence, and how it suddenly looks big enough to accommodate two people.

The dramatic timing from the Stefano script could not be better. Just after viewers learn that Sam Loomis is a man of sincerity with the best of intentions toward Marion, an aristocratically beautiful blonde woman arrives in the store and immediately confronts him. She introduces herself as Marion's sister Lila and expresses her concern that Marion has disappeared and not been heard from in a week. This disclosure reveals to viewers the time frame involved. Lila's urgent demeanor is conveyed by the statement, "Look, if you two are in this thing together, I don't care, it's none of my business, but I want to talk to Marion and I want her to tell me it's none of my business and then I'll go."

The discussion becomes tense and Sam realizes that Lila is a serious young woman who demands the facts and will brook no nonsense. Vera Miles, in the role of Lila, resembles Janet Leigh in that the two possessed an aristocratic beauty and finely chiseled features. Miles, a rare example of a beauty contest winner who made a successful transition to the ranks of leading lady, demonstrated loyalty and steadfastness of purpose playing the wife of Henry Fonda's character when he was accused of crimes for which he was innocent in Hitchcock's semi-documentary 1956 release *The Wrong Man*. In *Psycho* she exhibits the demeanor of a determined detective as she enters the scene and sharply questions her sister's lover. Under contract to Hitchcock for much of the fifties, Miles impressed the director with what he termed her "still waters run deep" performing demeanor.

As tension mounts, Lila begins to blame Sam for her sister's disappearance. Her questioning is reminiscent of a detective's and the session is interrupted by the appearance of a private detective, Milt Arbogast. The role of Arbogast would prove a springboard for the New York City–born Martin Balsam, who would secure a Best Supporting Actor Oscar for the 1965 film *A Thousand Clowns*. He explains his reason for being there, hoping to find Marion and the money she took.

The scene involves important interaction between the three key principals of the second part of the film in which solving the mystery of Marion's disappearance is the objective. The important factors are: Sam's commitment to Marion; Lila's revelation to Sam about Marion's disappearance, coupled with her stated suspicions about him; and Arbogast's disclosure that Marion's employer has no intention of prosecuting his secretary for embezzlement and is concerned only that she return the missing funds.

Norman's Behavior Under
Pressure Contrasted with Marion's

Hitchcock was a director of meticulous contrasts. These contrasts were used to enhance the high suspense level to which he constantly aspired. With *Psycho* being a film presenting in a thought-provoking fashion the pitfalls of a modern problem-filled society with a pronounced emphasis on Puritanism, it was only natural for Hitchcock to make the most of an opportunity to present two people under stress after having committed crimes.

As stated, Janet Leigh came apart at the seams after embezzling funds. Her incompetence stemmed from the tension of being a criminal on the run. It would be reasonable to conclude that guilt was the catalyst of such nervous and consistently bumbling activity since, after deciding to return to Phoenix to return the money and face the consequences of her actions, a different person emerged when she sought to provide the counsel of a sympathetic sister to Norman Bates. When Norman became fidgety and temporarily truculent her coolness was admirable and she maneuvered the conversation toward an amicable conclusion. The Marion Crane who emerged from Janet Leigh's performance during the supper conversation with the deeply conflicted Norman Bates was a woman with a cool native intelligence who spoke with common sense and logic.

The contrast revealed between Bates and Crane as criminal types is vast. Bates exudes a boyish charm in his crucial conversations with Arbogast and Loomis, hoping to divert them from success in their inquiries. There was no guilt in his case, and, according to the case history presented at the close of the film, he had every reason to believe that he was a loyal son protecting his mother, rather than a ruthless serial killer.

Balsam, playing the role of a savvy investigator, initially is treated to Norman's boyish charm and offered some candy corn. The immature and confused Bates proves no match for a mature man who makes a living investigating people for insurance companies. When the detective becomes convinced that something strange is going on inside the house Norman kills him after catching him unaware on the staircase. He is hacked to death in the manner of Marion Crane and his body and car are disposed of in the same manner, leaving the team of Sam Loomis and Lila Crane.

Psycho's Ultimate Face Off

After Sam and Lila sign in at the Bates Motel as man and wife, sensing that something is amiss with Arbogast as well as Marion, they are determined to succeed in their investigation. The film's ultimate face off occurs when a highly motivated Loomis, sensing that Norman is responsible for the disappearance of the woman he loved and intended to marry, sharply questions the hotel proprietor in his office.

Given Hitchcock's propensity for staying atop the movie scene, then signing to roles performers who excel in comparable character situations, it is likely that John Gavin aroused the director's interest for the role of Sam Loomis in *Psycho* as a result of a solid performance opposite Universal's most popular actress, Doris Day, in the 1960 suspense thriller *Midnight Lace*, produced by Ross Hunter and directed by David Miller. Miller had succeeded brilliantly with a similar Joan Crawford vehicle, *Sudden Fear* (1952). Both films' popular leading ladies are being stalked by their husbands, who hope to kill them, inherit their riches, then resume life with the women who assisted them in performing their deadly deeds.

In the case of *Sudden Fear* the audience is aware of the duplicity of the husband (played by Jack Palance) and his girlfriend, portrayed by Gloria Grahame. With David Miller's later retooling of the same essential plot, there is one basic difference between *Midnight Lace* and the earlier Crawford success. The difference stems from the fact that in *Midnight Lace* the conspiracy launched by unfaithful husband Rex Harrison is unrevealed, and the film takes on the air of a who-done-it.

The subject matter of the film, along with the fact that Doris Day, star of one of Hitch's jackpot winners of the fifties, *The Man Who Knew Too Much*, was appearing, provided ample incentive for the director to view *Midnight Lace*. John Gavin, who had received a Promising New Star Golden Globe in 1958, received a career boost by being cast in the upscale Ross Hunter film shot in London.

Gavin plays a sincere and reliable Irish construction boss working on the building next door to the flat where Doris Day resides. He falls in love with Day and is there to rescue her from harm's way when Harrison, in concert with girlfriend and co-conspirator Natasha Parry, makes his final attempt to kill her. Gavin's role is similar to that of the determined Sam Loomis, who genuinely cares for Marion and after her disappearance is determined to move heaven and earth to find her.

The showdown conversation with Perkins provides an opportunity for Hitchcock to pit a force of good determined to succeed in Loomis against a badly disturbed man seeking to hide the truth at all costs. The performers effectively use body language and expressions to reveal their dissimilarities of character and purpose. Loomis appears straight and tall, in the manner of a lawman serving the cause of righteousness, while Bates's boyish immaturity increases as the scene progresses. Sam's suspicion that Norman holds the key to learning what happened to Marion prompts him to become increasingly aggressive in his questioning. If Gavin is straight and tall, Perkins is devious and wilting. He becomes evasive and pouts in the manner of a boy who has done wrong and is on the verge of being found out. Perkins, while thin, stood above six feet, but through intelligent body language one can see him shrink as the scene develops, while six-footer Gavin seems to visibly grow.

Eventually Perkins asks Gavin to leave, and after he realizes that Miles has disappeared and might be in the house where the film's big secret lies, he takes Gavin by surprise and knocks him out, then moves quickly toward the house. He knows that Miles must be stopped. She has entered the same forbidden realm that Martin Balsam previously traversed.

The Lawman, His Wife and a Bygone Era

As explained in the *Vertigo* analysis, much comparative history revolved around the new San Francisco that Gavin Elster was eager to abandon and that of a century earlier. The scam that Elster pulled on James Stewart extended the contrast between San Francisco past and present in that Kim Novak was pretending to be under the influence of a dead woman who lived in the preceding century. While *Psycho* underscores numerous problems and tensions of American society heading into the 1960's, and flails at Puritanism, the presentation of Fairvale, the residence of Sam Loomis, along with the introduction of two important character performers, invites viewers to make *Vertigo*-like contrasts between past and present.

While most of the characters of *Psycho* are presented as immersed in various forms of difficulty, John McIntire, as Fairvale's Sheriff Al Chambers, and Lurene Tuttle as Mrs. Chambers, appear as representatives of a different, decid-

edly gentler society. They convey the look, dress and feel of homespun familiarity. When Sheriff Chambers is approached by the determined duo of Sam
Loomis and Lila Crane, his first instinct, as well as that of his wife, is to believe
that Norman Bates is not involved in criminal activity. This belief stems from
faith in community, as emphasized by Mr. and Mrs. Chambers mentioning how
long they have known Norman. Sheriff Chambers acknowledges that Norman
is a loner and realizes he is peculiar, but, after all, this is someone who was born
and bred in Fairvale. Norman Bates is someone they have known all of their lives,
a product of their community.

The meeting involving Sam and Lila with the Chambers following Sunday church service is also reflective of a kinder and gentler America. After the
Chambers follow the local custom of greeting the minister following services,
an invitation is extended by Mrs. Chambers to Sam and Lila to come by for
Sunday dinner. Her folksy, motherly manner appears to suggest that perhaps
some socialization will bring this attractive couple together. The Sunday dinner
invitation again harkens back to a gentle and hospitable society that is still alive
in Fairvale.

The Stefano script delineates the contrasting circumstances between order
and anarchy, between trust and doubt, characteristic of Hitchcock's distinction
drawing. While Sheriff and Mrs. Chambers would mention the length of time
that Norman Bates has been a part of the local community, stating doubt concerning wrongdoing, the same comment coming from a policeman in a film noir
drama set in New York, Los Angeles or Chicago would appear less credible, since
he would lack close personal involvement that the Chambers had with Bates.

McIntire and Tuttle as Symbols

McIntire and Tuttle, as Sheriff and his wife, rang particularly true as symbols of an honest and more straightforward society than that evidenced elsewhere
in *Psycho* due to their television personas. Just as Hitchcock held budget costs
down by using his television crew from his popular *Alfred Hitchcock Presents*, he
was able to frugally cast performers in *Psycho* by employing names and faces
familiar to television viewers.

Martin Balsam, then establishing a presence on such top live dramatic,
nationally televised programs such as *Playhouse 90* and *Climax*, was one example. McIntire was another, having attracted attention as a regular on the television series *The Naked City*. His exposure in *Psycho* did him no harm in enabling
the character performer to be cast to replace the recently deceased Ward Bond
as wagon master in 1961 in *Wagon Train*, while six years later he took over from
Lee J. Cobb in a starring role in another western series, *The Virginian*.

Lurene Tuttle was a legend in her own time among Hollywood insiders.
One of the industry's top drama coaches as well as a stellar character actress, Tut-

tle was saluted for her instructional assistance and inspiration by Helen Hunt in her Best Actress Academy Awards acceptance speech for *As Good as It Gets* (1997), co-starring Jack Nicholson, who won in the Best Actor category.

This author can personally vouch for her teaching excellence in that I was a former student of this talented lady, whose sensitivity and warmth made friends wherever she went. Lurene, who at one point taught in the communications department at the University of Southern California, combined dramatic readings with listening sessions examining the voices and inflections of performing geniuses. Richard Burton was a particular favorite. "His sounds are so rich and varied," she explained.

The veteran character performer gained fame among the nation's television viewers appearing opposite Leon Ames in the successful mid-fifties TV series *Life with Father*, a family drama set in New York in the latter part of the nineteenth century. Before that she had appeared as the faithful secretary Effie to Howard Duff in the popular radio detective series, *Sam Spade*. She would later secure an Emmy nomination as a regular on the popular television sitcom *Julia*, with Diahann Carroll and Lloyd Nolan from 1969 to 1971.

One strong possibility exists in determining why Lurene Tuttle was cast as the sweet and supportive wife to John McIntire in *Psycho*. In the brilliantly acerbic 1957 film noir classic about the hard hitting side of the journalism and public relations businesses in New York City, *Sweet Smell of Success*, Tuttle was cast as a supportive wife. She was in but one scene, playing the wife of radio acting veteran Lawrence Dobkin, but it was one of the most impactful of the film. Ruthless public relations operative Tony Curtis seeks to arm twist a favor from Dobkins and threatens blackmail through revealing details of an extra-marital affair. Tuttle strikes back hard, denouncing Curtis for his wicked opportunism as she tells him icily that she knew about the event in question and had long ago forgiven her husband.

Hitchcock almost surely saw the biting noir drama directed by fellow Britisher Alexander MacKendrick. Tuttle's tart handling of Curtis in the manner of a teacher sternly reprimanding a wayward student while maintaining the posture of a supportive and forgiving wife would surely have impressed Hitchcock in that the scene represented the kind of morality conflict evidenced in so many of his films. A point of irony to which Hitchcock could relate was that *Sweet Smell of Success* ultimately became a classic after being praised by critics and largely ignored by audiences at the time. This was reminiscent of the path traversed by *Vertigo* en route to classic status.

Another reason for Hitchcock to be familiar with *Sweet Smell of Success* is that it was based on a story by Ernest Lehman, who adapted it to the screen along with Clifford Odets. Lehman's productive collaboration with Hitchcock on the cleverly suspenseful screenplay for *North by Northwest* has already been mentioned. Lehman will surface anew in his second project with Hitchcock in the director's final film, *Family Plot*.

Bates Unmasked and
Was Psycho a Who-Done-It?

Norman Bates is ultimately unmasked in a final showdown. The psychotic killer recognizes that Lila, like Arbogast before her, will solve the mystery if she is able to spend any time in the forbidden confines of the Bates manor, which resembles an eerie mausoleum rather than a residence containing flesh and blood human beings. Attired as the long departed Mrs. Bates, the knife-wielding assailant seeks to snuff out the life of Lila Crane, but is prevented by Sam, who was fortunately knocked unconscious only briefly after Norman took him by surprise. Bates is, appropriately enough, shorn of knife and wig at the same dramatic moment that Sam is repelling his attack.

Since *Psycho* is a film clearly divisible into two parts, as is *Vertigo*, Hitchcock's comparative reference to the two films which were so comprehensively laced with psychological meaning is apt. While discussing *Vertigo* in an interview with Charles Higham and Joel Greenberg it was earlier revealed why Hitchcock believed in concentrating on suspense and avoiding last minute revelations. He knew that the question arose regarding *Psycho*'s second half, as the triumvirate of Arbogast, Lila, and Sam seek to determine what happened to Marion. Could the final 75 minutes of *Psycho* be called a who-done-it?

"In the case of *Psycho*, it's an *explanation*, not a denouement, of *how* this boy came to be that way," Hitchcock told Higham and Greenberg. "The film is really over." Hitchcock then went on to explain, as was earlier reported, that in suspense one is trading ten seconds of surprise for a continuing situation wherein a story's creator has all the time one wishes to tell a story. "It's an intellectual exercise," Hitchcock explained. "There's no emotion in a whodunit. They're wondering if it's the butler or whoever. But give them all the information at the beginning and they'll say: 'How are they going to find out about him?' They've a more intellectual kind of excitement going for them."

In the case of Norman Bates, riveted viewers knew that something was amiss, and did observe the murders of Marion and Arbogast, but were misled by the fact that the knife-wielding killer wore a dress and appeared to have the hair of a woman, which was actually a wig. There was therefore a surprise element, and, unlike with Kim Novak in *Vertigo*, viewers were unaware of circumstances and never cognizant of the double identity thread that embodies each film. Kim Novak performed as Madeleine Elster and Judy Barton, while Anthony Perkins performed a dual role as dutiful son and actual killer under the identity of Mrs. Bates. The difference was deliberate deception in the Elster-Barton characterizations and schizophrenic insanity in the case of Perkins, who, as explained by Simon Oakland at the film's conclusion, had convinced himself that his mother was alive, with the confirmation being highly personal as he assumed her identity along with his own.

The post–Marion Crane part two of *Psycho* was a who-done-it in the eyes of the three individuals seeking to resolve her disappearance. Viewers learned that Norman, rather than being the faithful son seeking to shield his presumably killer mother from harm's way, was a sharply conflicted personality assuming two identities.

While *Psycho* was not a who-done-it in the British tradition of Agatha Christie or Arthur Conan Doyle, with a Hercule Poirot, Miss Marple, or Sherlock Holmes using shrewd deductive logic to narrow down a challenging list of suspects to ultimately resolve crimes, the second segment of the film clearly contained the kind of surprise twist concerning the killer's persona that rendered it a different type of story than that described by Hitchcock as the kind of intellectual exercise embodied by *Vertigo*, where the basic crime elements are known and the fascination lies in seeing the loose ends being tied together.

A Documentary-Style Ending

Simon Oakland, cast as Dr. Richmond, appears in a documentary-type explanatory role at the end of the film. His function is to explain what Norman Bates is all about. He separates fantasy from reality in etching the gruesome image of an immature man who, when his mother takes a lover, cannot tolerate competition for her emotions and kills both of them. Bates's role as Hitchcock's ultimate mamma's boy is one of an individual so totally drawn to his mother that, after killing her, he cannot abide living with the reality that he ended her life.

Once Norman Bates adopted the persona of his mother he intervened on her behalf whenever he believed that a rival for her affections had surfaced. Such was the plight of Marion Crane when the Norman side of Bates's schizoid makeup became attracted to her. It remained for the mother side to take over and immediately destroy a potential rival.

The film ends on an interesting twist. After Simon Oakland explains the reasoning behind Norman Bates adopting his mother's persona and carrying the jealous rage he feels on her behalf to the level of murder, the scene shifts to the incarcerated psycho killer in his cell. Covered by a shawl and convinced he is Mrs. Bates, an interior monologue is heard in which the mother figure of the killer proclaims her innocence. The determination to prove her innocence is so strong that she will not even swat the fly bothering her, proving that any murder charge is unjustified.

The casting of Oakland to play the role of Dr. Richmond was another example of Hitchcock selecting a talented actor on the rise. A trained violinist, the Brooklyn-born Oakland decided to set his sights on the theater in his hometown. He secured Broadway roles before gravitating to Hollywood. In the 1958 Susan Hayward Academy Award–winning vehicle, *I Want to Live*, Simon Oakland played a role that could well have prompted Hitchcock to cast him in *Psycho*.

Oakland plays an opportunistic reporter who initially sensationalizes the murder case in which Hayward is charged but ultimately changes his tactics when he becomes convinced of her innocence and champions her cause.

Oakland proved that he could play an assertive authority figure, and he strikes the correct note in *Psycho*, coolly explaining details concerning the schizophrenic killer's psyche in an intellectually correct and never emotional manner. Two of Oakland's subsequent showcase character roles came in Steve McQueen films. In *The Sand Pebbles* (1966) he emerges as McQueen's enemy on the Navy ship they inhabit, while in *Bullitt* (1968) he serves as a police captain and the blonde actor's superior officer. In the tradition of *Psycho* performers, Oakland distinguished himself on television. During one five-year period he appeared as a regular on four series, including the popular *Kolchak: The Night Stalker*, starring Darren McGavin.

Why the Midas Touch of Psycho?

With *Psycho* Alfred Hitchcock had more than met the expectations of Paramount Studios in taking a low budget project, and turning it into a box office bonanza that spawned sequels over the decades, a cottage industry, and popular attractions at two of the nation's notable theme parks. As for the immediate cash impact of the horror film blockbuster, Hitchcock took a half-million-dollar budget and a 36-day shooting schedule and created a cinematic phenomenon that, at the end of 1960, its debut year, according to the *Hollywood Reporter's* list of grosses, took in $11,200,000, a staggering profit in view of its cost.

Psycho was beaten at the box office that year only by Ken Annakin's *Swiss Family Robinson*, made for Walt Disney Productions, which was filmed on location in Tobago. It was called one of the most difficult films ever produced by Disney and contained the largest assortment of animals ever assembled for one film. Two British directors, Annakin and Hitchcock, delivered the two top financial winners of 1960 with films that were markedly different, a family adventure film that took over six months to complete (in the case of *Swiss Family Robinson*) and a swiftly made and inexpensive *Psycho*.

Why did *Psycho* achieve the popularity it has enjoyed through the years? Hitchcock admitted his own bafflement on the topic. He would have anticipated the type of response the film generated for one of his prestige films like *Vertigo*, or the blockbuster that combined dazzling color and special effects along with one of filmdom's leading superstars, Cary Grant, *North by Northwest*. There is something intriguing about the scaled-down *Psycho* generating the type of sustained acclaim it has garnered, coming on the heels of Hitchcock's glitzy films of the fifties, anchored by such box office stalwarts as Grant, James Stewart, Doris Day and Grace Kelly.

In analyzing Hitchcock's success as a filmmaker one must stress the importance of timing. A great filmmaker needs to have his or her finger on the public pulse to succeed on an extended level over an entire career. While Hitchcock has been credited with launching a financial bonanza for horror movies, it has been pointed out by astute film historians that the team of Samuel Arkoff and James Nicholson had begun to earn dividends in the genre by the late fifties at American International Pictures. The cinema was Hitchcock's life and he had reason to be aware of the early achievements of AIP, and would, as someone with a record of bringing his films in frugally and on schedule, recognize, as did Arkoff and Nicholson, that the horror genre could be used advantageously in a low budget context.

If Hitchcock was indebted to Arkoff and Nicholson for helping to show him the way, they were more than compensated by the benefits they derived from Hitchcock placing the genre on the major international scene with the triumph of *Psycho*. By 1963 American International had, through exploring a low budget strategy (with horror films a major staple), graduated to doing a prestigious film in the genre, *The Raven*, based on the poem by Edgar Allan Poe. Vincent Price forged a new career starring in this and other AIP horror films. Roger Corman moved up the ranks as well as the film's director while casting newcomer Jack Nicholson in a role. British leading lady Hazel Court, who starred in episodes of *Alfred Hitchcock Presents*, also found a home at AIP appearing in films opposite Price.

Television and the Soap Opera Factor

Television was beneficial to Hitchcock in enabling him to cut costs in the filming of *Psycho*. The medium that had generated such awesome impact in the fifties and prompted certain movie figures such as David O. Selznick to believe that it would ultimately spell doom for the motion picture industry did not terrify Hitchcock, his former partner. As a shrewd pragmatist who adjusted with the times, Alfred Hitchcock, rather than lament the impact of television as had certain pessimists within the film industry, benefited from it on a major scale.

Hitchcock had secured a niche as a presence in his films through using an approach adopted by British filmmakers in the age of silent films to enhance frugality by appearing in his own films. Now he was able to achieve star status on his popular *Alfred Hitchcock Presents* television series. An entertaining comedian to many who knew him socially, Hitchcock began to take longer turns before the camera on television by presenting stories he sometimes directed and whose development he closely supervised, as well as making comments at the end of the show. At the conclusion of one episode involving a fearsome killer Hitchcock explained in his folksy Cockney manner, "The killer was apprehended after leaving the scene of his last crime a few minutes later. He was arrested for failing to yield a right of way."

As a director whose pockets were constantly jammed with Roman candles to be used to generate suspense, working within the intimate and brief compass of black and white television served to sharpen his dramatic instincts. Since stories had to be told within a briefer period of time and budgetary restrictions also provided limitations, including the number of characters and settings involved, Hitchcock could not help but develop a greater feel for stories emphasizing the plights of ordinary people, often in macabre settings and circumstances. A touch or more of the horror side of filmmaking could engage audiences while complying with time and monetary restrictions.

Considering the foregoing, it is understandable how and why the soap opera has become such a rousing success. The intimate seeing eye of television, bringing stories into the living rooms of Americans from all walks of life, provided a natural vehicle for engaging viewers in the same manner as a Hitchcock film in which he drained every ounce of suspense while his audience sat attentively, awaiting the next Roman candle from his seemingly endless arsenal.

One of the natural elements generating continuing popularity for programs such as *The Guiding Light, The Young and the Restless, General Hospital* and *All My Children* through the years has been the serial element of presenting a bit at a time and leaving the audience wishing for more and speculating on what might happen next. Much of this basic soap opera type format was utilized in *Psycho*. This was particularly evident in the first 45 minutes of the film in which audiences are engaged by the tormented psyche of Marion Crane and what steps she will ultimately take in her relationship with Sam Loomis, as well as resolving the issue of the $40,000 with which she has absconded.

The principles of soap opera that engage audiences on a regular basis are presenting figures that audiences can readily identify with, and placing them in continuing circumstances, much like the Saturday matinee serials in which key suspenseful events determine their fates. While soap operas have the advantage of a week to week, year to year continuity that a single film cannot match, the element of steadily changing circumstances and familiar characters, augmented in the case of *Psycho* by an additional horror story shock element, are ingredients that, if properly handled, have the potential to generate rousing box office figures.

Was *Psycho* a Middle Class *Vertigo*?

A case can be made that *Psycho* represented a middle class person's *Vertigo*, and that the earlier film represented an upper class, artier version of the 1960 film that combined salable elements of the horror and soap opera genres. Hitchcock regular Bernard Herrmann scored both films. The works reveal contrasting objectives. *Vertigo*, with its emphasis on the most beautiful scenic elements in and near San Francisco, from art galleries to giant redwoods, revealed a classical Herrmann with a symphonic score, accented during the love sequences between James Stewart and Kim Novak, that reminded Donald Spoto of Richard Wagner and his brilliant composition *Tristan and Isolde.*

Psycho was a film that, rather than concentrating on elegant scenery and Nob Hill San Francisco affluence, reflected a substantial mood swing away from the spectacular color scenery of *Vertigo.* From the first scene, when Marion meets Sam in the stark and simple seedy Phoenix hotel room for a quick lunchtime sexual interlude, we become part of the struggling middle class searching for meaning in what at times appears to be hopeless circumstances. This is further accented when Sam recognizes Marion's desire for a normal married life with a family, but painfully points out the burdensome reality of life in the small town of Fairvale, living in the back room behind his hardware store amid the economic discomfort of sending regular alimony checks to a wife he bitterly acknowledges lives in another country and enjoys a more comfortable lifestyle than his own.

The Joseph Stefano script carefully details an important aspect of the film, the plight of many struggling American middle class individuals moving into a new decade, while a horror story twist is implemented after Janet Leigh meets Anthony Perkins. Bernard Herrmann's responsibility was to provide a musical score that meshed with the film's basic story objectives. The great musical craftsman did not disappoint. The contrasts between his earlier elegant *Vertigo* score and that of *Psycho* are profound.

Herrmann asserts unique mastery over two key dramatic scenes. The sound of loud screeching violins is heard as Marion Crane drives in a rainstorm, tormented by the dimensions of her act of embezzlement. While she listens to imaginary interior monologue conversations in which her plight is discussed, the violin sounds are heard. They indicate that all is far from well in Marion's world as her psyche is tormented by her quick decision to steal $40,000 and leave Phoenix. Due to her upset state and the rainy conditions, she accidentally strays from the highway, as a result of which she sees the neon sign for the Bates Motel on what was the old main highway.

The screeching violins are again heard in the famous shower murder scene. The sound is akin to a flock of shrieking birds exhibiting discontent as they fly overhead. Considering the use of birds in *Psycho* (in their stuffed state as well as that of pictures on the wall), the similarity could well have been by design. Consider also that in the early sixties Hitchcock would make another film revealing that all is far from well, and that the forces of nature can prove destructive — *The Birds*, which will be examined in the next chapter.

Hitchcock as Star and a Major Publicity Force

Appearing before a national audience weekly as host of *Alfred Hitchcock Presents* provided the director with more visibility than he had ever previously known during his long career. Americans now knew Hitchcock as a bona fide star in his own right. The two top star figures heading the most popular Sunday night television programs in America were Alfred Hitchcock and Loretta Young. It must have greatly delighted Hitchcock that he shared the Sunday spotlight with the glamorous hostess of *The Loretta Young Show*, a former Best Actress Oscar winner for *The Farmer's Daughter*. Young, along with serving as hostess, would also star in episodes. Hitchcock developed a star presence of his own by hosting his presentations, some of which he directed, while regularly helping to shape story content.

Hitchcock's star was in full orbit as the sixties dawned, and he used his extended presence to help sell *Psycho*. He starred in a famous trailer in which he, despite denying that the film was in any way a who-done-it, borrowed from an advertising concept used to sell films and books by heightening suspense. The trailer featured Hitchcock at his salesman's best as he advanced two important points. The film's director explained that, due to the suspenseful ingredients of his unique film and to prevent impinging on audience concentration, nobody would be seated once a performance of *Psycho* began. The second point that Hitchcock stressed was in seeking a solemn and binding commitment from audience members not to reveal the ending of *Psycho*.

The trailer, along with the publicity it generated, served the purpose intended by Hitchcock. Discussion abounded and curiosity was aroused concerning the film's content. Why had Hitchcock sought to impose such a rule on audience patrons? What was it about the film's content that prompted the veteran director to beseech patrons not to reveal details of *Psycho*'s conclusion?

Hitchcock generated interest by placing himself squarely in the picture. He became salesman and talking point at the same time. This was, after all, a period when Madison Avenue assumed paramount importance by delivering its messages in visual images to citizens throughout the nation sitting before their television screens. While it is impossible to estimate just how much business Hitchcock generated through his clever sales tactics, the film's awesome commercial success, unprecedented for a film of its type and budget, suggests a high level of success.

10

The Master in Maturity

Anything is possible on film, my boy!—Alfred Hitchcock to Ken Annakin on the set of *The Birds*.

Despite the depth of Alfred Hitchcock's creative imagination, it is doubtful that as a youngster sitting in the dark and fascinating confines of London cinema houses, lost in the thrill of film and dreaming of what it would be like to one day be a part of the exciting process, he ever conceived of the stardom he would achieve in the fifties.

His star power on popular Sunday night television programming found him every bit the visible presence as one of Hollywood's most glamorous stars, the popular Loretta Young. His clever and acerbic comments were awaited with keen anticipation by a national television audience. Just as film audiences had paid close attention in anticipating his brief on-screen appearances, his caustic commentary in introducing and concluding his Sunday evening dramas was eagerly anticipated in view of the fact that, maintaining the old stage axiom, he always left his audience begging for more. His appearances were timed so that he would never overstay his welcome. The introductory capacity was ideal for maintaining interest in Hitchcock not only on television, but also in his film efforts.

Hitchcock's involvement with *Alfred Hitchcock Presents* enhanced his image as a distinguished elder statesman of film. When Hitchcock launched his venture into television he enlisted the assistance of Joan Harrison, one of the two prominent women in his film career, the other being his wife Alma. Harrison, after working with Hitchcock and Alma in developing scripts during his London phase, had seen an opportunity to strike out on her own as a film producer and signed a contract with RKO.

Harrison's producing career crested in 1947 with two brilliant efforts that unfortunately were ahead of their time and, as a result, were not acknowledged by film audiences in the main until years later. Harrison gave Jane Greer her entry to stardom in *They Won't Believe Me*, directed by Irving Pichel, which also

starred Robert Young and Susan Hayward. Greer related, "The film was a financial flop for years because the public would not accept Robert Young playing a
cad who deceived his wife by womanizing. It was a pity because it was one of
his greatest dramatic roles."

The timing of Harrison was advantageous to RKO since Greer, following
positive exposure provided by Harrison, in her next film rendered the most memorable performance of her career as ruthless and dangerously beautiful Kathie
Moffett, the femme fatale who destroys both Robert Mitchum and Kirk Douglas in *Out of the Past*, directed by Jacques Tourneur. "I will always be grateful to
Joan Harrison for giving me my big chance," Jane Greer recounted.

Ride the Pink Horse was, like *Out of the Past*, another cinematically fascinating film noir entry from RKO that was released in 1947. It starred Robert
Montgomery and was also directed by the prominent actor who preceded Ronald
Reagan as president of the Screen Actors Guild. The film's exotic Mexican location, albeit supposedly set in New Mexico, gave the movie a further air of authen-
ticity, along with the tight script and excellent characterizations, beginning with
Montgomery's portrayal of a returning World War II soldier intent on avenging
the death of his best friend. Harrison also collaborated on the script with seasoned veteran Ben Hecht.

Harrison, who joined Hitchcock initially at the age of 21, had been educated at Oxford University and the Sorbonne. While with Hitchcock she received
two Academy Award nominations for Best Screenplay for two 1940 releases done
in collaboration with the director, *Rebecca* and *Foreign Correspondent*. Her return
to the Hitchcock fold to work on his television series was part of a trend that
saw many others from the performing ranks who had worked with the director
doing the same, providing the program with a distinct déjà vu feel. Harrison
shared producing credits with another familiar name from Hitchcock films, Norman Lloyd, the Nazi spy nemesis of Robert Cummings in *Saboteur* who gained
screen immortality by plunging off the Statue of Liberty.

For his television series Hitchcock used familiar actors, past and future, from
his film productions, particularly on those episodes that he personally directed.
His first, which aired on October 2, 1955, entitled "Revenge," starred Ralph
Meeker, who achieved distinction in the noir triumph of that same year, *Kiss
Me Deadly*, directed by Robert Aldrich. Promising newcomer Vera Miles assumed
the female lead, and would later star in Hitchcock's *The Wrong Man* and *Psycho*.
Joseph Cotten, who starred in one of the director's favorite films, *Shadow of a
Doubt*, starred in the second Hitchcock-directed drama of that same year, "Break-
down." In that same production a tall, slender young aspiring actor who had
recently arrived in Hollywood from Dallas received a small role. His destiny
ultimately resided not in acting but in television production, thanks to a propensity for creating winning series (such as *Charlie's Angels* and *Dynasty*). That was
Aaron Spelling.

One exceptionally busy performer who had been a Hitchcock mainstay was fellow Britisher John Williams. A suave authority figure, Williams starred in many of the dramas personally directed by Hitchcock. Also receiving work in several Hitchcock television dramas was prominent former stage actress Patricia Collinge, who had played Joseph Cotten's sister and Teresa Wright's mother in *Shadow of a Doubt*. As for Teresa Wright, she starred in two segments of the program during its final year of 1964.

Hazel Court and Hitchcock

Among the British performers provided with an opportunity to appear frequently in Hitchcock television presentations was Hazel Court, a dazzling redhead who was signed in her teens by a Gainsborough Studios talent scout while performing in her native Birmingham. After moving to America she would become famous as an AIP regular in horror films, starring opposite Vincent Price, as well as for her frequent television appearances. One indelible memory of Hazel's productive career was her first performance before the cameras for Alfred Hitchcock.

"Hitchcock always directed the first episode of a new season," Court recalled. "I appeared in a segment called 'Arthur' opposite Laurence Harvey. We were cast as husband and wife."

Harvey had recently distinguished himself playing an angry and intensely determined young man from an impoverished background eager to quickly climb the ladder to fame in a small English factory town. *Room at the Top*, directed by Jack Clayton, depicted Harvey as a man emotionally torn between his desire to succeed and his romantic instincts. He marries Heather Sears, the daughter of the richest man in town, and forsakes the woman he passionately loves, played by Simone Signoret. Signoret's unforgettable performance as a woman so crushed over lost love that she ultimately commits suicide earned her an Academy Award for Best Actress. Harvey was nominated for an Oscar himself, and also received a nomination from the New York Film Critics Circle.

Despite the status he then enjoyed, the heady atmosphere of starring in a television drama under the legendary Hitchcock produced a frank admission from the rising young British star. "When we were waiting to begin," Court related, "Larry Harvey told me, 'You know, I'm scared!' I answered immediately, 'Well, so am I!'"

The anticipation was the most difficult part for Court and Harvey. At one point she asked Hitchcock a question about interpreting her character. "He told me, 'Don't worry about it,'" the leading lady recalled with a chuckle. "Hitchcock relied so much on the camera and the shots he had thought out in advance, and believed that everything would work out fine."

Hazel Court's recollection was comparable to the statement Gregory Peck made years later that he was nervous during *Spellbound* and had hoped for more direction from Hitchcock on how to play his role. Hitchcock was so thorough in his pre-production preparation that he could often envision just how a particular performer would look and sound before the camera. Often a performer grasped for motivation as to how to play a particular scene, particularly someone trained in the Stanislavsky method so popular in New York stage drama training, as with Peck. Hitchcock, as noted earlier, was not a method advocate and believed that the camera held the answer regarding the ultimate objective of acting. As long as a performer looked and sounded right he was not about to rock the boat.

One statement made by Court about Hitchcock revealed another aspect of his directing methods. "Alfred Hitchcock had a great sense of humor," Court related. "He was a great raconteur. He loved telling stories and was telling them all the time." Hitchcock's storytelling skills served him well. He certainly knew that the quickest way to destroy a good performance before a camera was through tension. By telling stories he could accomplish something beyond personal satisfaction and enjoyment. A good story can work wonders in achieving a general state of relaxation and well-being, by which it is easier to concentrate on rendering a solid performance before the camera.

Hazel Court Finds
Love on a Hitchcock Set

Hazel Court was frequently used in Hitchcock productions. One of her leading men was Roger Moore, who would go on to screen fame as James Bond; but the episode that premiered May 25, 1958, entitled "The Crocodile Case" (co-starring distinguished British character actor Denholm Elliott), proved more personally significant than all the others.

Don Taylor was a rising young director who caught Hitchcock's attention. As frequently occurred on the series, Taylor was invited to direct a series of segments during a brief span of time. "The Crocodile Case" was Taylor's fourth assignment during the first half of 1958. As an actor Taylor had been the first romantic interest in the blossoming career of another Taylor, Elizabeth, having played the fiancé of the brunette beauty, cast in the role of the daughter of Spencer Tracy and Joan Bennett, in *Father of the Bride* (1950). One year later Don and Elizabeth Taylor were reunited as a young married couple (and expectant father and mother) in *Father's Little Dividend*. Both films were directed by Vincente Minnelli. Don Taylor also received solid notices as the young partner of veteran New York policeman Barry Fitzgerald in Jules Dassin's 1948 film noir triumph, *The Naked City*.

"I met Don Taylor when he directed me in 'The Crocodile Case' on *Alfred Hitchcock Presents*," Hazel recalled. "I later married Don Taylor, so I naturally have sentimental feelings for the program. Hitchcock gave me a part and I met my future husband."

Hazel Court ultimately gave up her film career after performing opposite Vincent Price in *The Masque of Red Death* in 1964. While devoting time to her marriage and family, Court also found time to develop her talent as a sculptor. As for Taylor, he benefited from the experience and showcase of Hitchcock's popular television series. He carved a niche for himself in science fiction and directed *Escape from the Planet of the Apes* in 1971, as well as the 1977 screen adaptation of the H.G. Wells novel *The Island of Dr. Moreau*. The latter film, starring Michael York and Barbara Carrera, has become a cult classic among sci-fi aficionados.

In the cases of Hazel Court and Don Taylor, Hitchcock's frequent practice of providing talented young people a showcase opportunity on a popular nationally televised series extended even one step beyond the norm. In this case the Master provided a springboard to romance and ultimately marriage.

The Birds: Armageddon and Rebellion

Hitchcock's low budget blockbuster *Psycho* involved far more than a horror story about a schizophrenic serial killer. Hitchcock, as a sensitive filmmaker attuned to his times, recognized the turbulent uncertainty of an America headed into the sixties with a Cold War raging.

In 1962 America and the Soviet Union came perilously close to nuclear war during the Cuban Missile Crisis. As Robert F. Kennedy wrote in his account of that momentous October, entitled *Thirteen Days*, "We were eyeball to eyeball and the other guy blinked." Recent disclosures from Robert McNamara, the Secretary of Defense during that tense period, revealed that the United States and Soviet Union had come closer to a nuclear confrontation than had been previously recognized.

Even before the Cuban Missile Crisis Americans were sufficiently concerned about the prospect of nuclear conflict that many, particularly the affluent, built bomb shelters. An intense debate developed over whether building bomb shelters sent a dangerous message by indicating preparation for a conflict that critics maintained would result in a global cataclysm, and that such preparations increased tensions by creating anxiety on the part of the Soviet Union by prompting its leaders to believe that the shelters were a first step toward the conflict that would follow. Bomb shelter advocates responded that such a claim was absurd, and they were doing no more than preparing for a tragic eventuality should it come, which was a different matter from provoking such an action.

With nuclear testing proceeding, a debate ensued over the effects of Strontium 90 and radioactive fallout. This was part of a broader ecology issue that revolved around the ultimate fate of planet earth beyond the prospect of Armageddon via nuclear war.

Rachel Carson had a profound impact on society in the sixties with her naturalist writings and warnings about future dangers from upsetting the elements. She has been called the mother of the environmentalist movement. After growing up in rural Pennsylvania, Carson studied at the Woods Hole Marine Biological Laboratory in Massachusetts and received a masters in zoology from John Hopkins University in Baltimore in 1932. In 1952 Carson's prize-winning study of the ocean, *The Sea Around Us,* was published. This was followed three years later by *The Edge of the Sea.* In 1962 that the distinguished biologist caught the attention of an American president with the publication of her best known and top selling work, *Silent Spring.* Disturbed by the profligate use of synthetic chemical pesticides after World War II, Carson reluctantly altered her focus from marine biology to warn the public about the long-term effects of misusing pesticides, challenging the practices of agricultural scientists and the government, and calling for a change in the way humankind viewed the natural world.

Carson was attacked by the chemical industry and in certain government quarters as an alarmist. Undeterred, she spoke out courageously to remind humankind that it is a vulnerable part of the natural world and subject to the same damage as the rest of the ecosystem. In testimony before Congress in 1963 Carson called for new policies to protect human health and the environment. President Kennedy read *Silent Spring* and was influenced by it. A concerned Kennedy paid heed to Carson's warnings and called for the testing of the chemicals mentioned in her book.

Regrettably, neither Carson nor Kennedy would have much longer to labor in the environmentalist vineyards. Kennedy was assassinated in Dallas on November 22, 1963, while Carson died in 1964 after a long battle against breast cancer.

In retrospect it is evident that Rachel Carson's warnings invest her with posthumous prophet status. She saw in advance the destructive results of an imbalance between wanton materialism and human considerations. Many scientists believe that the Greenhouse Effect has heated up the ocean and caused more hurricanes than ever before. The recent destructive pattern of Hurricane Katrina and the devastation visited upon residents of New Orleans, Biloxi and Gulfport provide a dire example of the ultimate price to be paid by society for failing to heed scientific warnings.

The timing of the publication of *Silent Spring* amid concurrent highly publicized warnings by Carson occurred in the framework when Hitchcock was involved in various stages of *The Birds.* The book was published in 1962, while the film debuted the following year. Carson was the first ecological whistleblower. Hitchcock was so shrewd and meticulous that it is difficult to conceive of anything escaping his notice. With the massive attention given to Carson's best-seller, along with the attendant international publicity concerning her well-publicized congressional testimony, interviews and lectures, it would be virtually inconceivable for her viewpoint and widely expressed concepts to escape Hitchcock's consciousness. The subject of upsetting the ecosystem and the forward thrust of ecology for the first time squarely and successfully into the political process occurred at the very time that Alfred Hitchcock was deeply immersed in one of his most daring projects, *The Birds*.

Annakin's Visit to the Set of *The Birds*

Ken Annakin and Alfred Hitchcock were ranked first and second in box office receipts for 1960 with *The Swiss Family Robinson* and *Psycho*, respectively. The two British directors met briefly for the only time on the set of *The Birds*.

"I think that *Psycho* has to be remembered because of Janet Leigh's performance, in a way like Tippi Hedren in *The Birds*," Annakin remarked. "You can almost say that Hitch was running out of great human-thriller subjects after *Vertigo* and *North by Northwest*, yet he was still experimenting."

Annakin's comment about experimentation segues into the film Hitchcock was at work on when he met him for the only time. "Tippi Hedren invited me onto the set of *The Birds* one day and introduced me to Hitch," Annakin recalled. "He was clearly involved in instructing his special effects guys in placing the birds where he wanted them. I think I passed a remark that he was almost attempting the impossible. He turned to me with a rather condescending smile and said, 'Nothing is impossible on film, my boy.' As he turned away I nodded, because that is the principle after years of directing that I act upon myself."

The M Girls of Mystery

Tippi Hedren was a New York fashion model that Alfred Hitchcock saw in a television commercial and signed to a contract. Considering her finely chiseled features and natural elegance, it was understandable that she would be compared to Grace Kelly, not to mention the string of highly publicized Hitchcock blondes starting with Madeleine Carroll and extending to Kelly, Kim Novak and Eva Marie Saint.

Hedren's character in *The Birds*, Melanie Daniels, is an enigma that Mitch Brenner (Rod Taylor), after falling in love with her, has not even begun to figure out by fadeout. Hedren would be back before the cameras shortly after *The Birds* in Hitchcock's next film, the 1964 release *Marnie*. Once again she would play an enigmatic character, a kleptomaniac running away from a tortured past, as love interest Sean Connery seeks to unravel the many mysteries surrounding her.

An interesting thread concerning the Hitchcock ladies of mystery from his mature phase, in which reviewers and historians have plunged into psychological exploration, is that the women of mystery all had names that began with the letter M. Tippi Hedren, for instance, scores a double with Melanie from *The Birds* and Marnie from the film of the same name. The women of mystery can be analyzed accordingly, in chronological sequence:

1) Madeleine Elster, played by Kim Novak in *Vertigo*. While it can be argued that Judy Barton was the actual name of the character and that she was only masquerading as Madeleine Elster, the Hitchcock dramatic focus was on the make-believe character. The film's penetrating psychological uniqueness stemmed from the fact that James Stewart was driven by a synthetic creation. *Vertigo*'s ultimate point of irony, coming at the film's conclusion, was that Stewart, finally understanding the reality of what had occurred, tells Novak, "He [Elster] made you over like I did, but better." Madeleine Elster looms as the unforgettable image, the unattainable, the woman who never was but is desperately sought after by an enthralled Scottie Ferguson.

2) Marion Crane, played by Janet Leigh in *Psycho*. Leigh's Marion is far removed from the Nob Hill, dinner at Ernie's world of Madeleine Elster. Hitchcock, in his low budget triumph, transformed his world of psychologically frustrated characters from upper crust San Francisco to bread and butter Phoenix, with a beautiful secretary in her early thirties meeting her handsome boyfriend during her lunch break at a seedy motel for quick sex.

Hitchcock exploits his audience with one of his grandest of all teases as he invites them into Marion Crane's world and shows them the temptation to which she is subjected. A rich man who has had plenty to drink and is openly flirting with her scoffs at the riches he possesses, dismissing them as seemingly insignificant baubles. When Marion decides to take the money and run, hoping that it will provide the grist to start a new life, she becomes so rattled with uncertainty that she might as well be wearing a sign announcing her guilt. Her stumbling conduct with a sheriff's deputy and used car dealer prompt viewers to wonder what will happen to her. When she finally encounters the bizarre motel proprietor played by Tony Perkins viewer curiosity is enhanced all the more.

Marion Crane therefore assumes a different mystery aura than the Svengali-driven Madeleine Elster of *Vertigo* and the dual troubled personas of Melanie and Marnie, played by Tippi Hedren. Marion is the traditional American working woman confronted by temptation and yielding temporarily to it in hopes not of leading a life of Nob Hill privilege, but one with sufficient footing to enable her to marry and have a family.

3) Tippi Hedren as Melanie Daniels in *The Birds*. The opening scene of the film shows Hitchcock's impish side, in which he teases viewers with a highly unconventional meeting between two attractive people destined to fall in love who seem incapable of understanding just how such a mutual human state of bliss is achieved. It is a scene in a pet store in which Rod Taylor and Tippi Hedren are in perpetual disagreement and are seemingly more concerned about tricking each other than anything else. What makes this such an inventive scene is that, at the same time,

one can see a pattern of mutual attraction amid all the negative currents and the prevailing uncertainty of Melanie and what she represents. She remains a fascinating question mark throughout the film, as will be explained. Taylor, as Mitch Brenner, while finally realizing that he loves her, is also realistic enough to know that she remains an enigma.

4) Tippi Hedren as Marnie Edgar in *Marnie*. Once more we have a thoroughly confounded male suitor, this time played by Sean Connery, falling in love with a woman of mystery. He recognizes that it is futile to hope to understand Marnie since she cannot understand herself. Connery's character, Mark Rutland, who came from a wealthy publishing family with a rural estate near Philadelphia, became caught up in the intrigue of Marnie. The irony was that the knowledge of her unsavory past added to her allure. Lil Mainwaring, played by Diane Baker, was from Rutland's social milieu and bored him compared to the enigmatic unpredictability of Marnie. As Hitchcock revealed, "The basic theme of *Marnie* was a fetish of a man wanting to go to bed with a thief." The film was one of four Hitchcock pictures dealing with the sex-theft complex that, in addition to *Marnie*, included *To Catch a Thief* and *Psycho*, and concluded with Hitchcock's final film, *Family Plot*.

Symbolic Poem or Social Commentary?

The Birds has promoted some of the most spirited debate over the intent of Hitchcock. Donald Spoto discussed the film with a great Italian director, who stated his reasons for admiring *The Birds*. "Federico Fellini called it an apocalyptic poem and affirmed it as his own favorite among Hitchcock's works and one of the cinema's greatest achievements," Spoto wrote.

In relation to the United States going to the brink of nuclear war with the Soviet Union during this same period, and the start of the ecology movement generated by the penetrating observations of Rachel Carson, certain observers see *The Birds* as a critical commentary regarding where humankind stood early in the 1960s. The attack from the air in the form of the large flocks of birds that hostilely invade the previously quiet and idyllic Bodega Bay are seen as a symbolic reference to nuclear war.

Those who believe that the film is to be interpreted for its symbolism state that if an apocalypse was what Hitchcock was attempting to construct a film around, the obvious ending would be the destruction of the planet, as exemplified by Stanley Kramer's *On the Beach* four years earlier. These individuals point instead to the problems pertaining to the key performers in the film, who are directly linked to the symbolism displayed through the angry behavior of the birds.

Hitchcock's choice of *The Birds* represents a look back into his earliest Hollywood period. *The Birds* was adapted from a story by Daphne du Maurier, author of the gothic novel *Rebecca*. The unassuming du Maurier preferred the quiet of Cornwall in South England to bustling London, yet wrote arrestingly about turbulence and unrest. Hitchcock took her story and adapted it into his own deep and foreboding poetic image. He was assisted in the process by Evan Hunter, who had catapulted to fame in his late twenties when director-screenwriter Richard Brooks adapted his novel based on his teaching experiences, *Blackboard Jungle*, to the screen in a 1955 hit starring Glenn Ford and Sidney Poitier. Hunter adapted his own novel to the screen for the 1960 release *Strangers When We Meet*, directed by Richard Quine and starring Kirk Douglas and Kim Novak. In 1961 a Hunter novel dealing with juvenile delinquency, *The Young Savages*, was filmed by John Frankenheimer, with a compelling performance by Burt Lancaster.

Hunter was a writer who focused his efforts on criminal activity among juveniles and adults on the streets of New York City. Under the name of Ed McBain, prolific author Hunter developed a sturdy and faithful readership for his 87th Precinct novels, in which vigilant police officers seek to rid New York's meaner streets of crime.

While at first glance some observers might conclude that Hunter was treading in different water when adapting du Maurier's story to the screen, broader analysis provides a different answer. The mean streets of Bodega Bay are substitutes for New York City, with a unique kind of criminal epidemic afoot, extending beyond a familiar cops-and-robbers milieu.

Bodega Bay is a town under siege, with birds forming an unlikely criminal gang. Hunter was familiar with the kind of tense restlessness resulting from such a siege, but from a previously different context that was more limited than the reign of anarchy caused by the strange twist of nature prompting a series of bird attacks. This was a new kind of social anarchy for Hunter, with the criminal element possessing wings, supplying the visual Hitchcock, aided by his brilliantly inventive cinematographer Robert Burks, with unlimited cinematic possibilities.

A Human Failure of Understanding

In one important thematic respect *The Birds* closely parallels *Psycho*. Each film was marked by a distinctive human failure of understanding amid a sea of anarchy. It is easy to see Hitchcock as a skillful manipulator showing a world awash in social anarchy. It was previously noted how something was amiss in the basic characters of *Psycho*. There was a prevailing failure to connect. Even the film's symbol of wealth, the oil man whose $40,000 Janet Leigh decides to take, seems overwhelmed by it all and anything but happy over his affluent status.

This human failure to understand is made clear in the first scene of *The Birds*. In the manner of skilled film craftsmen, the team of Hitchcock and Evan

Hunter present a scene through which the story's basic elements are intelligently threaded. The bird theme is established in a scene set in a pet shop in which Mitch Brenner (Rod Taylor) appears, seeking to buy some birds as a birthday gift for his younger sister. When the shop's owner steps into the back of the store, Melanie Daniels (Tippi Hedren), who had come into the store previously, assists Brenner and immediately makes mistakes, indicating that she lacks knowledge of birds and is operating under false pretenses.

Brenner makes it immediately plain why he is taking such delight in exposing Melanie's ruse. He informs her that he is an attorney and had seen her in court in a case where her propensities as a practical joker were revealed.

Hitchcock would never again expose viewers to such a compact microcosm of a film's totality as in the case of *The Birds*. Before Melanie even enters the pet store she observes menacing swarms of sea gulls overhead, providing the setting for what lies ahead. As she enters Davidson's Pet Shop, Melanie walks by exiting customer Alfred Hitchcock. With so much information packed into the first scene it makes logical sense to have the director make his cameo appearance just before the initial conflict arises. The pair of terriers pulling the director along are his own dogs Geoffrey and Stanley.

What sights and sounds await Melanie Daniels and moviegoers upon entering the pet store? Screeching caged birds. As soon as the shopkeeper, Mrs. Mac-Gruder, played by Ruth McDevitt, steps away, Melanie seeks to play a prank on Mitch Brenner after he enters the store and expresses an interest in buying two lovebirds for his younger sister's birthday. The colloquy establishes the relationship between a spoiled young socialite and a virile, standoffish male. The irony is that a scene in which two attractive people are flirting during their first meeting revolves around circumstances in which the woman is seeking to deceive the man by playing a trick on him, while he in turn delivers periodic insults grounded in the reality of knowing who Melanie is and what she represents.

Informative Bird Talk

A colloquy transpires that is important to the film's evolution. Mitch, a San Francisco attorney, demonstrates his logical train of thought in questioning Melanie during her period of posing as a pet store saleswoman and authority on the subject of birds:

> MITCH: Doesn't this make you feel awful ... having all these poor little innocent creatures caged up like this?
> MELANIE: Well, we can't just let them fly around the shop, you know.
> MITCH: No, I suppose not. Is there an ornithological reason for keeping them in separate cages?
> MELANIE: Well certainly, it's to protect the species.
> MITCH: Yes, I supposed that's important, especially during the moulting season.
> MELANIE: That's a particularly dangerous time.

Mitch: Are they moulting now?
Melanie: Some of them are.
Mitch: How can you tell?
Melanie: Well, they get sort of a hangdog expression.

The dialogue is instructive in that the feelings and status of birds as seen within human society are discussed. Viewers are prepared for the concerted action that will follow from the birds of Bodega Bay. Mitch next asks to see a canary. Melanie obliges, but accidentally releases the bird into the air. The act of the canary flying through the air in the shop represents at least a temporary loss of control on the part of the humans seeking to confine it, a preview of what is to occur later in Bodega Bay. When the bird lands in an ash tray Mitch covers it with his hat and slips it back into its cage.

Melanie in a Gilded Cage

The acerbic Mitch Brenner decides that the time has arrived to inform the beautiful practical joker that he recognizes her and that he is not fooled by her conduct. Mitch speaks with sarcastic succinctness and clever symbolism. "Back in your gilded cage, Melanie Daniels."

Mitch ultimately expresses the root of his displeasure with Melanie, at the same time informing her that he has not been fooled by her pretense. Mitch lets it be known that he saw Ms. Daniels in court after a practical joke perpetrated by her resulted in the smashing of a plate glass window. "The judge should have put you behind bars," Mitch informs her bluntly.

It is established early that Melanie is basically a dilettante and spoiled rich man's daughter. This is the demeanor she displays in the film's important first scene. Mitch's smile reveals a sadistic delight in putting the spoiled beauty in her place.

Such treatment could be expected to infuriate such a well dressed and egotistical beauty. The barbs clearly find their target and Melanie feels both infuriated and insulted, but her attraction to Mitch persists nonetheless. Such a reaction is consistent with certain conceited and spoiled beauties. While Melanie, at the movie's outset, smiles rather than exhibiting disgust when a wolf whistle is directed toward her, and is well aware of her impact on the opposite sex, a man like Mitch Brenner represents a challenge.

While many men have presumably thrown themselves at the beautiful Melanie Daniels, Mitch Brenner, as a cocky, self-confident-to-the-point-of-egotistical attorney piques the interest of the blonde dilettante because he treats her differently. His insulting demeanor makes him a formidable challenge. This would not be the case were it not for his handsomeness and virile manner, along with his perceptive intelligence.

After their mutually antagonistic but flirtatious first meeting, Melanie, rather than forgetting about the insulting Mitch, runs out of the store to catch up with the intriguing attorney. She is too late but is able to copy the license plate of his car as he drives away.

Melanie then demonstrates the qualities that prompt men to generally convenience her when she telephones the office of the newspaper of which her father is publisher. She implores a city desk journalist to find out who the man is, turning on the soothing charm.

In little more than one complete scene the thread of the entire film has been established. It takes a master of Hitchcock's stripe to pull off such a convincing achievement. Here is all that has been revealed:

1) The dynamism and charisma of Melanie, living lavishly off of her father's wealth and accustomed to being sought after by the opposite sex.
2) The foreboding message of gulls congregating, which generates an expression of concern from Melanie.
3) The status of birds and their natural uninhibited state contrasted with confinement.
4) The attraction of two people impeded by an inability to coalesce emotionally and intellectually, a theme that will be extended to other relationships within the film.
5) The determination of the mysterious Melanie to pursue the equally enigmatic Mitch, despite insults, which results in an awkward romantic relationship wherein they never begin to understand each other or their surroundings.

Enter Bodega Bay

A woman of mystery, Melanie Daniels decides to utilize the element of surprise in her pursuit of Mitch Brenner. She decides to buy two lovebirds as a surprise gift for the younger sister Mitch had mentioned. After obtaining Mitch's name and address she stops by his apartment in downtown San Francisco, where she's told by his neighbor across the hall, played by veteran character actor Richard Deacon, that he has left for the weekend for Bodega Bay, as is his normal custom. When Deacon observes that she was intending to drop off the birds at Mitch's door he comments that it would not be a good idea to leave them there for an entire weekend. She agrees and makes her next stop Bodega Bay.

The Birds is a film that begins on a Friday afternoon and ends as the following Tuesday evening is beckoning. When one analyzes all that occurs within such a brief span of time, the film, in many respects, assumes the air of a breakneck thriller. *The Birds* could be classified as a murder mystery. The attacking birds of Bodega Bay serve as culprits, with no explanation ever provided for their conduct. Once more Hitchcock invites viewers to fill in the blanks.

It is interesting to note that this was the one film in which Hitchcock collaborated with a screenwriter who sprang to fame writing about juvenile delinquency (with *Blackboard Jungle*). Evan Hunter, unlike any other Hitchcock writer, was geared to fast-paced crime fiction. It could therefore be said that once more Hitchcock had shrewdly found the right person for the job. If one substitutes humans in the unique role fulfilled by the birds in the film, then the elements are present for a breakneck crime-style thriller.

Melanie alights for Bodega Bay in her silver sports car with the lovebirds in tow. The career of Alfred Hitchcock creatively combines elements of the past with those of the present. Bodega Bay, which Richard Deacon tells Melanie is "up the coast about sixty miles north," evokes memories of a film from Hitchcock's early Hollywood phase that he termed one of his favorites. *Shadow of a Doubt* was filmed in Santa Rosa, the closest town of significant size to Bodega Bay. References are made in the film to the Santa Rosa Police Department. Hitchcock exclaimed during the time of the filming of *Shadow of a Doubt* that one of the reasons why the movie occupied a place on his list of personal favorites was that his job, and the entire production, was made easier due to the level of local cooperation. Foremost on that list was the Santa Rosa Police, who cooperated with Hitchcock's requests in every regard.

Another city situated close to Bodega Bay that is mentioned in the film is Santa Cruz. Hitchcock filmed *Shadow of a Doubt* during a troubling period — his mother was gravely ill and ultimately died in the city where he was born and raised, which was under siege by the Luftwaffe. He began to feel an affinity for the area, and bought a home in Santa Cruz that became his relaxing retreat.

Taylor as Hedren's Perfect Contrast

The relationship of Melanie Daniels and Mitch Brenner is unique in that the mutual attraction exists, with the pair serving as foils, but at film's end there is no indication that they begin to understand each other. To present this kind of ambiguous romantic relationship developed by the team of Alfred Hitchcock and Evan Hunter requires selective casting. Tippi Hedren is effective as the spoiled and enigmatic Melanie Daniels, while Rod Taylor rings true as her counterpoint-romantic interest.

The Australian Taylor, a Sydney product, possesses the perfect blend of qualities to make him both an ideal romantic partner and sometime combative opponent of Hedren's character. Ex-model Hedren is convincing as a beautiful and spoiled rich girl, as well as dilettante and practical joker. The strengths of Taylor as a leading man render him an ideal match for Hedren in a difficult relationship that requires creative fine tuning.

Taylor, in screen appearances, developed a cultivated cosmopolitan accent to go along with his broad-shouldered, ruggedly virile look. This sophisticated virility plays well opposite the trickery and obfuscation of Hedren in *The Birds*. The very name of Rod has a virile sound, and the actor's choice of moniker stemmed from the fact that at the outset of his career he faced a dilemma similar to that of British actor Stewart Granger, whose real name was James Stewart. Given the same name as an immortal Hollywood superstar, his name was promptly changed to Stewart Granger. Rod Taylor initially bore the same name as the Nebraska adonis from MGM, Robert Taylor, hence the change to Rod.

In the manner of so many performers used by Hitchcock during the period of the late fifties and early sixties, when television was so prominent and provided regular exposure that proved marketable in cinema, Rod Taylor was a television mainstay — as the dashing leading man of adventure in the 1961 television series *Hong Kong*. In 1960 he had attracted attention in director George Pal's adaptation of the H.G. Wells science fiction classic, *The Time Machine*, sharing star billing with Yvette Mimieux and Alan Young. The same year that *The Birds* was released Taylor won Jane Fonda from Robert Culp in *Sunday in New York*.

Three Birds and Taylor?

Recalling once more that the Cockney slang name for women is "birds," the film, which has that moniker in the title, could alternatively be called *Three Birds and a Bloke*, using the appropriate slang for a man. The allegory shaped by Hitchcock in concert with Evan Hunter involved the relationships of Rod Taylor with three women. In each case the problems are enormous and are never resolved.

When Melanie arrives in Bodega Bay with the lovebirds she intends to bestow on Mitch as a gift for his younger sister, she stops at the home of Annie Hayworth (Suzanne Pleshette) after learning that she is a friend of Brenner's. The daughter of the managing director of Brooklyn's Paramount Theater, Pleshette groomed herself for an acting career at Finch College and Syracuse University. Her career was jump started when she was cast to replace Anne Bancroft as star of *The Miracle Worker* on Broadway. While continuing to perform regularly on film after *The Birds*, Pleshette would ultimately earn her career mark and obtain her highest level of recognition between 1972 and 1978 on the popular television series, *The Bob Newhart Show*.

Pleshette always excelled in playing a glamorous cerebral type, which is appropriate for Bodega Bay's school teacher Annie Hayworth. Innovative wheeler dealer Melanie Daniels introduces herself to Hayworth and entices her to let her stay in the spare bedroom in her house. Melanie, at the very time she is starting an enigmatic romantic relationship with Mitch Brenner, learns that Annie Hayworth was once romantically involved with Mitch Brenner.

The school teacher admits that Mitch is the reason she left San Francisco for Bodega Bay, as well as the reason why she remains in the small town. She then brings into the discussion the third woman with whom Mitch has a close personal association, his mother. Annie explains that since Mitch's father died, Mitch's mother has feared any strong attachment on her son's part toward any woman due to her fear of abandonment.

Hayworth explains to a curiously attentive Melanie that even though the romance has long passed, she prefers to remain in Bodega Bay to be Mitch Brenner's friend. She feels good being around him, and the mother who stood in the way of romantic fulfillment with Mitch is now on good terms with her since she no longer feels threatened by his former girlfriend.

Too Independent for a Mamma's Boy

Portraying Mitch Brenner's mother, Lydia, is the distinguished London-born star of stage and screen Jessica Tandy. Her selection harkens back to *Shadow of a Doubt* and its geographical proximity to Bodega Bay. Tandy's long-time husband and frequent stage co-star, Hume Cronyn, who was also born in London — but in London, Ontario Province, Canada — made his cinema debut in *Shadow of a Doubt* in a prominent feature role as Herbie Hawkins, the next door neighbor to the Newton family.

Lydia is delighted to inform Melanie, whom she immediately recognizes as a rival for her son's affections, that Mitch enjoys spending weekends in the quiet solitude of Bodega Bay and away from the rat race of bustling San Francisco. The mother cleverly scores on two fronts simultaneously, revealing her son's devotion toward her while hurling a barb at the cosmopolitan city by the bay where Melanie Daniels lives as a rich and spoiled socialite with nothing more to do than take a semantics class at the University of California at Berkeley, socialize, and sponsor a young Korean boy through school.

While Mitch Brenner is clearly attentive and loving toward his mother, his independent standoffishness is also in evidence. He reveals himself to be a sturdy man of independence who, while demonstrating proper devotion to his mother, continues to function as his own man. Hitchcock and Hunter explore the same mamma's boy syndrome visited in his previous films, while drawing a distinction. None of the three women who are drawn to Mitch will ever be able to assert any kind of dominant hold on him. As the characters develop on screen there is an emerging tacit understanding among all the principals that the masculine, clever, and resourceful Mitch will remain very much his own man.

When Lydia has an opportunity to speak with her son alone she concedes that Melanie Daniels is striking to the eye, but clearly sees her beauty as a threat rather than an indication of good taste on her son's part. Mrs. Brenner reveals what she has heard about the wealthy San Francisco society girl's trip to Rome — Melanie jumped into a fountain totally nude.

A Fellini Touch?

Mitch reveals the craftiness of an intelligent lawyer as he confronts Melanie with the information his mother provided. He does so after offering to see her in San Francisco, chiding that he has a lot of free time and perhaps they could go swimming, since he has heard that this is an activity of which she is fond. Melanie's response is that she was pushed into the fountain and that she was fully clothed at the time. She concedes that she was running with a wild crowd, leaving the impression that she was victimized by a prank in the midst of drinking.

The fountain being alluded to is almost certainly the famous Trevi Fountain. It was immortalized on film in the 1954 blockbuster filmed on location in Rome, *Three Coins in the Fountain*, starring Clifton Webb, Dorothy McGuire and Rosanno Brazzi, and directed by Jean Negulesco. The film's title relates to the old tradition of throwing coins into the famous fountain in concert with making a wish.

It was earlier mentioned that Donald Spoto had been told by Federico Fellini that *The Birds* was his favorite film, citing its fascinating allegorical content. The allusion to Melanie either jumping, or being pushed, into the (presumably Trevi) fountain calls to mind the Fellini classic *La Dolce Vita*, starring Marcello Mastroianni and Anita Ekberg, which was celebrated with Cannes Film Festival top honors and became an international favorite. The 1960 film addressed the rebellion and sexual experimentation of the period as exemplified by the "beautiful people" of the eternal city's jet set. The film emphasized the hedonism of Rome's aristocratic society and was set in the posh Via Veneto, the city's equivalent of Fifth Avenue in New York.

It took anything but an expansive stretch to envision Hitchcock and Hunter positing Melanie Daniels' lifestyle in Rome as synonymous with *La Dolce Vita* and Via Veneto–based hedonism. Viewers are compelled to await periodic clues, and brief ones at that, to learn anything about Daniels.

During dinner at the Brenner home a sudden conversational turn exposes Mitch as somewhat less than the idealistic social critic who earlier denounced Melanie for her practical joking and basic devil-may-care attitude toward life. The words, delivered with plenty of bite, emanate from Mitch's sister Cathy. An embarrassed Lydia is incapable of stopping the blunt verbal onslaught. Mitch denounced Melanie's attitude and complained that she did not receive jail time for her practical joke. Cathy zeroes in on the quality level of Mitch's legal practice.

> CATHY: Mitch knows a lot of people in San Francisco. Of course, they're mostly hoods.
> LYDIA (rebuking): Cathy!
> CATHY: Well, Mom, he's the first to admit it. He spends half his day in the detention cells at the Hall of Justice.
> LYDIA: In a democracy, Cathy, everyone is entitled to a fair trial. Your brother's practice...
> CATHY: Oh, Mom! Please! I know all that democracy jazz. They're still hoods.

A great deal has been revealed within a brief conversational compass. A notable trait of youngsters, particularly noteworthy of the brighter of their number, is to spill the unvarnished truth in a manner that frequently confounds their elders, who prefer more delicate circumlocutions to blunter verbal sallies. After all of Mitch's preaching to Melanie at their first meeting in the downtown San

Francisco pet shop about social responsibility, his sister candidly reveals him as a criminal syndicate legal mouthpiece.

The operative word clearly identifying Mitch's activities is "hoods." Can there be any misunderstanding over what is meant? Hitchcock was known for his meticulousness and there is no ambiguity in what the candid young Ms. Brenner says. The term hoods in police and crime drama parlance refers to organizational activity, specifically mob actions. Remember also that Evan Hunter was a New York City author who made his living writing about the meaner side of its streets.

Cathy Brenner was letting Melanie know that her brother made his living as a mob lawyer. This disclosure brings us full circle as viewers analyze Mitch's sharply critical comments concerning Melanie's practical jokes in a new light. This shrewd invocation reflects once more on the insincerity and moral ambiguity of modern society, which is often summarized in one word — hypocrisy.

The Difference Between Allegory and Amateurism

A pronounced thematic thread of *The Birds*, amounting to an acceleration from *Psycho*, was the inability of humans to emotionally and physically connect, focused principally on Mitch Brenner's relations with his mother, Melanie and Annie Hayworth. With the attacks of the birds in Bodega Bay we have traveled beyond the twisted morality of Madison Avenue and quiz show fraud of the late fifties, and Janet Leigh seeking to desperately find herself as she stumbles as a cumbersome thief, searching for happiness in her life with the man she loves, to the Hitchcock and Evan Hunter version of the world standing at the abyss, with the apocalypse quickly beckoning.

The irony is that the Hitchcock approach would in lesser hands be immediately labeled as conspicuous amateurism. One of the most fundamental criticisms separating the amateur from the professional filmmaker is that of characterization. Filmmakers are frequently criticized for failing to properly define their characters. The difference in *The Birds* is that there is a conscious effort to only partially flesh out the characters. Rather than a byproduct of a filmmaker's shortcomings, Hitchcock and Hunter have made it a deliberate point to present people who do not know and understand each other. This pattern occurs within a carefully constructed allegory defining flaws in the human condition.

An Allegory Within an Allegory and the Tides as a Harbinger

The Birds can be easily described as one allegory operating within the womb of a second allegory. In the manner of a sociology professor describing social strata, one can deduce that the allegory's first level involves the character interrelationships earlier described. Here are people groping for meaning and purpose in the midst of properly failing to understand one another. This allegorical tier has been carefully drawn in the film.

The film's initial allegory fits succinctly within the thematic cocoon of a broader allegory. This second allegory develops a solid nexus. The nexus embodies the basic understanding that if we on the one hand cannot successfully interact as human entities, the dangers of the second apocalyptic and highly foreboding allegory emerges. Contained within the apocalyptic allegory is the harsh message: "If we cannot learn to live with each other then humanity will perish."

While the action sequences that received the greatest attention from reviewers and filmgoers were the ingeniously presented attacks by the birds as they terrorized the residents of Bodega Bay, from a thematic and allegorical standpoint the movie's linchpin is a scene at the local restaurant, the Tides, in which a cross section of individuals representing various walks of life and differing viewpoints discuss what has happened. A near delirious Melanie describes a ferocious attack on the school children as they sought to run home from Bodega Bay School. One red-sweatered young girl falls and her eyeglasses shatter, providing one of the film's most effective close-ups. The young girl, played by Suzanne Cupito, grew up to be a prominent television beauty who starred in the popular series *Dallas* under the name Morgan Brittany.

Melanie is challenged in her account of events by Mrs. Bundy, the local ornithologist, who explains why such an attack could not have occurred. Mrs. Bundy is played by veteran British character actress Ethel Griffies. When Melanie reports that an attack was launched against the schoolchildren by crows and blackbirds, Mrs. Bundy, a chain smoker attired in a tweed suit and wearing a beret, emphatically disputes her claim. "I would hardly think that either species would have sufficient intelligence to launch a massed attack," Griffies retorts. "Their brain pans are not big enough.... Birds are not aggressive creatures, Miss. They bring beauty into the world. It is mankind, rather, who insists upon making it difficult for life to exist on this planet."

Birds constitute a substitute for humankind and the ongoing debate of the early sixties as to where the planet was headed. Cinematically, Stanley Kramer's *On the Beach* explored an ongoing scientific debate over the potential of nuclear weaponry and whether or not a nuclear conflict would result in the planet's extinction. Linked to that question was whether the United States should be actively pursuing international disarmament and the destruction of nuclear weapons, as Norman Cousins and the Committee for a Sane Nuclear Policy advocated, or whether such weaponry served as a necessary deterrent from the worst case scenario envisioned by "ban the bomb" activists. Dr. Edward Teller, considered one of the fathers of the hydrogen bomb, adhered to the deterrent viewpoint.

The brief dialogue exchange between Tippi Hedren and Ethel Griffies encompasses much of sixties society. The ecology movement and the imprint of Rachel Carson is evident through the statement that it is "mankind," not the birds, "who insists on making it difficult for life to exist on this planet."

Later, after being convinced that the birds had indeed launched a cohesive assault on Bodega Bay's citizenry, Mrs. Bundy reflects anything but confidence. She sits, head drooping, at the Tides, saying nothing and sobbing desperately, her hopes crushed. Her character would appear to embody the glowing side of nature, optimistic that humankind can surmount obstacles and will operate with the angels rather than the devils of its nature, only to discover that the destructive side has predominated.

Ethel Griffies is another example of Hitchcock astutely using great British talent in character roles. Born in 1878, Griffies made her London stage debut at 21 in the year of Hitchcock's birth. In 1924 at the age of 46 she made her Broadway debut. In 1963, the same year as the release of *The Birds*, Griffies was showcased by John Schlesinger in his inventive British coming of age film *Billy Liar*, which helped open up star vistas for its young leads Tom Courtenay and Julie Christie. As with so many of Hitchcock's performers from the fifties onward, Griffies made a substantial mark in television. A frequent guest on the *Merv Griffin Show*, she would regale the program's host, his regular sidekick, Britisher Arthur Treacher, and audiences with tales of her colorful 80-year show business career.

A Drunk Warns of the Approaching Apocalypse

Another skillful script invocation from the revealing scene at the Tides is a warning of an approaching apocalypse from the establishment's most inebriated customer. The question arises as to why Hitchcock and Hunter chose to have the Biblical declaration delivered by the town drunk. One point that can be raised is that, due to his state, others are less likely to pay attention. Tragedies, particularly in the realm of international politics, arise from individuals failing to pay heed to warnings. Another point that bears consideration is that so often alcohol produces a truth serum reaction. In Hitchcock's profession, as he surely knew, stories are rife in Hollywood about potential film transactions destroyed when details that would have been otherwise suppressed were blurted out under the liberating effects of alcohol consumption.

Karl Swenson, portraying the drunk, picks the perfect time to launch his apocalyptic warning. It comes following Ethel Griffies's assurance that birds are incapable of coalescing for attack. Swenson then delivers his foreboding message:

> DRUNK: "It's the end of the world." Thus sayeth the Lord God unto the mountains and the hills, and the rivers and the valleys. Behold I, even I shall bring a sword upon ya. And I will devastate your high places. Ezekiel, Chapter Six.
> WAITRESS: Woe under them that rise up early in the morning that they may follow strong drink.
> DRUNK: Isaiah, Chapter Five. It's the end of the world.

A fresh viewpoint is expressed in the discussion by Charles McGraw, a veteran RKO performer signed early in his career by Howard Hughes, who later became famous portraying the old Humphrey Bogart role of Rick in the 1955 television series version of the famous film, *Casablanca*. McGraw assumes the role of the pragmatic Bodega Bay citizen concerned about the small town's economy. He is cast as Sebastian Sholes, a boat owner. When he tells Mrs. Bundy, with notable concern, that sea gulls capsized one of his boats and "practically tore the skipper's arm off," Bundy remaining the ardent defender of the creatures, explains, "The gulls went after your fish, Mr. Sholes."

The Voice of Destruction

Allegorical conflict is presented via Mrs. Bundy's defense of the birds as tranquil creatures. She clashes with an angry salesman in a business suit, played by Joe Mantell.

While Bundy believes that birds are benign, harmless creatures that provide benefits to civilization, Mantell's salesman sees them as destroyers. It appears that Hitchcock and Hunter are allegorically presenting two distinctly different viewpoints of humanity, as represented by the birds. After ordering a strong drink, salesman Mantell sharply intones, "Kill 'em all!" He refers to gulls as scavengers. "Get yourselves guns and wipe them off the face of the earth," he barks, providing a quick armageddon solution. Mrs. Bundy responds that this would be virtually impossible considering the number of birds living throughout the world. The angry and determined salesman remains undeterred, however, exclaiming, "Kill 'em all. Get rid of them. Messy animals."

The term "he who lives by the sword shall perish by it" appears very much in play in the sequence after the salesman leaves the Tides. The salesman who proposes wiping the birds "off the face of the earth" becomes a victim himself. At the Capitol Oil Company, located near the restaurant, attacking birds have previously knocked a man to the ground. As a result of that incident gasoline begins flowing from a gas nozzle. When the salesman, unaware of circumstances, lights a cigar he burns his fingers with the lighted match. When the match drops in the path of the flammable liquid a chain reaction ensues, causing an explosion that takes his life. Once again an armageddon or nuclear cataclysm scenario, or a combination of each, occurs, and with the added irony of the adamant and hostile salesman being the victim.

Hedren as a Mysterious Force

In a powerful, allegorical film, one of the most intriguing unanswered questions among many is the mysterious character of Melanie Daniels that Tippi Hedren plays with an enigmatic touch. A spoiled San Francisco rich girl, she slides in and out of situations, certainly being noticed, but never successfully analyzed. Aside from playing pranks, enjoying drunken international partying, and flirting with Mitch Brenner, what is she really all about?

In one powerfully dramatic moment at the Tides, the hotbed of armageddon theory, a local mother with two small children has been driven into a near-hysterical state by the attacks of the birds. The mother, played by New Zealand–born character actress Doreen Lang, makes a connection between the attacks and the arrival of the mysterious stranger Melanie. Lang begins asking her where she came from and why she came to Bodega Bay. The verbal abuse becomes increasingly pronounced, concluding with the woman accusing the mysterious visitor of prompting the attacks, noting that they began after her arrival.

By that point Melanie Daniels is in an agitated state of her own. After the mother has reached her zenith of shrillness and accused Melanie of causing the savage bird attacks, she responds. Her manner of self-defense is more in the nature of a desire to be left alone than anger over being accused. There is a glassy-eyed look, akin to a woman under some form of hypnotic trance, as she reaches out and slaps the woman, after which she retreats into the arms of Mitch.

Tippi Hedren in *The Birds* emerges from the closest big city and arrives in the small town of Bodega Bay just before armageddon-like events. Significance can be drawn from her relationship to Annie Hayworth, who had, like her, been drawn to Bodega Bay by the also enigmatic Mitch, remaining there to be near him even after the last romantic flame existing between them had long been extinguished.

The relationship between the two women is brief and shrouded in the kind of mystery and second-guessing that signifies this allegorical film. Melanie sees Annie initially to obtain directions to the Brenner home. The resourceful blonde then secures the local teacher's permission to stay at her home. When Mitch believes that Melanie has come to Bodega Bay to see him, Melanie concocts a story about being Annie's friend. The tale breaks down upon minimal cross examination when the San Francisco trial attorney puts his talents to work.

Ultimately the woman who shares an interest in and fascination with the same man saves Melanie's life during a ferocious bird attack. In the process of aiding Melanie the school teacher loses her own life.

Despite the attacks, Melanie endures, though barely, as evidenced by her demeanor as Mitch helps her from his house and prepares to take her to a hospital. The story that began on a Friday afternoon at a downtown San Francisco pet shop, with Melanie showing a distinct curiosity about Mitch and exhibiting a desire to get to know him, ends on the following Tuesday, with film audiences every bit as perplexed concerning her and what she is all about as when she appeared in the first scene. Much emotion and drama are packed into five days.

Hitchcock's Ultimate "Fill in the Blanks" Film

Hitchcock's propensity to invite moviegoers to fill in the blanks concerning important elements of his films is invoked at its crowning summit in *The*

Birds. The lives of the characters portrayed by Taylor and Hedren, as well as those they encounter from both the human and winged worlds, are entwined in labyrinthian mystery. In the process nobody seems to interact, save the birds and their savagely cohesive assaults.

What prompts the winged creatures to go on such a destructive rampage? No answer is forthcoming. In the Hitchcock tradition, fill in the blanks yourself and experience the compelling drama and stunning special effects in the interim.

Ub Iwerks received the film's lone Academy Award nomination—for Special Effects. Hitchcock pulled off his dazzling feat of visually presenting furious attacks of birds on humans by filming each group independently, then putting them together. In this impressive achievement Hitchcock made a movie on two intersecting levels. He presented a horror story in which citizens of a small Northern California town are inexplicably attacked. The film can be appreciated on that level alone, although, to receive full benefits, the audience must consider the horror special effects attack element as that of an allegory.

While some critics have cautioned against drawing a parallel between the bird attacks and the plight of the world, with the prospect of nuclear war and potential environmental cataclysm, noting that ultimate destruction did not occur for Bodega Bay or the world lying beyond it, one important element must not be overlooked. Hitchcock chose not to complete the film with the traditional "The End" conclusion. What are we to make of Hitchcock's decision? A reasonable conclusion would be that it is up to viewers and the rest of society to fill in the ultimate blank. As Mitch helps a badly shaken Melanie to his car and toward medical aid, it should be noted that the birds are still very much a cohesive force, perched in what would appear to be quiescent abeyance.

The final unresolved blank was dumped into the symbolic lap of humanity. During this peak of Cold War activity, when the United States and the Soviet Union came the closest to a nuclear exchange than at any point in history, the crafty film master was presenting a lull—but was it preceding a storm? This was the last blank to be fill in by citizens of the world.

The Demise of Selznick

In 1965 Alfred Hitchcock was honored by the Hollywood Producers Association for his cinema contributions. Serving as master of ceremonies for the evening was David O. Selznick. The two creative titans of film had patched up any differences relating to their often stormy days of joint filmmaking and had become close. Selznick, who had not produced a film in almost ten years, the last being *A Farewell to Arms*, starring his wife Jennifer Jones and Rock Hudson, let his continuing disenchantment with the film history show by unleashing some negative barbs. Those in attendance noticed that his thoughts rambled and he did not appear well.

This was Selznick's last public appearance. He died shortly thereafter in the Beverly Hills office of his lawyer, succumbing to a heart attack. The final barbs he delivered during an evening devoted to Alfred Hitchcock's mastery provided a concluding note of irony to their fascinating relationship.

Selznick had correctly prophesied the obituary of his death. He had scaled the apogee of his power while still in his thirties as the producer of *Gone with the Wind*. The classic film would thereafter serve as the lurking shadow looming over his shoulder. David O. Selznick was the last of the reigning giants of the old studio film process of Irving Thalberg in which the producer was the dominant presence. Projects were assigned and directors worked with writers to turn out finished products in the minimal time frames. Selznick reigned when producers were king.

Alfred Hitchcock was the definitive pragmatist, a man of his time, whatever the rules of that period dictated. He used the very instrument that Hecht believed would administer the Hollywood cinema's coup de grace with superb effectiveness. By becoming a television celebrity Hitchcock was able to sell his products with greater effectiveness. While Selznick and others condemned the new medium, believing it would ensure Hollywood's downfall, pragmatist Hitchcock converted television to his advantage.

Considering the respective mind sets of the two film giants, it appears inevitable that they would part company after Hitchcock concluded the work for which he had been contracted on *The Paradine Case*.

So many performers appeared in Hitchcock's films during the final two decades of his career who had distinguished themselves on the smaller living room screens of America that one sensed a recognition of the Master that the process could work in two ways. While film producers bemoaned a citizenry of stay-at-homes glued to the small screens, Hitchcock kept things interesting for them through his advertisements as a major television personality who showed their television favorites on screen. Here was a pragmatist who had successfully bridged the gap between film and television and profited.

A Final Trip to England

Alfred Hitchcock returned to the city where he was raised and achieved his initial success as a director, and with a project that once more showed that he was a craftsman in touch with his times. *Frenzy* was filmed in London and enabled Hitchcock to vault past recent disappointing box office results for *Marnie* (1964), *Torn Curtain* (1966) and *Topaz* (1969).

Torn Curtain, starring Paul Newman and Julie Andrews, and *Topaz*, with Austrian James Bond–type Frederick Stafford heading the cast, served as illustrations of Hitchcock's keen awareness of current trends. *Torn Curtain* was a spy adventure set in danger-shrouded East Berlin. The city's strategic Iron Curtain

In Sober Reflection — Alfred Hitchcock and Austrian leading man Frederick Stafford sit in rapt concentration between scenes of the director's final film about intrigue, *Topaz* (1969). The film was set in the period leading up to the Cuban Missile Crisis. Stafford plays a French secret agent. Stafford's film reputation stemmed from his portrayal of a James Bond type in a European series of international thrillers.

setting adjacent to the West's beacon of hope, West Berlin, played up the ongoing conflict between dueling world philosophies. *Topaz,* adapted from a bestseller by Leon Uris, involved America's clash with Fidel Castro's Cuba amid the Cuban Missile Crisis.

The early seventies was a period in which America would finally extricate itself from Vietnam and Cold War adversaries. Realizing the peril of the kind of nuclear holocaust that came frighteningly close to realization in the sixties, the U.S. government undertook weapons control talks. The historic Strategic Arms Limitation Treaty, known popularly by the acronym SALT, was signed by representatives of the United States and the Soviet Union in 1972.

With the two superpowers striving to check the spread of nuclear weapons and maintain "trust but verify" postures, a new type of more personalized violence began to assert itself in world cinema, but this type of criminal activity was less personalized than in the thirties crime films starring James Cagney and

Creative Cake — Creativity abounded with Alfred Hitchcock, extending even to production parties. Hitchcock is flanked by the stars of *Topaz*, West German leading lady Karin Dor and Austrian leading man Frederick Stafford, far right, while he cuts a unique cake made to represent a copy of the bestselling novel by Leon Uris from which the 1969 release was adapted.

Edward G. Robinson. Rather than a killing involving rival gangs, and battles between gangs and police, this was more reflective of the individualized and depersonalized nuclear world epitomized in major cities.

Eastwood and Spaghetti Westerns

In the early sixties Clint Eastwood, star of the *Rawhide* television series, went to Italy and teamed up with Italian director Sergio Leone to rock the international film community with three cheaply made westerns that made them rich and famous. Eastwood, soft spoken and low key, was the antithesis of the fast talking, bullying James Cagney gangster figure who provided a pervasive presence from the thirties to the fifties. His was the voice of quiet authority, the strong, silent type who took charge.

The depersonalized nature of the process was evidenced by the fact that the first two films of the trilogy that quickly became known under the genre name of spaghetti westerns, *A Fistful of Dollars* (1964) and *For a Few Dollars More* (1965), cast Eastwood as "the Man with no Name." The cash ringing trilogy ended with the 1966 film, *The Good, the Bad and the Ugly.*

Eastwood, who had grown up in Northern California's Bay Area in Oakland, returned to his roots to play San Francisco detective Harry Callahan in a series of successful films, beginning with the 1971 jackpot success *Dirty Harry*, directed by Don Siegel. Successful sequels followed with *Magnum Force* (1973) and *The Enforcer* (1976). The films tapped into citizen resentment over the impact of urban crime, with a hamstrung Callahan willing to adopt unorthodox tactics beyond those permissible in the police manual. The most famous phrase to emanate from the popular series reflected rebellious determination in the face of frustration as Dirty Harry intoned with quiet determination, "Go ahead and make my day."

This theme of addressing citizen frustration at the urban level produced major results when Charles Bronson was cast as a liberal architect living in New York City who takes the administration of law and order into his own hands after his wife is brutally murdered and his daughter raped and left in a comatose state. In the 1974 hit *Death Wish*, directed by Britisher Michael Winner, New York City police call Bronson's character "the Vigilante," while his revenge taken against the city's criminal elements prompted spontaneous cheers and bursts of applause from audience members. Bronson became an international superstar with his portrayal, as three sequels featured him in the same role.

While Hitchcock remained a filmmaker of his time who was well aware of trends, he also was very much his own artist and shaped projects with his distinctive touch. The characters and projects that made international superstars of Clint Eastwood and Charles Bronson fell into the successful genre mold. In approaching *Frenzy* Hitchcock demonstrated a keen awareness of the influence of violence in the seventies' filmmaking process but shaped a film that bore thematic similarity to *Psycho* and *The Birds*. The prevailing anarchy of modern society stands at the core of *Frenzy*.

Returning Home, and Devourers and the Devoured: Frenzy

As Hitchcock neared the end of his long and productive career he took the opportunity to return to the city where he was born, grew up, and achieved his first professional success. Not only did Hitchcock return to his native London, his story is set in surroundings familiar to his youth. Hitchcock's father was a greengrocer, and much of *Frenzy*'s story and filming revolves around the busy grocers' stalls in colorful Covent Garden in Central London, the area where Liza

Serial Killer's Residence — This front view of 3 Henrietta Street in Central London's colorful Covent Garden was the residence of serial killer Bob Rusk, played by Barry Foster, in the 1972 release *Frenzy*. Alfred Hitchcock returned to his native London to make this film, the second to last of his career, followed only by *Family Plot*.

Doolittle of *Pygmalion* and *My Fair Lady* fame sold flowers and spoke with a strong Cockney accent before being transformed into an elegant lady by Professor Henry Higgins.

Hitchcock was a noted gourmet known for lecturing young men in the film business with whom he worked, like Gregory Peck and John Michael Hayes, about the proper strategic blends of food and wine. *Frenzy* is a film consisting of devourers and the devoured. The film's initial scene contains some of the wickedest irony the Master ever unleashed on screen.

The tranquil opening, with overhead shots of the Thames and the Tower Bridge in the city's eastern area near the financial district, constitutes the lull before the storm. Eventually the camera comes to rest on a group of people standing next to the Thames as a prominent local political figure, Sir George, played by John Boxer, tells his listeners proudly, "Ladies and gentlemen, I'm pleased to tell you that these ravishing sights [of the area] will soon be restored to you," and that the Thames "will be clear of industrial effluents, free of the waste products with which we have for so long polluted our rivers and canals."

His positive oration is then interrupted by the discovery of what the audience learns is the latest in a series of London serial strangling deaths as a naked woman's body is observed floating to shore. Standing amid the group of listeners and viewers is Hitchcock, wearing a traditionally British bowler hat. As part of the group, he is on-camera longer than in any of his other films, which featured "now you see him, now you don't" appearances that only the most alert audience members might catch. Perhaps the difference is that Hitchcock believed this would be his final London film and a longer camera appearance was justified.

Two Stories Unite and One More Mamma's Boy

The story construction developed by Hitchcock in concert with British playwright and scenarist Anthony Shafer bears a similarity to *Strangers on a Train*. A variant of the same principle would then be used in Hitchcock's final film, *Family Plot*. In *Strangers on a Train* viewers saw two stories evolve from the perspectives of the deranged Bruno Anthony, played by Robert Walker, and his intended victim Guy Haines, portrayed by Farley Granger. The bisected segments blended thematically toward the unified result, with the most dramatic sequences generally involving the film's two leading characters together.

Frenzy explores the activities of greengrocer Bob Rusk and down at his heels former Royal Air Force flying ace Richard Blaney, played by Barry Foster and Jon Finch respectively. The two men are presumed by Blaney to be friends, but serial killer Rusk eventually frames him for the murders the greengrocer actually committed.

Early in the film Rusk looks out the window of his Covent Garden flat next to his grocer's stall and calls down to Blaney as he walks on the street below. He introduces the older woman next to him as his mother.

The team of Hitchcock and Anthony Shafer explain to filmgoers at the film's outset where greengrocer Bob Rusk, falls psychologically. The simple introduction of his mother, along with other information, puts him in the "mamma's boy" category of psychotic killer Bruno Antony in *Strangers on a Train*. The additional information was furnished while Blaney sits in a pub drinking. Situated nearby are two well dressed London upper-class types. They mention the latest in the series of murders of strangled women, in this case the same body that was washed ashore at the film's opening.

The major element of the conversation relates to the psychological makeup of serial killers of women. It is noted that these individuals cannot achieve sexual release in a normal fashion, and can only gain orgasmic satisfaction when they are killing their victims. As a strangler this killer would achieve satisfaction at the moment of ultimate power when he has snuffed out the life of his victim.

Seventies Voyeurism

When Rusk makes Brenda Blaney, the former wife of Richard, his next strangling victim, we see the wise words from the pub conversation confirmed. Brenda Blaney, played by Barbara Leigh-Hunt, expresses revulsion from the moment that Rusk enters her office. We learn soon enough why she finds him so repulsive. She runs a matrimonial service and bluntly tells Rusk, who uses an assumed name, that she can do nothing for him since his expressed sexual tastes are too bizarre to be accommodated.

Foster plays the scene brilliantly as he gradually reveals Rusk's bestial side. At the point when Brenda is dismissing him he reveals, with a lurid smile, that she actually represents his ideal type. Realizing that her life hangs by a tenuous thread, Brenda feigns an interest in her depraved customer, agreeing to have lunch with him. He humiliates her by exposing her breasts and openly drools at the combination of exposed flesh and her trembling body.

It is informative to note the significant changes between the voyeurism Hitchcock reveals in the chilling scene where a necktie killer lusts after one more female victim and that from a famous earlier film. *Frenzy* debuted 18 years after Hitchcock's voyeuristic *Rear Window* (1954). Prevailing censorship codes would never have permitted anything as raw and graphic as the demented Bob Rusk engaging in his own sordid peep show before killing his victim. It was daring enough for Hitchcock to nimbly run the voyeurism of *Rear Window* past fifties censors, with James Stewart's avid fixation with the neighbor he never met, Miss Torso.

Brenda Blaney ultimately realizes that her demented customer is the London serial strangler when he removes his tie. The camera reveals that Bob Rusk, as was communicated in the informative pub conversation, achieves sexual gratification by killing his victim. In presenting such a scene of raw and chilling realism, Hitchcock was taking advantage of the period's relaxed codes, along with presenting graphic violence as reflective of the times.

Brenda becoming Rusk's metaphoric lunch culminates with the killer calmly taking a bite out of Brenda Blaney's apple. Note that an apple was the forbidden fruit in the Garden of Eden.

Finch and Granger Similarities

Jon Finch as Richard Blaney falls into the suspect category after his ex-wife is strangled, as had Guy Haines (Farley Granger) after his spouse's death in *Strangers on a Train*. Haines arouses suspicion due to a loud argument with his wife at the record store where she works, culminating in shouts and Haines angrily shaking her.

Blaney's demeanor is more likely to arouse suspicion than that of Haines, since Blaney has virtually gone to seed after a stellar career as an RAF pilot. He is fired from the pub where he works on the pretext that he was robbing the till, when in reality the dismissal stemmed from jealousy by the pub's owner over barmaid Barbara Jane "Babs" Milligan's (Anna Massey) preference for Blaney. The rattled and out of work Blaney then shows up at his ex-wife's office and argues loudly enough for the alert secretary in the next room to hear them. When his ex-wife pities him enough to treat him to dinner at her club he launches into a juvenile temper tantrum, observed by a roomful of diners.

Suspicions concerning Blaney extend even beyond his temper tantrums in front of his ex-wife. Before he realizes that his ex-wife has slipped some money into his empty pockets, Blaney spends the night at a local Salvation Army. He learns of his good fortune only after his closest bunk mate picks his pocket, being alertly observed and thwarted by Blaney. Blaney's blanket was a potato sack, which extends its scent to his clothes. When the following day he entices girlfriend Babs Milligan to a rendezvous at a Bayswater area hotel he sends the clothes out for cleaning. The potato sack scent will later come back to haunt him in connection with the film's most unforgettable scene, which once more harkens back to *Strangers on a Train*.

Blaney's rendezvous with the barmaid turns out to be their last. Bob Rusk agrees to do her a good turn and allow her a place to stay. When she becomes his next victim Blaney becomes all the more logical a suspect, given his close romantic links to the last two strangling victims. A friend, Johnny Porter (Clive Swift), offers to allow him to accompany he and his wife to Paris, where they are slated to open a British pub. The opportunity sours when Richards's wife Hetty, played by Billie Whitelaw, makes it plain from the outset that she cannot stand Finch, nixes the proposal. Initially Hetty Porter expresses confidence that Blaney was the killer. After circumstance proves that he could not have killed Milligan she convinces her husband that they cannot afford the prospect of being considered accessories after the fact and being dragged into a murder scandal. Blaney's volcanic temper erupts once more as he calls the Porters "bastards" and storms out of their flat overlooking Hyde Park, once more alone as a city-wide dragnet closes in on him.

One of Hitchcock's Most Memorable Scenes

Rusk's murder of Milligan sets into motion circumstances resulting in one of the most memorable, not to mention uniquely creative, scenes of Hitchcock's career. In any kind of memory association game pertaining to *Frenzy* the response likely to overwhelm all others would be, "Oh yes, the film with the body and the potato sacks."

The theme of devouring and being devoured extends to the film's intensely unique scene, revolving around food and the Covent Garden market. Rusk decides to dispose of victim Milligan by placing her inside a lorry, among bags of potatoes to be transported outside London.

A hitch in Rusk's plan develops when, at the time the lorry driver emerges and is set to drive the vehicle out of the city, the killer realizes that a key piece of evidence rests literally in Milligan's hand and could implicate him as her killer. In her struggle to resist death, Milligan reached out and pulled off Rusk's personalized tie clasp bearing the letter "R." That the letter R is also the first letter of innocent suspect Richard Blaney's first name was almost assuredly intended by Hitchcock and Shafer.

The ensuing struggle by Rusk bears resemblance to one of the key scenes of *Strangers on a Train* in that it involves the tantalizing Hitchcock tactic of teasing viewers into rooting for a vile killer in the interest of enhancing suspense. In *Frenzy*, rather than planting a damaging piece of evidence to implicate an innocent victim, Hitchcock reverses the principle as killer Rusk desperately seeks to remove a piece of evidence that could implicate him in the murder. Hitchcock outdoes even himself in wringing every bit of suspense from the effort of Rusk to pry the tie clasp from the death grip of Babs Milligan.

The first Hitchcock ploy to extend suspense occurs when the lorry driver emerges and drives off while Rusk tugs desperately at the tie clasp. His effort is made understandably more difficult through being in a vehicle moving at a brisk speed along a highway. Much uncomfortable jostling occurs as the body twists and turns. It bounces around, so does Rusk, and so do the sacks of potatoes. At one point the dust that has been stirred in the confined area from the frenzied activity causes Rusk to sneeze. The sound arouses suspicion from the lorry driver.

The Hitchcock propensity for throwing up obstacles to enhance suspense flourishes with another ploy. In Rusk's struggling efforts to extricate the tie clasp from Milligan's rigor mortised fingers, some of the potato sacks fall out of the truck and onto a busily traveled highway. A driver from another vehicle warns the lorry driver about the dropping potato bags, prompting him to stop and launch an impromptu inspection. Rusk is able to hide behind the sacks in the darkness and avoid detection.

Ultimately the killer is able to pry the tie clasp loose and exit the lorry when its driver stops at a roadside restaurant. Rusk is then able to do more than merely implicate Blaney. When the on-the-run Blaney, having nowhere else to go, visits Rusk, the man Blaney considers his friend offers to allow him to stay at his flat. Rusk leaves him long enough to summon the first police officer he sees, turning Blaney in.

The Food Element as Comedy

The use of food as a thematic tool is extended by Hitchcock and Shafer to the level of comedy. The rapidly paced story of a Jack the Ripper–type figure murdering London women runs the risk of exhausting a viewer's grimness quotient unless some relief is furnished. This is done through the element of comedy, lightening up the story and preventing an otherwise thematic heaviness from overwhelming audiences.

Blaney is taken to dinner by his ex-wife the night before she is strangled by Rusk, who invites her to lunch before symbolically digesting her as his own midday repast. The crucial effort to remove incriminating evidence from the death grip of Milligan's hand occurs amid sacks of potatoes.

The comedic element enters the food scene when Alec McCowen, cast as Chief Inspector Oxford, the case's lead investigator, must deal with his zany wife in the midst of a gourmet French cooking spree. He is initially seen happily devouring a large English breakfast in his Scotland Yard office. Viewers later learn why he so positively praises the solidity of the full English breakfast to his colleague. Back home at his London flat he suffers through inadequate and poorly prepared repasts cooked up by his wife, played by Vivien Merchant. He spits out some quail she has served with fanfare as soon as she leaves the room. Humor joins with the macabre when the chief inspector discusses details of the criminal devouring his female victims while the inspector seeks to rid himself of his wife's "gourmet" food without her observing.

The selections of McGowen and Merchant to play key roles again displayed Hitchcock's use of some of Britain's finest British character talent. McCowen was a noted British stage star with a penchant for Chekhov. His two key film performances came in 1972 with *Frenzy* and *Travels with My Aunt*, in which he performed opposite Maggie Smith in director George Cukor's screen adaptation of Graham Greene's novel. McCowen's character undergoes a transformation in the latter film when the bookish accountant not only is taught how to enjoy life by his eccentric "aunt," but ultimately learns that she is actually his mother.

Vivien Merchant was known throughout Britain as not only a talented actress, but as the wife (at the time *Frenzy* was filmed) of prestigious playwright Harold Pinter, a union that ended shortly thereafter. She appeared in some of her husband's plays, notably *The Homecoming*.

Merchant's celebrated film debut came in a key companion role in director Lewis Gilbert's 1966 adaptation of Bill Naughton's novel and one person play, *Alfie*, which helped propel Michael Caine to the front ranks of international stardom. As a practicing Catholic throughout his life, whose films are frequently built around major morality issues, Hitchcock was bound to have been moved by the manner in which abortion was handled in the film's most powerful scene. When womanizer Caine meets sexually starved Merchant (whose husband is confined to a sanatorium), entices her into a sexual interlude, the result of which is a pregnancy. The previously hedonistic-to-the-point-of-indifference Caine develops a new appreciation for life following the sad abortion proceeding at his flat, with Denholm Elliott performing brilliantly — in his only scene in the film — as the abortionist.

The mastery of the delicate role of a sensitive woman submitting to an abortion secured Most Promising Newcomer honors for Merchant, as well as Best Supporting Actress by the National Board of Review, along with Oscar and Golden Globe nominations in that same category. Hitchcock challenged her depths by providing Merchant with an opportunity to play a role in *Frenzy* reminiscent of delightfully zany American comedienne Billie Burke. Her role as the would-be gourmet chef who falls far short of the mark netted her a Best Supporting Actress nomination from the New York Film Critics Circle.

Surprise Twist Ending

While Hitchcock, in a discussion about *Vertigo*, stated his disinclination toward surprise twist endings, it was noted that he used such a device in *Psycho* by revealing that the presumed woman murdering people was none other than the demented Norman Bates. In *Frenzy* the raging insistence of innocence on the part of fall guy Richard Blaney convinces veteran police inspector Oxford that the protestations might be true.

Blaney is so enraged by becoming the victim of his presumed friend that he cares not one whit about his own life, but only for taking vengeance on the man who set him up. Aided by fellow prison hospital ward inmates, Blaney is able to escape following a faked suicide attempt carried out to get him to the infirmary and hopefully one step closer to freedom. After the prison guard in the ward is given sleeping pills in his coffee and falls into a deep slumber, Blaney escapes.

The infuriated Richard Blaney has declared his intention to kill Rusk enough times that there is no doubt concerning his destination after making his escape. The film's climax comes in the form of a meeting of its two major characters, Blaney and Rusk, each an element of the dual-structured story by Hitchcock and Shafer. Police Inspector Oxford, the investigator and force of law and order, forms a symmetrical threesome with the killer and his presumed friend and ultimate victim. Hitchcock, a master of the delicate science of merging comedy into drama, reveals the relieved expression on Oxford's face (as he's about to be subjected to yet another of his wife's "gourmet" meals) when he learns that his suspicions concerning Rusk's guilt and Blaney's innocence have been confirmed by an identification of the killer from a waitress at the truck stop where Rusk alighted from the lorry after retrieving his tie clasp. The inspector's gastronomical relief is contrasted with Vivien Merchant's expression of keen disappointment that intervening police business prevents him from finishing the "gourmet meal" she so carefully prepared.

A Grand Tease

The swiftly paced drama ends in Rusk's Covent Garden apartment and involves a grand tease before the film's three male principals meet. Inspector Oxford, realizing that the enraged escapee Blaney is intent on carrying out his threat to kill Rusk, determines to arrive at the flat before the vengeance-seeking victim. Realizing that the evidence exists to convict the actual killer, the police inspector hopes to save Blaney from jeopardizing his future freedom by an act of revenge.

A homicidally furious Blaney arrives shortly before Oxford and believes he has received his coveted opportunity for revenge. He observes an object lying in bed, covered from view. Blaney releases his pent-up frustrations by driving a crowbar repeatedly against the presumably sleeping Rusk. It appears to the audience that the arriving Oxford is too late to save Blaney, whose run of ill luck never seems to cease.

When the blanket covering the apparently sleeping Rusk is pulled off, the grand tease is accomplished. What the audience observes is another dead woman, Rusk's latest victim. Blaney and Oxford do not even have an opportunity to communicate. Their attention is seized by the sound of approaching footsteps.

Rusk, notably bereft of tie, arrives pushing a trunk. Nothing is said. Any dialogue would be superfluous. The camera's all-seeing eye reveals the perfect ending. An astonished killer is caught shortly after the murder of his most recent victim bearing the trunk into which he intended to place the body. Whereas many suspense films would have ended with a ferocious struggle between the two antagonists, Hitchcock ends on a note of silent irony as the startled killer, realizing the game is up, exchanges a long stare with the film's symbol of authority and the designated fall guy.

A Documentary Flavor

Hitchcock's casting strategy in *Frenzy* was reminiscent of *Psycho*. By selecting performers below the rank of the superstars who had graced his earlier films, Hitchcock was providing *Frenzy* with the flavor of a "you are there" documentary experience, similar to that of *Psycho*. Considering that he was selecting a cast from the land of Shakespeare, the casting process became a festival festooned with dramatic riches.

On the subject of Shakespearian drama, Hitchcock's selection of Jon Finch to star as the innocent dupe came shortly on the heels of his starring role as Macbeth in the 1971 film version of the play directed by Roman Polanski.

The selection of Barry Foster as the demented strangler and ostensible friend of Blaney provides the perfect dramatic mix in a film that shifts back and forth between the two characters. Foster is one decade older than Finch, and Hitchcock is content to exploit that difference as the greengrocer appears on the surface to be more mature than the down-on-his-luck former RAF hero. Hitchcock cleverly builds on the angry tension within Blaney, leading to temper tantrums, to construct contrasting images of an apparent killer out of control whose life is in shambles, and a stable businessman who looks calm and collected in his business suits — until he reveals himself in the office of Blaney's ex-wife as the misogynist killer he actually is.

Barry Foster, like Jon Finch and so many British performers, had an impressive stage background rooted in Shakespeare, with *Hamlet* as his favorite role. Foster became a familiar face on British television and in America over the Public Broadcasting System for his lead role in the series *Van der Walk*. He portrayed the Dutch crime-solving detective in the series set in Amsterdam, a major departure from his role as a serial killer in *Frenzy*.

Anna Massey and Barbara Leigh-Hunt also possessed long British stage resumes. Massey had acting in her blood as the second child of performers Raymond Massey and Adrienne Allen. She developed a reputation for brilliant performances in television remakes of cinema classics, such as *The Corn Is Green* (1979), playing Miss Ronberry; as Mrs. Danvers in the 1981 remake of *Rebecca*; and as Betsy in the 1985 reprise of *Anna Karenina*. She was also one of the stars of the British sitcom *Nice Day at the Office*.

Barbara Leigh-Hunt made her first professional stage appearance while still a student at the Old Vic. The same year that *Frenzy* was released she played Catherine Parr in *Henry VIII and His Six Wives*, a feature film adaptation of the BBC miniseries.

There are two other casting notes to include concerning *Frenzy*. The receptionist at the Coburg Hotel in Bayswater, where Richard Blaney has his sexual rendezvous with Babs Milligan, was Elsie Randolph. Four decades earlier she played comic relief in Hitchcock's *Rich and Strange*, as the meddlesome ship passenger constantly pestering married couple Henry Kendall and Joan Barry. Clive Swift, the henpecked Johnny Porter who wanted to assist Blaney after learning he was unjustly accused of the murders, played the same type of role in the 1990s comedy series *Keeping Up Appearances* opposite overbearing social climber Hyacinth Bucket, played by Patricia Routledge.

A Writer with a Hot Hand

Frenzy was adapted to the screen from the novel *Goodbye Piccadilly, Farewell Leicester Square* by Arthur La Bern. In typical Hitchcock fashion, the novel was selectively retooled to suit the director's style of showcasing scenes highlighted by imaginative camera work while providing the legendary story twists and turns to keep the audience on edge. Hitchcock shrewdly opted for a British playwright with a hot hand at the time that *Frenzy* was in the planning stages.

A suspense author and a former barrister, Shafer's career reached its apogee with his play *Sleuth*, which ran for 2,359 performances in London's West End, then transferred to Broadway, where it played 2,000 performances and secured a Tony Award. The film adaptation of *Sleuth* appeared in 1972, the same year that *Frenzy* debuted. It featured a brilliant *mano a mano* contest between Laurence Olivier and Michael Caine. The younger performer Caine recalled later how he told the venerable performer Olivier, who would ultimately reach the House of Lords, "Take your best shot, Larry!"

Shafer, whose twin brother Peter penned the highly successful play *Equus*, found a screenwriting niche in adapting Agatha Christie works to the screen. He adapted *Death on the Nile* (1978) and *Evil Under the Sun* (1982), as well as providing uncredited work on the 1974 release, *Murder on the Orient Express*.

Visiting an Important Hitchcock Location

On March 30, 2004 this author had the opportunity to visit the location of the flat where Barry Foster, as greengrocer Bob Rusk, committed some of the murders, as well as stored bodies of victims. The 3 Henrietta Street location of

Revisting Hitchcock Site—Author William Hare is taken on a tour of a famous Hitchcock site during a 2004 London trip, by Philippa Rimmer, assistant manager of the Eurospan Group. Eurospan, a book distribution company, occupies the office space at 3 Henrietta Street in Central London. They stand in what was the flat occupied by Barry Foster, playing serial strangler of women Bob Rusk, in the 1972 Hitchcock film, *Frenzy*. Through the window Convent Garden can be observed. At the time the film was made the area was a bustling market site where fresh fruits and vegetables were sold.

the flat is one floor above what used to be the bustling grocery stalls of the Covent Garden market scene. Hitchcock visited Henrietta Street long before making *Frenzy*. In the 1920s he visited playwright Winifred Ashton, who wrote as Clemence Dane, in her flat situated over a publishing office.

The flat where Bob Rusk resided is now occupied by the Eurospan Publishing Group, a book distribution company. The office overlooks the throbbing Henrietta Street activity of Covent Garden, where the grocers' stalls were situated at the time *Frenzy* was filmed.

Hitchcock's Final Film

After returning to London to film *Frenzy*, Hitchcock put the capstone on his legendary career by finishing at his final home, Universal Studios, with a flourish unanticipated even for the creative and unpredictable director. At 75 Hitchcock had seemingly done it all, but, as he would be quick to remind any-

Hitchcock's Final Film — Director Alfred Hitchcock poses with the stars of his final film, the 1976 Universal release *Family Plot*, at a press conference prior to the start of principal photography. Hitchcock is flanked, left to right, by female stars Barbara Harris and Karen Black. Standing above them, left to right, are Bruce Dern and Roy Thinnes. Just prior to the start of filming, Roy Thinnes was replaced by William Devane.

one who made such a suggestion, his active mind was still creating, while his studio was more than willing to assist in the process.

On May 19, 1975, Hitchcock added another chapter to his book of macabre humor by staging a press luncheon for his 53rd and what proved to be final film, which at the time was called *Deceit* but would eventually be changed to *Family Plot*. The story's plot line was closely linked to a devious murderer who killed his adopted parents and provided an extra headstone for himself, with the difference being that his grave site contained no body. As a result, the press luncheon that drew more than 150 domestic and foreign press members, along with the film's stars and the director himself, was held in the bizarre (but thematically correct) setting of a cemetery high on a hill on Universal's back lot. The press members, and stars Karen Black, Bruce Dern, Barbara Harris and Roy Thinnes, the last of whom would be replaced by William Devane, mingled in a somber outdoor graveyard setting and dined luxuriously with the director at a huge banquet table spread with a black tablecloth.

Among the press contingent covering the event for *Hollywood Studio Magazine* was movie writer Robert Kendall. The visit brought back memories of Kendall's days as an actor when he launched his film career replacing Sabu in *Song of Scheherazade*, starring Yvonne De Carlo, Jean Pierre Aumont and Brian Donlevy. He shortly thereafter appeared in *Casbah*, starring Tony Martin, De Carlo and Marta Toren.

"I have been invited to many luncheons over my 25 years in the Hollywood press contingent," Kendall remarked, "but never before had I been invited to enjoy a luncheon in a cemetery setting. Leave it to Alfred Hitchcock, the suspense master, with his macabre sense of humor to stage such an event. Bloody Marys were served and later, during a graveyard stroll, press members were surprised and shocked to find tombstones with their names and years of birth imprinted on the tombstones."

Female servers were costumed as widows in mourning wearing black dresses with black hats and veils. Bartenders wore black armbands. An old-style horse-drawn hearse was kept in readiness, while the graveyard was designated as "H Cemetery" with a sign noting "Lunch Served Today."

"Hitchcock made a dramatic entrance in a long black limo," Kendall recalled. "As Hitch emerged from his limo a broad smile formed on his face. Flash bulbs popped and television cameras captured the dramatic moment. Casually, Hitch walked over to his bust, which had been placed atop a marble pedestal, and dramatically wrapped his hands around the neck, as if he were strangling himself. He then explained the graveyard setting's connection to the film."

Hitchcock's Final Press Conference

If Hitchcock's final film inspired an offbeat and thoroughly fascinating luncheon, Universal did the same with the Master's final press conference for his last film. The closed circuit television presentation took place at NBC Studios in Burbank. It occurred March 23, 1976, just prior to the release of *Family Plot*. Sixty cities from across the United States were involved in the effort, with major reception points being the Plaza Hotel in New York City, the Registry Hotel in Dallas and the Continental-Plaza Hotel in Chicago.

Robert Kendall covered that memorable event as well for *Hollywood Studio Magazine*. "Everyone was served brunch along with impressive black notebooks," Kendall said, "with Hitchcock's profile outlined in gold, along with a glass crystal ball, with the head of Hitchcock, with one eye winking from inside the crystal ball."

Once the closed circuit hookup was ready Hitchcock was introduced by a Universal representative and immediately proceeded to reveal his working process. "First, I put the entire film down on paper," Hitchcock explained in a business-like manner. "People say, 'Don't you improvise on the set?' I say, 'Certainly not. It's cheaper to work this way. It's quieter to plan every detail in advance.'"

Alfred the Perfectionist — Alfred Hitchcock was a perfectionist, as exemplified by the meticulous craftsmanship exhibited during his 53-film career. He is seen here lining up a shot for an upcoming take.

A media representative from the Plaza Hotel in New York inquired about Hitchcock's directing style. "Once an actress came to me tearfully and said, 'You are not directing me,'" the director recalled. "I explained to her, 'The only thing I do is tell you when you are doing it wrong.'"

A representative at the Continental-Plaza Hotel in Chicago asked Hitchcock, "What was it like working with Ingrid Bergman?" Hitch smiled and related, "Ingrid was nervous about a scene we were doing in *Spellbound*. I told her, 'It's only a movie, Ingrid!' We both laughed." The Swedish star relaxed and shooting resumed.

A Reuters International News Service representative in Burbank asked Hitchcock about retirement. A puzzled look formed on Hitchcock's face and he asked, "What's that?"

In that *Psycho* was one of Hitchcock's most popular films it was no surprise that a media representative from Chicago would ask about the most widely shown scene from all his movies, the shower murder. "I've never been a believer in violence," Hitchcock explained. "*Psycho* was filmed in black and white, so I wouldn't show blood running from the bathtub in technicolor. Violence doesn't contribute cinematically."

A film critic from New York asked, "Do you feel at times there isn't much left in suspense?" Hitchcock quickly replied, "A suspense movie is giving the audience information in advance. There is a great deal of difference in surprise and anticipation. Most people make mystery films as 'mystifying films.'"

A media representative at Dallas' Registry Hotel posed the question, "Has real life drama made it difficult to keep pace in a film with what is really happening?" Hitchcock nodded in agreement, then explained, "We're fighting headlines all the time. I don't think of *Family Plot* by saying I want to make a movie about kidnapping. I thought of the project as two sides of a triangle meeting at a certain point. The two sides generally come to their apex. Climax takes place when the totally unrelated elements are brought together."

The director then fielded a question relating to camera technique. "I see the camera as the person who sees something," Hitchcock explained. "In *Family Plot* one whole sequence is composed of people in a car. Close-ups of the people are shown and the road ahead. We photograph the emotions of the individuals in the car, not focusing primarily on the road ahead."

In response to being asked what was his favorite movie, Hitchcock responded, "*Shadow of a Doubt*. We got to know the price of everything. We got all the details and shot the whole film in Santa Rosa. The people in the town gave us a tremendous amount of help. It also satisfied me in this respect — melodrama."

"What's it like to be Alfred Hitchcock?" someone asked. "I'm somewhat of a loner," responded the director. "I don't flaunt myself in public. I suppose I must be honest and say it is very pleasant when the film is good, but it is very unpleasant when the picture is a failure. Frankly, that's miserable!"

A New York media representative asked Hitchcock, "What's your favorite reading?" He replied quickly, "Raymond Chandler, Dashiell Hammett, John Buchan and Agatha Christie."

Aware of one famous Hitchcock trait, a Burbank media representative asked, "What was your favorite practical joke?" Hitchcock recounted with a laugh, "It was in London at a hotel where I gave a dinner party for Gertrude Lawrence. All of the food was blue. Blue cream soup, blue trout, blue peaches, blue ice cream."

During the mid-seventies it was being reported in the media that Janet Leigh had been receiving hate mail relating to her starring role in *Psycho*. Robert Kendall asked Hitchcock if he had any explanation for the hate mail. "I cannot understand why Janet Leigh gets hate mail from her *Psycho* appearance," a perplexed Hitchcock replied. "After all, she was the victim. It has never happened with any other movie I made."

Hitchcock's humor came into play when he mentioned receiving a letter from a man in France who told him he had a serious problem. He read a portion of the letter: "My daughter saw the French film *Diabolique* and now she won't take a bath. Then she saw *Psycho* and now she won't take a shower. Our daughter is very difficult to have around now. What should I do?" Hitchcock recounted his reply: "I'd send her to the cleaners."

Psychic phenomena formed an integral part of *Family Plot*'s storyline. Robert Kendall asked Hitchcock if he believed in such phenomena. "Not really, but hunger, yes!" the director succinctly responded.

Asked about other films he liked on a comparable scale to *Shadow of a Doubt*, Hitchcock quickly responded by naming *The 39 Steps*, *Rear Window*, *The Lodger*, *Family Plot* and *Vertigo*. When he was asked if he was losing weight, Hitchcock told his questioner, "I'm losing it talking to you."

One critic present at the Burbank location began by complimenting Hitchcock on how well he looked and wishing him a long life. At that point a troubling question was posed. "What would you like on your tombstone?" Hitchcock was asked. There was an immediate hush in the NBC Burbank Studio. The director had a heart condition that necessitated his wearing a pacemaker at that juncture of his life. The expressions of the other media representatives indicated they thought the question thoroughly tactless. It came from a representative noted for impropriety. Hitch took it all in stride, bowing his head as if in deep meditation. Slowly he raised his head. He finally replied in a profoundly serious tone, "I want this in quotes — 'You can see what can happen if you are not a good boy.'"

"At that point, the media gave Alfred Hitchcock a standing ovation in Burbank, New York, Chicago and Dallas," Robert Kendall related. "For two hours Alfred Hitchcock had taken on the critics under hot TV studio lights. He kept us all thoroughly entertained with his wonderful wit and sense of humor. He had enchanted us with his quick response to any question. He gave us keen insight into movie making that will always place Alfred Hitchcock in a category all by himself— master of movie suspense."

In addition to becoming America's prevailing master of ceremonies with his witty television appearances on his popular *Alfred Hitchcock Presents* series, the director had a long record of media appearances and interviews with book and magazine authors. His shrewd repartee made him a media favorite, and, typically enough, the more appearances he made the better he became as an accomplished master of epigrammatic humor.

The Concept of the Story Board

In his Burbank news conference Hitchcock quickly zeroed in on a familiar area, his concern with detailed planning before filming commenced. His ability to see the film in his head before approaching the set helped Hitchcock to finish ahead of schedule and save studios money. Hitchcock was one of two masters of his time in the story board concept of filmmaking. The other was another reigning film legend — Walt Disney.

Ken Annakin functioned as a top Disney director during the same period of the fifties when Hitchcock was making some of his most successful films. As earlier mentioned, Annakin's *The Swiss Family Robinson* and Hitchcock's *Psycho* stood one and two respectively as the top cinema grossers for 1960. Annakin launched his successful Disney period with two films starring Richard Todd as Robin Hood, *The Story of Robin Hood* and *The Sword and the Rose*, released in 1952 and 1953 respectively. Annakin's successful 1959 release, *The Third Man on the Mountain*, was Walt Disney's favorite film. The productive Disney experience was followed in 1965 by Annakin's international blockbuster, *Those Magnificent Men in Their Flying Machines*, for which he directed and co-authored the screenplay with Jack Davies, earning an Oscar nomination for Best Original Screenplay.

"My first experience in storyboarding was through Walt Disney," Annakin recalled. "When I got the job of directing, I was presented not only with the script, but a complete book of pictures illustrating that script. I was told it had been supervised and prepared by Carmen Dillon, a wonderfully skilled British woman who was Disney's designer-art director. I was told that Walt had guided her and okayed everything and that I must stick to 'the pattern' laid out."

The story board technique was integral to the Disney system, and Annakin initially was jolted by an abrupt change of pace from techniques he had successfully employed previously. "My first thoughts when I discovered this 'condition' was to almost resign," Annakin explained, "because over a ten year period I had already made a dozen feature movies with mostly success! I felt the director should decide the shape and look of any movie — and of course that is true. But I learned the value of story boards on *Robin Hood* and continued to use them ever after, but of course prepared under my direction and collaboration."

Setting the Scene—Film craftsman Hitchcock knew what he wanted on a film set. He is seen, cigar in hand, setting up a scene. Hitchcock's extensive preparation prior to shooting, aided by his story board technique, enabled him to complete projects frugally. This prudent practice made Hitchcock a popular figure with studio executives.

Annakin outlined the benefits of the story board approach used by Hitchcock and Disney:

> Storyboarding helps in many, many ways. First of all, you can experiment with the visual ways you are going to tell your story, instead of working it out on the set. This can save masses of money. You can hand out various pages of a story board to your cameraman, assistants, special effects people so they know what you are aiming at visually. This contributes very much to the team spirit of your crew.
>
> This is the way I work, and I believe Hitchcock worked the same way, though it is possible he always made the actors fit into his visual concept quite strictly. Another Disney director, Harold French, who made *Rob Roy* for Disney when J. Arthur Rank would not release me, stuck strictly to every visual in his story board. Obviously one can do that, but the actors cannot really "come into your team," especially in the way they do in a Mike Leigh *Vera Drake* movie.

Annakin made a point commensurate with one frequently made about Hitchcock's frugality in filmmaking and the positive result it had on producers and production companies. "Of course, most producers adore having the movie laid out in a story board," Annakin observed. "It is a great help in budgeting, and when they view rushes they can tell whether the movie is working out okay, that is if they are true filmmaker producers, and not just financiers."

Hitchcock and Actors

Hitchcock's anecdote about reassuring Ingrid Bergman with "Ingrid, it's only a movie" has become one of the most quoted of the film industry. Hitchcock's reflections at his final NBC Studios press conference concerning his relations with performers dovetail with the comments of Ken Annakin and British leading lady Hazel Court.

"I always heard," Annakin said, "that Hitchcock, being a designer and great visual conceiver, made his actors fit into the shots exactly as he planned, and it was up to them to create their special characters. There is no doubt that the system worked for most of his stars."

Hitchcock's Best Film?

The question regarding Hitchcock's favorite film, along with his response, bears scrutiny. While Hitchcock singled out *Shadow of a Doubt* as his "favorite film," one must ask if his favorite film was necessarily his best film. He consistently referred to the 1943 release as his "favorite movie experience" for reasons explained earlier. If there is one element that warms a director's heart above all others it is an error-free environment buttressed by devoted individuals intent on making the production a success. So often the best laid plans erupt in turmoil when problems arise during a production, and they occur without warning in some of the most delicate and unpredictable circumstances.

On the subject of Hitchcock's greatest film it would be advisable to heed the conclusions of the tandem that, through joint experience, has probably invested the most time studying and analyzing the director's work. Donald Spoto spent long periods of time interviewing Hitchcock and wrote two definitive works about him, one dealing with his life and times and the other analyzing each of his films. Australian film historian Ken Mogg, as webmaster of the popular *MacGuffin* Internet site, continues the challenging analytical pursuit of Hitchcock's art and perpetuates his reputation to increasing numbers of new fans interested in the great director. Mogg also provided one of the definitive Hitchcock works, not only analyzing each of his films, but also providing a survey of the noted writers who worked with the director, and an analysis of Hitchcock's television series and the impact it generated. These two paramount Hitchcock authorities selected *Vertigo* as the Master's greatest effort. This author agrees with their conclusion.

In analyzing a motion picture — or anything else — a conclusion need be based on the sum total of key factors. The total number of points predicated on the selected factors should accordingly stand as best. After analyzing key factors, *Vertigo* stands as number one. The film was magnificently mounted in Technicolor that took advantage of colorful San Francisco locations, a cosmopolitan city long regarded as one of the most photogenic by cinematographers. The film starred the world's most popular next door neighbor, James Stewart, a Hitchcock favorite as well, playing the role that made him famous, but with an important psychological twist — that of being used by a diabolical puppet master unlike any villain in film history.

The suave villain played by Tom Helmore behaved throughout the film as the perfectly cultivated gentleman — while in the process of ruining three lives. The lives he destroyed were those of his real life wife, the beautiful blonde temptress who convinced practical-minded ex-cop John Ferguson that she was possessed by the spirit of a woman who had lived a century earlier and, ultimately, Stewart himself. Could anyone remotely conceive of the Ferguson depicted at the end of *Vertigo* as anything but a truly broken man?

The dual roles played by Kim Novak was a unique feature in its own way, as effective as the performance of Tom Helmore. Novak became such an ideally performing tool (and victim) of the diabolical Gavin Elster that, as Judy Barton, she could not rise to the level of elegance and sophistication she seemed to achieve effortlessly when puppet master Gavin Elster was passing her off to retired police lieutenant John Ferguson as his beautiful blonde wife Madeleine.

To these superbly innovative story elements and impeccable plot execution one must add the combined visual and audio effects. The dazzling Technicolor scenery of San Francisco was superbly enhanced by the scenic redwood area near the city, culminating in the idyllic beauty of San Juan Batista Mission. The dazzling score by Bernard Herrmann, reflective of Richard Wagner, is the final ingredient to be added to the mix.

Hitchcock's Favorite Authors

Hitchcock's list of authors mentioned at the NBC news conference was anything but a surprise. The spy thrillers of John Buchan were popular in the London of Hitchcock's day, so the choice of his popular work *The Thirty-Nine Steps* for a film was understandable. Hitchcock was not a filmmaker with clearly defined messages in the manner of Stanley Kramer, but in instances where certain social or historical trends were in evidence the Britisher's instincts took him in comparable directions to message director Kramer. The Britain of the mid-thirties was rife with concern over the rise of Hitler's Third Reich and the prospect of war.

Agatha Christie was a popular British author in the detective suspense mold. Hitchcock selected her, along with the two American authors credited as architects of the hard-boiled school of fiction, former San Francisco Pinkerton detective Dashiell Hammett and the man who emulated his style and exceeded him in substance, Raymond Chandler, who, despite all the rewrites and writers involved, received screen credit with Czenzi Ormonde for one of Hitchcock's greatest masterpieces, *Strangers on a Train*.

Another popular English detective author of Hitchcock's youth whose books he read was Arthur Conan Doyle, who achieved lasting international fame writing about the exploits of a detective on London's Baker Street with a stratospheric IQ named Sherlock Holmes.

The nemesis of Holmes was the fiendish Professor Moriarity, who also possessed superior intelligence. Could Hitchcock, a reader of the Holmes novels as a youngster in London, have been thinking of Professor Moriarity when he helped construct the character of the intelligent and thoroughly ruthless Gavin Elster, along with some other of his suave villains?

The use of sources from childhood reading is reminiscent of William Shakespeare centuries earlier. A visit to the Shakespeare home in Stratford-upon-Avon on Henley Street where the Bard was born and raised contains textbooks studied by him, possibly while attending the King Edward VI Grammar School in his home town. *Plutarch's Lives*, which traced the lives and analyzed the characters of famous Greeks and Romans, were used as textbooks during Shakespeare's student days. They formed a nucleus for Shakespeare's historical plays that, like Plutarch's works, stressed the often complex character constituencies of the individuals of the historical milieus they depicted. Character analysis was the key ingredient in Shakespeare's dramatic works, along with the conflicts developing from the actions of the personae. To Shakespeare, plot is secondary to dramatic conflict and characterization.

A comparable analysis can be made in Hitchcock's case. A classic illustration was his conflict with Raymond Chandler when they worked on the screenplay of *Strangers on a Train*. Chandler believed that the basis of a screenplay resided in the emphasis on story development and was flabbergasted when Hitchcock's perspective emerged. If Shakespeare could use *Plutarch's Lives* as a formative basis for plotting, then Hitchcock could do the same with suspense influences from his youth.

What Chandler, coming from the perspective and experience of a writer of detective novels and magazine stories, did not realize was that Hitchcock, as illustrated by his frequent and instructive MacGuffin analogy, was a visual genius who operated from the root assumption stated by director Rouben Mamoulian as "What we have is a camera." Mamoulian's point was that the camera separated film from other forms of artistic expression.

Hitchcock's intimacy with the camera and his recognition that it was the perpetual constant, the glue that held filmmaking together, made him a natural for the most voyeuristic works, as represented by his two classics from his productive 1950s period, *Rear Window* and *Vertigo*. In the case of Hitchcock, to understand his craft, one needs to catapult beyond story elements to the scenic twists and turns, the Roman candles, that kept audiences glued to their seats while the Master, as a modern technological Puck, sustained his grand tease.

Variety Weighs In

Film industry organ *Variety* weighed in with one of its patented catchy headlines for the Hitchcock news conference: "Hitchcock Puts Tongue in Cheek for Coast-to-Coast Crix Sesh." The accompanying story by correspondent Joseph McBride focused on some of the director's succinct gems, which in Hitchcock's case embodied a treasure chest of riches.

Hitchcock revealed that it had taken two years of work, from scripting through editing, to put *Family Plot* together. "Most of the time was spent trying to avoid the clichés," Hitchcock explained. "That seems to be the one thing that obsesses me in making a picture."

The subject of symbolism produced some interesting comments. The director conceded that he does sometimes employ symbols, "but I don't think in a very conscious way." When one critic professed to find symbolism in wall smudges around a light switch in *Family Plot*, Hitchcock commented dryly, "A switch is a symbol of light." He conceded to conscious symbolism with the train-entering-a-tunnel ending of *North by Northwest* with the comment, "I think that comes under the heading of pornography ahead of its time."

John Simon of *New York Magazine* discoursed on religious symbolism in *Family Plot*, which prompted the director to respond, "Mr. Simon, I don't think I'm that religious." When another questioner wondered why Karen Black in the film keeps her blonde wig in a refrigerator, Hitchcock provided a cool answer: "Because when she went to put it on it was nice and cool."

Structure and Meaning in Family Plot

Despite the fact that *Family Plot* revolves around kidnapping for profit, Hitchcock professed no particular interest in the subject. He explained that he found more enjoyment in working out the construction problems involved in a story with "two sides of a triangle meeting at a certain point."

The director volunteered "a possible influence by the paintings of [Piet] Mondrian" in an overhead angle of Bruce Dern pursuing Katherine Helmond through a maze-like cemetery. "I felt it was a fresh way of doing a small chase," he explained.

Hitchcock expressed his belief that a director's style should be personal and consistent. "Self-plagiarism is style," he revealed. "You can't be one minute like Cezanne and the next minute like Grandma Moses."

One critic expressed the view that the verbal exposition in the opening scenes of *Family Plot* violated Hitchcock's dictum against "photographs of the people talking." The Master launched a detailed response:

"You're dealing with what you call a springboard situation. It must be laid out perfectly clearly to the audience, and that calls for a certain amount of explanation, words and so forth.

"The audience must be made comfortable at the beginning, so when you've given them all the information they require, then you can start being purely cinematic and telling your story in pictures."

About Women's Lib

In 1976, the year of the release of *Family Plot*, women's liberation was a major political and social issue, with spokespersons like Gloria Steinem, Bella Abzug and Betty Friedan receiving attentive audiences. When a critic complimented the director for creating a rare good female role for Barbara Harris during a period in which women performers were seeking parts of greater depth and meaning, Hitchcock's response showcased his scintillating wit:

"Well, you know, the use of women in pictures is historical and inevitable. What was the serial in silent days? 'The Perils of Pauline.' Nobody was interested in the perils of George.

"[French playwright Victorien] Sardou said 'torture the woman'—in a piece of dramatics—and the trouble today is today we don't torture the women enough. Maybe it's due to women's lib; they can look after themselves more than they used to."

A Practical Joker

The subject of Hitchcock's propensity for practical jokes, synchronous with his delight in teasing film audiences with his control and mastery over suspense elements, was a natural topic for the pre-release *Family Plot* news conference. British filmmaker Val Guest can readily attest to Hitchcock's flair in that direction based on personal experience when they had adjoining offices at Gainsborough Studios in the Islington section of North London.

Guest, who had blossomed as a young writer doing scripts for the famous British comedian Will Hay, expanded to a wide repertoire that included science fiction and war drama. His 1961 science fiction release *The Day the Earth Caught Fire*, with Edward Judd, Janet Munro and Leo McKern, was an international success. In addition to directing the film, Guest co-authored the screenplay with Wolf Mankowitz, and secured a British Academy Award in the writing category. That had been preceded by the 1957 sci-fi hit *Quatermass II*, starring Brian Donlevy. A number of Guest's screen hits starred his beautiful wife, American-born Yolande Donlon. They included *80,000 Suspects* (1963), which also starred Claire Bloom and Richard Johnson, *Mr. Drake's Duck* (1951), also starring Douglas Fairbanks, Jr., *Penny Princess* (1952), also starring Dirk Bogarde, and *They Can't Hang Me* (1955), also starring Terence Morgan.

Guest was also one of the directors of the James Bond spoof *Casino Royale* (1966), with a large international cast including comedy geniuses Peter Sellers and Woody Allen, as well as sexy Ursula Andress and the venerable Orson Welles. In 2001 his career memoir, *So You Want to Be in Pictures: From Will Hay to Hammer Horror and James Bond*, was released.

"That infamous practical joker Alfred Hitchcock [had an] office next door to mine at Gainsborough Studios in Islington, where he was making *The Lady Vanishes*," Guest recounted. "He, too, borrowed money from this struggling screenwriter [Guest]. It was late Saturday, the banks were closed, he said, and he needed some floating cash. Could I loan him ten pounds and he'd repay it after the weekend. And I did. Came Monday, Tuesday, Wednesday, but no sorely needed ten pounds. Until late Friday afternoon when there was a tap on my office door. It opened to reveal the Gainsborough pageboy. 'Mr. Hitchcock says thank you,' he announced, dragging in two heavy sacks with ten pounds' worth of farthings. With four of them to the penny and 240 pennies to the pound that made it 9,600 farthings to be exact. Getting them to the bank was another story."

Val Guest was, like Hitchcock, a creative film innovator. Practical joker Hitchcock's act spawned a desire for retaliation on the part of Guest, who made a shrewd plan of his own. "I heckled my friends for any old, unused keys they had lying around in drawers," Guest explained. "I tied a separate tag on all 200 of them." Guest wrote a message on the key tags: HITCHCOCK—143 BROMPTON ROAD—FINDER WILL BE REWARDED.

"Then we dropped them all over London," Guest revealed. "In buses, trains, parks, greyhound tracks.... It was ten days before there was any reaction from Hitch. Then one morning my office door was pushed open and his pink, round face poked around it. 'Just tell me,' he said mournfully. 'How many bloody keys did you drop?'"

Ending with a Spoof

Hitchcock's propensity toward practical jokes coheres with his dazzling brilliance as a film craftsman to keep audiences on edge with his spoofs. It served as a form of poetic justice for Hitchcock to end his celebrated career with a grand spoof, covering similar ground that he had traversed in his great classic

Laughing Hitch—Alfred Hitchcock enjoys a laugh on the set between takes. The director was known for enjoying jokes, especially of the practical variety.

Vertigo, but spun in a different direction. In *Vertigo*, brilliantly incomparable villain Gavin Elster used the psychic world as a grand con to hatch a skillful and ultimately successful murder plot, with his wife as victim. In *Family Plot* Barbara Harris's exploitation of psychic phenomena is cast in a comedic light. Her role as a phony psychic leads to some of the most inventive comedy of Hitchcock's career.

Alfred Hitchcock remained forever on top of his game where sociological trends were concerned. The Southern California scene of the mid-seventies where he worked and resided was summarized by a baseball wife who, after her husband was traded from the Los Angeles Dodgers and the family returned to their Midwest roots, penned a memoir of the period in which she bluntly stated, "In L.A. everybody seemed to ask two questions: Where are you from and what sign were you born under?"

That succinct comment tapped into the current Southern California scene in that the area was notable for its inherent rootlessness, with individuals streaming in from other locales and frequently leaving not long thereafter without leaving a trace; and there seemed to be a natural curiosity about the psychic world on the part of many Southern California residents. It would be revealed in the eighties that Ronald and Nancy Reagan, president and first lady, were fascinated by the topic, with Nancy seeking advice from astrologers.

Tabloids during the seventies contained numerous ads and columns by psychics and astrologers, while those involved in the film world were particularly rife with psychic interest. This had been the land to which European psychiatrists had migrated and found profitable in the post–World War II period. Hollywood's elite paid large sums of money to open up unexplored areas of the unconscious mind, with Selznick and Hitchcock tapping into that energy to produce *Spellbound*. The same type of curiosity rampant among the Hollywood creative set that spawned a mighty post-war interest in psychotherapy and psychiatrists generated a keen interest in psychic phenomena and psychics in the seventies.

A brilliant audience hook is extended in *Family Plot*'s first scene as Barbara Harris pulls out all stops as a struggling phony medium seeking to please a wealthy older woman, played by Cathleen Nesbitt. The session proves ultimately fulfilling in a way that provides Harris with an opportunity to tap into Nesbitt's largesse beyond her psychic performances. Julia Rainbird (Nesbitt) seeks to locate a long lost relative and leave her vast estate to him. If Blanche (Harris) could locate him she would receive a handsome reward of $10,000.

Barbara Harris's comedic skills were utilized early with Chicago's Second City troupe. Harris, born Sandra Markowitz and raised in the Chicago suburban of Evanston, scored big on Broadway in the Lerner and Lowe musical hit *On a Clear Day You Can See Forever*. She won a Tony Award for her performance in the musical *The Apple Tree*. Harris made her film debut playing a social worker in *A Thousand Clowns* (1965) and received a Best Supporting Actress Oscar nomination in the 1971 comedy *Who Is Harry Kellerman and Why Is He Saying Those Terrible Things About Me?*

The casting of Cathleen Nesbitt marks another instance of Britisher Hitchcock tapping the highly fluid wellspring of the English stage to fill an important character role. Nesbitt's first experience on London's West End scene occurred in 1910 in a revival of Arthur Wing Pinero's *The Cabinet Minister*. In 1915, while appearing with the Irish Players, Nesbitt journeyed to America and appeared in a Broadway production of John Millington Synge's *The Playboy of the Western World*. She returned to England in 1919 and performed in a variety of roles on stage and in film before making her American cinema debut in *Three Coins in the Fountain* (1954). Two years later she played Mrs. Higgins in *My Fair Lady* on Broadway.

Nesbitt was a regular on the 1963 television sitcom *The Farmer's Daughter*, playing William Windom's mother, and played an octogenarian drug addict in *The French Connection II* (1971). In 1981, at the age of 92, Nesbitt reprised her role of Mrs. Higgins in the Broadway revival of *My Fair Lady*. Her autobiography, *A Little Love and Good Company*, was published in 1973.

The film's riveting opening scene presents a dynamic contrast between medium Blanche and Julia Rainbird. The scene is reminiscent of many being played out at the time in the Los Angeles area. Opportunistic psychics sought to latch on to wealthy older women, who sought contact with bygone relatives. In this case the objective supplied the story's motivational nexus since the wealthy woman sought contact with her nephew, Edward Shoebridge, to bestow her riches on him.

Mogg's Memorable Moment

Australian Ken Mogg's eventful trip to California in 1975 saw him explore key Hitchcock film locations in California at Mission Dolores and Bodega Bay. The future webmaster of the *MacGuffin* Internet site saw film history unfold in watching a scene from Hitchcock's last film shot at Universal.

"I watched Hitchcock direct a scene [set] at an airport," Mogg recalled about the memorable evening. "Hitchcock was by then 76 and unwell. Filming was scheduled to start after sunset on a back lot at Universal. An airport office, with three or four steps leading up to it, had been erected beside a strip of asphalt representing a tarmac. Only the front part of the ground floor was actually built. The remainder of the building as seen in the film is a small matte painting by the gifted Albert Whitlock.

"Whitlock and his team arrived early to take measurements and to line up an establishing shot with cinematographer Leonard South. With dusk came a noticeable drop in temperature. At last, Hitchcock arrived in a chauffeur-driven, heated limousine. He stayed inside it for maybe ten minutes, watching with evident approval the preparations for shooting. An assistant director conversed with him through the window. Someone told me that even standing beside the car you might feel hot!"

Hitchcock emerged from the limousine and moved slowly, though unassisted, to his director's chair. Last minute activity continued all around Hitchcock. "There was no fuss, no calling out," Mogg remembered. "Hitchcock seemed mentally alert as ever. This was during the first month of shooting. Hitchcock noticed that a defusing scrim on one of the lights had come loose and was casting almost imperceptible shadows on the tarmac. A grip was sent up a ladder to hold the scrim during shooting."

Two police cars serving as props were parked to the left of the scene. Just before the camera was ready to roll someone went from one car to the other affixing license plates. "Apparently some regulation prohibited the plates from being brought out until just prior to shooting," Mogg concluded.

The establishing shot involved Karen Black disguised in a blonde wig, accompanied by an airport security officer, walking quickly across the tarmac and entering a brightly lit office. "I watched all of this action from a position immediately behind Hitchcock," Mogg noted. "Between takes, Hitchcock would tutor Karen Black in the mysteries of film technique. She seemed happy to ask him leading questions. 'Why do we need this shot at all?' she asked. 'Why not just go directly inside the building?' To which Hitchcock answered in his lugubrious drawl: 'It's like with the trombones in the orchestra, you see. We can't just let them blare out in-dis-crim-in-ate-ly, can we?'"

Shooting continued into the night. Another prop, a helicopter, stood nearby. It would be used when Black, carrying the ransom diamonds for which her character had come, took off, holding an airport pilot at gunpoint. "I was told that the cockpit of the helicopter would later be filmed on a sound stage," Mogg recalled.

One Final Suave Villain

Hitchcock's tradition of the suave villain began with Godfrey Tearle as Professor Jordan, the man with the missing finger, in *The 39 Steps*, and carried forward to the Claude Rains and James Masons along the way. The image would resurface in the director's last film in the person of William Devane. It will be recalled that at the pre-filming press reception at Universal Roy Thinnes was ticketed to play the role of the ruthless criminal who fakes his own death and assumes the identity of sophisticated jewelry store owner Arthur Adamson.

Robert Kendall attended both the 1975 reception and the satellite news conference prior to *Family Plot*'s release one year later. "I had spoken with Roy Thinnes at the Universal reception and was favorably impressed," Kendall related. "He was very congenial. After the news conference one year later I had the opportunity to talk for a few minutes with Hitchcock without any other media people present. I found Hitchcock very down to earth and polite. I was curious about why Roy Thinnes was replaced and asked Hitchcock about it. 'Roy Thinnes was such a nice fellow that I finally decided that it would be hard for people to imagine him as a killer and a kidnapper,' Hitchcock explained."

The response to Kendall's question harkens back to the experiment Hitchcock performed on the busy streets of downtown Beverly Hills with Joseph Cotten, preparing for his role as another suave villain (in *Shadow of a Doubt*). In preparing for his role, Cotten became troubled as he searched for a character type to emulate. While Hitchcock put Cotten at ease on that occasion by revealing that killers essentially looked like anybody else, his selection of Devane to replace Thinnes reveals a belief that, while killers could resemble anyone, it is also true that certain individuals look and act more suspicious than others. With Thinnes, were he playing the Gregory Peck role in *The Man in the Gray Flannel Suit* (1956), one could easily envision him telling his boss "no thanks" and opt-ing for more time with his wife and family in suburban New York City rather than living virtually full time in the Big Apple's rapacious corporate jungle; whereas with William Devane it would be readily cognizable, in contrast, for him to grin smugly and tell his boss, "Chief, I'm getting itchy, it's time for a takeover!"

The Albany-born Devane received a classical foundation in the acting craft as an alumnus of the American Academy of Dramatic Art, and attracted early attention as a performer with the New York Shakespeare Festival. Devane received a major career break performing in the biting anti–President Lyndon Johnson off–Broadway satire *MacBird* in 1967. A physical resemblance to President John F. Kennedy provided Devane with an opportunity to star in the miniseries *The Missiles of October*. The series aired in 1974 and might have been the springboard toward Hitchcock's hiring of Devane for *Family Plot*. Hitchcock might well have been attracted by the miniseries' topic of the 1962 Cuban Missile Crisis, which served as the subject matter for the director's 1969 film *Topaz*.

Devane's superb performance as Arthur Adamson, the ruthless killer-kidnapper-jewelry store owner in *Family Plot*, more than likely helped make another major career opportunity available — a starring role as hard drinking, two-fisted Sergeant Milt Warden in the 1979 miniseries *From Here to Eternity*, based on the James Jones bestseller and directed by Buzz Kulik. Ironically, in the miniseries Devane became involved in a triangle with Roy Thinnes, the unfaithful husband Captain Dana Holmes, whose beautiful wife Karen, played by Natalie Wood, seeks some badly needed affection in the arms of her spouse's First Sergeant. Thinnes's role as an unsympathetic philanderer and opportunist was a departure from his wholesome image.

In the manner of so many of Hitchcock's performers from the fifties onward, Devane would gain lasting fame as a television regular. He played duplicitous State Senator Gregory Sumner in the ABC hit series *Knot's Landing*, which premiered in 1983 and afforded Devane steady work until its cancellation one decade later.

Ernest Lehman Returns

Screen adaptation was the hallmark of definitive professional Ernest Lehman. He worked in mutually satisfying concert with Hitchcock on *North by Northwest* and would be reunited with the Master for *Family Plot*, an adaptation of the novel *The Rainbird Pattern* by Victor Canning. After striking box office and critical acclaim with *North by Northwest*, Lehman became one of Hollywood's busiest screenwriters in the interim preceding *Family Plot*, with a varied array of interesting credits to his name, such as *From the Terrace* (1960); *West Side Story* (1961); *The Prize* (1963); *The Sound of Music* (1965); as producer and screenwriter for *Who's Afraid of Virginia Woolf?* (1966); as producer and screenwriter of *Hello,*

Dolly! (1969); and as producer, director and screenwriter of *Portnoy's Complaint* (1972).

The script that Lehman developed dealt with character contrasts within conflicting groups. The clashing forces are two teams consisting of a male and female. As will be seen, Lehman, in concert with Hitchcock, keeps the swiftly paced story moving as the forces finally converge with a misunderstanding on the chief villain's part making him erroneously believe that he stands in imminent danger of having his real identity, the one he has taken great pains to bury, revealed.

In an interview with John Brady, screenwriter Lehman reveals that, as so many Hitchcock historians contend, many of the perceived symbols attributed to the director in his films are non-existent. Some of the claims relate to Freudian interpretations, while Lehman cites two instances from *Family Plot* outside that realm that are nonetheless wide of the interpretive mark.

"Hitch and I used to laugh sometimes when we read about the symbolism in his pictures, particularly in *Family Plot*," Lehman said. "By mistake a propman had two pieces of wood set up so that they looked vaguely like a cross, and the car goes downhill and crashes through a field, goes through a fence and knocks over the cross. So some learned New York critic commented: 'There's Alfred Hitchcock's anti–Catholicism coming out once again.'"

The critic's conclusion must have been news to Hitchcock, a practicing Roman Catholic throughout his entire life. Lehman then provided another example of erroneously-attributed symbolism, this time within the international film community:

"When I was at the Cannes Film Festival with *Family Plot*, Karen Black, Bruce Dern and I attended a press conference, and some French journalist had the symbolism of the license plate in the picture all worked out: 885 DJU. He had some *elaborate* explanation for those numbers. When he got through explaining it, I said, 'I hate to tell you this, but the reason I used that license plate number was that it used to be my own, and I felt it would be legally safe to use.'"

Two Couples and a
Cool Blonde with a Twist

The script woven by experienced craftsman Ernest Lehman worked on two levels that ultimately came together, wherein resolution occurred. Two couples stood at the story's apex. Adamson (William Devane) plotted the deaths by fire, made to look like an accident, resulting in his own apparent demise. Devane then changed his identity from Edward Shoebridge to Arthur Adamson. He sought to achieve riches by kidnapping important people and demanding large ransoms, which he shrewdly collected in expensive jewels.

Devane's confederate and romantic interest is Karen Black. Like Barbara Harris, Black had Chicago roots. After studying drama at Northwestern University, Black enjoyed a meteoric rise in the film industry at the same time as Jack Nicholson, as they both performed in the celebrated sixties rebellion message films *Easy Rider* (1969) and *Five Easy Pieces* (1970). Black received Golden Globe and New York Film Critics Circle Best Supporting Actress honors for the latter film, in which she plays a good-hearted but dim-witted waitress. The seventies were Black's peak period, as she secured a Best Supporting Actress Golden Globe for *The Great Gatsby* (1974) and starred in two prominent 1975 releases, John Schlesinger's *The Day of the Locust* and Robert Altman's *Nashville*.

Karen Black, who was born Karen Blanche Ziegler in Park Ridge, Illinois, might have secured her role in *Family Plot* at least in part through screenwriter Ernest Lehman. It was Lehman who directed her in the 1972 release *Portnoy's Complaint*, which he adapted from the Philip Roth novel, as well as producing.

The dramatic tension springing from Black's relationship with Devane in *Family Plot* results from her being a reluctant crime participant. He explains that after they complete two more jobs that an enriched retirement glowingly awaits them. That objective becomes complicated when Adamson (Devane) becomes convinced that they need to do away with Blanche (Barbara Harris) and George (Bruce Dern). Fran (Black) balks over becoming involved in murder, while Adamson undertakes the option in the manner of a determined CEO laying off workers through outsourcing. To Adamson, it is all in a day's work.

Karen Black could be called the last in the series of Hitchcock cool blondes begun with statuesque British beauty Madeleine Carroll in *The 39 Steps*. To label her as such would, however, require careful qualification. In the film, brunette Black serves as go-between for Adamson in his contact with ransom-paying relatives of victims he has kidnapped (with his female partner's assistance). To confuse authorities, Arthur Adamson has his partner don a blonde wig, making her a cool blonde during kidnapping sessions.

A Chicago Review

It would be understandable if upstate New Yorker William Devane felt like the odd man out among the talented quartet heading the casting of *Family Plot*. The performer playing the suave villain was from New York's capital city, while all three of the others performers hailed from Chicago. Completing the quartet was Bruce Dern. An irony stemming from the film's casting relates to the fact that, had Chicagoan Roy Thinnes not been replaced by Devane, *Family Plot* would have emerged as an all–Chicago review.

Bruce Dern teamed with former Second City trouper Barbara Harris to supply valuable comedy relief and keep a story focused on murder and kidnapping exploits from becoming too heavy. Dern clashes with Harris over her activities as

Unlocking a Family Mystery — Hitchcock sits as George (Bruce Dern) seeks to unravel the mystery of Edward Shoebridge, played by William Devane, in *Family Plot*. Dern examines the headstone of what is supposed to be the final resting place of Shoebridge, but ultimately learns that the gravesite contains no body and that Shoebridge has assumed the name of Adamson. Hitchcock's final film explored deception in a manner comparable to the spy thrillers of his earlier years, as Adamson pulls off a sting while George and girlfriend Blanche (Barbara Harris) attempt to locate Shoebridge.

Madam Blanche, Spiritualist; and when she becomes unflaggingly determined to find missing heir Edward Shoebridge, he becomes concerned that his concentration on sleuthing (to assist her in earning the $10,000) might cost him his job as a cab driver. In typical Hollywood fashion, George (Dern) terms himself an "actor" and explains that the cab driving job is only until he can become established in his real career. As prominent members of the Hollywood film community, Hitchcock and Lehman were well aware of the dilemmas confronting performers trying to break into the business.

The clashes between Harris and Dern are hilarious; at one point, when she is desirous of sex and he is tired from hours of driving his cab, he explains with exasperation that he is "too pooped to pop." One of the film's comic high points occurs when George needs Blanche's car to follow up a lead in the pursuit of the elusive Edward Shoebridge. He enters the back door while she is in the midst of a psychic session with an enthralled patron. As a means of meeting him in the kitchen and chastising him for jeopardizing a "reading" and the business of a client, Madam Blanche pretends to be pursuing the spirit of the departed husband of her patron into that portion of the house. Following a brief conversation, in which a miffed Blanche provides George with her car keys, she maneuvers her way back to the living room, never breaking stride and continuing to speak in the voice and manner of the departed husband. The client then asks anxiously, "Well, did you find him?"

Bruce Dern emerged from a background that would suggest a career in law or government rather than in acting. The actor's grandfather was Henry Dern, who, after serving two terms as governor of Utah, was tapped by incoming President Franklin Delano Roosevelt to serve as Secretary of War, a position which he occupied until his death in 1936. Dern's uncle Archibald Macheish won three Pulitzer Prizes in poetry, was also a distinguished playwright, and finished at the top of his graduating class at Harvard Law School. As for Dern's father, he was a prominent partner of the La Salle Street law firm in Chicago's Loop, headed by Adlai Stevenson, who served as governor of Illinois, was a two-time Democratic Party presidential nominee, and served as America's United Nations Ambassador under presidents John F. Kennedy and Lyndon B. Johnson.

When Dern was ready for prep school he was sent to Choate School in Connecticut, where the list of past students included future President John F. Kennedy. He later was a student at Pennsylvania University, where the slender, long-limbed Dern distinguished himself as a middle distance runner.

Dern surprised his family when he decided to forsake academic pursuits for studies at New York's Lee Strassberg Actors' Studio. There followed a lean period in which Dern, an atypical lead who fell more into the category of offbeat character type, was provided with an opportunity to appear in some Roger Corman low budget horror films through the assistance of his friend Jack Nicholson. During that same period Dern's career was also assisted by Hitchcock, who provided him with acting opportunities in his television series. Hitchcock also cast him as the unfortunate sailor in the flashback sequence of his 1964 release *Marnie.*

Just as the seventies proved to be the key decade for Karen Black, the same applied to Dern. Following a breakthrough role in the 1972 release *The King of Marvin Gardens*, starring his friend Nicholson and Ellen Burstyn, Dern secured a Golden Globe nomination for Best Supporting Actor two years later in *The Great Gatsby.* Two years after his stellar performance in *Family Plot*, Dern received Academy and Golden Globe nominations for Best Supporting Actor for his work opposite fellow former Actors' Studio student Jane Fonda and Jon Voight in Hal Ashby's probing drama about the Vietnam War, *Coming Home.* Dern received a coveted Silver Bear Award for Best Actor from the Berlin International Film Festival for the 1983 release, *That Championship Season.*

Contrasting Villains

In addition to being a film rich in contrasts and tensions existing within the two couples who are the main characters, *Family Plot* offers a brilliantly developed contrast between the suave villain played by Devane and his partner in crime, who carried out the murder of Arthur Adamson's adopted parents in a fire Adamson masterminded to set himself free. Long Island–born character performer Ed Lauter invested the role of Maloney the garage mechanic with the proper degree of sinister persona mixed with a burning hostility toward what he perceives as the injustices of life.

When George learns that the burial plot beneath the headstone of Edward Shoebridge contains no remains, he poses as a lawyer and questions Maloney at his gas station. Once George leaves, Maloney pays a visit to Adamson at his jewelry store.

The meeting between the suave villain who does the plotting and the crude killer who executes the crimes is one of the most dramatic of the film, and reveals what initially appears as a significant contrast to be, on further scrutiny, similarity. Whereas Adamson wears tailored suits, Maloney dresses modestly and has dirt under his fingernails, being an automobile mechanic and gas station proprietor. In addition, Maloney is plain spoken and ungrammatical compared to sophisticated Adamson, but the mutual antipathy between the two men is based not on their differences but on similarities.

The Long Island–born Lauter, who began his show business career as a comedian, conveys a menacing demeanor that serves him well in roles such as that of Maloney. Maloney resents Adamson for pretending to be something he is not, a polished gentleman, and recognizes that at bottom they are one and the same — ruthless opportunists willing to kill. Adamson, on the other hand, is reminded of who and what he is by the appearance of Maloney. The gas station owner is aware of Adamson's real identity and persona, which Adamson has taken great pains to eradicate.

Maloney's attempt to remove the curious nuisances George and Blanche from the scene results in an action sequence reminiscent of a concept explored ambitiously in late sixties cinema, but with a twist. British director Peter Yates had previously added appreciable interest to two well received crime dramas by including brilliant chase sequences. The 1967 film *The Great Train Robbery* has the criminals leading their police pursuers through the streets of London. One year later Steve McQueen, portraying a plain clothes detective, pursues a vehicle driven by a criminal through San Francisco in *Bullitt*.

The stellar and cinematically dazzling event of *Family Plot* emerges when Maloney uses his mechanical skills to cause a brake fluid leak in Harris's car, with Dern behind the wheel. To make the scene more cinematically fascinating, Hitchcock has Dern lose control of the car on a winding mountainous pass. The car's own downward momentum makes it accelerate. George ultimately has the presence of mind to use the emergency brake and steer the car off the road. It topples over and is standing upside down when the car comes to a halt — with Blanche's foot pushing against George's head.

After they have barely had time to climb out of the car and walk along the same highway where they almost lost their lives, the determined Maloney surfaces anew, this time attempting to run them both over. In the attempt, as he seeks to avoid collision with a vehicle coming from the opposite direction, he loses control and his vehicle plunges down a narrow mountainous expanse, after which it explodes and Maloney loses his life.

The opportunistic Adamson, after reading about Maloney's death, has mixed emotions. On the one hand he is delighted that his partner is dead, so he will not be able to plague him anymore. On the other, he is disgusted that Maloney had not disposed of Cabbie and Medium. His dirty deed minister is gone, and Adamson is left to be his own enforcer.

Existential Irony

The point wherein the two stories converge at the film's conclusion contains biting existential irony. Adamson, haunted by an impoverished childhood, engages in a plan to kill his adoptive parents and establishes a new persona, with a focus on success. His desire to achieve great wealth causes him to become a kidnapper, demanding ransom in the form of expensive jewels. Resentment concerning his past has become a motivator in choosing a well known church prelate as his last kidnap victim, believing that the clergyman had mistreated him during his youth. Misunderstanding prompts Adamson to believe he must kill George and Blanche, believing that they seek to blackmail him since they are aware that he is actually Edward Shoebridge and has assumed a new identity in Arthur Adamson. Devane meets Harris for the first time when he is on his way, along with Black, to deliver their victim in exchange for the specified ransom. Adamson then learns that his criminal enterprise was unnecessary and that he stood to inherit a large fortune. Far from being a young man of impoverished circumstances, he actually belonged to one of the city's wealthiest families.

Could Adamson's circumstances change through one meeting with a woman he earlier perceived as a blackmailer but is actually someone serving as a conduit for delivering a fortune to him? The opportunity swiftly passes, as the archbishop, clad in clergyman vestments, tumbles out of the car in which he lies unconscious after being given a shot by Adamson. At that point Adamson decides that he must subdue and later kill Harris after his victim has been delivered to the ransom payers.

A Concluding Wink
from Harris and Hitchcock

The Master's final film concluded with incredibly shrewd and historically appropriate symbolism. The director, noted for concocting spoofs and using MacGuffins to fool audiences while perpetuating suspense, ends *Family Plot* by having Blanche use her wits to save her life and apprehend criminals Adamson and Fran. The fact that the team of George and Blanche stumbled around the field of investigation, never knowing they were pursuing a dangerous criminal until the end of the film, was an example of babes-in-the-woods types thrown into a situation beyond their comprehension. Hitchcock explored this phenomenon via Robert Donat's character in *The 39 Steps*. Once Blanche is captured by Adamson and given a shot, with the intent of temporarily subduing and then killing her, her craftiness and survival instincts come into play. The woman who billed herself as Madam Blanche, Spiritualist, had made her living through acting. Her experience ultimately enables her to save her own life. When Adamson seeks to subdue her, Harris pretends to be unconscious. She ultimately sees her chance, as Adamson prepares to kill her, to shock the killer momentarily with a blood curdling cry reminiscent of one of her psychic renderings, then darts out of the room and slams the door shut, at which point partner George is able to lock both Adamson and Fran within the isolated area they use to hold kidnapping victims captive.

While Blanche was playing possum she was able to learn the secret of where the jewels extracted as ransom payment were stored — in the living room chandelier. George had been so disgusted by his girlfriend's psychic performances that he informed her that, absent the research he did on her behalf to provide her with information on her clients to use in her dramatic sessions, she was as psychic as a slice of salami. She then convinces him at the film's conclusion that she was truly psychic by feigning a trance and leading him to the missing jewels, which would bring a huge reward from the authorities. George gasps in disbelief that Madam Blanche really is psychic.

As for Barbara Harris playing Madam Blanche, she shares her secret with her audience. With George in a state of amazement over Blanche's seemingly authentic psychic powers, the camera closes in on her as she smiles knowingly and winks at the audience. The Master has carried out his final spoof. Using the marketing skills he honed narrating his *Alfred Hitchcock Presents* dramas, Hitchcock included a head shot of himself winking in *Family Plot* publicity advertisements. Shown inside a chandelier, he substituted himself for the winking Barbara Harris at the film's close.

There was good news and bad regarding *Family Plot*. The good news involved Hitchcock ending his career with such an inventive and entertaining film. The bad news is that there would be no more Hitchcock films. The team of Dern and Harris, bickering but uniting to solve a mystery, was reminiscent of the superbly matched

The Master Explains—Seated in his familiar director's chair, Hitchcock holds court between scenes of the filming of *Family Plot*. Hitchcock's succinct and colorful conversational manner, often interspersed with a tinge of irreverence, made him good copy and an eminently quotable figure. In his mature years he developed a penchant for selling his films with mass media advertisements laced with wry humor.

duo of Robert Donat and Madeleine Carroll in *The 39 Steps* 41 years earlier. If Hitchcock found a winning success formula he was shrewd enough to remold it with appropriate fine tuning for extensive use through the years.

Annakin's Overview

As a young man growing up in West Beverley in the English north country of Yorkshire, Ken Annakin watched Hitchcock's films of his London period. After the war, provided with an opportunity to launch a career of his own through the efforts of the other famous British director during Hitchcock's London phase, Carol Reed, Annakin followed the same path of Hitchcock in becoming a prominent director initially on his home soil, then embarking for America to continue his career.

"As for my personal Hitchcock favorites, I still find *Rebecca* gripping," Annakin revealed. "*Notorious*, the twisted love affair between Grant and Bergman, has so much suspense and intrigue that it absolutely holds you in a choke-hold. *Strangers on a Train* involves a twisted sadomasochistic plot where Hitch drags you along to accept murder, arousing the very deepest emotions in human beings. *Dial M for Murder*, this is not deep-digging Hitchcock, but the almost perfect example of putting a well worked out stage play on film shows that Hitch was not all twisted and delving into madness. It has often been said that *Vertigo* is about Hitch revealing himself and his inner thoughts about his wife, played by Kim Novak. The scenes between James Stewart and Novak are enthralling, and Hitch introduced new camera techniques of zooming in and out to establish the feeling of vertigo."

Fellow director Annakin admired one distinctive Hitchcock film for its inventiveness, while applying it to a similar effort of his own. "Hitchcock's greatest experiment technically was in *Rope*, where he put the movie together with 8-minute takes," Annakin said. "It was quite remarkable and was never done before or since. I think he was trying to get the effect of scenes developing as they do on a theater stage. I was fascinated and tried to shoot one sequence this way in Somerset Maugham's *Quartet* (1949) in 'The Colonel's Lady' segment that I directed, where, in this London club room, everyone was discussing the love story book that the Colonel's wife has written. It was a perfect place to use the long-take technique, but I couldn't make it drag out to a full eight minutes as Hitch did — and he did it ten times over!"

Annakin's choice for the most representative example of Hitchcock bringing his bag of tricks and technical expertise to full fruition is a film that was one of his biggest money makers, along with garnering a large share of critical praise. "I would say that the peak of Hitch's filmmaking and choice of subject matter, containing suspense, black humor, implied sexual goings-on and political machinations, is *North by Northwest*," Annakin concluded. "This has them all! Cary Grant is superb. It is a perfect movie adventure, superior to the efforts of us all today!"

Ken Annakin then concluded with an overview of Hitchcock: "I would say that Hitch was completely self-centered, full of ideas, and determined to plough his own route. I have spoken to actors who worked with him, and they all indicate that he expected them to grasp the part, milk it, and correct the playing to Hitch's brusque orders, if what they were doing didn't fit in exactly to his concept. Shall we say a lot of us directors have some parts and qualities Hitch possessed, but no one has had as full a bag of tricks and interests as he had."

When asked what an aspiring director might learn from the films of Alfred Hitchcock, Annakin's answer was succinct and to the point. "An aspiring director may learn bits of techniques and how Hitch created a thrill, but it will only be a morsel, because no one has ever been 'so full of it' as Hitch — nor probably ever will be."

Alfred Hitchcock secured the Academy's prestigious Thalberg Award in 1967 and was nominated five times in the directorial category for *Rebecca* (1940); *Lifeboat* (1944); *Spellbound* (1945); *Rear Window* (1954); and *Psycho* (1960). *Vertigo*, a film that knowledgeable historians place in the top rank of cinema achievement (in a class with Orson Welles's *Citizen Kane*), didn't earn him a Best Director's nomination. The technologically advanced *Rope* was also bypassed, along with such brilliantly crafted works as *Shadow of a Doubt*, *Strangers on a Train*, and the blockbuster Ken Annakin found to be Hitchcock's most representative work, *North by Northwest*.

The fact that Hitchcock never won an Academy Award in the Best Director category represents the Academy's deficiency rather than any shortcoming of the Master. The industry is riddled with examples of political machinations, with many such activities revolving around the Academy and the coveted Oscars bestowed annually on award night. With a career consisting of so many brilliant works combining technical virtuosity, brilliant story development, dazzling thrills and rich entertainment value, it is inconceivable, absent politics, that Hitchcock would fail to win even once.

As each new generation recognizes his special magic, Hitchcock assumes a posture of notable public recognition. With cinema enthusiasts throughout the world viewing his films with avid interest, Hitchcock looks down at the flurry of activity from the great beyond, winking and exclaiming, "I fooled you again, didn't I? I hope you enjoyed it."

He came, he saw, he continues to conquer. Alfred Hitchcock wove a unique magic all his own. Admired but never emulated, he was a unique filmmaker with an unceasing supply of MacGuffins and Roman candles.

Bibliography

All-Movie Guide. Internet Film Site and Database. www.allmovie.com.

Annakin, Ken. *So You Wanna Be a Director?* Sheffield, England: Tomahawk, 2001.

Armes, Roy. *A Critical History of British Cinema.* Harcourt, 1989.

Arts and Entertainment Network, "Murder He Wrote," Biography of Raymond Chandler, 1997.

Auiler, Dan. *The Hitchcock Notebooks: An Authorized and Illustrated Look Inside the Creative Mind of Alfred Hitchcock.* New York: HarperCollins, 2001.

_____. *Vertigo: The Making of a Hitchcock Classic.* New York: St. Martin's Press, 1998.

Behlmer, Rudy, editor. *Memo from David O. Selznick.* New York: Avon Books, 1972.

Bergan, Ronald. *Anthony Perkins: A Haunted Life.* London: Little, Brown, 1995.

Brady, John. *The Craft of the Screenwriter.* New York: Simon and Schuster, 1981.

Buchan, John. *The Thirty-Nine Steps.* London: William Blackwood and Sons, 1915. Reprint, with an Introduction by Christopher Harvie, Oxford: Oxford University Press, 1999.

Cotten, Joseph. *Vanity Will Get You Somewhere.* San Francisco: Mercury House, 1987.

DeRosa, Steven. *Writing with Hitchcock: The Collaboration of Alfred Hitchcock and John Michael Hayes.* New York: Faber and Faber, 2001.

De Rosso, Diana. *James Mason: A Personal Biography.* Oxford, England: Lennard Publishing, 1989.

Dirks, Tim. The Greatest Films. Internet Film Site and Database, filmsite.org.

Drazin, Charles. *In Search of the Third Man.* London: Methuen, 1999.

Durgnat, Raymond. *A Long Hard Look at* Psycho. London: British Film Institute, 2002.

_____. *The Strange Case of Alfred Hitchcock.* London: Faber and Faber, 1974.

Fairbanks, Douglas, Jr. *The Salad Days.* New York: Doubleday, 1988.

Fontaine, Joan. *No Bed of Roses.* New York: Morrow, 1978.

Friedrich, Otto. *City of Nets: A Portrait of Hollywood in the 1940s.* New York: Harper and Row, 1986.

Gottlieb, Sidney. *Alfred Hitchcock Interviews.* Jackson, Mississippi: University of Mississippi Press, 2003.

Guest, Val. *So You Want to Be in Pictures: From Will Hay to Hammer Horror and James Bond.* London: Reynolds & Hearn, 2001.

Hanna, Thomas. *The Thought and Art of Albert Camus.* Chicago: Regnery, 1958.

Hare, William. *Early Film Noir: Greed, Lust and Murder Hollywood Style.* Jefferson, North Carolina: McFarland, 2003.

_____. "The Ken Annakin Story." *Films of the Golden Age*, Fall 1998.

_____. *L.A. Noir: Nine Dark Visions of the City of Angels.* Jefferson, North Carolina: McFarland, 2004.

_____. "Rouben Mamoulian: Impeccable Style." *Films of the Golden Age*, Spring 1999.

_____. "Sir Carol Reed: The Man Behind 'The Third Man.'" *Films of the Golden Age*, Winter 2000–2001.

Hecht, Ben. *Gaily, Gaily.* New York: Doubleday, 1963.

Higham, Charles. *Celebrity Circus.* New York: Delacorte Press, 1979.

_____, and Joel Greenberg. *The Celluloid Muse: Hollywood Directors Speak.* Chicago: Regnery, 1969.

_____, and Roy Moseley. *Cary Grant: The Lonely Heart.* New York: Harcourt, 1989.

Hiney, Tom. *Raymond Chandler: A Biography.* New York: Atlantic Monthly Press, 1997.

The Internet Movie Database. Internet Film Site and Database. www.imbd.com.

Kendall, Robert. "Hitchcock *Family Plot* Pre-Release News Conference." *Hollywood Studio Magazine*, June, 1976.

Lacey, Robert. *Grace.* New York: Putnam, 1994.

Leff, Leonard J. *Hitchcock and Selznick: The Rich and Strange Collaboration of Alfred Hitchcock and David O. Selznick in Hollywood.* New York: Weidenfeld and Nicolson, 1987.

Leonard, Maurice. *Mae West: Empress of Sex.* New York: Birch Lane Press, 1992.

MacFarlane, Brian. *An Autobiography of British Cinema.* London: Methuen, 1997.

MacShane, Frank. *The Life of Raymond Chandler.* New York: Dutton, 1976.

Maltin, Leonard, editor. *TV Movies and Video Guide.* New York: Signet, 1990.

McBride, Joseph. "Hitchcock *Family Plot* Pre-Release News Conference." *Variety*, March 24, 1976.

McGilligan, Patrick. *Alfred Hitchcock: A Life in Darkness and Light.* New York: Regan Books, 2004.

_____. *Fritz Lang: The Nature of the Beast.* New York: Griffin, 1998.

Milne, Tom. *Mamoulian.* Bloomington: Indiana University Press, 1969.

Mogg, Ken. *The Alfred Hitchcock Story.* London: Titan Books, 1999.

Morley, Sheridan. *James Mason: Odd Man Out.* London: Weidenfeld and Nicolson, 1989.

Perry, George. *The Films of Alfred Hitchcock.* London: E.P. Dutton, 1965.

Rothman, William. *Hitchcock: The Murderous Gaze.* Cambridge, Massachusetts: Harvard University Press, 1982.

Sackett, Susan. *The Hollywood Reporter Book of Box Office Hits.* New York: Billboard Books, 1990.

Schickel, Richard. *The Men Who Made the Movies.* New York: Atheneum, 1975.

Server, Lee. *Screenwriter: Words Become Pictures.* Pittstown, New Jersey: Main Street Press, 1987.

Speck, Gregory. *Hollywood Royalty: Hepburn, Davis, Stewart and Friends at the Dinner Party of the Century.* New York: Carol Publishing, 1992.

Spoto, Donald. *The Art of Alfred Hitchcock: Fifty Years of His Motion Pictures.* New York: Anchor Books, 1992.

_____. *The Dark Side of Genius: The Life of Alfred Hitchcock.* Boston: Little, Brown, 1983.

_____. *Notorious: The Life of Ingrid Bergman.* New York: HarperCollins, 1997.

Taylor, John Russell. *Hitch: The Life and Work of Alfred Hitchcock.* London: Faber and Faber, 1978.

Thomson, David. *A Biographical Dictionary of Film.* New York: Morrow, 1976.

_____. *Showman: The Life of David O. Selznick.* New York: Knopf, 1992.

Truffaut, François. *Hitchcock.* London: Secker and Warburg, 1968.

Wakeman, John, editor. *World Film Directors: Volume One, 1890–1945*. New York: H.W. Wilson, 1987.
Wapshott, Nicholas. *The Man Between: A Biography of Carol Reed*. London: Chatto and Windus, 1990.
Wood, Robin. *Hitchcock's Films Revisited*. New York: Columbia University Press, 1989.

Personal Interviews

Ken Annakin, September 17, 2004 and February 15, 2005.
Hazel Court, September 20, 2004.
Robert Kendall, April 12, 2005.
Ken Mogg, May 22 and June 9, 2005.

Index